The Viking Age in Scotland

The Viking Age in Scotland

Studies in Scottish Scandinavian Archaeology

Edited by Tom Horne, Elizabeth Pierce
and Rachel Barrowman

EDINBURGH
University Press

Edinburgh University Press is one of the leading university presses in the UK. We publish academic books and journals in our selected subject areas across the humanities and social sciences, combining cutting-edge scholarship with high editorial and production values to produce academic works of lasting importance. For more information visit our website: edinburghuniversitypress.com

© editorial matter and organisation Tom Horne, Elizabeth Pierce and Rachel Barrowman, 2023, 2024
© the chapters their several authors, 2023, 2024

Edinburgh University Press Ltd
The Tun – Holyrood Road
12(2f) Jackson's Entry
Edinburgh EH8 8PJ

First published in hardback by Edinburgh University Press 2023

Typeset in 10.5/12.5 Adobe Sabon by
IDSUK (DataConnection) Ltd
A CIP record for this book is available from the British Library

ISBN 978 1 4744 8582 1 (hardback)
ISBN 978 1 4744 8583 8 (paperback)
ISBN 978 1 4744 8584 5 (webready PDF)
ISBN 978 1 4744 8585 2 (epub)

The right of Tom Horne, Elizabeth Pierce and Rachel Barrowman to be identified as editors and the contributors to be identified as the authors of this work has been asserted in accordance with the Copyright, Designs and Patents Act 1988, and the Copyright and Related Rights Regulations 2003 (SI No. 2498).

Contents

List of Tables	viii
List of Figures	ix
List of Abbreviations	xii
Acknowledgements	xiii
The Contributors	xiv
Preface	xvi
A Dedication to Colleen Batey	xviii
Foreword by Judith Jesch	xix

    Before *Vikings in Scotland*: A Brief History of Viking-Age Archaeology in Scotland   1
    Olwyn Owen

Part I. The Arrival of the Vikings and Native–Norse Interactions

1. *Landnám* and Landscape in Viking Orkney   13
David Griffiths

2. What Does *Landnám* Look Like? Excavations at Swandro and Old Scatness   29
Stephen J. Dockrill and Julie M. Bond

3. The Tarbat Peninsula in Northern Pictland: Portmahomack as a Case Study in Native–Norse Interaction during the 9th to 11th Centuries   43
Cecily Spall

4. Echoes of Native–Norse Relationships in the Archaeology at St Ninian's Isle, Shetland   57
Rachel Barrowman

Part II. Scandinavian Settlement

5. The Use of Space in Norse Houses: Some Observations from the Hebrides   75
Niall Sharples

6. Hamar and Underhoull, Unst: Settlement in Northernmost Scotland 85
Julie M. Bond and Stephen J. Dockrill

7. Investigating the Origins of Steatite Vessels across the Viking Diaspora 98
Amanda K. Forster and Richard E. Jones

8. Machair Bharabhais, Leòdhas: A Scandinavian Settlement in its Context 112
Mary MacLeod Rivett and Trevor Cowie

Part III. Place-names: Interactions with the Landscape

9. Norse Settlement in the Southern Hebrides: The Place-name Evidence from Islay 123
Alan Macniven

10. Understanding the Norse Period through Place-name Evidence: A Case Study from the Island of Mull 135
Alasdair C. Whyte

11. The Church and Gaelic–Norse Contact in the Hebrides 143
Thomas Owen Clancy

Part IV. Environmental Impact and Land Use

12. Isotope Zooarchaeology in Viking Scotland: Previous Research, Possibilities and Future Directions 155
Jennifer R. Jones

13. Feasts, Food and Fodder: Viking and Late Norse Farming Systems in Scotland 170
Ingrid Mainland

14. Norse Shielings in Scotland: An Example of Cultural Contact 189
Ryan Foster

Part V. Power and the Political Landscape

15. *Thing*-sites and the Political Landscape in the North 197
Alexandra Sanmark

16. The Brough of Birsay, Orkney 213
Christopher D. Morris

17. The Earl's Bu, Orphir, Orkney 223
Colleen E. Batey

18. Revisiting Tuquoy – Still Full of Surprises . . . 229
    Olwyn Owen

19. The Lewis Hoard of Gaming Pieces – Evoking and
    Reassembling a Viking Past? 239
    Mark A. Hall and David H. Caldwell

Part VI. Economy and Exchange

20. The Viking-Age Silver and Gold of Scotland 251
    James Graham-Campbell

21. The Galloway Hoard 262
    Martin Goldberg

22. Viking and Norse Bullion Economies in Scandinavian
    Scotland 276
    Tom Horne

23. Small Finds, Big Questions: Two Decades of Research
    on Combs in Viking-Age Scotland 289
    Steven P. Ashby

Part VII. Death and Burial

24. The 'Pagan Norse Graves of Scotland' Research Project 299
    *James Graham-Campbell, Caroline Paterson and
    Stephen Harrison*

25. Swordle Bay, Ardnamurchan: A Viking Boat Burial 308
    Colleen E. Batey

26. Carrick, Mid Ross: A Viking Cemetery on Loch Lomond 313
    Colleen E. Batey

    Afterword: Major Advances and Future Directions 322
    Colleen E. Batey and James Graham-Campbell

Index 328

Tables

4.1	Archaeological sequences from the 1955–9 and 1999–2000 excavations	61
6.1	Radiocarbon and archaeomagnetic dates from the sites of Hamar and Underhoull	89
7.1	Tuquoy samples	105
7.2	Iceland samples	107
13.1	Relative frequency of cattle, sheep/goat and pig at Late Iron-Age, Viking, Norse and Late Norse sites in the Northern Isles	180
13.2a	Culling profiles for sheep/goat	181
13.2b	Culling profiles for cattle	182
15.1	List of all potential *thing*-sites identified in Scotland	199

Figures

0.1	Brough of Birsay, Orkney	2
1.1	Sites discussed in text	15
1.2	Excavation at Buckquoy, Birsay, Orkney, from the east, with House 4 in the foreground	16
1.3	Norse longhouse at Jarlshof, Shetland	20
1.4	Longhouse at East Mound, Bay of Skaill, Orkney under excavation	20
2.1	Iron-Age village at Old Scatness with the Iron-Age, Pictish and Viking structures numbered	31
2.2	Iron-Age and Viking steatite, showing the discrete concentrations of Viking-Age steatite in the buildings discussed	33
2.3	Steatite line sinker (SF 1570) found in the deliberate infill of Pictish Structure 5	34
2.4	Iron-Age and Norse settlement at Swandro in relation to the Pictish and Viking cemetery at Westness on Rousay	37
3.1	Portmahomack on Tarbatness and sites mentioned in the text	44
3.2	Layout of the 8th-century monastic settlement	44
3.3	Evidence for the burning horizon across the Northern Workshops	47
3.4	Post-raid activity across former monastic settlement	48
3.5	Clay and stone moulds from post-raid metalworking	50
3.6	Map of place-names and Norse material around the Tarbat peninsula and inner Moray Firth	51
4.1	The sandy tombolo to St Ninian's Isle and the site of the excavations	58
4.2	Location of St Ninian's Isle	58
4.3	Combined plans published by Small, Thomas and O'Dell and Cain, a sketch made by Thomas, and Helen Nisbet's 1959 excavation sketch	60
4.4	Late Norse burial SK5	64
5.1	The sequence of large houses on Mound 2	76

5.2	The interior of House 2	77
5.3	The floor layers inside House 3	81
6.1	Map of Unst, Shetland, showing the main Norse sites mentioned in the text	86
6.2	Hamar, House 1	88
6.3	Upper House, Underhoull	92
6.4	The carved steatite (soapstone) figurine from Upper House, Underhoull	94
7.1	Location of steatite quarries and archaeological sites	101
7.2	Simple typology of steatite vessels	102
7.3	Changing trends in the use of Norwegian and Shetland vessels in the North Atlantic	103
7.4a	La/Yb vs Dy/Yb plot of the samples from Tuquoy and Iceland	106
7.4b	La/Yb vs Dy/Yb plot of the quarry samples on Shetland	106
8.1	Machair Bharabhais: location map	113
8.2	Plan of Norse site prior to excavation	113
8.3	Plan of main excavation area showing location of structures A and B	115
9.1	The Isle of Islay	124
9.2	Stephen MacDougall's (1749–51) *Map of the Island of Islay*	127
9.3	Distribution of Islay farm-names by language background and ON farm-names and 'Land Capability for Agriculture'	128
9.4	Distribution of other ON place-names and topography	129
10.1	Places in south-east Mull mentioned in this chapter	137
11.1	Map by W. F. H. Nicolaisen of place-names containing *cill* in Scotland	145
11.2	Early medieval cross from the graveyard at Kilmuir, North Uist	147
12.1	Bone collagen $\delta^{13}C$ and $\delta^{15}N$ values from isotope evidence of cows, sheep and red deer	158
12.2	Bone collagen $\delta^{13}C$ and $\delta^{15}N$ values from pigs and dogs	160
13.1a	Relative frequency (%NISP) of cow, sheep/goat and pig in Late Iron-Age Northern Isles	176
13.1b	Relative frequency (%NISP) of cow, sheep/goat and pig in Viking, Late Norse and medieval faunal assemblages from the Northern Isles	177
13.2a	Culling strategy for sheep in Late Iron-Age, Viking and Late Norse Orkney	178
13.2b	Culling strategy for cattle in Late Iron-Age, Viking and Late Norse Orkney	179
14.1	Distribution map of Old Norse shieling-names in Britain	190
15.1	Dingieshowe on a narrow isthmus on the Orkney Mainland	200
15.2	The potential *thing*-site at Edin in the Isle of Bute	201

15.3	The correlation between the Icelandic *thing*-sites, mid-19th-century pathways and taxed farms named in sources from the 17th century and earlier	203
15.4	The presumed location of the outdoor assembly site and booths at Tinganes in Tórshavn on Streymoy, Faroe Islands	205
16.1	Brough of Birsay from the south-east at the Point of Buckquoy	214
16.2	Brough of Birsay from the west	215
16.3a	Decorated copper alloy mount RF 979	219
16.3b	Face of stone RF 2761	219
17.1	Location of Orphir on Scapa Flow, Orkney	224
17.2	Identified structural elements of the horizontal mill	226
18.1	Cross Kirk and the site of the Norse settlement from the air	230
18.2	Part of the hall during excavation in 1983	231
18.3	Interpretation of the earth resistivity survey results	234
18.4a	The waterlogged 'pit' during excavation in 1988	237
18.4b	Some of the worked wood from the waterlogged 'pit'	237
19.1	Some of the Lewis Hoard laid out for chess	240
19.2a–d	The four 'berserkir' pieces from the Lewis Hoard	242
20.1	Distribution map of the Viking-Age silver and gold hoards of Scotland	252
21.1	Trewhiddle-style pectoral cross	263
21.2	The lower deposit of silver bullion	264
21.3	Three-dimensional digital model of the vessel	268
21.4	Anglo-Saxon metalwork from within the vessel	269
22.1a	Insular mount weight	278
22.1b	Oblate spheroid weight	278
22.1c	Cubo-octahedral weight	278
23.1	Diagnostic markers: 'native' and Norse comb forms	290
23.2	Comb in situ at Skaill Bay, Orkney	291
24.1	Distribution map of the pagan Norse graves of Scotland	301
25.1	Location map of the Swordle burial, Ardnamurchan	309
25.2	Line drawing of the sword from the burial	311
26.1	Location of Carrick, Mid Ross, Loch Lomondside	314
26.2	Viking-Age graves, those with grave goods and those without, within the penannular ring-ditch	316

Abbreviations

aDNA	Ancient DNA
BAR	British Archaeological Reports
CANMORE	Computer Application for National Monuments Record Enquiries. Compiled and managed by Historic Environment Scotland (https://canmore.org.uk/) (formerly RCAHMS NMRS database)
CT	Computerised Tomography
HES	Historic Environment Scotland
HMSO	Her Majesty's Stationery Office
IAM	Inspector of Ancient Monuments
ICP-MS	Inductively Coupled Plasma Mass Spectrometry
NABO	North Atlantic Biocultural Organisation
NGR	National Grid Reference, Ordnance Survey
NMRS	National Monuments Record for Scotland
NMS	National Museums Scotland
NSA	New Statistical Account
OIr	Old Irish
ON	Old Norse
OS	Ordnance Survey
OSA	Old Statistical Account
RCAHMS	Royal Commission on the Ancient and Historical Monuments of Scotland
SUERC	Scottish Universities Environmental Research Centre
TT	Treasure Trove
XRF	X-Ray Fluorescence spectroscopy

Acknowledgements

The organisers of the *Vikings in Scotland: 20 Years On* conference, held on 5–7 December 2018 at the University of Glasgow, are grateful to all of the speakers and session chairs for making the event such a success. This conference was only possible due to the generous financial contributions from a number of societies and institutions, especially Historic Environment Scotland. The organisers are also grateful to the following: the Department of Archaeology and the Centre for Scottish and Celtic Studies at the University of Glasgow, the Hunter Archaeological and Historical Trust, the Scottish Society for Northern Studies, the Viking Society for Northern Research, the Glasgow University Research Incentivisation Fund, Scotland's Archaeology Strategy, Glasgow Archaeological Society, the Glasgow City Council Lord Provost's Office for hosting a civic reception at Kelvingrove Art Gallery for conference delegates, and the Glasgow Convention Bureau.

Outside of the main conference, thanks are due to Dr Martin Goldberg and Dr Adrián Maldonado at National Museums Scotland for arranging a tour and behind-the-scenes display of Viking artefacts; Frazer Capie and Friends of Govan Old for hosting the keynote address by Professor Judith Jesch and a reception among the early medieval stones housed in the church; and Glenmorangie Company for refreshments at the Govan reception.

The editors of this volume would like to thank Colleen and James for their support and enthusiasm for this publication, as well as their multiple contributions. We hope this will be a suitable continuation to the legacy of *Vikings in Scotland: An Archaeological Survey*.

The Contributors

Dr Steven P. Ashby Senior Lecturer, Archaeology, University of York

Dr Rachel Barrowman Research Associate (Archaeology), University of Glasgow

Dr Colleen E. Batey Visiting Reader of the University of Highlands and Islands; Visiting Fellow St John's College, and Honorary Fellow, Archaeology, University of Durham

Dr Julie M. Bond Senior Lecturer, School of Archaeological and Forensic Sciences, University of Bradford

Dr David H. Caldwell Independent researcher

Prof. Thomas Owen Clancy University of Glasgow

Trevor Cowie Independent researcher; formerly National Museums Scotland

Dr Stephen J. Dockrill Reader in Archaeology, School of Archaeological and Forensic Sciences, University of Bradford

Dr Amanda K. Forster Director of Operations, DigVentures Ltd

Dr Ryan Foster Independent researcher

Dr Martin Goldberg Principal Curator of Medieval Archaeology and History, Scottish History and Archaeology department, National Museums Scotland

Prof. James Graham-Campbell Emeritus Professor of Medieval Archaeology, University College London

Prof. David Griffiths Director of Studies in Archaeology, Department for Continuing Education, University of Oxford

Dr Mark A. Hall Collections Officer, Perth Museum and Art Gallery

Dr Stephen Harrison Senior Lecturer in Archaeology, University of Glasgow

Dr Tom Horne Affiliate Researcher (Archaeology), University of Glasgow

Prof. Judith Jesch, FBA Professor of Viking Studies, University of Nottingham

Dr Jennifer R. Jones Lecturer in Archaeology, School of Natural Sciences, University of Central Lancashire

Dr Richard E. Jones Honorary Lecturer in Archaeology, University of Glasgow

Dr Alan Macniven Department of European Languages and Cultures: Scandinavian Studies, University of Edinburgh

Prof. Ingrid Mainland UHI Archaeology Institute, Orkney College, University of the Highlands and Islands

Prof. Christopher D. Morris Emeritus Professor of Archaeology, University of Glasgow

Olwyn Owen Visiting Reader, Archaeology Institute, University of the Highlands and Islands

Caroline Paterson Centre for Open Studies, University of Glasgow

Dr Elizabeth Pierce Affiliate Researcher (Archaeology), University of Glasgow

Dr Mary MacLeod Rivett Senior Casework Officer, Historic Environment Scotland

Prof. Alexandra Sanmark University of the Highlands and Islands

Prof. Niall Sharples Professor of Archaeology, Cardiff University

Cecily Spall Field Archaeology Specialists: Heritage

Dr Alasdair C. Whyte Lord Kelvin/Adam Smith Research Fellow in Celtic Onomastics, University of Glasgow

Preface

In the two decades since James Graham-Campbell and Colleen Batey published *Vikings in Scotland: An Archaeological Survey*, a tremendous amount of research and publication has taken place. The twentieth anniversary of the book offered an excellent opportunity to provide an update in light of the countless excavations, scientific advances, historical and place-name studies and postgraduate theses that had been produced since 1998. This was partly inspired by a day conference held in honour of Barbara Crawford in 2007 (Woolf 2009) to celebrate twenty years since the publication of *Scandinavian Scotland* (Crawford 1987). The resulting *Vikings in Scotland: 20 Years On* conference was held in December 2018 at the University of Glasgow. Scholars from around the UK and abroad shared their latest research on the Viking Age in Scotland, and the papers in this book are a result of that conference.

The format of this volume is different from James and Colleen's book in that each chapter is a separate paper authored by a conference speaker. Rather than feature a few select papers, the editors of this volume opted to include as many papers as possible from the conference to cover as much ground as one volume can. As a result, the papers in this volume are slightly shorter than in many volumes, and short chapters on specific sites are meant to illustrate wider concepts discussed in the volume. Many excellent monographs and reports about these sites that have been produced or are nearing publication can provide more detailed information.

The keynote speaker from our conference, Judith Jesch, begins this volume with a tribute to Colleen. Subsequently, Olwyn Owen provides an historical overview paying homage to a key strength of *Vikings in Scotland*, namely an accessible overview of the recent research on Viking-Age Scotland. Thereafter, the book follows thematic sections which begin with first contacts and Norse settlement in 'Arrival of the Vikings and Native–Norse Interactions', 'Scandinavian Settlement' and 'Place-names: Interactions with the Landscape', then to 'Environmental Impact and Land Use'. The updated research continues with sections on 'Power and the Political Landscape' and 'Economy and Exchange'.

Finally, 'Death and Burial' discusses a particularly fruitful area of recent archaeological discovery in Scotland. Fittingly, James and Colleen close the book with 'The Future of Scottish Viking Studies', demonstrating that now, as in 1998, their method is to look to the future, encouraging present and forthcoming generations to share their expertise and joy in the study of Viking and Norse Scotland.

We would like to thank James and Colleen for their support throughout the process. We would also like to thank Edinburgh University Press for agreeing to publish this volume more than twenty years after similarly publishing *Vikings in Scotland*. As papers in this volume demonstrate, James and Colleen's book is still very relevant to research in Viking-Age Scotland today.

Tom, Elizabeth and Rachel

Crawford, B. E. 1987 *Scandinavian Scotland*. Scotland in the Early Medieval Ages 2. Leicester: Leicester University Press.

Woolf, A. (ed.) 2009 *Scandinavian Scotland – 20 Years After. The Proceedings of a Day Conference held on 19th February 2007*. St John's House papers 12. St Andrews, Fife: The Committee for Dark Age Studies, University of St Andrews.

Editors' Note on 'Viking (Age)' and '(Late) Norse'

The term Viking Age is defined in this volume as dating to around 800 to 1050, and the Late Norse 1050 to 1350, with the proviso that the Viking Age can be extended to between 750 and 1100 (see Jesch 2015: 7 and Morris 2021: 37–8), and the Late Norse period to around 1450, particularly in the Northern Isles. The terms Viking and Norse are also sometimes used more generally as cultural terms.

References

Jesch, J. (2015) *The Viking Diaspora*. Medieval World Series. London: Routledge.

Morris, C. D. (2021) *The Birsay Bay Project Volume 3. The Brough of Birsay, Orkney Investigations 1954–2014*. Oxford and Philadelphia: Oxbow Books.

A Dedication to Colleen Batey

This volume is dedicated to Dr Colleen Batey in recognition of her years of teaching and her many contributions to the study of the Vikings in Scotland and across the North Atlantic. Colleen's focus on the Vikings, particularly their artefacts, continued throughout her career, and she has directed and worked on many high-profile archaeological sites, including the Brough of Birsay, Orkney; Freswick Links, Caithness; the Earl's Bu, Orkney; Hofstaðir, Iceland; and also, the early medieval site at Tintagel, Cornwall.

After being awarded her PhD from the University of Durham with a thesis evaluating the evidence for Vikings in Caithness, Colleen went on to lecture in archaeology at the University of Leeds (Continuing Education) and then University College London, before moving to Glasgow. She was appointed Curator of Archaeology at Glasgow Museums, and British Curatorial Advisor for the Smithsonian Institute, Washington, DC touring exhibition, *Vikings: The North Atlantic Saga*. She was also given visiting appointments at the Archaeological Institute of Iceland, Reykjavík and Hunter College, New York and was Guest Curator for the Hunterian Museum, Glasgow. Latterly, she went on to take up an appointment as lecturer at the University of Glasgow, where she taught and mentored many students who have gone on to make their careers in Viking archaeology.

In addition to her academic work, Colleen has spent many summers lecturing on expedition ships about the archaeology of their destinations from the Baltic to Canada, including many UNESCO World Heritage Sites.

Colleen retired from teaching at the University of Glasgow in 2019 as Senior Lecturer. She is remembered fondly by her many former students for her wit and her willingness to make time for students of all levels. She now lives in Orkney near a Norse archaeological site, is a Visiting Reader at the University of the Highlands and Islands and is writing up her excavations at the Earl's Bu. She is active in many Viking projects throughout Scotland and continues to encourage and inspire early career researchers and colleagues. It is a pleasure to dedicate this volume to her.

Foreword
Judith Jesch

Scotland has always played a major part in both public and academic understandings of the Viking Age (usually defined as 750–1050 CE) and its aftermath. Scandinavian Scotland was linked south to England and the European continent, south-west to Ireland, north-west to the Faroes, Iceland, Greenland and North America, and east to the Norwegian homeland from which many Scandinavian Scots are thought to have come. Unlike many of these other regions in the western Viking world (with the exception of the new polities of Faroe and Iceland), Scotland retained formal and political, as well as cultural and linguistic, connections with Scandinavia well beyond the end of the Viking Age, until 1266 in the Hebrides and 1468/9 in the Northern Isles. As a result of the longevity of its Scandinavian contacts, it is arguably Scotland that best fits the model of a 'Viking diaspora', extending throughout the Viking Age and into what is generally known as the 'Late Norse' period.

It was thus no accident that the very first Viking Congress was held in Shetland in 1950. The publication of the papers from that meeting (Simpson 1954) set the tone for a lively interdisciplinary conversation between archaeologists, historians, philologists, onomasts, art historians and academics from other disciplines which continues today and in which Colleen Batey has had a central role. It was at the 1989 Viking Congress in Caithness and Orkney that I first met Colleen, a fellow Durham graduate, who had already established herself as an expert on the Viking and Late Norse archaeology of Caithness at the previous Viking Congress (Batey 1987). I remember Colleen as a lively guide on excursions to Freswick and Robertshaven in Caithness and Orphir in Orkney, as well as presenting a paper on the Viking and Late Norse graves of Caithness and Sutherland. After the Congress, I was asked to join Colleen and Chris Morris in editing the proceedings (Batey et al. 1993) and I well remember a long, hard but convivial weekend in Glasgow preparing the final version for submission to the Press. Just how we managed it all in those days before email or electronic documents is a mystery to me now, for back then even those who had a newfangled personal computer still mailed in a typescript which we then sent on to the Press for typesetting. Given the size and complexity of the volume, we and the Press did well, I think, to get it out in time for the next Congress in 1993.

Colleen's work on the Late Norse site at Freswick Links, based on excavations going back to 1979, culminated in the full site report published in 1995 with Chris Morris and James Rackham (Morris et al. 1995). However, lest anyone think that she was only interested in northern Scotland, or the Late Norse period, three years later Colleen and James Graham-Campbell published the book celebrated at the conference from which the papers in this volume derive (Graham-Campbell and Batey 1998). The combination of a site and a finds specialist was ideal for the archaeological and Viking-Age focus of the book, though the authors give due acknowledgement to both non-archaeological evidence and the interest of the later period. The papers in the present volume pick up on many of the themes of *Vikings in Scotland*, while also presenting new approaches and disciplines, and are a fitting tribute to Colleen's long career, many publications, gift for collaboration and central role in presenting Scandinavian Scotland to the world.

References

Batey, C. E. (1987) Viking and Late Norse Caithness: The archaeological evidence. In J. Knirk (ed.), *Proceedings of the Tenth Viking Congress, Larkollen, Norway, 1985*. Oslo: Universitetets Oldsaksamling, 131–48.

Batey, C. E., J. Jesch and C. D. Morris (eds) (1993) *The Viking Age in Caithness, Orkney and the North Atlantic*. Edinburgh: Edinburgh University Press.

Graham-Campbell, J. and C. E. Batey (1998) *Vikings in Scotland: An Archaeological Survey*. Edinburgh: Edinburgh University Press.

Morris, C. D., C. E. Batey and D. J. Rackham (eds) (1995) *Freswick Links, Caithness: Excavation and Survey of a Norse Settlement*. Inverness and New York: Highland Libraries in association with the North Atlantic Biocultural Organisation.

Simpson, W. D. (ed.) (1954) *The Viking Congress: Lerwick, July 1950*. Edinburgh: Oliver and Boyd.

Before *Vikings in Scotland* – A Brief History of Viking-Age Archaeology in Scotland

Olwyn Owen

It was well over forty years ago that Colleen Batey and I first crossed the causeway to the beautiful Brough of Birsay (Figure 0.1). We will be forever grateful for that magic time of discovering Orkney, Vikings and archaeology – all within the same few weeks of digging on the Brough. That first encounter was in the mid-1970s, by which time excavations led by Morris and Hunter were underway (see Morris, this volume). Soon after, Morris extended his fieldwork to Birsay village and the Point of Buckquoy, where Ritchie (1977) had recently unearthed a sequence of Pictish dwellings overlain by Norse buildings, reviving the perennial controversy about what happened to the Picts when Scandinavians first arrived. In retrospect, this work heralded a new age of discovery and research about Norse Scotland, which culminated some twenty years later in Graham-Campbell and Batey's comprehensive review of the archaeological evidence in *Vikings in Scotland* (1998) and has continued ever since. In the 1970s, though, our understanding was still fairly rudimentary.

The Northern Isles were invariably the focus of early research and had fared better than any other part of Scotland in terms of attention given; but it is salutary now to recall how few settlement sites were known then, even in Orkney, let alone investigated. In 1977, Ritchie lamented the 'amazingly small body of evidence'. In his overview of Viking Orkney published in 1985, Morris concluded: 'it is not yet possible to generalise about the settlement evolution of the area in the Viking period'.

The Brough of Birsay, in common with many monuments in the Northern Isles, had been examined by antiquarians, and was then partly excavated by the Ministry of Works before and after the Second World War to display the site (Morris, this volume). These interventions were something of a mixed blessing: on one hand, they made sites accessible and better known; on the other, they often 'cleared' rather than excavated sites, and sometimes inappropriately consolidated these important

Figure 0.1 Brough of Birsay, Orkney.

monuments. The results were also more likely to translate into guidebooks than full archaeological accounts, if they appeared at all.

The Earl's Bu in Orphir (Batey, this volume) has a long history of interventions. *Orkneyinga Saga* (Chapter 66: Taylor 1938) makes clear that the famous round church and earl's hall were situated close together, which prompted several antiquarian attempts to locate the hall. Johnston believed he had found it in his excavations from 1899–1901 and went to great lengths to marry the saga's description of the hall with the features he uncovered, but it is clear he was looking at several different structures (see Batey, this volume). The site was purchased in 1939 by Walter Grant, and excavation commenced by 'two labourers'. Unfortunately, the only surviving records of this work comprise a single plan and an incomplete site book, which at least furnishes an insight into the site's complexity. The reason for dwelling on the sorry tale of excavations at the Earl's Bu before 1978 (when Batey began her excavations of the Norse mill) is not only because the site is so important in the history of the earldom, but also because it explains why the remains laid out today are almost unintelligible. It is a cautionary tale about the dangers of searching for archaeological evidence to corroborate information in *Orkneyinga Saga*.

Despite all this work in Orkney, since the 1950s it is arguably Jarlshof in Shetland that has dominated our picture of settlement. The results of

Hamilton's excavations, published in 1956, provided the template for a Viking farmstead with its sequence of rebuilt longhouses and outbuildings – and arguably still do today. This site, too, had suffered several early interventions after its discovery in 1897, and Hamilton's interpretation was hindered by lack of publication of this earlier work, as well as by the complexity of this multi-period settlement. The site is ripe for reassessment, and Hamilton's seven Viking and Late Norse phases should be treated with caution. Nonetheless, when Wainwright published his seminal overview of Scandinavian settlement in the Northern Isles in 1962, he cemented the significance of Jarlshof to the study of Scandinavian Scotland: 'For a picture of a Viking settlement in the Northern Isles we are at present dependent almost entirely upon Jarlshof. Fortunately, Jarlshof gives us a very full picture' (Wainwright 1962: 147).

A handful of other Norse sites in the earldom were excavated during the 1960s and '70s. Small's 1962 excavation of a single Norse farmstead at Underhoull, Unst, Shetland, led him to develop an influential model of the environmental factors determining the location of Viking settlements (Small 1966; 1968). In the mid-1970s, work on the Brough of Deerness, Orkney, gave an early insight into Norse chapels and the process of Christianisation (Morris and Emery 1986); while at Skaill in Deerness, Gelling directed a long-running project from 1963 to 1981. Skaill is putatively associated with an important character in *Orkneyinga Saga*, Thorkel Fostri (the fosterer), who played a pivotal role in the story of his foster-son, the mighty Earl Thorfinn. The multi-period settlement at Skaill spanned the Late Bronze Age to the post-medieval period. The degree of survival and complexity of the Norse buildings were impressive, but the short seasons and excavating the same building sometimes many years apart must have impeded interpretation. Unfortunately, Gelling died in 1983 and left an incomplete record. However, a paper he had delivered at a 1981 conference was published after his death (Gelling 1984) and is the only significant report on Skaill written by Gelling himself. Thankfully, the project was brought to publication by Gelling's colleagues at Birmingham University (Buteux 1997), but some of the lacunae in the site record have inevitably affected our understanding.

In general, our understanding of Norse settlement has been bedevilled by a lack of, or long delays in, publication – a problem that persisted through the 1970s, 1980s and beyond. It is hard to believe now, but, in those pre-developer funding days, it was normal not to commence post-excavation until fieldwork was complete, which significantly delayed publication of multi-season projects and contributed to a major backlog in publication – one only tackled seriously from the 1990s.

By the 1980s, several major multi-season projects were underway, notably at Pool in Sanday and Tuquoy in Westray, Orkney. Pool produced a plethora of important new information, including unexpected evidence of the earliest Norse arrivals effectively squatting in abandoned Pictish buildings (Hunter 2007: 121–68), a picture repeated in the 1990s at Old Scatness, Shetland (Dockrill, this volume); while Tuquoy cast new light on a high-status settlement with its zenith in the 12th century (Owen, this volume). Crawford's twenty-year campaign of excavations at The Biggings, Papa Stour, Shetland, from 1977 to 1990, was a research-led interdisciplinary project, which, among much else, uncovered the remains of a so-far unique wooden *stofa* (Crawford and Ballin Smith 1999). The Late Norse settlement at Sandwick in Unst, excavated by Bigelow from the late 1970s, was more typical of a Late Norse farmstead in terms of both its findings and the coastal erosion threatening the site (Bigelow 1985; 1987).

The dearth of reference so far to any part of Scotland other than the Northern Isles reflects the relative sparsity of research and knowledge from elsewhere much before the millennium. In *Vikings in Scotland* (1998), Graham-Campbell and Batey list only The Udal in North Uist (an important settlement still not adequately published: Crawford 1977) and Drimore in South Uist (Maclaren 1974) as excavated settlements in the Western Isles, though they also describe tantalising traces at eroding midden sites such as Barvas (see MacLeod Rivett and Cowie, this volume). This situation has improved markedly with important results from sites excavated recently at Bornais and Cille Pheadair, South Uist (Sharples 2005; 2021; Parker Pearson 2018).

It is equally surprising to realise that the only other confirmed Norse settlements known in mainland Scotland in 1998 were Freswick Links and Robert's Haven in Caithness, and Whithorn in Galloway, though each cast new light on the period. Freswick, for example, dug in the 1930s and '40s, and revisited in the 1970s (Batey 1987; Morris et al. 1995), produced a sequence of Norse settlement and extended our understanding of the Orkney earldom geographically. Barrett's work at Robert's Haven provided an early insight into the importance of fishing and the stockfish trade in the Late Norse period (Barrett 1997), which has become a major theme at several sites dug more recently, including Quoygrew, Westray (Barrett 2012) and St Boniface, Papa Westray (Lowe 1998); while Whithorn demonstrated the role of the Norse in a proto-urban settlement in Scotland, not unlike that in Dublin (Hill 1997). The 1990s also saw the 're-discovery' of a collection of early medieval sculpture at Govan on the Clyde (Ritchie 1994), including a remarkable group of five hogback stones, which prompted new archaeological work investigating this power centre and the relationship between Scandinavians and Strathclyde Britons (Owen and Driscoll 2011).

The other types of archaeological evidence available for Viking Scotland, notably pagan graves, had invariably been discovered by accident, most of them in antiquity and poorly recorded. Despite the comparative dearth of known settlement sites, the west of Scotland has produced some very wealthy graves, such as the burial at Kiloran Bay, Colonsay, discovered in the 1880s (Anderson 1906–7), a dispersed cemetery at Ballinaby, Islay (Anderson 1879–80; Edwards 1933–4) and another cemetery at Cnip, Uig, Lewis (MacLeod et al. 1916; Dunwell et al. 1995). The Kiloran Bay grave was reasonably well recorded by contemporary standards, but finders in antiquity were generally more concerned to recover artefacts and skulls than to record the graves themselves. In mainland Scotland, Viking graves, and sometimes cemeteries, have been discovered from Caithness (Reay, for example: Batey 1993) to Argyll (Ardnamurchan: Harris et al. 2017) to East Lothian (Auldhame: Crone and Hindmarch 2016).

Orkney has by far the largest concentration of pagan graves from Scandinavian Scotland, and its most extensive burial place is on the Links of Pierowall, Westray. Unfortunately, the Pierowall burials were revealed piecemeal through erosion and sand-blow from the 17th to the 19th centuries, and the surviving antiquarian sources and artefacts give a confused picture (Thorsteinsson 1968). Most of the artefacts and human remains are lost, although a few pieces survive in museums. Painstaking research by Graham-Campbell (see Graham-Campbell et al., this volume) has revealed evidence of thirty-three graves, but there are likely to have been more, perhaps many more, indicating the presence of a market by this excellent harbour (Owen 2005).

Viking graves excavated to modern standards include the boat burial at Scar, Sanday, with its three individuals (Owen and Dalland 1999), and the burial of a boy at Balnakeil, Durness, Sutherland (Batey and Paterson 2013). The first grave found at Westness, in Rousay, Orkney – a richly accompanied woman buried with a newborn infant and a superb Celtic brooch (Stevenson 1989) – was discovered accidentally in 1963 when a cow was being buried. In the late 1970s and early '80s, Kaland returned to Westness and dug an entire Pictish and Norse cemetery, which has yielded the remains of over thirty individuals, with graves dating from the 7th to 11th centuries (Kaland 1993; Sellevold 1999). Meanwhile, scientific advances continue to cast light on older and not-so-old discoveries, as, for example, the recent DNA analysis of the three burials in the Scar boat, which strongly suggests that this elderly woman, a man in his thirties and a child aged about ten were a family group – mother, son and grandson. Graham-Campbell and Paterson's forthcoming compendium of pagan Norse graves in Scotland will doubtless cast further light on many of the burials discovered in times gone by (see Graham-Campbell et al., this volume).

Similar problems of serendipitous discoveries in antiquity and poor recording afflict the evidence of Viking-Age gold and silver hoards and single finds. The Skaill Hoard, for example, was discovered in 1858 by a boy fossicking in a rabbit burrow. Well over a hundred silver objects and coins, weighing over 8kg in total, were dug up and dispersed among the finders. It was only thanks to the efforts of George Petrie that most of the hoard was recovered soon afterwards, though items were still making their way to the National Museum as late as 1981. Against this background, the Galloway Hoard, recovered in 2014, is remarkable not only for its contents, but also because it was retrieved mainly by professional archaeologists and has an archaeological context (Owen 2015; Goldberg and Davis 2021; Goldberg, this volume). Graham-Campbell's (1995) invaluable study of Viking-Age gold and silver in Scotland brought together all the available evidence for the (then known) thirty-four hoards and twenty-five single finds of treasure, and prompted further research into specialist aspects, such as ring-money (see also Graham-Campbell, this volume).

Runic inscriptions have received similar comprehensive treatment, in this case by Barnes, with his work on the thirty-three (minimum) inscriptions in Maeshowe standing as a particular highlight (Barnes 1994). Jesch has produced an equally impressive body of philological work over forty years, focused on the sagas and skaldic poetry (for example, Jesch 2005); while various authors, from Nicolaisen (1976) onwards, including Fellows-Jensen (for example, 1984) and the late Doreen Waugh (for example, 1991), have continued to extract new information from the copious Scandinavian-derived place-names from northern and western Scotland.

Several scholars sought to bring all this evidence together before *Vikings in Scotland* was published, notably Crawford, whose *Scandinavian Scotland* (1987) was rooted in historical, linguistic, literary and archaeological research, and remains a model of the interdisciplinary work so essential for any serious investigation of the impact of the Norse. Today this is such a 'given' that it hardly needs stating, but in the 1970s and '80s, it was neither accepted wisdom nor easily achieved: the networks and mechanisms for collaborations were simply not in place. The need for an interdisciplinary approach was recognised as long ago as 1950, when the Viking Congress was initiated to bring together scholars from Britain, Ireland and Scandinavia and to promote collaboration between different disciplines; but the Congress was only partly successful in this endeavour over succeeding decades (Smith 2016). These days, of course, there is a much wider range of technical, scientific, environmental and other considerations, which adds to the challenge of achieving true interdisciplinarity, but also adds significantly to the potential information yield of modern excavations and discoveries. More popular accounts also began to appear in the 1990s, such as Ritchie's *Viking Scotland* (1993) and Owen's *The Sea Road* (1999), both focused mainly on archaeological evidence.

The two decades since *Vikings in Scotland* was published have seen a leap forward in the number, type and geographical range of investigations and associated research into the enduring impact of Scandinavian colonisation. Some types of monuments, such as *thing-* sites, markets and landing places, were almost entirely unexplored in 1998, but are now topics of considerable interest, while studies of artefacts and palaeoenvironmental evidence have multiplied to great effect in the last twenty years. Clearly, much remains to be discovered, but these days every project seems to add a new dimension to our understanding of this multifaceted and fascinating period. The papers in this volume give but a glimpse of the diverse and important work now underway.

References

Anderson, J. (1879–80) Notes on the contents of two Viking graves in Islay, discovered by William Campbell Esq, of Ballinaby . . . *Proceedings of the Society of Antiquaries of Scotland* 14, 51–69.

Anderson, J. (1906–7) Notice of bronze brooches . . . With description, from notes by the late William Galloway, of a ship-burial of the Viking time at Kiloran Bay, Colonsay. *Proceedings of the Society of Antiquaries of Scotland* 41, 437–50.

Barnes, M. P. (1994) *The Runic Inscriptions of Maeshowe, Orkney.* Runron 8, Uppsala Universitetet.

Barrett, J. H. (1997) Fish trade in Norse Orkney and Caithness: a zooarchaeological approach. *Antiquity* 71, 616–38.

Barrett, J. H. (ed.) (2012) *Being an Islander: Production and Identity at Quoygrew, Orkney,* AD *900–1600.* Cambridge: McDonald Institute Monograph.

Batey, C. E. (1987) *Freswick Links, Caithness: A Reappraisal of the Late Norse Site in its Context.* British Archaeological Reports, British Series 179 (2 vols). Oxford: BAR publishing.

Batey, C. E. (1993) The Viking and Late Norse graves of Caithness and Sutherland. In C. E. Batey, J. Jesch and C. D. Morris (eds), *The Viking Age in Caithness, Orkney and the North Atlantic.* Edinburgh: Edinburgh University Press, 148–64.

Batey, C. E. and C. Paterson (2013) A Viking burial at Balnakeil, Sutherland. In L. Webster and A. Reynolds (eds), *Early Medieval Art and Archaeology in the Northern World. Studies in Honour of James Graham-Campbell.* Leiden: Brill, 631–61.

Bigelow, G. F. (1985) Sandwick, Unst and the Late Norse Shetland economy. In B. Smith (ed.), *Shetland Archaeology: New Work in Shetland in the 1970s.* Lerwick: The Shetland Times Ltd, 95–127.

Bigelow, G. F. (1987) Domestic architecture in medieval Shetland, *ROSC (Review of Scottish Culture)* 3, 23–38.

Buteux, S. (1997) *Settlements at Skaill, Deerness, Orkney: Excavations by Peter Gelling of the Prehistoric, Pictish, Viking and Later Periods, 1963–1981.* University of Birmingham/British Archaeological Reports British Series 260. Oxford: BAR publishing.

Crawford, B. E. (1987) *Scandinavian Scotland*. Scotland in the Early Medieval Ages 2. Leicester: Leicester University Press.

Crawford, B. E. and B. Ballin Smith (1999) *The Biggings, Papa Stour, Shetland: The History and Archaeology of a Royal Norwegian Farm*. Society of Antiquaries of Scotland monograph 15. Edinburgh: Society of Antiquaries of Scotland.

Crawford, I. A. and V. R. Switsur (1977) Sandscaping and C14: The Udal, North Uist. *Antiquity* 51, 124–36.

Crone, A. and E. Hindmarch with A. Woolf (2016) *Living and Dying at Auldhame: The Excavation of an Anglian Monastic Settlement and Medieval Parish Church*. Edinburgh: Society of Antiquaries of Scotland.

Dunwell, A. J., T. G. Cowie, M. F. Bruce, T. Neighbour and A. R. Rees (1995) A Viking Age cemetery at Cnip, Uig, Isle of Lewis. *Proceedings of the Society of Antiquaries of Scotland* 125, 719–52.

Edwards, A. J. H. (1933–4) A Viking cist-grave at Ballinaby, Islay. *Proceedings of the Society of Antiquaries of Scotland* 68, 74–8.

Fellows-Jensen, G. (1984) Viking settlement in the Northern and Western Isles – the place-name evidence as seen from Denmark and the Danelaw. In A. Fenton and H. Pálsson (eds), *The Northern and Western Isles in the Viking World: Survival, Continuity and Change*. Edinburgh: John Donald Publishers, 148–68.

Gelling, P. S. (1984) The Norse buildings at Skaill, Deerness, Orkney, and their immediate predecessor. In A. Fenton and H. Pálsson (eds), *The Northern and Western Isles in the Viking World: Survival, Continuity and Change*. Edinburgh: John Donald Publishers, 12–39.

Goldberg, M. and M. Davis (2021) *The Galloway Hoard: Viking-Age Treasure*. Edinburgh: National Museums of Scotland.

Graham-Campbell, J. (1995) *The Viking-Age Gold and Silver of Scotland (AD 850–1100)*. Edinburgh: National Museums of Scotland.

Graham-Campbell, J. and C. E. Batey (1998) *Vikings in Scotland: An Archaeological Survey*. Edinburgh: Edinburgh University Press.

Graham-Campbell, J. and C. Paterson (forthcoming) *Pagan Norse Graves in Scotland*.

Hamilton, J. R. C. (1956) *Excavations at Jarlshof, Shetland*. Edinburgh: HMSO.

Harris, O. J. T., H. Cobb, C. E. Batey, J. Montgomery, J. Beaumont, H. Gray, P. Murtagh and P. Richardson (2017) Assembling places and persons: A tenth-century Viking boat burial from Swordle Bay on the Ardnamurchan peninsula, western Scotland. *Antiquity* 91 (355), 191–206.

Hill, P. (ed.) (1997) *Whithorn and St Ninian: The Excavation of a Monastic Town 1984–91*. Stroud: The Whithorn Trust and Sutton Publishing.

Hunter, J. with J. M. Bond and A. N. Smith (2007) *Investigations in Sanday, Orkney, Volume 1: Excavations at Pool, Sanday. A Multi-period Settlement from Neolithic to Late Norse Times*. Kirkwall: The Orcadian Ltd.

Jesch, J. (2005) Literature in medieval Orkney. In O. Owen (ed.), *The World of* Orkneyinga Saga: *The Broad-cloth Viking Trip*. Kirkwall: The Orcadian Ltd, 11–24.

Kaland, S. H. H. (1993) The settlement of Westness, Rousay. In C. E. Batey, J. Jesch and C. D. Morris (eds), *The Viking Age in Caithness, Orkney and the North Atlantic*. Edinburgh: Edinburgh University Press, 308–17.

Lowe, C. E. (1998) *St Boniface Church, Orkney: Coastal Erosion and Archaeological Assessment*. Edinburgh: Sutton Publishing and Historic Scotland.

Maclaren, A. (1974) A Norse house on Drimore machair, South Uist. *Glasgow Archaeological Journal* 3, 9–18.

MacLeod, D. J., W. Gibson and J. Curle (1916) An account of a find of ornaments of the Viking time from Valtos, Uig, in the island of Lewis. *Proceedings of the Society of Antiquaries of Scotland* 50, 181–9.

Morris, C. D. (1985) Viking Orkney: A survey. In C. Renfrew (ed.), *The Prehistory of Orkney BC 4000–1000 AD*. Edinburgh: Edinburgh University Press, 210–42.

Morris, C. D. and N. Emery (1986) The chapel and enclosure on the Brough of Deerness, Orkney: Survey and excavations, 1975–1977. *Proceedings of the Society of Antiquaries of Scotland* 116, 301–74.

Morris, C. D., C. E. Batey and D. J. Rackham (1995) *Freswick Links, Caithness: Excavation and Survey of a Norse Settlement*. North Atlantic Biocultural Association monograph 1 and Highland Archaeology monograph 1. New York and Inverness: NABO.

Nicolaisen, W. F. H. (1976) *Scottish Place-names: Their Study and Significance*. London: Batsford.

Owen, O. (1999) *The Sea Road: A Viking Voyage through Scotland*. Edinburgh: Canongate Books.

Owen, O. (2005) Scotland's Viking 'towns': A contradiction in terms?. In A. Mortensen and S. V. Arge, *Viking and Norse in the North Atlantic* (= Proceedings of the Fourteenth Viking Congress). Tórshavn: Faroese Academy of Sciences in collaboration with Historical Museum of the Faroe Islands, 297–306.

Owen, O. (2015) Galloway's Viking treasure: The story of a discovery. *British Archaeology* 140, 16–23.

Owen, O. and M. Dalland (1999) *Scar: A Viking Boat Burial on Sanday, Orkney*. East Linton: Tuckwell Press.

Owen, O. and S. T. Driscoll (2011) Norse influence at Govan on the Firth of Clyde, Scotland. In S. Sigmundsson (ed.), *Viking Settlements and Viking Society* (= Proceedings of the Sixteenth Viking Congress). Reykjavík: University of Iceland Press, 333–46.

Parker Pearson, M., M. Brennand, J. Mulville and H. Smith (2018) *Cille Pheadair: A Norse Farmstead and Pictish Burial Cairn in South Uist*. Oxford: Oxbow Books.

Ritchie, A. (1977) Excavations of Pictish and Viking-Age farmsteads at Buckquoy, Orkney. *Proceedings of the Society of Antiquaries of Scotland* 108, 174–227.

Ritchie, A. (1993) *Viking Scotland*. London: Batsford and Historic Scotland.

Ritchie, A. (ed.) (1994) *Govan and its Early Medieval Sculpture*. Stroud: Sutton Publishing Ltd.

Sellevold, B. J. (1999) *Picts and Vikings at Westness: Anthropological Investigations of the Skeletal Material from the Cemetery at Westness, Rousay, Orkney Islands*. NIKU Scientific Report 010. Oslo: Norsk institutt for kulturminneforskning.

Sharples, N. (ed.) (2005) *A Norse Farmstead in the Outer Hebrides: Excavations at Mound 3, Bornais, South Uist*. Oxford: Oxbow Books.

Sharples, N. (ed.) (2021) *The Economy of a Norse Settlement in the Outer Hebrides: Excavations at Mounds 2 and 2A, Bornais, South Uist*. Oxford: Oxbow Books.

Small, A. (1966) Excavations at Underhoull, Unst, Shetland. *Proceedings of the Society of Antiquaries of Scotland* 98, 225–48.

Small, A. (1968) A historical geography of the Norse Viking colonisation of the Scottish Highlands. *Norsk Geog Tidskrift* 22, 1–16.

Smith, B. (2016) 'An idea original and sympathetic': Viking Congresses and their transformations, 1950–2013. In V. E. Turner, O. Owen and D. J. Waugh (eds), *Shetland and the Viking World* (= Proceedings of the Seventeenth Viking Congress, Lerwick). Lerwick: Shetland Heritage Publications, 1–6.

Stevenson, R. B. K. (1989) The Celtic brooch from Westness, Orkney, and hinged-pins. *Proceedings of the Society of Antiquaries of Scotland* 119, 239–69.

Taylor, A. B. (trans.) (1938) *The* Orkneyinga Saga: *A New Translation with Introduction and Notes*. Edinburgh: Oliver and Boyd.

Thorsteinsson, A. (1968) The Viking burial place at Pierowall, Westray, Orkney. In B. Niclasen (ed.), *Proceedings of the Fifth Viking Congress*. Tórshavn: Feroya Landsstyri, Torshavnar Byrad, Foroya Frooskaparfelag, Foroya, 150–73.

Wainwright, F. T. (1962) The Scandinavian settlement. In F. T. Wainwright, *The Northern Isles*. Edinburgh: Nelson, 117–62.

Waugh, D. J. (1991) Place-name evidence for Scandinavian settlement in Shetland. *ROSC (Review of Scottish Culture)* 7, 15–23.

Part I

The Arrival of the Vikings and Native–Norse Interactions

The historical sources for the start of the Viking Age in Scotland are sparse at best and comprise only occasional mentions of raids in the Irish historical sources. The resulting view that violent Viking raids or invasions occurred around 800, which were then followed by land-taking (*landnám*) and settlement, dominated archaeological thought at the time of the publication of *Vikings in Scotland*, although this was starting to change (Griffiths, this section). The Scandinavian arrivals could be identified in the archaeological record, particularly in the Northern and Western Isles of Scotland, with pagan graves furnished with weapons, grave goods and sometimes boats or horses, bowed longhouses, and an increased use of steatite vessels and the expansion of fishing. However, there was still a lot to be learnt about the nature of the initial contact between the native populations in Scotland of Picts, Gaels, Angles and Britons, and about the processes by which this transitioned to land-taking, naming and settlement (Graham-Campbell and Batey 1998: 23–4, 54, 72–4, 93–5).

Both leading up to the publication of *Vikings in Scotland* and beyond, arguments have ranged from total genocide of the native populations on the one hand, to peaceful coexistence within an incoming, but ultimately dominating, Scandinavian culture on the other (see Barrett 2008). The research included in this section demonstrates that the situation is far more nuanced than has always been appreciated. Norse impact varied among different areas, and the increasing recognition of continuity and change in the archaeological record demonstrates that the reality of native–Norse interaction was complex, something also mirrored in place-name studies (Macniven, Whyte and Clancy, all this volume).

As Griffiths illustrates, there is a noted gap in radiocarbon dates from northern and western Scotland spanning the likely period of first Viking arrivals to the later 10th century, whereas evidence for architecture and landscape use is clearly identifiable as Scandinavian. He suggests this may be the result of an intermediate period of transition, which Dockrill and Bond (this section) have also identified at Old Scatness, Shetland and suggest that this process was complex and continued for some time.

Within this context, Spall (this section) describes the evidence for razing by fire of the 8th-century Pictish monastic settlement of Portmahomack in the Tarbat peninsula between 780 and 810. Seen by the excavators as evidence for an otherwise undocumented Viking raid, this chapter gives us a stark picture of the reality of destruction and the probable fragmentation of Pictish landholdings along the inner Moray Firth. In contrast, a strong argument for continuity is provided by excavations at the chapel and burial ground on St Ninian's Isle, Shetland (Barrowman, this section), where new analyses have led to a re-evaluation of the original interpretations of violent Viking incursions into the site around 800. Instead, a continued loyalty to the site by both the native Pictish and incoming Norse populations is evidenced despite seismic changes of belief and culture.

References

Barrett, J. H. (2008) The Norse in Scotland. In S. Brink and N. Price (eds), *The Viking World*. Abingdon: Routledge, 411–27.

Graham-Campbell, J. and C. E. Batey (1998) *Vikings in Scotland: An Archaeological Survey*. Edinburgh: Edinburgh University Press.

Chapter 1

Landnám and Landscape in Viking Orkney
David Griffiths

The Viking heritage of Orkney and Shetland is widely and justifiably celebrated. Norse place-names abound in the landscapes and seascapes of the Northern Isles, to the virtual exclusion of other linguistic origins. Saints' dedications and other local traditions hark back to the islands' Norse earldom association with Scandinavia, prior to their transfer to Scotland in 1468–71. The *Orkneyinga Saga*, composed in Iceland around 1200, gives the origin of the Earldom of Orkney as happening in the reign of Harald Fairhair of Norway, around 870, although there are grounds for suspecting this to be a retrospective claim. The saga describes Harald's expedition to rid the islands of plundering Vikings (ethnicity unspecified) who had become a problem for Norway (Pálsson and Edwards 1978: 26). However, its coverage of events only becomes fully fledged from the time of Earl Sigurd II (960–1014), and there were political reasons in the context of 1200 for the advocates of Norwegian rule in the North Atlantic to 'back-date' its claim (Griffiths 2019; 2020). As argued below, the imprint of Scandinavian influence on the landscape of the Northern Isles may be a somewhat later development than traditionally supposed.

Eighteenth- and 19th-century antiquarians excavated in and around prehistoric monuments, and were not unaware of the legacy of the 'Danes' (Graham-Campbell 2004), but the Viking era in the Northern Isles was not a significant academic concern for excavation until more recently. *Orkneyinga Saga* was first translated into English as late as 1873 (Goudie et al. 1873), but it took yet longer for a search for the Viking presence to enter archaeological consciousness in a systematic way. An upsurge of nationalist-minded Viking scholarship in Scandinavia, particularly in Norway after its independence from Sweden was achieved in 1905, was undoubtedly influential, yielding the *Viking Antiquities in Great Britain and Ireland* series of volumes largely researched in the 1920s and published in 1940. Home-grown scholars of that era, notably J. Storer Clouston, and later Hugh Marwick, focused their attentions on documenting the physical and toponymic legacy of Norse rule. To Marwick, the Viking arrival was as bloody and complete as his scholarly Norwegian counterparts would have wished to hear: truly an ethnic cataclysm (Smith 2003: 145–6). The period of 'Culture History' in early to mid-20th-century archaeological scholarship emphasised invasion and conquest and the movements and migrations of peoples as explanations for culture change. This has been an enduringly powerful framework for academic research. It has produced an emphasis on the Viking Age as a total or near-complete break with the past, a recast or even supplanted society, and a 'colonial' presence introducing Scandinavian practices to virtually every sphere of life and death.

Despite there being no tangible evidence for early Viking raids in Orkney or Shetland (Griffiths 2019; 2020: 320–1), in common with the dates of early raiding which are historically attested elsewhere in Britain, there was for long a widespread acceptance that the critical moment of transition in the Northern Isles occurred with violent Viking raids or invasions around 800 followed by relatively synchronous Viking settlement (the *Landnám* – the taking or naming of land); from then on, Scandinavian dominance has been perceived to be profound. When *Vikings in Scotland: An Archaeological Survey* was published, these concepts and dates remained mainstream, although the beginnings of revisionist thinking were appearing (Graham-Campbell and Batey 1998: 54; see also Buteux 1997: 261–4 and Barrett et al. 2000). Twenty years on, there are yet greater grounds for questioning the continuing hold of the 'colonial invasion' concept. Was the early Viking arrival really such a dramatic and sudden watershed? – the 'Big Bang' theory as described by Barbara Crawford (1995: 139) – changing everything within a few years? (and need this idea necessarily be opposed to a universal counter-theory of peaceful assimilation?). Could it instead have been more of a slow, ragged process, perhaps involving undocumented episodes of violence on a local scale and some negotiation, with, in its early phase, cultural convergence between pre-Viking and Viking populations? Moreover, rather than the *landnám* happening largely at the start of the Viking presence, could episodes of political takeover, major societal change and immigration have occurred somewhat later, well within what we understand to be the Norse period? Could it therefore have taken a much longer and more incremental self-generating process for the landscape and culture of the islands which we recognise today as 'Scandinavian' to take shape?

Continuity, change and the early Viking presence in Orkney and Shetland

Vikings in Scotland: An Archaeological Survey lays out the means by which we document and understand the Viking presence. 'The Norwegian

Figure 1.1 Sites discussed in text.

Background' sets the scene for regional surveys in Scotland, followed by pagan Norse graves, settlements, the economy, hoards, runic inscriptions, sculpture, and influences on the church. The Northern Isles loom large throughout the book's coverage. Architecturally, much attention has been given to the differences between the rounded building forms of the pre-Viking era, notably Iron-Age brochs, wheelhouses and 'cellular' Pictish buildings, and the rectilinear longhouse style of domestic building commonly associated with the Viking presence. Pictish habitations underwent modifications of use, style and material culture which archaeologists have associated with the arrival of Scandinavian settlers, but there is then often seen a hiatus in locus and time before more substantial longhouse-based settlement forms emerge from the later 10th century onwards. In some cases, this activity takes place on (most often peripheral) parts of mounded sites which had been previously occupied, whereas in others it occurs on new sites, situated away from previous occupation. *Contiguity* of placement does not necessarily equate to *continuity* of occupation. Furnished pagan burial plays a particular role in these transitions, as will be discussed below.

Over the past fifty years, the most influential excavation for charting the transition from Pictish to Viking eras in Orkney has been the site of Buckquoy (Figure 1.2), near the end of the peninsula forming the northern

Figure 1.2 Excavation at Buckquoy, Birsay, Orkney, from the east, with House 4 in the foreground. Reproduced with kind permission of Anna Ritchie.

extent of Birsay Bay, on Orkney's West Mainland. This was excavated as a rescue project by Anna Ritchie in 1970–1 (Ritchie 1977). A settlement mound then perched on the edge of an eroding cliff-face, its physical position is now gone, but the influence of its published findings remains, and its interpretation was subject to a reappraisal by Ritchie and others in 2003 (Brundle et al. 2003). In the primary report of 1977, a relative scheme of phasing was developed, where Ritchie outlined five phases of occupation, two in association with cellular-type buildings and three subsequently with buildings of a more rectilinear plan. An orthodoxy emerged, which is conveyed in *Vikings in Scotland* (Graham-Campbell and Batey 1998: 160–1), that the latter three phases of occupation were indicative of a Norse occupation of the site. The 2003 reappraisal began to cast this interpretation in a more ambiguous light, quoting examples such as the Howe, near Stromness, where Iron-Age and Pictish buildings displayed rectilinear traits, and conversely where more rounded features have been observed in diagnostically Norse buildings, notably those on the neighbouring Brough of Birsay (Brundle et al. 2003: 96). The majority of the finds from Buckquoy were Pictish or Insular in type, and the later settlement phases did not produce a haul of typical bone pins, combs, beads and steatite such as might now be expected from a Viking settlement site in the Northern Isles, casting further doubt on their Norse attribution of the later phases. The authors of the 2003 reappraisal restated their belief that the later occupation phases were Norse, but their words convey a more equivocal tone than did the 1977 site report. Anna Ritchie has confirmed to the author that in the light of yet another generation of scholarship on early medieval Scotland having occurred in the interim, she now readily accepts the likelihood of a Pictish attribution for all of the occupation phases marked by both cellular and rectilinear buildings at Buckquoy (Ritchie, pers. comm. January 2021).[1]

In the most recent post-occupation phase (6) at Buckquoy was found a furnished burial of pagan type of a mature male above the remains of House 3. This included a cut halfpenny of Eadmund of Wessex (940–6), a date which must surely be the *terminus post-quem* of date of the burial deposit, despite a confusingly early radiocarbon date of the mid-first millennium AD, taken from human remains which were thought to be associated with the burial, but which may have come from an intrusive bone from an earlier deposit (Barrett 2003: 103). The furnished burial's mid-10th-century date chimes with other burials inserted in pre-Viking settlement mounds, which were then not subject to further Norse activity (see below).

The Brough of Birsay, a prominent tidal island a short distance off the western end of the Buckquoy peninsula, was described by Graham-Campbell and Batey as 'an embryonic [Pictish] power base which was taken over by the Vikings' (Graham-Campbell and Batey 1998: 11). On its eastern, landward-facing side, the roofless stone shell of the church known as the Norse earldom's first 'cathedral' of the early 12th century stands amid an extensive spread of Norse domestic and industrial structures, which overlie more structurally fleeting Pictish deposits containing important pre-Viking metalworking evidence. A cracked but complete Type II Pictish-style symbol stone was unearthed during excavations in 1935. There are signs in Birsay's long history of archaeological activity that the area's later political importance as a centre of the earldom may have affected interpretations of its central or unusual status in the preceding Pictish and early Viking periods, producing a caveat offered by Anne Brundle who discussed what she saw as its 'unimportance' in the Pictish era (Brundle 2005). A final publication by Christopher Morris of excavations on the Brough from 1954 onwards has recently appeared (Morris 2021; Morris, this volume). Commenting on her reappraisal of radiocarbon dates from Morris's excavations, with regard to the Pictish–Viking transition, Zoë Outram states: 'the earliest period of occupation was recorded on the Brough of Birsay in Sites I, III, IV North and South and in Room 5. The dates for the remains assessed within these areas spanned 665 cal AD to 1210 cal AD, which was refined to span *735 cal AD to 1190 cal AD* following the production of modelled estimates. This could be used to suggest that the initial Scandinavian occupation in Birsay occurred at the earliest within the *eighth century* but as late as the *twelfth century*' (Outram 2021: 560). The likelihood is somewhere in the middle of this range.

At the southern end of Birsay Bay, a large but badly deflated sandy settlement mound known as Saevar Howe was ineptly dug into in 1862, when a long-cist cemetery was identified along with pre-Viking artefacts, and was subjected to a smaller but more orderly rescue excavation in 1977, which identified walls and finds which were interpreted as denoting Norse and pre-Norse phases of occupation, but no trace of the cemetery was found (Hedges 1983). The date and precise nature of the transition between the phases and whether they were consecutive or separated by a hiatus was uncertain, although a silver penny of Burgred of Mercia (866–8) was found, associated with the earliest part of the trend towards a rectilinear building style.

At Pool, on Sanday, a large multi-period settlement mound excavated by John Hunter between 1983 and 1988, there was also some apparent evidence of settlement continuity from the Pictish to Viking periods towards the end of a long occupation sequence which begins in the Neolithic (Hunter 2007). Hunter's chapter 5, on the critical Phase 7 ('Interface and Scandinavian Settlement') is prefaced with a quotation from George Mackay Brown giving lyrical expression to a violent invasion by blond Scandinavians. The early part of Phase 7 (7.1) is still Iron-Age or Pictish in character, with compact, rounded buildings, but the succeeding sub-phase (7.2) saw the creation of longer, more sub-rectilinear buildings in two discrete areas on the north-eastern and southern peripheries of the main prehistoric settlement mound (Structures 25–28). The foundations of (Phase 7.2) Structure 25, a timber building, rest on part of the rounded, Iron-Age-style Structure 18, from Phase 7.1, indicating that Structure 18 had gone out of use. Nevertheless, Hunter postulated that there was an overlap in occupation between phases 7.1 and 7.2. Although preservation and therefore interpretation for Phase 7.2 were compromised by plough damage, Hunter was confident in drawing the conclusion that it marked the onset of Scandinavian occupation at the site, stating that Structure 25 'differed fundamentally from associated or earlier local styles', representing 'a fundamental change in cultural ethos' (ibid.: 123). The possibility of endogenous change explaining the Phase 7.2 building types at Pool was apparently not considered or favoured as an interpretation, perhaps showing the enduring power of the culture-historical paradigm in the minds of excavators. The onset of critical cultural change at Pool was argued, on the basis of five radiocarbon dates (Hunter 2007: 140), to the early date of the late 8th to early 9th century, despite calibration problems being referred to, and the materials dated not being mentioned in the report (thus preventing a view being taken on whether longevity of use, or the marine reservoir effect, might have skewed this chronology earlier than the time they might truly represent). A key element in Hunter's interpretation was the introduction of artefacts including steatite whorls and bone pins, together with flax- and ironworking evidence which are generally accepted to be more characteristic of Norse settlements, although the cultural signals from Phase 7 were mixed. The subsequent (and last) phase at Pool, Phase 8, did see a shift and reordering of the site towards a more pronounced Scandinavian cultural signature, with a well-preserved longhouse (Structure 29), a 'Late Norse' phase whose onset Hunter suggested had occurred in the 'late tenth or early eleventh century' (ibid.: 147). Phase 8 does not appear to be integrated in any way with Phase 7, suggesting rather than Hunter's preferred term 'reorganisation' (implying ongoing activity), a reuse of the site following a hiatus may in fact have taken place.

'Transitional' phases between Pictish and Norse identified at Buckquoy and Pool are also evident on comparable sites in Shetland. At Old Scatness, an extensive multi-period site near the southern tip of Mainland, with an Iron-Age broch and other structures, modifications to existing architecture and material culture, associated by their excavators with an early Norse presence, were initially imposed within the structure of pre-Viking wheelhouses, Structures 6 and 11. Internal space was reordered, hearths were modified, ironworking activity was detected and flagged floors introduced, leading their excavators to state that 'The Viking settlement at

Old Scatness was well-established by the beginning of the 10th century AD and probably by the late 9th century' (Bond and Dockrill 2016: 11). A fragmentary longhouse (Structure 4) appeared on part of the existing settlement mound, parts of the substantial Iron-Age structures, including a broch, were apparently altered to some extent, and there was a spread of fish middens of a type recognisable at Late Norse settlements elsewhere (Dockrill et al. 2010: 88–92). The authors of the 2010 Old Scatness report linked the onset of Norse occupation to the nearby and previously excavated site at Jarlshof (ibid., 95–7).

A similar site to Old Scatness in many respects, but with more pronounced Norse and later occupation (Figure 1.3), Jarlshof was extensively excavated before and after the Second World War, and promptly published in the 1950s (Hamilton 1956). At the end of the wheelhouse era, a number of small, simple sub-rectilinear buildings emerged which were located upon, but acentral to, the large prehistoric settlement mound (Phase I), whereas the succeeding Phase II saw much larger and more identifiably Norse-style longhouse construction, the two phases forming a remarkable parallel to Pool's phases

Figure 1.3 Norse longhouse at Jarlshof, Shetland. Andrew Jennings, used with permission.

Figure 1.4 Longhouse at East Mound, Bay of Skaill, Orkney under excavation, from the east. D. Griffiths.

7 and 8. J. R. C. Hamilton, the author of the comprehensive and well-crafted 1956 report, dated the start of Phase I as around the familiar (see above) historical watershed of 800, but lacking the facility of radiocarbon dating or statistical modelling, the site's phasing and chronology remain, as noted by Graham-Campbell and Batey in 1998, in need of re-examination. Elsewhere in Shetland, excavations of part of a multi-period settlement site at Norwick, Unst, have produced five radiocarbon determinations which, along with Norwegian-sourced steatite objects, suggest a relatively early phase of Viking occupation, possibly well within the 9th century, although there are some caveats about this possibility expressed in the interim publication (Ballin Smith 2013: 229). Norwick was identified as a Viking settlement on artefactual grounds, although there was also evidence of flagged floors and drains. The building remains were fragmentary but appear to lack some of the attributes of 'classic' longhouse settlements elsewhere in Unst, such as Underhoull, Hamar and Belmont, which are dated to a considerably later phase of the Viking Age (Bond and Dockrill 2016: 8).

The picture which emerges from the multi-period settlement sites briefly outlined above is of an intermediate phase of gradual adoption of architectural and artefactual traits which have been interpreted as Norse introductions, but aspects of which equally well could be endogenous adaptations. Material culture is portable, and architecture is subject to repeated modification and innovation. No society which is in any way connected to the outside world remains static in these respects. At Pool, Old Scatness and Jarlshof, an intermediate phase where pre-Viking buildings were used as foundations and to some extent remodelled, with a changing economy and material culture, was followed by a more pronounced Norse phase, but the case for direct contiguity between these phases remains uncertain. The spread of Later Norse longhouses on the Brough of Birsay, at Jarlshof and Phase 8 at Pool may essentially be new settlements of the mid-10th century onwards, in these cases taking advantage of abandoned but prominent locations rather than forming a direct evolution of their preceding phases. In the 1997 publication of excavations undertaken by Peter Gelling in 1963–81 at Skaill, Deerness, on Orkney's East Mainland, Simon Buteux stated that the evidence did not suggest much continuity between Pictish and Viking periods, despite the fact that the latest pre-Viking phase of buildings included rectilinear examples (Buteux 1997, quoted in Graham-Campbell and Batey 1998: 170). Although, like Jarlshof, the dating parameters of the site's phases are not supported by radiocarbon or other absolute dating chronologies and therefore subject to doubt and revision, Buteux perceptively divided the character of the Norse occupation into the 'pioneer', 'consolidation' and 'establishment' phases (Buteux 1997: 261–5).

Marking and establishing the Norse landscape

It is inevitable that many favoured settlement locations will attract repeated settlement over time, but the use by Norse settlers of older sites for occupation or burial does not present a consistent picture, nor was their settlement confined to existing foci. The situation appears to this author far more complex, nuanced and varied than a theory of appropriation of positions of existing power by incoming groups may suggest (see, for example, Leonard 2012; McLeod 2015). At Buckquoy, the settlement phase of the mound probably ended before the Phase VI pagan grave was inserted. It represents not a new beginning on that site, but the ending of a story reaching back into the pre-Viking period. Rather than an annexation by incoming peoples, it arguably represents a form of commemorative closure of an abandoned mound.

The Broch of Gurness (or Aikerness) on the Evie shore of Orkney's West Mainland was, prior to excavation in the 1930s, a large amorphous settlement mound accumulated around a well-preserved Iron-Age broch. The site evidently had some secondary Pictish and, less convincingly, Norse occupation; a building said to be from each era is reconstructed near its visitor centre, and in 1935 a roughly incised Class 1 Pictish symbol stone was found on top of a wall flanking the central passageway into the broch. At least two Viking burials were found among the latest deposits at the site, the better preserved of which was in a most prominent position at the outer limit of the entrance passage to the broch (Hedges 1987: 73). Other broch sites in Orkney, such as the Howe, near Stromness, and Lamba Ness on Sanday, have produced secondary Viking burials, as have sites of pre-Viking occupation and middens, such as at Brough Road (south of Red Craig), Birsay, 'Knowe of Moan', Harray, The Knowe of Swandro on Rousay, and Styes of Brough on Sanday (Morris 1989: 109–42; McLeod 2015: 2–4). At Swandro, a Late Norse longhouse settlement is located a short distance away from the (evidently somewhat earlier) Viking burial site, and at Brough Road, midden material accumulated evidently from Viking settlement activity somewhere nearby, but thus far we know of no evidence of such burials being focal foundation deposits for ongoing occupation. This indicates that, as at Buckquoy, such secondary pagan burials can be seen as an 'end event' for pre-Viking or indeed much earlier habitations which remained visible as features in the landscape, perhaps as an act of closure (as suggested by the prominent placement of the Gurness entrance passage burial, for instance), but were not intended to take over these particular locations for the purpose of continued use.

At rarer cemetery sites, such as Moa Ness, Westness, Rousay, furnished Viking burials were inserted among an established spread of unfurnished inhumations. Whether this is an indication of violent conquest or of cultural transition and continuity has been debated (the latter seems more likely), but chronologically, most attention on Westness has been focused on the start of the intrusive phase which is thought to have started in the 9th century. Stable isotope analysis on some of the Westness furnished burials has revealed that those individuals sampled were far from being uniformly Scandinavian in biological origin (Montgomery et al. 2014). The end-dates of Viking burial at Westness have been less remarked upon, but these could be significant in marking the changing cultural landscape. Sometimes, ends can be as important as beginnings. Other prominent Viking burials in Orkney have been dated to long after the putative start of the Viking Age. In the case of the boat burial at Scar, Sanday (Owen and Dalland 1999), radiocarbon dating on human remains in one case gave a date of 980–1260 cal AD, with the mean of three dates being 1060±40 BP, giving a probable overall date on radiocarbon grounds for the grave deposit in the mid- to later 10th century (the artefacts point towards somewhat earlier in the 10th century, but this difference could be explained by these having been in circulation for some time before the burial).

At the Bay of Skaill, Sandwick, an eroding, probably prehistoric settlement mound a short distance west of the Neolithic 'village' of Skara Brae was the site of a single furnished Viking burial, which James Graham-Campbell in a recent reappraisal has dated to no earlier than the first half of the 10th century (Graham-Campbell 2019a). Graham-Campbell also drew attention to a further possible Viking grave in Sandwick, indicated by a find prior to 1851 of a ringed-pin from a 'tumulus', the identification of which is uncertain. The location of any pre-10th-century Viking settlement at this prominent bay remains unresolved. A broch at Verron at the northern edge of the bay is a possible candidate for a 'transitional' site, as yet untested by excavation. Near Verron stands the former parish church of St Peter, from the graveyard of which a Viking bone strap-end decorated in the Borre style was retrieved during grave-digging in the early 1930s (Paterson 2019). The origins of the church site may date back at least to the Viking Age, as suggested by this find, especially if the theory (Lamb 1993) that the 'Peterkirks' of Orkney had a Pictish origin is accepted, but this theory has been challenged in favour of a 12th-century date (for example, Clancy 2012). Immediately south of the church is a prominent cluster of large sandy settlement mounds, the largest of which is called 'The Castle of Snusgar', a name first attested in the 1795 *Old Statistical Account* but likely to be of Norse origin. The environs of this mound, probably on its eastern flank, were the scene in 1858 of the discovery of the Skaill Hoard, which remains the largest identifiably Viking silver hoard in Scotland, the deposition of which has been dated to between 960 and 980 (Graham-Campbell 2019b: 296).

The author's own excavations at Snusgar and neighbouring East Mound (Griffiths et al. 2019) exposed two clusters of longhouses, with their main phases of occupation (Phases 2–4) dating to the later 10th to early 11th centuries. In this case, sixty AMS radiocarbon dates were obtained, giving a strong chronology anchored mostly on carbonised grain samples and refined by Bayesian modelling. In contrast to interpretations of other, previous excavations which tend to have been given long occupation phase durations of a century or more, the duration of these occupation phases was shown to be remarkably short, with major changes coming about within a generation at most. Both Snusgar and East Mound were new sites of longhouse occupation founded on open sandy grassland, in the case of Snusgar beginning contemporaneously with, or very shortly after, the deposition of the hoard. Was the hoard itself a foundation deposit in a new place, for a new phase of settlement?

Both of the Bay of Skaill excavations produced artefacts of bone, steatite, glass and amber, together with flaxworking, in the case of East Mound accompanied by ferrous metalworking, all of which accord with assemblages interpreted elsewhere (such as at Pool and Scatness) as indicative of Viking settlement. 'Placed deposits' and structured middens were present at the sites (Harrison 2020). There are indications among the comb types, pins and pottery, indeed in the hoard itself, of a more pronounced Irish-Sea flavour to the material culture of the site, rather than a directly imported Norwegian one. The better-preserved of the two longhouse sequences, on East Mound (Figure 1.4), was constructed around a central hall, which not only was the earliest structure on the site but was an interior space of some size and distinction, leading to its interpretation as a *skáli*, a tax-gathering central farmstead, even possibly providing a clue as to the origin of the name of the bay itself. No human burials or even fragmentary remains, with the exception of a child's tooth, were found in these domestic contexts, the implication probably being that burials were located at the nearby church, and therefore that the occupation started later than the end of the pagan period. The (re)conversion to Christianity must surely be a factor in the apparent closure of older sites, and the opening up of new ones, near to churches, and in the redrawing of the landscape which we see emerging from the mid-10th century. A comparable picture is observed at Marwick Bay, just north of the Bay of Skaill, where floor and metalworking deposits in an eroding settlement mound on the coastline produced two radiocarbon dates in the range 770–980 cal AD, indicating a site of the Pictish to early Viking period, whereas two *skáli* names, Langskaill and Netherskaill (evidently denoting the division of an original Skaill farm), lie between 0.8 and 1km inland, implying a settlement shift and landscape reconfiguration somewhat later in the Viking period (Griffiths et al. 2019: 10, 107).

Conclusion

The later 10th century seems to have been a significant time of transition and settlement renewal in the Orcadian landscape, and may represent something of a political takeover, long after the one traditionally sought. The period 960–80 saw the deposition of the Northern Isles' most extensive silver hoard, a series of furnished burials in abandoned settlement sites, and the beginnings of new forms of occupation and economy, dominated by impressive longhouses. Some of these were founded in new locations close to churches, such as those at the Bay of Skaill, whereas others, such as at Pool, are sited in proximity to earlier phases of occupation but not necessarily in unbroken continuity. Prior to this time, changes towards rectilinear forms of building and a more varied material culture had occurred in the architecture and material culture of mounded settlements, but these could, I suggest, be interpreted as much as endogenous changes adapting to new realities and incoming contacts in the 9th century, rather than necessarily being expressive of the stamp of the dominant intruder, as so often stated in the past. In this respect, there is something very subtle and interesting waiting to be teased out of the available evidence, which could reveal new insights as to how the pre-Viking population responded and adapted to external stimuli.

The 'Scandinavianisation' of Orkney and Shetland, with their distinctive patterns of assembly, landholding and nomenclature, surely gained some initial traction in the later 10th century, but it took several more centuries for these traditions to become fully and widely adapted, acculturated and established. The late William P. L. Thomson, Orkney's most revered local historian in the modern age, took issue with the earlier views of Hugh Marwick and others that these attributes could be traced back to the early Viking Age, preferring to see them as taking shape in the 12th century (Thomson 2008: 5–24). The growth of Scandinavian influence, now reflected in the islands' celebrated cultural heritage, is not attributable to an 'all at once' event of the early Viking Age, but an incremental process lasting several hundreds of years. This was reinvigorated in the period after 1100 when deep-sea cod fishing opened up new markets and contacts, and a new influx of direct Norwegian influence is witnessed at fish-processing sites such as Quoygrew, Westray (Barrett 2012). The era of the developed medieval earldom, rather than the early Viking Age, should therefore be seen as the principal source of the Scandinavian cultural transformation of the landscapes of the Northern Isles.

Note

1. Since this paper was written, several new radiocarbon dates have been obtained from the Buckquoy material by Gordon Noble and Charlotta Hillerdal (University of Aberdeen), which appear to confirm that the main settlement phases are all pre-Viking (Gordon Noble, pers. comm.).

References

Ballin Smith, B. (2013) Norwick, Shetland's earliest Viking settlement? In V. E. Turner, J. M. Bond and A.-C. Larsen (eds), *Viking Unst*. Lerwick: Shetland Amenity Trust, 217–32.

Barrett, J. H. (2003) Appendix 2, The radiocarbon dates from Buckquoy, Orkney. In J. Downes and A. Ritchie (eds), *Sea Change, Orkney and Northern Europe in the Later Iron Age, AD 300–800*. Balgavies: Pinkfoot Press, 103–4.

Barrett, J. H. (2012) *Being an Islander. Production and identity at Quoygrew, Orkney, AD 900–1600*. McDonald Institute Monographs. Cambridge: McDonald Institute for Archaeological Research.

Barrett, J. H., J. R. Beukens, I. Simpson, P. Ashmore, S. Poaps and J. Huntley (2000) What was the Viking Age and when did it happen? A view from Orkney. *Norwegian Archaeological Review* 33, 1–39.

Bond, J. and S. J. Dockrill (2016) Viking settlement and Pictish estates. New evidence from Orkney and Shetland. In V. E. Turner, O. A. Owen and D. J. Waugh (eds), *Shetland and the Viking World: Papers from the Seventeenth Viking Congress*. Lerwick: Shetland Heritage Publications, 7–13.

Brundle, A. (2005) The unimportance of early Birsay. In O. Owen (ed.), *The World of Orkneyinga Saga*. Kirkwall: The Orcadian, 75–87.

Brundle, A., D. Home Lorimer and A. Ritchie (2003) Buckquoy revisited. In J. Downes and A. Ritchie (eds), *Sea Change, Orkney and Northern Europe in the Later Iron Age, AD 300–800*. Balgavies: Pinkfoot Press, 95–104.

Buteux, S. (1997) *Settlements at Skaill, Deerness, Orkney, Excavations by Peter Gelling of the Prehistoric, Pictish, Viking and Later Periods, 1963–81*. British Archaeological Reports (British Series) 260. Oxford: Archaeopress.

Clancy, T. O. (2012) Paradigms and problems of insular saints' cults. In S. Boardman and E. Williamson (eds), *The Cult of Saints and the Virgin Mary in Medieval Scotland*. Woodbridge: Boydell, 1–20.

Crawford, B. E. (1995) *Scandinavian Scotland*. Leicester: Leicester University Press.

Dockrill, S., J. Bond, V. E. Turner, L. D. Brown, D. Bashford, J. E. Cussans and R. A. Nicholson (2010) *Excavations at Old Scatness, Shetland, Volume 1, The Pictish and Viking Settlement*. Lerwick: Shetland Heritage Publications.

Goudie, G., J. Andersen and J. A. Hjaltalin (1873) *The Orkneyinga Saga*. Edinburgh: Edmonston and Douglas.

Graham-Campbell, J. A. (2004) 'Danes … in this Country': Discovering the Vikings in Scotland. *Proceedings of the Society of Antiquaries of Scotland* 134, 201–39.

Graham-Campbell, J. A. (2019a) The 1888 Skaill Viking grave. In D. Griffiths, J. Harrison and M. Athanson, *Beside the Ocean, Coastal Landscapes at the Bay of Skaill, Marwick and Birsay Bay, Orkney*. Oxford, Oxbow Books, 300–4.

Graham-Campbell, J. A. (2019b) The 1858 Skaill Viking-Age silver hoard. In D. Griffiths, J. Harrison and M. Athanson, *Beside the Ocean, Coastal*

Landscapes at the Bay of Skaill, Marwick and Birsay Bay, Orkney. Oxford: Oxbow Books, 293–9.

Graham-Campbell, J. A. and C. E. Batey (1998) *Vikings in Scotland: An Archaeological Survey*. Edinburgh: Edinburgh University Press.

Griffiths, D. (2019) Rethinking the Viking Age in the West. *Antiquity* 93(368), 468–77.

Griffiths, D. (2020) How Scandinavian was the Early Viking Age in the Northern Isles? In A. Pedersen and S. Sindbæk (eds), *Viking Encounters, Proceedings of the Eighteenth Viking Congress*. Århus: Århus University Press, 318–30.

Griffiths, D., J. Harrison and M. Athanson (2019) *Beside the Ocean, Coastal Landscapes at the Bay of Skaill, Marwick and Birsay Bay, Orkney, Archaeological Research 2003–2018*. Oxford: Oxbow Books.

Hamilton, J. R. C. (1956) *Excavations at Jarlshof, Shetland*. Edinburgh: HMSO.

Harrison, J. (2020) Settlement change in Viking and Late Norse Orkney c. 850–1200. Placed deposits in domestic contexts. In A. Pedersen and S. Sindbæk (eds), *Viking Encounters, Proceedings of the Eighteenth Viking Congress*. Århus: Århus University Press, 335–70.

Hedges, J. W. (1983) Trial excavations on Pictish and Viking settlements at Saevar Howe, Birsay, Orkney. *Glasgow Archaeological Journal* 10, 73–124.

Hedges, J. W. (1987) *Bu, Gurness and the Brochs of Orkney*. British Archaeological Reports (British Series) 165. Oxford: British Archaeological Reports.

Hunter, J. R. (2007) *Excavations at Pool, Sanday: A Multi-period Settlement from Neolithic to Late Norse Times*. Investigations in Sanday, Orkney 1. Kirkwall: The Orcadian.

Lamb, R. G. (1993) Carolingian Orkney and its transformation. In C. E. Batey, C. D. Morris and J. Jesch (eds), *The Viking Age in Caithness, Orkney and the North Atlantic: Proceedings of the Eleventh Viking Congress*. Edinburgh: Edinburgh University Press, 260–71.

Leonard, A. (2011) Vikings in the prehistoric landscape, studies in Mainland Orkney. *Landscapes* 12(1), 42–68.

McLeod, S. (2015) Legitimation through association? Scandinavian accompanied burials and pre-historic monuments in Orkney. *Journal of the North Atlantic* 28, 1–15.

Montgomery, J., V. Grimes, J. Buckberry, J. A. Evans, M. P. Richards and J. H. Barrett (2014) Finding Vikings with isotope analysis: The view from wet and windy islands. *Journal of the North Atlantic* Special Volume 7, 54–70.

Morris, C. D. (1989) *The Birsay Bay Project, Volume 1: Brough Road Excavations 1976–82*. University of Durham Department of Archaeology Monograph Series 1. Durham: Department of Archaeology, University of Durham.

Morris, C. D. (2021) *The Birsay Bay Project, Volume 3, The Brough of Birsay, Orkney, Excavations 1954–2014*. Oxford: Oxbow Books.

Outram, Z. (2021) Discussion of dating evidence based on radiocarbon evidence from sites around Birsay Bay. In C. D. Morris, *The Birsay Bay Project, Volume 3, The Brough of Birsay, Orkney, Excavations 1954–2014*. Oxford: Oxbow Books, 549–73.

Owen, O. and M. Dalland (1999) *Scar: A Viking Boat Burial on Sanday, Orkney*. Edinburgh: Tuckwell Press.

Pálsson, H. and P. Edwards (1978) Orkneyinga Saga, *the History of the Earls of Orkney*. Harmondsworth: Penguin Classics.

Paterson, C. (2019) A Viking-Age bone strap end from near St Peter's Kirk. In D. Griffiths, J. Harrison and M. Athanson, *Beside the Ocean, Coastal Landscapes at the Bay of Skaill, Marwick and Birsay Bay, Orkney*. Oxford: Oxbow Books, 304–6.

Ritchie, A. (1977) Excavation of Pictish and Viking-Age farmsteads at Buckquoy, Orkney. *Proceedings of the Society of Antiquaries of Scotland* 108, 174–227.

Smith, B. (2003) Not welcome at all: Vikings and the native population in Orkney and Shetland. In J. Downes and A. Ritchie (eds), *Sea Change, Orkney and Northern Europe in the Later Iron Age, AD 300–800*. Balgavies: Pinkfoot Press, 145–50.

Thomson, W. P. L. (2008) *Orkney, Land and People*. Kirkwall: The Orcadian.

Chapter 2

What Does *Landnám* Look Like? Excavations at Swandro and Old Scatness

Stephen J. Dockrill and Julie M. Bond

Research at two multi-period settlement mounds, Old Scatness (Shetland; Dockrill et al. 2010) and Swandro (Rousay, Orkney; ongoing, Bond and Dockrill 2016), suggests that many first-generation Scandinavian settlements occur at pre-existing Pictish settlements and associated landscapes. Both sites have settlement biographies that provide evidence for long sequences spanning the Early Iron Age to the Norse period, including evidence for *landnám*, or first settlement. Settlement on existing Pictish 'estates' (high-status settlements with associated agricultural land, often originating in the Iron Age or earlier) would provide access to both maritime and agricultural resources, and it is suggested that 'estate taking' may have been a means of procuring key locations.

The term *landnám* is used in several ways in archaeology; Cleasby in his Icelandic–English dictionary defined it as 'taking possession of land as settler, settlement' (Cleasby and Vigfússon 1874), while Danish palynologist Iversen used it in the 1940s to describe features in pollen diagrams which he thought indicated clearance of the landscape by incoming Neolithic farmers, and it is still used in this sense (Iversen 1941). In North Atlantic archaeology it is often used in the context of settlement of a presumed empty landscape by the Norse in Iceland or the Faroe Islands. Here we use it in preference to the more loaded term 'colonisation' to indicate initial Norse settlement.

Old Scatness, Shetland

The site of Old Scatness formed a focus of archaeological research in Shetland, with excavations taking place between 1995 and 2006 (Dockrill 2002; Dockrill et al. 2006, 2010). Old Scatness lies on the western coastline of Dunrossness, on the southern tip of Mainland Shetland. To the west is the Atlantic Ocean, and to the north-east, the natural harbour of the Pool of Virkie and the North Sea. The Old Red Sandstone sedimentary sequence is a continuation of the same geological sequence as Orkney and provides a fertile agricultural zone together with good building stone. A substantial Iron-Age village was built around an early broch, which formed the focal point of the settlement. The broch demonstrates a complex sequence of at least three main phases of use, the last of which extends into the Pictish period (Figure 2.1).

The Iron-Age and Pictish sequence at Old Scatness

Old Scatness had been partially truncated by roadworks on its northern circuit, allowing the full investigation of the stratigraphic sequences that both pre-dated and post-dated the construction event of the broch between 390 and 200 BC (calibrated 2 sigma: GU-11534), clearly associated with a stone-lined ditch which encloses the village. The symbolic strength of the defended settlement with the broch tower at its centre would have provided a subliminal statement of power (Dockrill et al. 2006; Dockrill et al. 2015: 478).

To the west of the broch were two large roundhouses with aisled piers around the circumference, forming the type of structure termed a 'wheelhouse'. At Old Scatness these large roundhouses (Structures 12 and 14) demonstrated a complex history of use, with their ancillary buildings and each with evidence for an upper floor; probably a partial mezzanine around the circumference of the buildings resting on the piers.

The site was reconfigured in the 1st century AD; the western wheelhouses were deliberately infilled and a new radial or wheelhouse form was constructed within the broch tower. High-status artefacts including Roman glass fragments, amber and metalwork are indications of a continuation of status (Dockrill et al. 2015: 492).

During the Late Iron-Age or Pictish phase (600–800) a variety of structural forms replaced the larger long-piered wheelhouses. These buildings were of varied form and included small cellular structures as well as triangular-piered wheelhouses with parallels to Wheelhouse 2 and cellular buildings of this period at Jarlshof (Hamilton 1956: 58–92). This phase represents changes to the village that took place between the beginning of the 5th century AD and the arrival of Scandinavian people in the 9th to 10th century.

The artefactual evidence from the Pictish settlement phase presents a continued narrative of wealth and status. An exceptionally well-carved Pictish Class I symbol stone showing a bear, probably forming part of an orthostat terminal to one of the piers in the secondary use of the wheelhouse, Structure 11, provides further evidence for status (Bond 2010). Agricultural wealth is also evident during the course of this period. Barley is of particular importance within the mixed economy. The excavation of a purpose-built corn dryer in the later phase of the

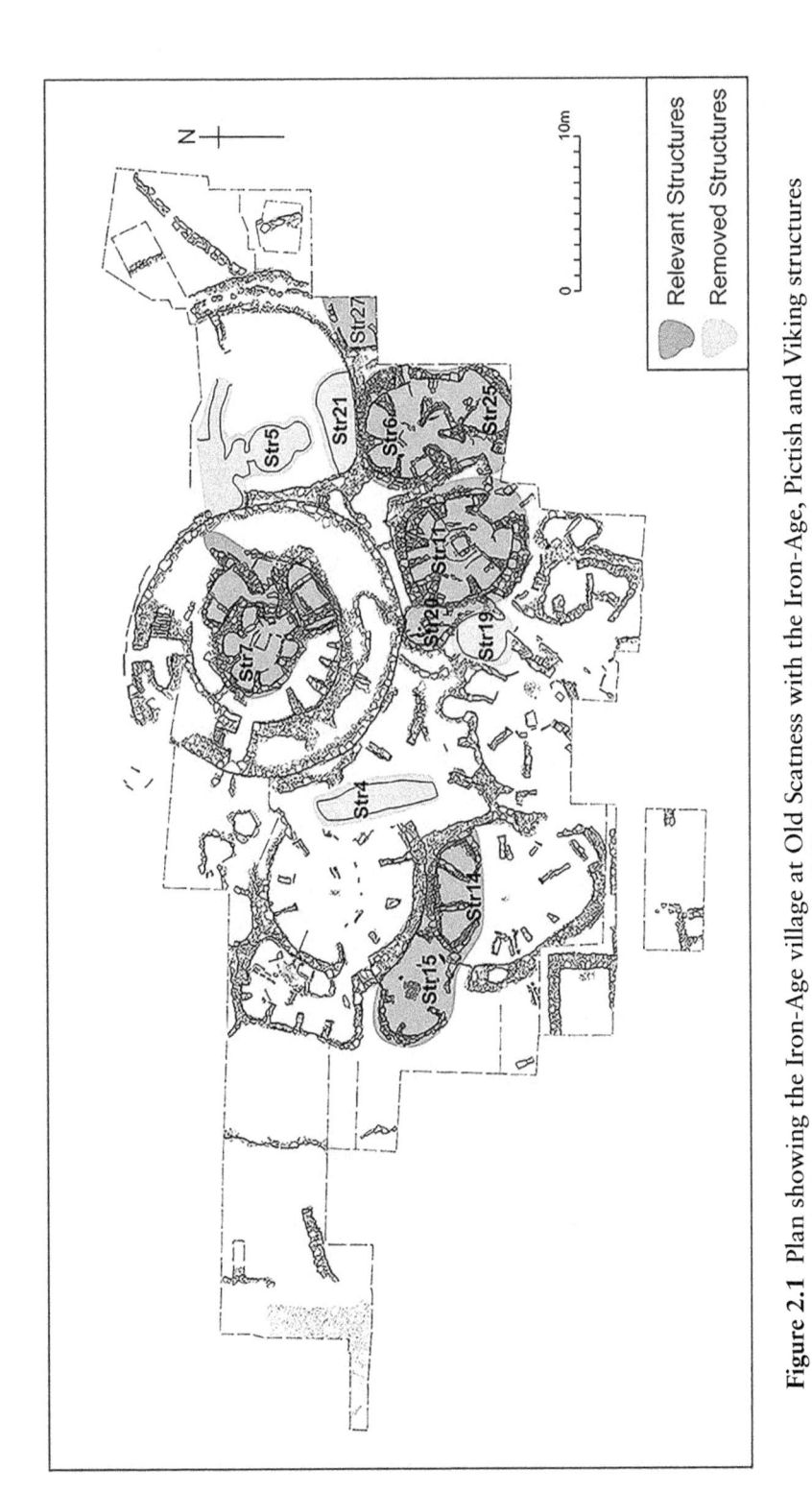

Figure 2.1 Plan showing the Iron-Age village at Old Scatness with the Iron-Age, Pictish and Viking structures numbered. Dockrill et al. 2010; © S. J. Dockrill/Shetland Amenity Trust.

large wheelhouse east of the broch (Structure 21) underlines the importance of this resource. This is also echoed in the presence of a man-made infield beyond the ditch around the settlement. These anthropogenic soils appear to have been carefully managed and added to throughout the Iron Age, forming an important resource.

The evidence for a Viking presence and settlement continuity

Old Scatness (Dockrill et al. 2010), Jarlshof (Hamilton 1956) and Pool on Sanday, Orkney (Hunter 2007) share the same problem in identifying the cultural change from Pictish to Viking and the nature of that change. Models have ranged from assimilation at the one extreme, to genocide at the other (for example, Ritchie 1974; Crawford 1981: 260; Lamb 1993; Morris 1998; Smith 2001). The evidence for the events that mark the interface between Pictish and Viking culture, changes in artefact assemblages and structural forms, in reality can be both fragmentary and ambiguous.

There is an emerging argument for early Viking settlers selecting wealthy pre-existing Pictish farms or estates (Bond and Dockrill 2010; 2016). Old Scatness provides an important body of data supporting this argument. The evidence for the initial Norse presence is discussed here by examining the depositional sequences in a number of Pictish buildings. The artefactual and environmental evidence, together with the contexts in which they were found, provide clearer evidence for cultural change from Pictish to Norse at Old Scatness. There is strong evidence for the modification of existing structures and a later phase of reorganisation of the settlement mound together with aspects of the cultural and palaeoeconomic evidence that appear to present a clear Viking identity.

The primary phase of reorganisation of the Pictish settlement was particularly visible in the archaeological record of the north-east side of the site. A number of Pictish buildings had been infilled with a mixture of rubble, midden and cultural material that was clearly Scandinavian in origin. Many of these artefacts were made of steatite (soapstone) (Figure 2.2).

One building (Structure 5) had been deliberately infilled up to the top of the surviving stonework. Within this deliberate infill of rubble and midden, the upper fill was of particular interest as it contained a steatite spindle whorl and a line sinker (SF1570: Figure 2.3). This line sinker was different from other Shetland examples in being a very finely carved dynamic boat shape; the closest parallel is from a male grave at Marvik, Suldal, in Norway, dated to c. 900–1000 (Foldøy 1995: 149). This line sinker suggests a dramatic change in fishing strategy to the exploitation of the fast-flowing tideway ('roost') around Sumburgh Head. This particular line sinker form differs from other forms found in Shetland

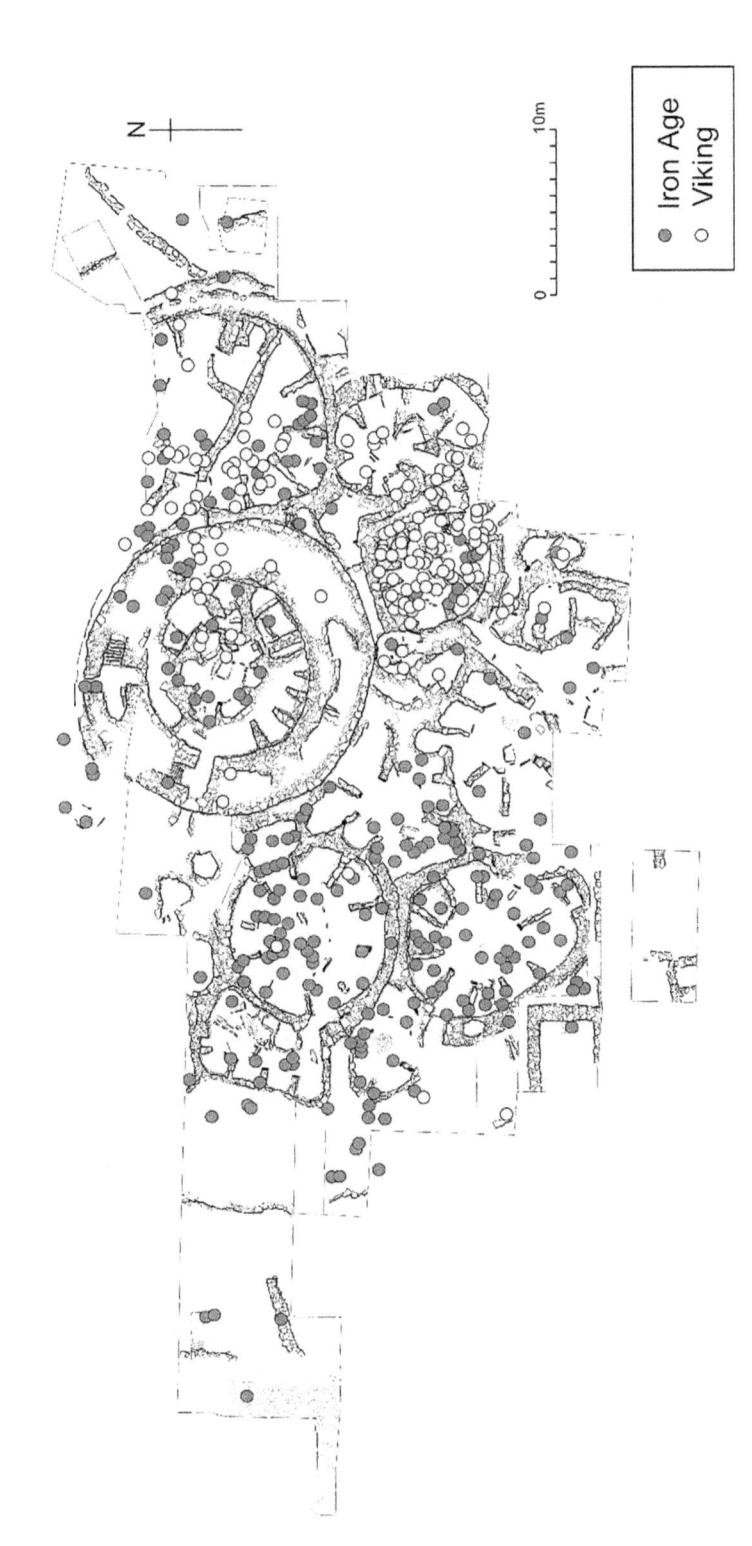

Figure 2.2 Distribution plan of Iron-Age and Viking-Age steatite, showing the discrete concentrations of Viking-Age steatite in the buildings discussed. A. K. Forster in Dockrill et al. 2010; © A. K. Forster/Shetland Amenity Trust, used with permission.

Figure 2.3 Steatite line sinker (SF 1570) found in the deliberate infill of Pictish Structure 5; a close parallel of a similar date was found in Marvik, Suldal, Norway. Photo: S. J. Dockrill.

which seem to be later, such as the examples within the Norse phase of Jarlshof (Hamilton 1956: 114, 117–18). A large quantity of charred cereal grain (hulled six-row barley, *Hordeum vulgare*, and cultivated oats, *Avena* sp.) together with seeds of flax (*Linum usitatissimum*) and weeds of cultivation were recovered from this infill. The appearance of flax as a new crop has been argued by Bond as being an indicator of Scandinavian culture in Orkney and Shetland (Bond and Hunter 1987; Bond 1994, 2007). Two radiocarbon dates for the same deposit suggest a date for deposition in the period 810–1020 cal AD at 95 per cent confidence level (these two radiocarbon AMS dates were derived from barley grains producing calibrated dates of 860–1020 cal AD [GU–14784] and 810–1020 cal AD [GU–14785]). At this period, the wall tops of this building appear to have been at the level of the contemporary ground surface. This surface was sealed by a distinctive but featureless mixed red-brown sandy loam, which included a silver coin of the Anglo-Saxon king Athelstan, minted in Chester or York, and likely to have been in circulation c. 930–970 (Dockrill et al. 2010). The Garthbanks Hoard, to the west of Old Scatness, also contained coins of Athelstan (Graham-Campbell 1995: 101).

Structural modification was also seen within a small Pictish wheelhouse, Structure 6. A steatite spindle whorl or bead (SF6446), a hexagonal flat-faced form with an open biconical perforation, was found on a paved surface in the northern cell of this building. This shows similarities to a 9th- to 10th-century example from Skaill in Deerness, Orkney (Porter in Buteux 1997). The hearth contained abundant fragments of corroded iron, which appeared to originate from an object (or objects) formed by thin iron plates, some with rivet holes, which had been placed on the hearth at or around the time of abandonment. Elsewhere in the building, a large quantity of iron fragments included nails of the type commonly referred to as clench or boat nails and the roves or plates used like washers on the opposite side of the planks (Bill 1994). Clench nails too are usually classed as Scandinavian rather than Pictish artefacts.

A number of fish bones, some clearly articulated and including parts of a large cod (around 700–800mm long), were associated with the iron plates in the hearth of Structure 6. Disarticulated bones included two cleithra (one chopped), probably from the same fish, and several head bones from a slightly smaller cod. The butchered cleithrum would suggest that the fish recovered with the iron was either salted and dried (a stockfish), partially dried by hanging outside (known as 'blown' fish in Shetland) or hung above a hearth to smoke. Stockfish were a staple in Shetland and Scandinavia until modern times (Nicholson 2010a). Burnt fish bones were also associated with the redeposition of ash from hearth rake-out within the wheelhouse.

To the west of the hearth, a significant assemblage of bird bones was found in association with bones from large fish. The remains of shag, greater black-backed gull and eider duck were identified (Nicholson 2010b). Knife cuts indicate that these birds were used for food rather than being accidental inclusions. North of the hearth, the butchered remains of at least one other greater black-backed gull were found.

This evidence is consistent with identifiable cultural change associated with the arrival of Scandinavian people. The modified wheelhouse in this late phase when considered with the contents is consistent with an interpretation for its use as a smokehouse or as a 'skeo' (for air-drying fish, bird and other meats). The presence of large quantities of fish and bird bone, some articulated, suggests that the later usage of this building may have been for food processing, preservation and storage, though large quantities of corroded iron may suggest the possibility of some ironworking having taken place here as well. The finding of a rotary grindstone just outside the doorway adds credence to this interpretation.

The infill of this wheelhouse contained a number of fragments of steatite sub-rectangular vessels. Forster has argued that the typological forms suggest that these finds are later than those infilling Structure 5 and Structure 11, discussed below (Forster 2010: Section 6.4 and Forster 2004: 196–205).

Pictish Structure 11 provides further compelling evidence for Scandinavian reuse. This building appears to have been deliberately slighted, with the removal of the orthostats at the ends of two of the triangular piers. One of these uprights may have been decorated with a Class 1 Pictish carving (the Pictish bear mentioned above). The building's floor surface was covered by rubble and midden which acted as bedding for a new paved surface. An AMS radiocarbon date for the midden infill provided a date of 710–980 cal AD (1175±45 BP; GU–9538). The repaved surface contained two parallel lines of orthostatic kerbs in alignment with the eastern entrance. Charred barley recovered from the compact clay bedding returned an AMS radiocarbon date of 780–1020 cal AD (1120±45 BP; GU–9545). A large quantity of flake and spheroidal hammer-scale was found, as well as larger fragments of slag and iron objects, suggesting a period of ironworking either in the building or close by. Subsequently the building was rapidly infilled with rubble and midden which contained classic soapstone vessel sherds and loom weights identical to those from Viking-period Jarlshof. In the material filling the passageway was found a schist hone of the kind described at Jarlshof as 'haunched hones' (Hamilton 1956: 114), probably from Eidsborg, Norway.

Above this infilling and within the shell of Structure 11, just below the surviving wall head, was a surface with a distinctive long hearth. The hearth consisted of a long strip of ash and burnt surface, running for some 2m roughly north–south with a large flat stone, heavily burnt and fire-cracked, at its southern end. This seems to be a long hearth (*langeldr*) characteristic of Viking longhouses. The contemporary surface adjacent to the hearth contained numerous artefacts which can be diagnostically associated with Viking culture. These finds included steatite vessel sherds, spindle whorls and a collection of over forty soapstone and mica schist loom weights, twenty-one of which were found together as a group, suggesting the location of a warp-weighted loom. These loom weights are similar to those found at Jarlshof (Hamilton 1956: 113–14). There was also an iron knife with a classic angle back typical of Viking knives (McDonnell 1998: 158). The area around the hearth was rich in the carbonised remains of flax. An archaeomagnetic date for the long hearth gives a last use between 850 and 960 AD (AM11), while the associated surfaces have been radiocarbon dated at 780–1020 cal AD (1115±45 BP; GU–8371) and 690–980 cal AD (1180±50 BP; GU–8376). It is probable that this floor surface belongs to a Viking building, perhaps timber, which succeeded Structure 11.

To the west of the demolished broch there were faint traces of a later building; the paving and single-faced wall elements suggested the fragmentary remains of a longhouse (Structure 4) on an approximate north–south axis. The stonework and paving were very similar to some of the Norse longhouse structures at Jarlshof; in particular, the remains of the central paving in House 1 and House 3 (Hamilton 1956: 108, 139).

None of this evidence is as obvious as the change from Iron-Age roundhouse to Viking longhouse which has been taken as the classic sign of Scandinavian arrival in the Northern Isles at sites such as Jarlshof or Pool. These are more subtle indications of an earlier period of takeover and reuse of the Pictish buildings before the later and more recognisable wholesale reorganisation of the settlement.

The Knowe of Swandro, Orkney

The Knowe of Swandro on the Orcadian island of Rousay (HY 3753 2966: Figure 2.4) consists of an eroding mound with obvious stone inclusions, which is situated immediately behind a boulder beach on the Bay of Swandro. On its eastern flank is the Norse settlement site known as Westness, excavated by the Norwegian archaeologist Sigrid Kaland in the 1970s (Kaland 1993). The mound may have been disturbed during Radford's investigation of the nearby Westness Norse houses in the 1950s or '60s (Wilson and Hurst 1964: 240). Assessment from 2010 and current excavations by the authors show that the Iron-Age settlement, as at Old Scatness, is long-lived, from at least Late Bronze Age/Early Iron Age to Late Norse (Bond and Dockrill 2016 and see https://www.swandro.co.uk for summaries).

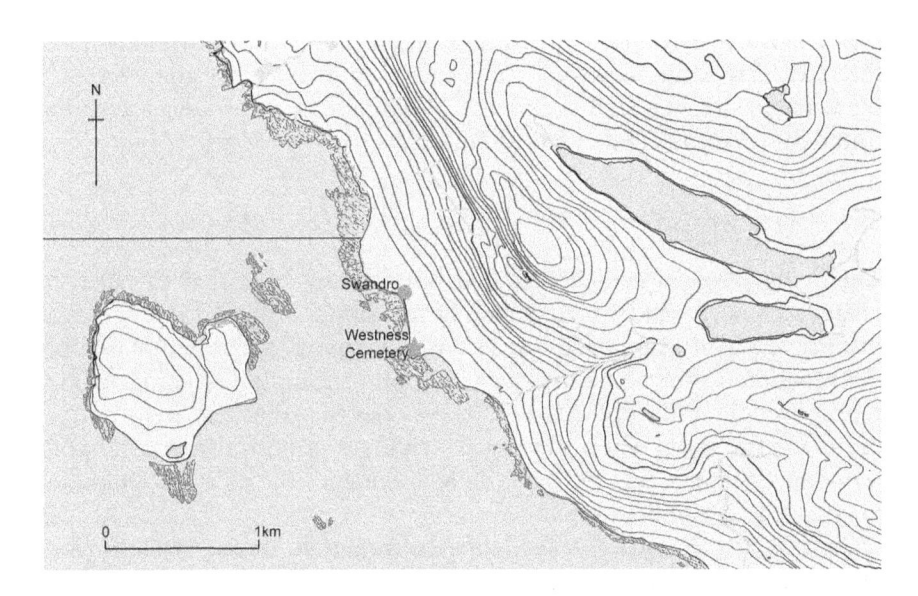

Figure 2.4 Location of the Iron-Age and Norse settlement at Swandro in relation to the Pictish and Viking cemetery at Westness on Rousay. L. D. Brown; © J. M. Bond and S. J. Dockrill.

The settlement, an Iron-Age and Pictish village focused on a monumental roundhouse forming the centre of the Knowe of Swandro, has been found to extend south-east under the Norse houses at Westness excavated by Sigrid Kaland. Thus, the Westness Norse houses are the latest phase of the Swandro multi-period settlement (Kaland 1993; Sellevold 1999).

The Pictish and Viking cemetery of Westness, on a nearby promontory, contains Pictish Christian burials succeeded by pagan Viking graves, indicating a continuity of 'place' in this landscape for both settlement and burial (Kaland 1993; Sellevold 1999). More recent isotopic research has demonstrated that the Viking burials were not of people native to the islands and were thus first-generation settlers (Montgomery et al. 2014).

Excavation of the Iron-Age settlement is producing strong evidence that the site was later levelled and within the upper fill of the entrance passage to the roundhouse, a *styca* of Eanred of Northumbria (a 9th-century king) was recovered, along with the bones of a domestic cat. The coin supports the possibility that the infill might be associated with Viking reorganisation of the settlement, prior to the construction of the later Norse longhouses.

To the east of the monumental roundhouse, the remains of a distinctive midden material with bands of winkle shell sealed an orange-brown midden layer with carbon flecking. This midden appeared very different to those excavated elsewhere relating to the Iron-Age sequence of deposits, particularly in the high concentrations of winkle shells present. A decorated spindle whorl made from a cattle femoral head and part of a decorated bone needle case were recovered from this midden. At the time of writing, we await radiocarbon dates for these contexts, but the evidence again suggests primary Norse settlement evidence is to be found in the Iron-Age and Pictish buildings.

Discussion

The archaeological evidence at Old Scatness suggests that the Pictish village was occupied by incomers of Scandinavian origin. There seems a distinct reorganisation of the settlement, evidenced by the demolition of the broch and other buildings and with other standing buildings being repurposed in radically different ways, disregarding the long native dry-stone tradition. There are distinct changes in both the cultural and economic assemblages, although there is evidence the native population may have had a limited input.

Steatite artefacts act as a key Norse cultural indicator at Old Scatness, with evidence of distinctive Viking and Norse forms, discussed in detail by Forster (2010: 258–303). Forster's study of steatite across the North Atlantic region has addressed the issue of typology and highlighted morphological characteristics that can be used in the identification of

Norwegian and Shetland vessels (Forster 2004). Forster's analysis of the distribution of vessels thought to be of Norwegian and Shetland origin was found to support the Old Scatness science-based chronology (Outram and Batt 2010: 99–130).

Old Scatness has several important lessons to convey about the date and nature of the initial Viking settlement in the Northern Isles. Other sites such as Pool and Buckquoy have demonstrated an initial 'interface' between Pictish and Viking, and it has been assumed that this was a short-lived transitional phase, followed relatively quickly by reorganisation of the settlement and replacement of the Late Iron-Age or Pictish structures with Viking-style longhouses. The evidence from Old Scatness seems to show that the 'transitional' phase may have been more complex, with the reuse and modification of existing buildings maintained for some time. The sequence of dates, from a variety of techniques and tied to a complex stratigraphic sequence, suggests that *landnám* for this site was prior to its reorganisation in the late 9th century. However, a plateau in the radiocarbon calibration curve precludes the exact dating of this event.

By the end of the 10th century the settlement at Old Scatness was clearly Scandinavian in character, with changes expressed in the material culture, architectural record and in the inherent 'lifestyle' of its occupants. Old Scatness and Swandro are part of an emerging pattern. We can add Pool, Buckquoy, Skaill, Jarlshof and Norwick, all multi-period sites (Hunter 2007; Ritchie 1977; Buteaux 1997; Hamilton 1956; Ballin Smith 2007), to this developing model. The appropriation of existing settlements seems to have been the norm, rather than the exception. These settlements are mostly on prime agricultural land, in many cases created by generations of former inhabitants (Dockrill 2002; Guttmann et al. 2003). Such old estates are, by definition, the successful ones, and therefore highly attractive to an incoming Norse population.

Acknowledgements

We would like to thank Historic Environment Scotland, Shetland Amenity Trust, Swandro-Orkney Coastal Archaeology Trust, Orkney Islands Council and Orkney Archaeology Society.

References

Ballin Smith, B. (2007) Norwick: Shetland's first Viking settlement? In B. Ballin Smith, S. Taylor and G. Williams (eds), *West Over Sea: Studies in Scandinavian Sea-Borne Expansion and Settlement Before 1300*. The Northern World, volume 31. Leiden: Brill, 287–98.

Bill, J. (1994) Iron nails in Iron Age and Medieval shipbuilding. *Crossroads in Ancient Shipbuilding*, 6, 73–6.

Bond, J. M. (1994) *Change and Continuity in an Island System: The Palaeoeconomy of Sanday, Orkney*. Unpublished PhD Thesis, University of Bradford.

Bond, J. M. (2007) The plant remains. In J. Hunter, *Investigations in Sanday, Orkney. Volume 1: Excavations at Pool, Sanday. A Multi-period Settlement from Neolithic to Late Norse Times*. Kirkwall: The Orcadian/Historic Scotland, 171–207.

Bond J. M. (2010) The Pictish bear carving from Structure 11. In S. J. Dockrill, J. M. Bond, V. E. Turner, L. D. Brown, D. J. Bashford, J. E. M. Cussans and R. A. Nicholson, *Excavations at Old Scatness, Shetland Volume 1: The Pictish and Viking Settlement*. Lerwick: Shetland Heritage Publications, 304–6.

Bond, J. M. and S. J. Dockrill (2010) Viking and Norse Settlement at Old Scatness. In S. J. Dockrill, J. M. Bond, V. E. Turner, L. D. Brown, D. J. Bashford, J. E. M. Cussans and R. A. Nicholson, *Excavations at Old Scatness, Shetland Volume 1: The Pictish and Viking Settlement*. Lerwick: Shetland Heritage Publications, 77–97.

Bond J. M. and S. J. Dockrill (2016) Viking settlement and Pictish estates: New evidence from Orkney and Shetland. In V. E. Turner, O. A. Owen and D. J. Waugh (eds), *Shetland and the Viking World: Proceedings of the Seventeenth Viking Congress, Lerwick*. Lerwick: Shetland Heritage Publications, 7–13.

Bond, J. M. and J. R. Hunter (1987) Flax-Growing on Orkney from the Norse Period to the 18th century. *Proceedings of the Society of Antiquaries of Scotland* 117, 175–81.

Buteux, S. (1997) *Settlements at Skaill, Deerness, Orkney: Excavations by Peter Gelling of the Prehistoric, Pictish, Viking and later Periods, 1963–1981*. British Archaeological Reports (British Series) 260. Oxford: Archaeopress.

Cleasby, R. and G. Vigfússon (1874) *An Icelandic–English Dictionary: based on the ms. collections of the late Richard Cleasby*. Oxford: Clarendon Press.

Crawford, I. (1981) War or peace – Viking colonisation in the Northern and Western Isles of Scotland reviewed. In H. Bekker-Nielsen, P. Foote and O. Olsen (eds), *Proceedings of the Eighth Viking Congress, Århus 24–31 August 1977*. Odense: Odense University Press, 259–70.

Dockrill, S. J. (2002) Brochs, economy and power. In B. Ballin Smith and I. Banks (eds), *In the Shadow of the Brochs: The Iron Age in Scotland*. Stroud: Tempus, 153–62.

Dockrill, S. J., Z. Outram and C. M. Batt (2006) Time and place: A new chronology for the origin of the broch based on the scientific dating programme at the Old Scatness Broch, Shetland. *Proceedings of the Society of Antiquaries of Scotland* 136, 89–110.

Dockrill, S. J., J. M. Bond, V. E. Turner, L. D. Brown, D. J. Bashford, J. E. Cussans and R. A. Nicholson (2010) *Excavations at Old Scatness, Shetland Volume 1: The Pictish Village and Viking Settlement*. Lerwick: Shetland Heritage Publications.

Dockrill, S. J., J. M. Bond, L. D. Brown, V. E. Turner, D. J. Bashford and J. E. Cussans (2015) *Excavations at Old Scatness, Shetland Volume 2: The Broch and Middle Iron Age Village*. Lerwick: Shetland Heritage Publications.

Foldøy, Ø. (ed.) (1995) *Museotec at the Museum of Archaeology, Stavanger: Finds of Rogaland from Ice Age to Middle Ages*. Norway, AMS Småtrykk 31. Stavanger: Arkeologisk Museum i Stavanger.

Forster, A. K. (2004) *Shetland and the Trade of Steatite Goods in the North Atlantic Region during the Viking and Early Medieval Period*. Unpublished PhD Thesis, University of Bradford.

Forster, A. K. (2010) Section 6.4 Steatite. In S. J. Dockrill, J. M. Bond, V. E. Turner, L. D. Brown, D. J. Bashford, J. E. Cussans and R. A. Nicholson, *Excavations at Old Scatness, Shetland Volume 1: The Pictish Village and Viking Settlement*. Lerwick: Shetland Heritage Publications, 258–303.

Graham-Campbell, J. (1995) *The Viking-Age Gold and Silver of Scotland*. Edinburgh: National Museums of Scotland.

Guttmann, E. B., I. A. Simpson and S. J. Dockrill (2003) Joined up archaeology at Old Scatness, Shetland: Thin section analysis of the site and hinterland. *Environmental Archaeology* 8, 17–31.

Hamilton, J. R. C. (1956) *Excavations at Jarlshof, Shetland*. Ministry of Works Archaeological Reports No. 1. Edinburgh: HMSO.

Hunter, J. (2007) *Investigations in Sanday, Orkney. Volume 1: Excavations at Pool, Sanday. A Multi-period Settlement from Neolithic to Late Norse Times*. Kirkwall: The Orcadian/Historic Scotland.

Iversen, J. (1941) Landnam i Danmarks Stenalder: En pollenanalytisk Undersøgelse over det første Landbrugs Indvirkning paa Vegetationsudviklingen. *Danmarks Geologiske Undersøgelse* II.række, 66, 1–68.

Kaland, S. H. H. (1993) The settlement of Westness, Rousay. In C. E. Batey, J. Jesch and C. D. Morris (eds), *The Viking Age in Caithness, Orkney and the North Atlantic*. Edinburgh: Edinburgh University Press, 308–17.

Lamb, R. (1993) Carolingian Orkney and its transformation. In C. E. Batey, J. Jesch and C. D. Morris (eds), *The Viking Age in Caithness, Orkney and the North Atlantic. Proceedings of the 11th Viking Congress*. Edinburgh: Edinburgh University Press, 260–71.

McDonnell, G. (1998) Irons in the fire – Evidence of ironworking on broch sites. In R. A. Nicholson and S. J. Dockrill (eds), *Old Scatness Broch, Shetland: Retrospect and Prospect*. North Atlantic Biocultural Organisation Monograph No. 2, Bradford Archaeological Sciences Research 5. Bradford: Department of Archaeological Sciences, 42–8.

Montgomery, J., V. G. Grimes, J. Buckberry, J. A. Evans, M. P. Richards and J. H. Barrett (2014) Finding Vikings with isotope analysis: The view from wet and windy islands. *Journal of the North Atlantic* Special Volume 7, 54–70.

Morris, C. D. (1998) Raiders, traders and settlers: The Early Viking Age in Scotland. In H. B. Clarke, M. Ní Mhaonaigh and R. Ó. Floinn (eds), *Ireland and Scotland in the Early Viking Age*. Dublin: Four Courts Press, 73–103.

Nicholson R. A. (2010a) Section 5.3 Fish and fishing from the Pictish to the Norse centuries. In S. J. Dockrill, J. M. Bond, V. E. Turner, L. D. Brown, D. J. Bashford, J. E. Cussans and R. A. Nicholson, *Excavations at Old Scatness, Shetland Volume 1: The Pictish Village and Viking Settlement*. Lerwick: Shetland Heritage Publications, 156–67.

Nicholson, R. A. (2010b) Section 5.4 The bird bones from the Pictish to the Norse centuries. In S. J. Dockrill, J. M. Bond, V. E. Turner, L. D. Brown, D. J. Bashford, J. E. Cussans and R. A. Nicholson, *Excavations at Old Scatness, Shetland Volume 1: The Pictish Village and Viking Settlement*. Lerwick: Shetland Heritage Publications, 168–71.

Outram, Z. and C. M. Batt (2010) Dating at Old Scatness. In S. J. Dockrill, J. M. Bond, V. E. Turner, L. D. Brown, D. J. Bashford, J. E. Cussans and R. A. Nicholson, *Excavations at Old Scatness, Shetland Volume 1: The Pictish Village and Viking Settlement.* Lerwick, Shetland Heritage Publications, 99–130.

Ritchie, A. (1974) Pict and Norseman in Northern Scotland. *Scottish Archaeological Forum* 6, 23–36.

Ritchie, A. (1977) Excavation of Pictish and Viking Age farmsteads at Buckquoy, Orkney. *Proceedings of the Society of Antiquaries of Scotland* 108, 174–227.

Sellevold, B. J. (1999) *Picts and Vikings at Westness: Anthropological Investigations of the Skeletal Material from the Cemetery at Westness, Rousay, Orkney Islands.* Oslo: NIKU Scientific Report 010, 1–62.

Smith, B. (2001) The Picts and the martyrs, or Did Vikings kill the native population of Orkney and Shetland?. *Northern Studies* 36, 7–32.

Wilson, D. M. and D. G. Hurst (1964) Medieval Britain in 1962 and 1963. *Medieval Archaeology* 8, 231–99.

Chapter 3

The Tarbat Peninsula in Northern Pictland: Portmahomack as a Case Study in Native–Norse Interaction during the 9th to 11th Centuries

Cecily Spall

Prior to the inception of the Tarbat Discovery Programme, which was designed to explore the archaeological site centred on St Colman's Church, Portmahomack, Ross-shire (Figure 3.1), the strongest Norse association from the site was a silver hoard deposited c. 1000, place-name evidence and historical references to Torfness (Tarbatness). Thirteen seasons of open-area excavation, field survey and a lengthy post-excavation phase have reframed the site as the first Pictish monastic settlement to be excavated (Carver et al. 2016). What Portmahomack offers to the subject of 'Viking Scotland' is how life in this frontier zone was modelled and shaped by politics and ideology in the 9th to 11th centuries, beginning with an abrupt interruption aligned with a hitherto undocumented Viking raid.

The Pictish monastery

The extensive archaeological site surrounding St Colman's Church was first identified from the air, appearing as a cropmark in the dry summer of 1984 (Figure 3.2). Excavation revealed the cropmark belonged to a complex water-collection system which simultaneously fed and enclosed a planned site. Between 1994 and 2007, a large T-shaped transect within the enclosure was excavated and the geography of the monastery was explored and defined. The monastery was founded at the site of a 5th- to 7th-century elite estate centre in c. 680 and flourished up until c. 780–810, when the trajectory of the site took a dramatic turn.

The Tarbat peninsula, long favoured for its natural attributes, sits between the Dornoch and Cromarty firths and enjoys sheltered access to the sea from the sandy bay at Portmahomack. Access between the firths can be made via the north–south portage across the peninsula during rough weather, as well as access to the Great Glen and its resources to the west. The peninsula boasts good-quality arable land, rare and highly

44 Cecily Spall

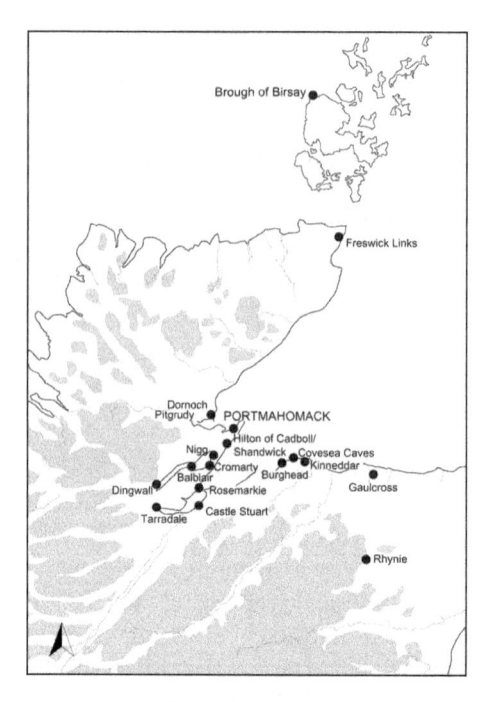

Figure 3.1 Location of Portmahomack on Tarbatness and sites mentioned in the text. © University of York/FAS Heritage.

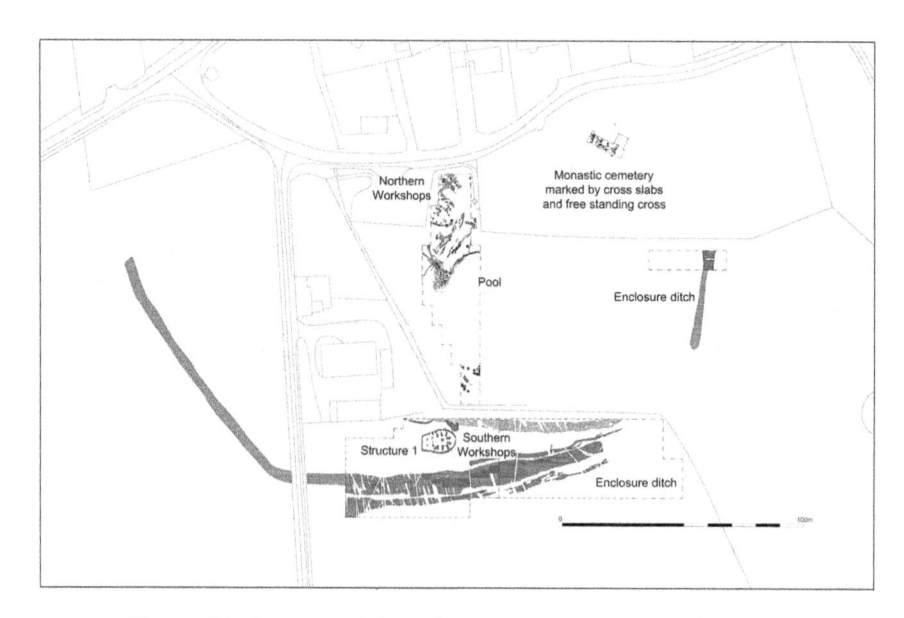

Figure 3.2 Layout of the 8th-century monastic settlement showing the enclosing ditch, location of cemetery and Northern and Southern Workshops. © University of York/FAS Heritage.

prized terrain in north-east Scotland, and enjoys low rainfall compared to adjacent areas, and turf and peat suitable for exploitation for fuel.

The monastic settlement lay undefended, on the raised beach overlooking the sandy landing bay. The monastic church and its cemetery, marked in the 8th century by three magnificent cross-slabs and a free-standing cross, occupied an area now under and around the present church. Beyond the cemetery, the site consisted of Northern Workshops on a large man-made terrace above a pool, with Southern Workshops beyond, immediately inside the banked and ditched enclosure.

The early medieval church building was not found, but a significant sample of the monastic cemetery was encountered and mapped. The burial ground was carefully maintained and constrained in its extent. In the years following the foundation of the monastery the burial ground received nearly sixty burials, almost wholly those of men, most of whom had died during middle or old age. Apart from simple burial, sometimes with a shroud, the head box or head support was the most prominent burial rite, and this was maintained up to the last burials in the cemetery. The cemetery was well organised with plots; many graves were marked by a simple cross-marked stone, fragments of which were recovered and reused in the fabric of the 12th-century church.

The Northern Workshops zone was demarcated by two large stone enclosure walls served by a kerbed and paved road flanked by wood-lined drains. This zone is best known for having preserved artefacts and ecofacts, allowing the identification of early medieval vellum-working for the first time in Britain. The economy of the monastery was based on cattle farming, with the bone assemblages reporting a regime geared to optimal meat production with dairying and the concomitant production of hides.

The Southern Workshops zone was dominated by a large timber and turf, hall-like building, Structure 1, which was host to highly skilled smiths producing exquisite composite items. Among the objects that appeared to have been made were items of deluxe ecclesiastical equipment comparable to those that constitute the Derrynaflan Hoard (Youngs 1989). The calibre of the sculpture, craft-working and economy of the monastery signals a significant and resource-rich establishment.

Around the turn of the 9th century, the Northern Workshops were destroyed by an intense fire, which could have been interpreted as the result of an accident if it were not for the character of the ensuing clear-up operation. The fire-destruction horizon was covered with hundreds of small chunks of smashed Pictish sculpture. Resumption of activity following this dramatic interlude looked quite different to that which had gone before, and the monastic mode was not to be reinstated.

The raid

The strata and artefactual evidence identified in this stratigraphic sequence converge towards a deliberate act against the monastery, and we have identified it as a raid effected by Vikings, although other protagonists are not ruled out.

Evidence for this 'event horizon' was very distinct archaeologically. The Northern Workshop's zone was affected by scorching apparent in the form of a 'skin' of burning which was discontinuous but touched almost everything above-ground (Figure 3.3). Burnt remains included charred turf walls, floor rushes, roof thatch and wicker hurdles collapsed in situ. The sandstone kerbs of the road, and the enclosing walls were also heat-affected. Other significant damage included the destruction of at least two of the four cross-slabs which surrounded the monastic church and cemetery; a sarcophagus and architectural masonry also met the same fate.

Something of the human experience was also recorded. The array of tools recovered – in many instances perfectly serviceable and probably highly valued – lay strewn on the surface of the working horizon as though hastily abandoned.

Within the cemetery, evidence for interpersonal violence was recorded, with incidences being greater in the post-raid period than before. Two burials included sword injuries; one individual suffered three massive blade blows to the head, all from behind, suggesting that he was fleeing from his attacker and fell to his knees before the fatal blow; another elderly male showed two injuries inflicted with a large blade in a face-to-face encounter, which he had survived.

The date of the raid has been modelled using stratigraphy, artefactual evidence and radiocarbon dating (Carver et al. 2016: 259–60). The sculpture included typological forms dated no later than the late 8th to early 9th century; a stick pin found immediately underlying the burning was of a type current at the time of the Viking raids. Many radiocarbon end-dates from the Northern Workshops were 95 per cent likely to be no later than about 780 and two dates converged on about 800. Metalworking hearths which followed the raid returned dates no later than 880, so the parameters were set broadly at between about 800 and 880 and perhaps as close as between 780 and 810.

These date parameters lie close to the first documented raid at Lindisfarne (793), which heralded the onset of the first Viking incursions, and those that followed soon after were recorded briefly in the *Annals of Ulster*, probably including the first of several raids at Iona (794) and Rathlin Island or Lambay (795) (*AU* U794.7 and U795.3). The date of the raid of Portmahomack lies close to this early wave, and overall the event can be modelled c. 800. Before this horizon was excavated, the

The Tarbat Peninsula in Northern Pictland 47

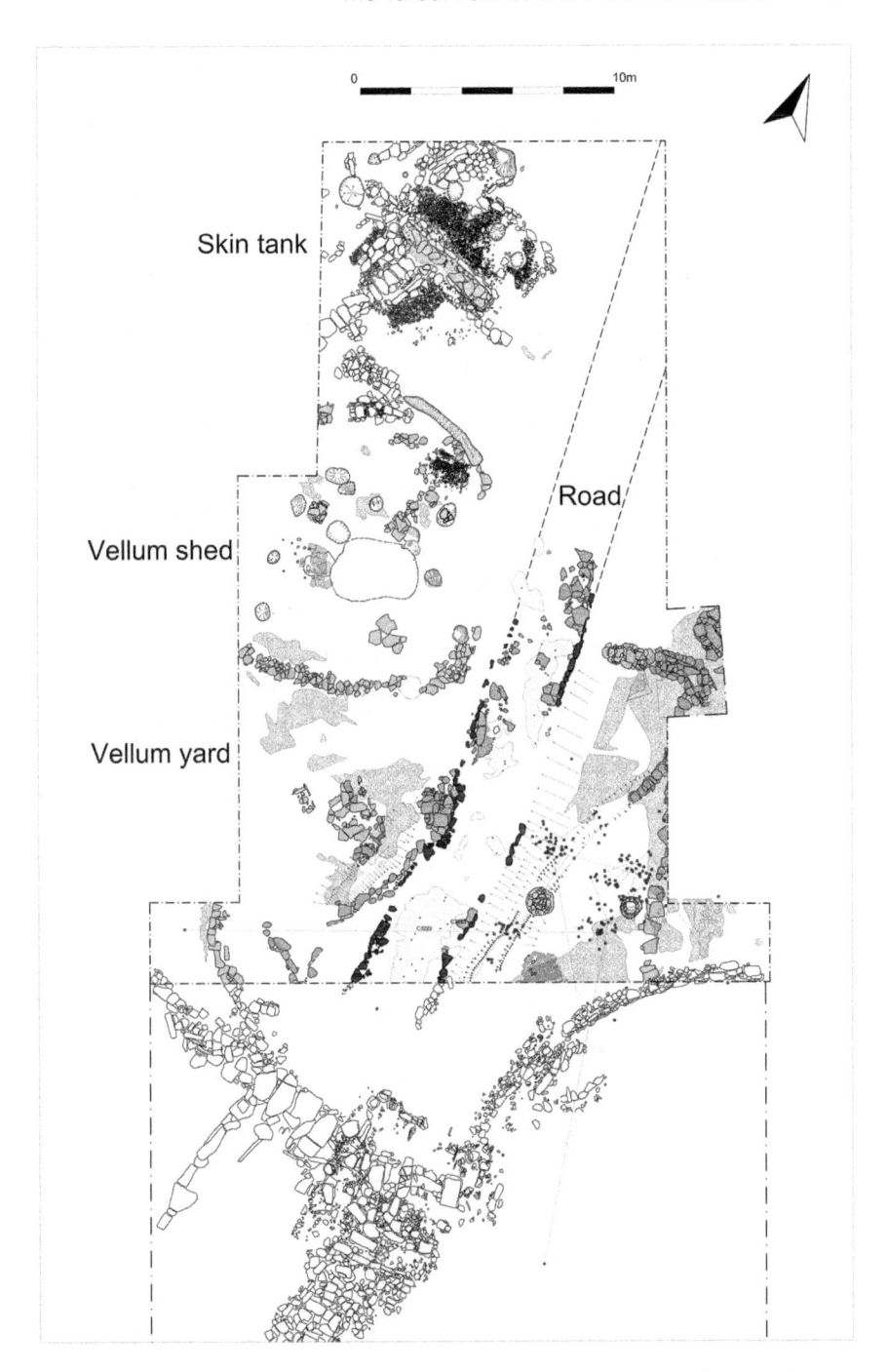

Figure 3.3 Evidence for the burning horizon across the Northern Workshops overlain by the location of smashed sculptural fragments. © University of York/FAS Heritage.

highly fragmented pre-existing sculptural corpus had prompted speculation of a destroyed monastery. Other sites in the Moray region, such as Kinneddar and Rosemarkie, remain candidates for monasteries which may have suffered a similar fate, particularly given the fragmentary nature of the sculpture (Henderson and Henderson 2004: 146, 212).

Post-raid activity

The aftermath of the raid was finely stratified; the burnt ruins of the Northern Workshops were levelled up using smashed sculpture and activity resumed (Figure 3.4). The sandstone paving of the road was broken up and added to a new surface of pebbles. To either side of the road an intense period of metalworking followed, with a hearth returning a radiocarbon date of 660–880 cal AD. To the west of the road, a stone-lined channel was built using broken pieces of a Pictish zoomorphic panel. Activity focused on non-ferrous casting of a variety of items and went hand in hand with a marked upturn in ironworking, including smelting and smithing.

Groups of crucibles were identified as forms in use before the raid but often of greater capacity, and XRF analysis signalled that they were used to cast leaded bronze. A group of large two-piece moulds were used to repeatedly cast large, leaded bronze items; these take an acorn-like form,

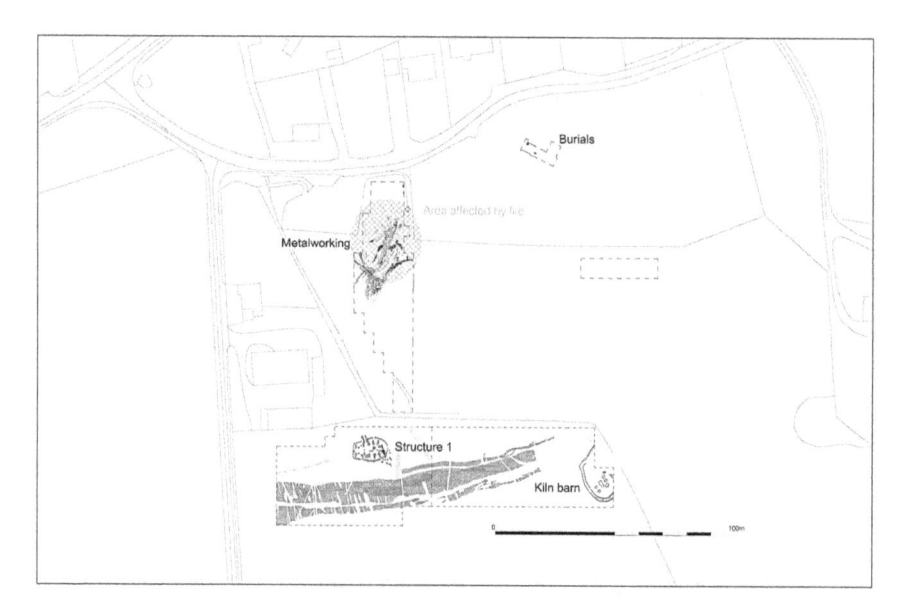

Figure 3.4 Layout of post-raid activity across the former monastic settlement. © University of York/FAS Heritage.

but cannot be directly paralleled. Without any other clear function or ornament, and involving a significant investment of solid metal, these are identified as possible weight moulds. Along with a group of stone ingot moulds and a lead weight, this evidence suggests a new emphasis on trade and standard weights previously lacking in the material assemblages (Carver et al. 2016: 270–6).

Who were the post-raid metal workers? The slightest of clues are there, but they can be viewed as equivocal and not a clear indication of ethnicity. The assemblage from the Pictish smithy at the Brough of Birsay provides several links to the Tarbat assemblage. Simple finger-ring moulds and a group of tabbed objects are strikingly similar (Figure 3.5) (Curle 1982: 34–5). A mould matrix bearing a Pictish 'dragon' was among the broken moulds and recalls the beast on the 'Dragon Stone' from the monastic cemetery enclosure.

Portmahomack produced an example of a painted pebble – one of the few artefacts that can be said to be culturally diagnostic of Pictish occupation. The Portmahomack example was stratified with post-raid metalworking dumps; it may indeed be residual from Period 2, but its presence is noteworthy at the site which was so remarkably well stratified in general. Whether the post-raid craft-working was a late Pictish initiative or one that harnessed the skills of craftsmen connected by long-lived technology and conservative artistic training is not clear.

Who were the post-raid farmers? Resumption of craft-working was short-lived, not seeing the end of the 9th century, whereas the farming appears to have endured for longer. The end of activity in this zone was marked by a grey blanket of windblown sand into which a pit was dug to receive the skinned and jointed skeleton of a cow, which has the feeling of a ceremonial leave-taking moment. The cow returned a date of 830–1020 cal AD and the soil over it produced a comb side plate of the 10th to 12th centuries.

A total of seventeen burials were made within the monastic cemetery following the raid. The community continued to use the head box and burials continued to be those of older men – by what arrangement this male-only population was maintained is not clear – but a continuing church community following burial practice of the monastic settlement seems to be implied. These burials diminish in frequency during the 9th to 10th centuries and appear to have ceased entirely by the 11th century. In this region, the head box appears to have passed into lay practice as witnessed at Balblair, where graves of men, women and children were made with this burial rite and the cemetery dated broadly to the 11th to 12th centuries (Reed 1995: 788).

The Southern Workshops were not affected by the fire of the raid, but craft-working ceased and the area was converted into a farm, managing quantities of grain which continued into the 10th and possibly into

50 Cecily Spall

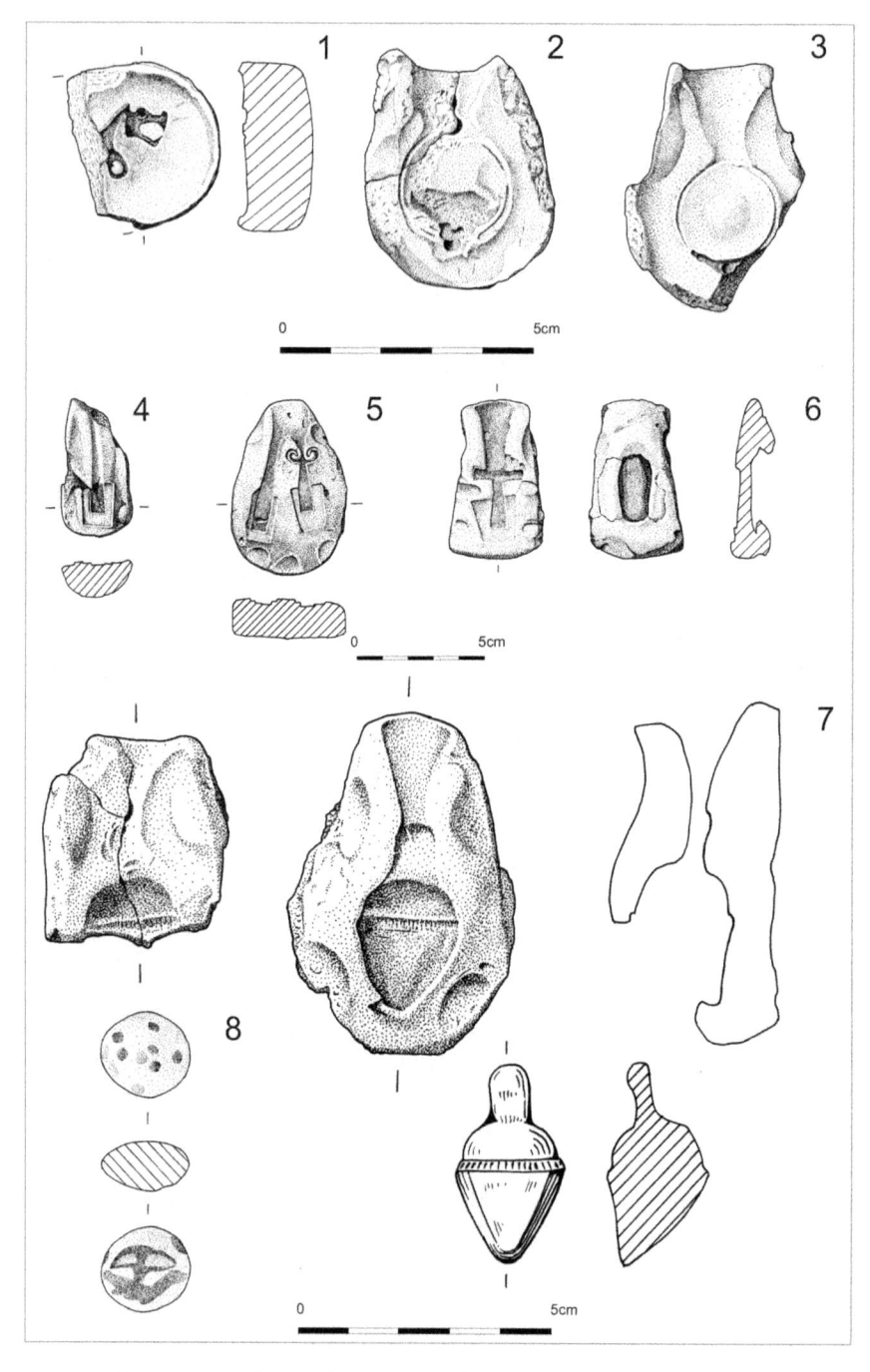

Figure 3.5 Clay and stone moulds from post-raid metalworking including tabbed items, possible weight moulds and bar ingots. © University of York/FAS Heritage.

the 11th century. Structure 1 was repurposed as a kiln-barn, signalling a notable change in the site economy; an upper floor was inserted and a stone-lined flue cut through the south wall, carbonised grain from which was dated to 1020–1210 cal AD, while a nearby ditch was backfilled by 1020. A further barn-like building, Structure 5, was built anew, and carbonised grain from its ditch returned a date of 890–1030 cal AD. This process of change may align with the distribution of Norse place-names on the peninsula that imply Norse farmsteads located on prime farmland coinciding with areas of soil improvement, perhaps signalling one of the most attractive characteristics of the monastic territory (Figure 3.6).

Hoard

The end-dates of the post-raid activity converge around 1000 to 1030, around the time when a hoard of Viking silver – two silver armlets and a group of silver pennies of Louis le Begue (877–879) and a penny of Edgar (959–975) – was buried in the monastic cemetery, no doubt during a time of unrest. James Graham-Campbell dates deposition of the hoard to c. 990 to 1000 (Graham-Campbell 1995: 143–4). Not long after, the Battle of Torfness was fought in c. 1035. Barbara Crawford places this great sea battle at the Tarbatness peninsula (Crawford 1987: 73). The battle saw Norse Earl Thorfinn the Mighty and his forces vanquish Moray leader Karl Hundison, and is a victory thought to have opened up the Dornoch and Cromarty firths to Norse settlement.

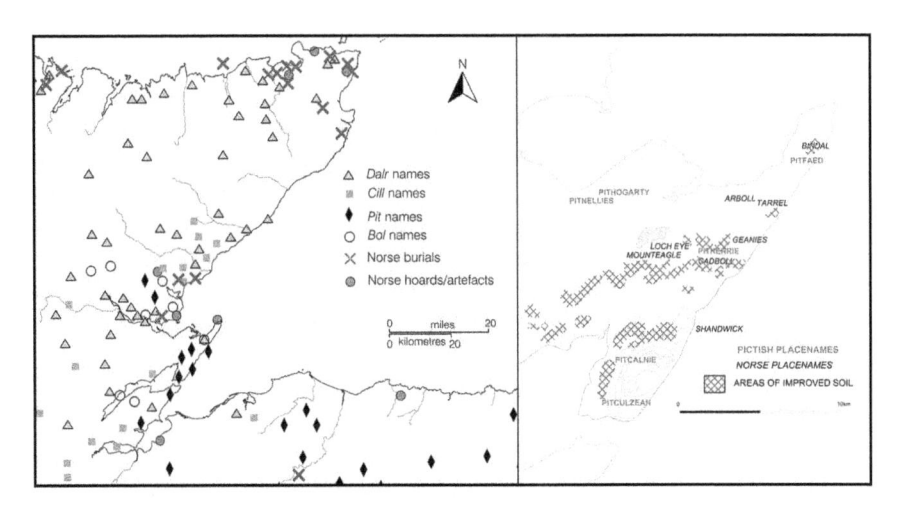

Figure 3.6 Map of place-names and Norse material around the Tarbat peninsula and inner Moray Firth (also showing areas of soil enhancement). © University of York/FAS Heritage.

Portmahomack in context

The raid on the monastery at Portmahomack belongs to the period when coastal monasteries were the focus of short, sharp incursions marking the beginning of the Viking Age in Britain. The activity that follows immediately at Portmahomack belongs to the end days of the Pictish kingdom in this frontier zone. The monastic mode was broken by the raid, and the political will was apparently not there to see it resume business as before. The cemetery continued to be used by a much-diminished community who continued monastic burial traditions. Judging by those who were buried there, life was harder, more violent, and eventually the community failed entirely.

Since publication in 2016, Portmahomack sits in a rapidly expanding Pictish context. Recent discoveries and reappraisal of sites in the inner Moray Firth all contribute to understanding of the nature and chronology of this zone. Important early medieval sequences are now known at Rosemarkie Caves, including an extraordinary deviant burial and metalworking signalling the rise of a power centre (5th to 7th century) (Birch 2018); at the enormous Pictish barrow cemetery at Tarradale on the Black Isle (5th to 6th century) (Grant 2020); and at Burghead fort where excavation is being rewarded with a consolidated chronology and archaeological sequence for the fort, including buildings, signals of an early church and evidence for fiery destruction as the end sequence (7th to 10th century) (Noble et al. forthcoming). Further discoveries of Pictish archaeology include proposed early dating of the two-part Pictish name symbols in Covesea Caves (4th to 5th century) (Armit and Bütser 2020); the 'Conan Stone', a new Pictish cross-slab from near Dingwall, perhaps signalling an early church site (8th century) (Brunskill 2019); and the recovery of more of the Gaulcross Hoard, supporting newly proposed dating and biography (5th to 6th century) (Noble et al. 2019: 103–18). All these discoveries add to the momentum initiated by Alex Woolf's proposal to move the Kingdom of Fortriu north of the Mounth (Woolf 2006) and the University of Aberdeen Northern Picts Project that increasingly casts the 'Problem of the Picts' in a new light.

Meanwhile, very little new Norse archaeology has been discovered since the 1990s. A fragment of hack-silver from the terminal of a ring-money bracelet can be noted from Pitgrudy, Dornoch (Hunter 2011: 104) along with a recently metal-detected copper-alloy Hiberno-Norse ring pin from Castle Stuart on the Moray Firth (O'Grady et al. 2016: 176; TT 159/09). At Dornoch a stratified early medieval sequence was contacted consisting of ditches and ironworking (8th to 9th century), a building and ironworking structures (late 9th to 10th century) and a large enclosure and pit containing burnt cereals (10th to 11th century) (Coleman and Photos-Jones 2008). The few associated unstratified finds tend towards Norse connections, including a polygonal bell paralleled at Freswick Links, a stick pin shaft, whalebone counter and weaving tool. Here too there is an archaeological sequence spanning the 9th to 11th century without clear cultural affiliations, but this side of the firth enjoys more Norse place-names and Norse material, including burials (Crawford 1995: fig. 3; Carver 2008: figs. 8 and 9).

Dingwall and Cromarty have been thought to represent early thanage sites of the 11th century and later. Dingwall specifically has long been held to represent the south-eastern frontier of Norse colonisation and influence, the place-name thought to derive from Old Norse 'þing-vǫllr', meaning field of the assembly. A natural terraced hill known as Gallowhill, on the western edge of the town, was traditionally identified as the *thing*-site and remains a site of interest as a possible execution place. However, detailed landscape research identified the site of a mound and level field located on a former tidal estuarine peninsula of the now-clogged River Peffery close to St Clement's Church. The site was much altered in the post-medieval period and was appropriated as a memorial to George Mackenzie, first Earl of Cromartie in the early 18th century by the addition of his grave and a large stone obelisk. Radiocarbon dates from excavation through the basal mound make-up returned dates spanning the 11th to 13th centuries (O'Grady et al. 2016). Interpretation of the archaeology and dates does not align easily with identification as a major Norse regional centre for legal organisation, but may reflect an enduring Norse influence.

So, what seems now to be the greater and continuing problem than the Picts is the succeeding 'Dark Age' of the 9th to 11th century during which this northern Pictish kingdom transitioned into Moray while repelling – to a greater or lesser degree – Norse intrusions which aimed to access both the Great Glen and regional timber supplies which could be accessed from river valleys (Crawford 1995).

The strata of available evidence types – geographical, historical, archaeological, toponymical – when layered upon each other contribute something to our understanding of native–Norse interaction (Carver 2008; Carver et al. 2016: 282–6).

Nicholas Evans notes that the Tarbat peninsula lacks *cill-* names and preserves an intriguing group of *pit-* names, perhaps indicating landholding continued under 'supervision of a different ecclesiastical establishment' after the raid (Evans 2019: 34). This may be reflected in the continued use of the monastic cemetery after c. 800, the continuity in craft technology if not products, and the painted pebble.

The identification of the Tarbatness peninsula as Torfness (Crawford 1987: 73) connects the area with Einar the Turfer, and his descendants Thorfinn and Sigurd, who fought with Moray leaders for supremacy. Einar the Turfer is recorded as being the first man to cut turf for fuel in

891–4 (died 910) (*OS*, ch. 7). Turf and peat had long been exploited on the peninsula; the claim does not suggest cultural fusion, but does point to the attractiveness of this rich and reliable fuel source.

Documentary and place-name evidence analysis led by Barbara Crawford show the southward extent of Norse-speaking settlement (*dalr, bol, arnat*) (Crawford 1987, 1995; Crawford and Taylor 2003). This wider distribution of place-names is reflected in recovered identifiably Norse artefacts, including pagan graves and diagnostic metalwork, sometimes recovered as hoards (see Figure 3.6) (Kruse 1992; Batey 1993; Graham-Campbell 1993; Carver 2008: fig. 8). On the Tarbat peninsula, the retention of the cross-slabs across the peninsula – at Hilton, Shandwick and Nigg – can be noted. These were not thrown down until the later post-medieval period and, in the instances of Shandwick and Hilton, were left to stand sentinel over sites which adopted Norse names. Perhaps their utility as wayfaring markers trumped their Pictishness in this maritime space. Norse place-names also coincide with areas of high-quality farmland, such as at Cadboll and Geanies. The isthmus of the peninsula at Loch Eye may include the Norse element – *eith* – perhaps suggesting the enduring importance of the portage, while Shandwick names a sandy landing bay.

Conclusion

The raid, if correctly attributed to a Viking strike, represents direct evidence of Pictish–Viking interaction, but what followed the raid appears to be a gradual, and not always entirely peaceful, fragmentation of the former monastic settlement and wider landholding. Perhaps for the same reasons the resource-rich Tarbat peninsula was endowed to a monastery, the territory also attracted Norse settlement. The Norse place-names, coincident with good farmland and strategic places, may indicate targeted exploitation and settlement, but are not indicators of rapid migration, takeover or cultural fusion. The evidence for higher levels of trauma in the post-raid burials points to a harder lifestyle, more competition for resources and more violence than was experienced before the raid, but not directly to native–Norse interaction. By the time the hoard was buried and the Battle of Torfness fought, intensive occupation at Portmahomack had faded away, with no clear evidence for supremacy of any group during the 9th to 11th centuries.

References

Armit, I. and L. Büster (2020) *Darkness Visible: The Sculptor's Cave, Covesea, from the Bronze Age to the Picts*. Edinburgh: Society of Antiquaries of Scotland.

AU Mac Airt, S. and G. Mac Niocaill (eds) (1983) *The Annals of Ulster (to AD 1131)*. Dublin: Dublin Institute for Advanced Studies.

Batey, C. E. (1993) The Viking and late Norse graves of Caithness and Sutherland. In C. E. Batey, J. Jesch and C. D. Morris (eds), *The Viking Age in Caithness, Orkney and the North Atlantic*. Edinburgh: Edinburgh University Press, 148–64.

Birch, S. (2018) Rosemarkie Caves excavations: Interpreting the results of three years of excavation, 2016–2018. Available at www.spanglefish.com/RosemarkieCavesProject/excavations2016-2018.asp [Last viewed: 5 November 2020].

Broun, D. (2005) The seven kingdoms in *De Situe Albaniae*: A record of Pictish political geography or imaginary map of ancient Alba? In E. J. Cowan and R. A. McDonald (eds), *Alba: Celtic Scotland in the Middle Ages*. Edinburgh: PLACE, 24–42.

Brunskill, A. (2019) 1,200-year-old Pictish cross-slab found. *Current Archaeology* 357. Available at https://www.archaeology.co.uk/articles/1200-year-old-pictish-cross-slab-found.htm.

Carver, M. O. H. (2008) Post-Pictish problems: The Moray Firthlands in the 9th to 11th centuries. Rosemarkie: Groam House Lecture for 2007.

Carver, M. O. H., J. I. Garner-Lahire and C. A. Spall (2016) *Portmahomack on Tarbatness: Changing Ideologies in North-east Scotland, Sixth to Sixteenth century AD*. Edinburgh: Society of Antiquaries of Scotland.

Coleman, R. and E. Photos-Jones (2008) *Early medieval settlement and iron-working in Dornoch, Sutherland: Excavations at The Meadows Business Park*. Scottish Archaeological Internet Report 28.

Crawford, B. E. (1987) *Scandinavian Scotland*. Leicester: Leicester University Press.

Crawford B. E. (1995) *Earl and Mormaer: Norse–Pictish relationships in Northern Scotland*. Rosemarkie: Groam House Lecture for 1994.

Crawford, B. E. and S. Taylor (2003) The southern frontier of Norse settlement in Northern Scotland. *Northern Scotland* 23: 1–76.

Curle, C. L. (1982) *Pictish and Norse finds from the Brough of Birsay 1934–74*. Society of Antiquaries of Scotland monograph series 1. Edinburgh: Society of Antiquaries of Scotland.

Evans, N. (2019) A historical introduction to the northern Picts. In G. Noble and N. Evans (eds), *The King in the North: The Pictish Realms of Fortriu and Ce*. Edinburgh: Birlinn, 10–38.

Graham-Campbell, J. (1993) The northern hoards of Viking-Age Scotland. In C. E. Batey, J. Jesch and C. D. Morris (eds), *The Viking Age in Caithness, Orkney and the North Atlantic*. Edinburgh: Edinburgh University Press, 173–86.

Grant, E. (2020) Barrow-loads of barrows: Excavating the Pictish cemetery at Tarradale on the Black Isle. Available at https://nosasblog.wordpress.com/2020/05/26/barrow-loads-of-barrows-excavating-a-monumental-pictish-cemetery-at-tarradale-on-the-black-isle/ [Last viewed: 5 November 2020].

Henderson, G. and I. Henderson (2004) *The Art of the Picts*. London: Thames and Hudson.

Hunter, F. (2011) Pitgrudy (Dornoch parish), metal detector find. *Discovery and Excavation in Scotland* New Series 12, 104.

Kruse, S. E. (1992) Late Saxon balances and weights from England. *Medieval Archaeology* 36, 67–95.

Noble, G., M. Goldberg, M. Alistair and O. Sveinbjarnarson (2019) (Re)discovering the Gaulcross hoard. In G. Noble and N. Evans (eds), *The King in the North: The Pictish Realms of Fortriu and Ce*. Edinburgh: Birlinn, 104–18.

Noble, G. et al. (Forthcoming) Excavations at Burghead Fort.

O'Grady, O. J. T., D. MacDonald and S. MacDonald (2016) Re-evaluating the Scottish *Thing*: Exploring a late Norse period and Medieval assembly mound at Dingwall. *Journal of the North Atlantic* Special Volume 8, 172–309.

OS Pálsson, H. and P. Edwards (trans.) (1981) *Orkneyinga Saga*. London: Penguin.

Reed, D. (1995) The excavation of a cemetery and putative chapel site at Newhall Point, Balblair, Ross and Cromarty, 1985. *Proceedings of the Society of Antiquaries of Scotland* 125, 779–91.

Woolf, A. (2006) Dún Nechtain, Fortriu and the geography of the Picts. *Scottish Historical Review* 85(2), 182–201.

Youngs, S. (1989) *The Work of Angels: Masterpieces of Celtic Metalwork, 6th to 9th centuries AD*. London: British Museum Press.

Chapter 4

Echoes of Native–Norse Relationships in the Archaeology at St Ninian's Isle, Shetland

Rachel Barrowman

The relationship between the native population and the incoming Norse has been one of the most contentious aspects of Viking-Age archaeology in Scotland over the last fifty years, with scholarship travelling back and forth between the two extremes of violent annihilation and peaceful assimilation, visiting various positions in between (see, for example, Morris 1998; Backlund 2001; Barrett 2003; Smith 2003). The archaeology at St Ninian's Isle has an important contribution to make to the debate, not least in suggesting that the picture is far more intricate than the two extremes would suggest.

St Ninian's Isle is a small island joined by a sandy tombolo (Figure 4.1) to the west coast of Dunrossness in south mainland Shetland (Figure 4.2). It is most well known for a hoard of Pictish silverware found in 1958 during excavations on the island led by Andrew O'Dell between 1955 and 1959, when his team excavated a myriad of Iron-Age to late medieval archaeological features from beneath up to 6m of windblown sand. Although short annual accounts and articles concerning the treasure were produced, the site was not published until 1973 by Alan Small, who had supervised there as a student (Small et al. 1973). Very little in the way of site records could be located, and the resulting volume unavoidably dealt primarily with the hoard; the account of the excavations themselves comprised only four pages, a plan and selected finds drawings, with Charles Thomas adding his own thoughts and a plan in relation to the sculptured stones (Thomas 1973). All that was known of a Viking-Age presence was the suggestion that the hoard had been buried in the floor of an early chapel on the site in the face of Viking raids around 800, and that four steatite cross-stones and a small hogback were found in the 1950s in the windblown sand that covered the site, with no record of their provenance (Thomas 1973: 13). References to St Ninian's Isle in Viking surveys have, as a result, had to concentrate on these tantalising morsels of information (Graham-Campbell and Batey 1998: 9, 14, 65, 227; also, for example, Crawford 1987: 128, 131, 159, 166; Morris 1990 (1994): 816–17).

Figure 4.1 The sandy tombolo to St Ninian's Isle and the site of the excavations, on the right-hand side of the photograph. Photograph by the author.

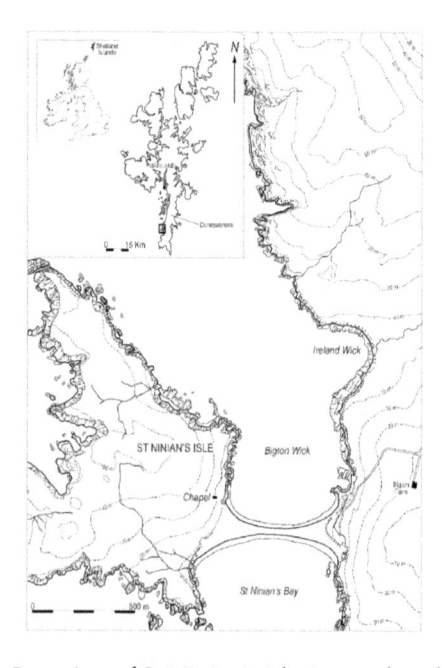

Figure 4.2 Location of St Ninian's Isle. Reproduced from Barrowman 2011, 2, Fig. 1.1.

Fieldwork, including excavation, was undertaken on the site in 1999–2000 as part of the Viking and Early Settlement Archaeological Research Project Shetland chapel sites survey (see Morris and Barrowman 2008). Subsequently the former Historic Scotland funded research and analysis of artefacts deposited with the Shetland Museum after Alan Small passed away, as well as site notebooks and slides held in the Shetland Archives, and as much of the 1950s material as could be found from other sources. Figure 4.3 is the resulting combined illustration of the 1950s work[1] with the features excavated in 1999/2000 superimposed onto it. With the completion of post-excavation work, it was possible to put forward a phased archaeological sequence into which many of the features excavated in the 1950s could be located and dated (see Barrowman 2011: 80–7, fig. 3.34). Reassuringly, the sequence was found to broadly support that put forward in the 1973 volume, although there were some important differences as it was found to be far more complicated and nuanced than was first suggested, especially around Phase III, the native/Norse 'interface' period (for the term 'interface', see discussion in Morris 2021: 37–8).

The Viking Age – populating the gap

In Table 4.1, the sequence proposed by Thomas is laid out on the left, and that of the 1999–2000 excavations on the right. It can be seen from this table that the Iron-Age occupation phases are well matched, as are the 'Burial ground, initially Pagan' and 'Phase III: Pre-Christian to Christian spiritual site'. Thomas' no. 3, 'Christian burial ground . . .', is again matched by recent work on the right. However, below this is Thomas' 'Viking hiatus' and an empty gap where the Viking Age should be. Thomas (and Small) suggested that the site was one of early Christian burial, with an accompanying church and shrine, which was then attacked and abandoned during the Viking raids (as evidenced by the burial of the hoard) and not used again as a burial ground until the Late Norse period (Thomas' no. 4 on the left in Table 4.1, over the top of the thick layer of windblown sand that had inundated the site). The new work completely revises this conclusion as it clearly shows that there was no gap or 'considerable interval' that corresponded to the Viking Age. In the new sequence (on the right in Table 4.1) the evidence for the transition from pagan to Christian is all encompassed in the same phase, as is the transition from 'native' to identifiably 'Norse' burials (Phase III). There was no evidence for a clear stratigraphical break in Phase III, and the huge inundation of sand did not actually occur until around the end of the 11th century, rather than immediately after the Viking raids at the turn of the 9th century. In particular, human remains from nine burials, including a group of six Norse-period Christian infant burials

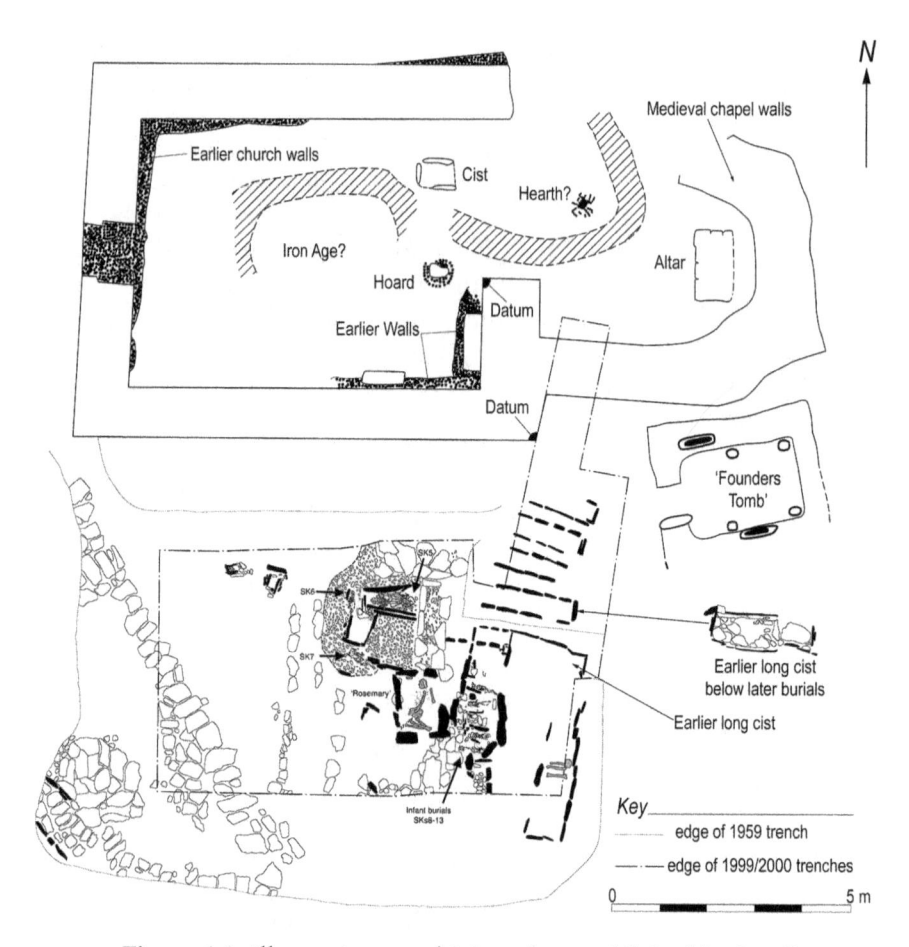

Figure 4.3 Illustration combining plans published by Small (1973, Fig. 5), Thomas (1973, Fig. 8) and O'Dell and Cain (1960, Fig. 1), a sketch made by Thomas and now in his archive, and Helen Nisbet's 1959 excavation sketch. Adapted from Barrowman 2011, 186, Fig. 5.1.

radiocarbon dated and statistically modelled to the 10th century (see below), were interred before the massive sand inundation took place, implying that far from a catastrophic 'hiatus' in the Viking Age, burial continued at the site during this period.

At the base of the excavated sequence on the site were the remains of cellular buildings pre-dating the 7th century (Phase II), and similar to small, cellular drystone buildings excavated at the Iron-Age settlement sites at Scalloway, Old Scatness and Kebister nearby (Sharples 1998; Owen and Lowe 1999; Dockrill 2003; Dockrill et al. 2010). After the desertion of this settlement, the area was used as a burial ground in the

Table 4.1 Archaeological sequences from the 1955–9 (Thomas 1973: 11–13, 33–9) and 1999–2000 excavations (Barrowman 2011). Based on Barrowman 2011: 187, Fig. 5.2.

1955–9 excavations (Thomas 1973, 11–13; 33–9)	1999–2000 excavations (Barrowman 2011) All radiocarbon dates calibrated at 2-sigma (see Outram 2011). *Can all be refined to sometime in the 10th century
Bedrock covered by thin layer of peat below church	*Phase I: Bedrock and unexcavated deposits*
1. Iron Age occupation Stone walls, rubble collapse, paved areas, occupation debris From first few centuries BC to 3rd/4th centuries AD	*Phase II: Iron Age occupation* Wall footings, paving and midden Late Iron Age up to 7th–8th centuries AD
2. Burial ground, initially Pagan 3rd/4th–6th/7th centuries Short- or medium-length slab cists with crouched inhumations, pottery and human bone fragments Large, crouched burial 'Rosemary' over wall	*Phase III: Pre-Christian/Christian spiritual site and burial ground. Norse/native interface* Short cists, cremations, paving, wall base and rubble mound Large, crouched burial ('Rosemary'): SUERC 5442: 655–775 cal AD
3. Christian burial ground with accompanying stone chapel and shrine Late 7th and 8th centuries Oriented extended inhumations in long cists Shrine posts and slabs (1–9), cross-marked stones (10–11) and (15)	Long cists ('Hubert' and 'Robert' respectively): SUERC 5440: 680–875 cal AD SUERC 5441: 780–995 cal AD Accompanying small church (corner post shrine(s) post found unstratified in sand but probably derive from this phase)
	Infant inhumation SK7: 670–880 cal AD
A 'considerable interval' or 'hiatus' resulting from the Viking raids Hoard buried c. 800 AD Windblown sand	Hoard buried some time from the 8th century onward Ogham inscription (unstratified; Forsyth 2011) Christian infant burials below low kerbed cairn and small cross-incised grave marker stones SK8 AA 45627: 730–990 AD* SK9 AA 45628: 705–975 AD* SK10 AA 45629: 890–1120 AD* SK11 AA 45630: 895–1155 AD* SK12 AA 45631: 880–1120 AD* SK13 AA 45632: 770–990 AD* Warrior burial in cist SK5: 1025–1220 cal AD Infant burial SK6: 1015–1210 cal AD
	Phase IV: Windblown sand inundation
4. Norse Christian chapel built early 12th century Small hogback stone (17) steatite cross-marked slabs (12–14) and cross frag (16) unstratified but found in top of sand	*Phase V: New chapel built end of 11th or in 12th century* Accompanied by narrow extended long cists
5. Chapel enlarged late 12th/early 13th century Chancel added, medieval cross-slab (18) porphyry stone (21) and possible cresset lamp (22) Burial ground continues in use until mid-19th century	Chapel enlarged and chancel added Demolished 1744 Burial ground continues in use until mid-19th century
	Phase VI: O'Dell's excavations 1955–9

Late Iron Age, with at least twelve cists containing cremations or burials found in 1958–9, set into midden layers covering the abandoned buildings (see O'Dell 1960; Small 1973: 7; Barrowman 2011: 47–50). Areas of stone pathways and paving were also excavated, contemporary with the short cists and similar to other Late Iron-Age sites in the Northern Isles, such as the structures pre-dating St Nicholas chapel on Papa Stronsay, which Ritchie interpreted as a pagan Pictish shrine (Ritchie 2003; Barrowman 2011: 57–9, 93–100, 192–4). St Ninian's Isle is thus a rare example of an excavated Late Iron-Age burial site in Shetland that existed prior to the arrival of the Norse, in an area with extensive evidence for a flourishing Late Iron-Age (Pictish) community.

It is within this same archaeological phase of 'pagan' burials that the first recognisably Christian burials are identified on the site. They consist of two long cists, located on photographs and in descriptions in the archive as having been excavated from below the sand inundation layer in 1959, and probably accompanying the early church building identified by O'Dell, into which the hoard was buried for safekeeping. A pre-Norse primary cross-slab (Thomas 1973: 28–9, 36, pl. viii) was found set upright at the west end of one of these cists, and a second cross-incised stone was found laid flat at the east end of the second when the area was re-examined in 2000 (see Barrowman 2011: 56, fig. 5a). The human remains excavated from these two cists were identified as being from an adult male and a juvenile aged 11–14 years old at death (Roberts 2011b) and were radiocarbon dated to 680–875 cal AD (1245±35 BP; SUERC-5440) and 780–995 cal AD (1125±35 BP; SUERC-5441) respectively (narrowed slightly to *695–880 cal AD* and *825–975 cal AD*; see Ashmore et al. 2011 and Outram 2011). This potentially places them into the early Viking Age, despite the marking of the burials with what Thomas describes as a pre-Norse primary cross-slab (Thomas 1973: 28).

A second group of Christian burials were found at the end of the final excavation season in 1959 when 'a number of box-like structures formed by stones set on edge which suggest further burials' (Small 1973: 7) were uncovered, under a low cairn of pebbles. This low cairn was set into the edge of a rubble mound that had covered an unaccompanied, north to south oriented, inhumation (named 'Rosemary' by the excavators in 1959; see Table 4.1 and Figure 4.2), which the recent work confirmed had been lying prone and tightly flexed (Barrowman 2011: 58–9; Roberts 2011b: 76). Radiocarbon dating of 655–775 cal AD (1305±35 BP; SUERC-5442; see Ashmore et al. 2011 and Outram 2011) places this inhumation in the Pictish period and after the spread of Christianity into north-west Britain, and yet there is nothing particularly Pictish or Christian about it. The distinctive Pictish burial form in northern Scotland has traditionally been recognised as a circular or square burial cairn, usually with a stone kerb, overlying an extended burial in a long cist covered by a layer of sterile sand (see, for example, Ritchie 1974: 32–3; Ashmore 1981; Close-Brooks 1984), with examples having been excavated in the Northern and Western Isles (such as Bigelow 1984; Morris 1989: 109–27; Mulville et al. 2003; Parker Pearson et al. 2018). However, work by Maldonado has demonstrated that long cists with no mounds are equally prevalent (with excavated examples from Westness and Buckquoy in Orkney, or Galson in Lewis, for instance; see Maldonado 2013). The St Ninian's Isle burial is similar in that it was once below a rubble mound and is of a similar date (particularly to Cille Pheadair, South Uist, dated to 620–780 cal AD), but unlike any of these examples, it is an extremely flexed burial in a short cist, and therefore remains unique for this period in Scotland, with little to compare it to in pre-Viking Orkney or Shetland.

In 2000, the six 'box-like structures' in this area were investigated and found to be contained within an outer kerb of upright stones. Four of the structures had small upright headstones surviving, two incised with double transom crosses. Sadly, six infant burials were discovered below these compartments, cut into the soil. It appeared at first that each compartment covered a burial, but on excavation, one was found to be empty below, and a second covered two burials, one truncating the other. In addition to this, over a hundred infant bones and fragments from the left-hand side of the body, with no element duplicated, were also identified in the soil sample from the immediate area of another of the infants, suggesting that there had once been a seventh, neonate infant displaced by the burial of a second adjacent to it (Roberts 2011a; Duffy 2011). These occurrences suggest that the infant burial complex was used over a considerable period of time and did not represent one event. The stratigraphical relationships were used by Outram (2011) to refine the range of radiocarbon dates through modelling to a *10th century* date for the death of all of the infants sequentially over time. Fisher also dates the cross-incised headstones stylistically to the Norse period (the late 10th or early 11th centuries) and draws comparisons in the square plaiting design to sculptured stones from nearby Papil (Fisher 2011: 124).

Cook's δ^{13} carbon isotope analysis of the skeletal material produced estimate values of less than 30 per cent (Cook 2011), not strongly indicative of a marine diet. In addition to this, Roberts' analysis of the six infants, SK8–13, ranging from neonates to 2 years 8 months, identified indications of rickets, such as porosity of the bone, poor mineralisation of the teeth and stunted growth, suggestive of Vitamin D deficiency. As all the infants were at an age when nutrition would normally have been derived from the breast milk of the mother, this has implications for the mother's health (Roberts 2011a). This seems strange when the population lived in a coastal environment, a source of marine food high in Vitamin D. Conversely, two further infants buried a small distance away in simple dug graves, SK6 (see Figure 4.3) dated to 1015–1210 cal AD (940±45; AA-45625) and SK7, 670–880 cal AD (1250±45; AA-45626), did not show any signs of rickets. Ultimately any further interpretation is only speculation with such a small sample size and only isotope estimates available, but an obvious suggestion is that the skeletal evidence indicates a sustained period of decline and poverty.[2] This may be due to environmental factors – windblown sand, first evidenced in small quantities in and around the early long cists, but culminating in a catastrophic inundation at the end of the 11th century onwards, may suggest increasingly stormy conditions that would have affected crop production. However, it is also possible that an element of economic or social control of resources may be in evidence here.

The latest-dated burial to be excavated from below the windblown sand was an adult male burial (SK5) found interred extremely flexed in one of the four short cists excavated to the south of the chapel. The cist (Figure 4.4) appeared to have been emptied in 1959, but in 2000, an inhumation was found still in situ, inserted into the base of the cist so extremely flexed that the cist had to be dismantled in order to excavate it. A small iron knife was included with the body, either as a grave good, or perhaps attached to clothing that was wrapped around the body

Figure 4.4 Late Norse burial SK5, in situ when first uncovered in Cist 303, with short cists 302 and 303 and infant burial SK6 adjacent, partially excavated. Photo: R. Barrowman (Barrowman 2011, 96, Fig. 4.5).

(Batey 2011: 131–2). A sequence of severe traumatic injuries had caused the individual's death, including a fracture to the left leg consistent with a blow from a very sharp blade, a number of skull fractures, and finally, having the head lifted and throat cut from behind by a knife (Roberts 2011a: 159–61). Despite being interred into a short cist, surprisingly the remains dated to 1025–1220 cal AD (895±45; AA-45624; modelled to *1020–1175 cal AD*; Bayliss 2011; Outram 2011). Potentially contemporary finds from the site include the unstratified collection of five 'Christian Norse' carved steatite stones from O'Dell's excavations, although these were found in the top of the windblown sand (see Thomas 1973), whereas SK5 and the short cist it was in were situated below it.

Analysis of the SK5 remains found that the articulation present suggested the remains were moved while extremely decayed but with enough of the ligaments present to be holding skeletal elements together, with a possible interpretation that they were recovered from a battle site elsewhere and brought back to St Ninian's Isle to be buried (Roberts 2011a: 159–60).[3] Interestingly, two burials from the 1950s excavations are described as being redeposited extremely flexed 'with the thigh bones touching the skull': a skeleton found in the pit dug in the 'Founder's Tomb' in 1957 but subsequently lost, and a burial code-named 'Elizabeth', identified in a box of human remains excavated from the site in 1959 and described as having been reburied with the thigh bones touching the skull (Barrowman 2011: 55–6, 59, 200). Frustratingly, the lack of further information means that little more can be added except that there are indications that SK5 was not the only 'translated' burial on the site.

Conclusion: Continuity of place and importance of local identity

The interment of the earliest dated, manifestly Christian, long cist burials on St Ninian's Isle into the same deposit as, and less than a metre away from, the short cists, rubble mound and paved pathways of a pagan burial site, demonstrates that the site continued to have a special significance after the advent of Christianity and remained significant to the population using it after conversion. The site itself may have been chosen as an early church site because it was already considered a special place by the local population who cremated or buried their dead there prior to the arrival of Christianity.

The translation of the Viking-Age/Late Norse burial remains SK5 to St Ninian's Isle to be interred suggests a continued strong loyalty of place, spiritually as well as perhaps culturally. This can be compared to the partially articulated 'bundle of bones' buried to the east end of the mortuary chapel at Whithorn (Hill 1997: 187–9).[4] The translation of relics is a common theme in both early Christian and later Norse conversion stories and histories, and it is perhaps O'Dell's own enthusiasm for this that has led to the term 'translation' being used. However, the relocation of at least one burial to the Isle, and the placing of short and long cists, and infant burials, within the same small area suggests that St Ninian's Isle continued to be considered a special place by the population(s) who chose to bury their dead and worship there at least sporadically (there is not enough evidence to confirm continuation) throughout the 8th to 11th centuries, from the pre-Norse to Norse periods, and from the pre-Christian to Christian.

The Isle is in an area that was not only rich in Pictish culture, as seen at nearby Old Scatness and Jarlshof, and in the ogham stone from St Ninian's Isle itself (Forsyth 2011), but also in early Christian material culture as first suggested by Thomas (1973). Early Christian sculpture from nearby sites such as Papil, Gungstie, Noss and Bressay across the sound of Ness, and also Mail, Cunningsburgh continue to illustrate that St Ninian's Isle was part of a vibrant early Christian landscape in the southern half of mainland Shetland in the 8th to 10th centuries (see Thomas 1971; Stevenson 1981; Turner 1998; Fisher 2002; Scott and Ritchie 2010; Barrowman 2011: 196; Forsyth 2011, 2020). Forsyth draws attention to the fact that by far the largest collection in Shetland of pre-Norse and Norse sculpture has been recovered from St Ninian's Isle, including three ogham-inscribed fragments, two of which are now lost (Forsyth 2011; 2020: 249). She concludes in her assessment of the St Ninian's Isle ogham stone and its place in the assemblage of ogham-inscribed stones from Shetland that 'the impression is of on-going participation in the Scottish ogham tradition over a potentially extended period, with a possible emphasis in the 10th century. That Shetland oghamists should still be part of the common tradition after the Norse adventus is perhaps surprising, yet it appears to be borne out by numerous parallels . . .' (Forsyth 2011: 23).

Certainly, the presence of 9th- to 11th-century burials at St Ninian's Isle means that whatever happened after the incoming Norse arrived in Shetland, there continued to be burials there, with no evidence for any hiatus until the catastrophic inundation of sand towards the end of the 11th century. This also means that there is less reason to think that the early church building was abandoned at this time; in fact, although the recent reassessment confirmed that the treasure was indeed dug into the floor of the earlier church building, there is no reason from the archaeological evidence alone why the treasure could not have been deposited after the 9th century (see discussion in Barrowman 2011: 201–3 and Graham-Campbell's analysis [2003: 13–21], which concludes that the hoard need not have been buried hurriedly). Although the St Ninian's Isle excavation archives and material assemblages contain only echoes of native and Norse culture, there are small but powerful glimpses left to us of the relationship between native and Norse, and the overriding sense is one of a continued loyalty to a local place by the native and incoming population, throughout changes in both belief and culture.

Acknowledgements

This paper, as given at the *Vikings in Scotland: 20 Years On* conference in 2018, was based on an extensively reworked version of a paper delivered at the *St Ninian's Isle Treasure: Fifty Years Since* conference, held in Lerwick in July 2008. Brian Smith, of the Shetland Museum and Archives, who organised that conference and invited me to participate, had hoped to publish the proceedings, but this had not proved possible. Since then, I have been able to mull over the points made in it and to further bring out aspects of my conclusions. I am very grateful to those who assisted with this, not least the late Anthony Charles Thomas, James Graham-Campbell, Colleen Batey and Christopher Morris, who were a support throughout the project, and to Christopher Morris and Katherine Forsyth, who read through a draft of this paper. Any faults or mistakes contained therein, however, are entirely my own.

Notes

1. I am grateful to James Graham-Campbell, who reminded me to include the portion of the west wall of the earlier chapel that appears on O'Dell's 1959 plan (published in O'Dell 1960, note 4, fig. 1), and that the west wall, while not on Thomas' published plan in the 1973 volume, is recorded on his original sketch-plan made after interviewing O'Dell and meeting with Alan Small while researching the carved stones from the site.
2. Interestingly, Thomas, when discussing a supposed 'hiatus' on the site, refers to 'a few surviving Christian islanders or Picts under the domination of pagan Norse landholders' (Thomas 1973: 13).
3. In this case the burial was either interred into an old cist, or the cist itself is not Iron Age, but Late Norse as suggested prior to completion of the post-excavation analyses (Barrowman 2003: 57). The archive notes, if taken at face value, attribute charred human bone fragments to this cist, so either this is an error, and they were animal bones deriving from the midden deposits below, or the charred bones were disturbed when SK5 was inserted.
4. I am grateful to Adrián Maldonado for drawing my attention to this.

References

Ashmore, P. (1981) Low cairns, long cists and symbol stones. *Proceedings of the Society of Antiquaries of Scotland* 110 (1978–80), 346–55.

Ashmore, P., R. Barrowman and C. Cook (2011) Radiocarbon dating of the Marischal Museum collection of human skeletal material. In R. C. Barrowman, *The Chapel and Burial Ground on St Ninian's Isle, Shetland: Excavations Past and Present*. Society for Medieval Archaeology monograph 32. London: Society for Medieval Archaeology, 79–80.

Backlund, J. (2001) War or peace? The relations between the Picts and the Norse in Orkney. *Northern Studies* 36, 33–48.

Barrett, J. H. (2003) Culture contact in Viking Age Scotland. In J. H. Barrett (ed.), *Contact, Continuity and Collapse: The Norse Colonization of the North Atlantic*. Studies in the Early Middle Ages. Turnhout: Brepols, 73–111.

Barrowman, R. C. (2003) A decent burial? Excavations at St Ninian's Isle in July 2000. In J. Downes and A. Ritchie (eds), *Sea Change: Orkney and Northern Europe in the later Iron Age AD 300–800*. Balgavies: Pinkfoot Press, 51–61.

Barrowman, R. C. (2011) *The Chapel and Burial Ground on St Ninian's Isle, Shetland: Excavations Past and Present*. Society for Medieval Archaeology monograph 32. London: Society for Medieval Archaeology.

Batey, C. E. (2011) Metals. In R. C. Barrowman, *The Chapel and Burial Ground on St Ninian's Isle, Shetland: Excavations Past and Present*. Society for Medieval Archaeology monograph 32. London: Society for Medieval Archaeology, 131–3.

Bayliss, A. (2011) Radiocarbon dating of human skeletal material from the 2000 excavation. In R. C. Barrowman, *The Chapel and Burial Ground on St Ninian's Isle, Shetland: Excavations Past and Present*. Society for Medieval Archaeology monograph 32. London: Society for Medieval Archaeology, 169–73.

Bigelow, G. (1984) Two kerbed cairns from Sandwick, Unst, Shetland. In J. P. G. Friell and W. G. Watson (eds), *Pictish Studies: Settlement, Burial and Art in Dark Age Northern Britain*. British Archaeological Reports British Series 125. Oxford: British Archaeological Reports, 115–29.

Close-Brooks, J. (1984) Pictish and other burials. In J. P. G. Friell and W. G. Watson (eds), *Pictish Studies: Settlement, Burial and Art in Dark Age Northern Britain*. British Archaeological Reports British Series 125. Oxford: British Archaeological Reports, 87–114.

Cook, G. (2011) Results of the bone stable isotope measurements. In R. C. Barrowman, *The Chapel and Burial Ground on St Ninian's Isle, Shetland: Excavations Past and Present*. Society for Medieval Archaeology monograph 32. London: Society for Medieval Archaeology, 179–80.

Crawford, B. E. (1987) *Scandinavian Scotland*. Scotland in the Early Middle Ages 2, Studies in the Early History of Britain. Leicester: Leicester University Press.

Dockrill, S. J. (2003) Broch, wheelhouse, and cell: Redefining the Iron Age in Shetland. In J. Downes and A. Ritchie (eds), *Sea Change: Orkney and Northern Europe in the Later Iron Age AD 300–800*. Balgavies: Pinkfoot Press, 83–94.

Dockrill, S., J. Bond, V. E. Turner, L. D. Brown, D. Bashford, J. E. Cussans and R. A. Nicholson (2010) *Excavations at Old Scatness, Shetland, Volume 1, The Pictish and Viking Settlement*. Lerwick: Shetland Heritage Publications.

Duffy, P. (2011) Disarticulated remains. In R. C. Barrowman, *The Chapel and Burial Ground on St Ninian's Isle, Shetland: Excavations Past and Present*. Society for Medieval Archaeology monograph 32. London: Society for Medieval Archaeology, 165–8.

Fisher, I. (2002) Crosses in the ocean: Some *papar* sites and their sculpture. In B. E. Crawford (ed.), *The Papar in the North Atlantic: Environment and History*. St John's House Papers, no. 10. St Andrews: Committee for Dark Age Studies, University of St Andrews, 39–57.

Fisher, I. (2011) The carved stones. In R. C. Barrowman, *The Chapel and Burial Ground on St Ninian's Isle, Shetland: Excavations Past and Present*. Society for Medieval Archaeology monograph 32. London: Society for Medieval Archaeology, 121–4.

Forsyth, K. (2011) An ogham-inscribed slab from St Ninian's Isle, found in 1876. In R. C. Barrowman, *The Chapel and Burial Ground on St Ninian's Isle, Shetland: Excavations Past and Present*. Society for Medieval Archaeology monograph 32. London: Society for Medieval Archaeology, 15–25.

Forsyth, K. (2020) Protecting a Pict?: Further thoughts on the inscribed silver chape from St Ninian's Isle, Shetland. *Proceedings of the Society of Antiquaries of Scotland* 149 (2019–20), 249–76.

Graham-Campbell, J. (2003) *Pictish Silver: Status and Symbol*. H. M. Chadwick Memorial Lectures 4. Cambridge: University of Cambridge, Department of Anglo-Saxon, Norse and Celtic.

Graham-Campbell, J. and C. E. Batey (1998) *Vikings in Scotland: An Archaeological Survey*. Edinburgh: Edinburgh University Press.

Hill, P. (1997) *Whithorn and St Ninians: The Excavation of a Monastic Town, 1984–91*. Stroud: Sutton.

Maldonado, A. (2013) Burial in early medieval Scotland: New questions. *Medieval Archaeology* 57, 1–34.

Morris, C. D. (1989) *The Birsay Bay Project Volume 1. Brough Road Excavations 1976–1982*. Department of Archaeology Monograph Series 1. Durham: University of Durham.

Morris, C. D. (1990) *Church and Monastery in the Far North: An Archaeological Re-evaluation*. The Jarrow Lecture 1989, Jarrow. Reprinted in *Bede and his World. The Jarrow Lectures*, Volume II 1978–1993, Aldershot 1994, 807–48.

Morris, C. D. (1998) Raiders, traders and settlers: The early Viking Age in Scotland. In H. B. Clarke, M. Ni Mhaonaigh and R. Ó. Floinn (eds), *Ireland and Scandinavia in the Early Viking Age*. Dublin: Four Courts Press, 73–103.

Morris, C. D. (2021) *The Birsay Bay Project Volume 3. The Brough of Birsay, Orkney investigations 1954–2014*. Oxford: Oxbow Books.

Morris, C. D. and R. C. Barrowman (2008) The Shetland Chapel-sites Project. Further investigations and résumé. In C. Paulsen and H. D. Michelsen (eds), *Símunarbók. Heiðursrit til Símun V Arge á 60 ára degnum, 5 september 2008*. Tórshavn: Fróðskapur, Faroe University Press, 166–92.

Mulville, J., M. Parker Pearson, N. Sharples, H. Smith and A. Chamberlain (2003) Quarters, arcs and squares: Human and animal remains in the Hebridean Late Iron Age. In J. Downes and A. Ritchie (eds), *Sea Change: Orkney and Northern Europe in the Later Iron Age AD 300–800*. Balgavies: Pinkfoot Press, 20–34.

O'Dell, A. C. (1960) *St Ninian's Isle Treasure. A Silver Hoard Discovered on St Ninian's Isle, Zetland on 4th July, 1958*. Aberdeen: Aberdeen University.

Outram, Z. (2011) Re-modelling of all dated samples to include those from the 1959 and 2000 excavations on St Ninian's Isle. In R. C. Barrowman, *The Chapel and Burial Ground on St Ninian's Isle, Shetland: Excavations Past and Present*. Society for Medieval Archaeology monograph 32. London: Society for Medieval Archaeology, 173–9.

Owen, O. and C. Lowe (1999) *Kebister: The Four-thousand-year-old Story of One Shetland Township*. Society of Antiquaries of Scotland monograph series 14. Edinburgh: Society of Antiquaries of Scotland.

Parker Pearson, M., M. Brennan, J. Mulville and H. Smith (2018) *Cille Pheadair: A Norse Farmstead and Pictish Burial Cairn in South Uist*. Sheffield Environmental and Archaeological Research Campaign in the Hebrides volume 7. Oxford: Oxbow Books.

Ritchie, A. (1974) Pict and Norseman in Northern Scotland. *Scottish Archaeological Forum* 6, 23–36.

Ritchie, A. (2003) Paganism among the Picts and the conversion of Orkney. In J. Downes and A. Ritchie (eds), *Sea Change: Orkney and Northern Europe in the Later Iron Age AD 300–800*. Balgavies: Pinkfoot Press, 3–10.

Roberts, J. (2011a) Articulated remains. In R. C. Barrowman, *The Chapel and Burial Ground on St Ninian's Isle, Shetland: Excavations Past and Present*. Society for Medieval Archaeology monograph 32. London: Society for Medieval Archaeology, 158–65.

Roberts, J. (2011b) Human remains from the 1955–1959 excavations: Articulated skeletons held in the Marischal Museum, Aberdeen. In R. C. Barrowman, *The Chapel and Burial Ground on St Ninian's Isle, Shetland: Excavations Past and Present*. Society for Medieval Archaeology monograph 32. London: Society for Medieval Archaeology, 76–9.

Scott, I. G. and A. Ritchie (2010) *Pictish and Viking-Age Carvings from Shetland*. Edinburgh: Royal Commission on the Ancient and Historical Monuments of Scotland.

Sharples, N. (1998) *Scalloway: A Broch, Late Iron Age Settlement and Medieval Cemetery in Shetland*. Cardiff Studies in Archaeology – Oxbow Monograph 82. Oxford: Oxbow Books.

Small, A. (1973) The site: Its history and excavation. In A. Small, C. Thomas and D. M. Wilson (eds), *St Ninian's Isle and its Treasure*. Aberdeen University Studies 152, 2 vols. Oxford: Oxford University Press, 1–7.

Small, A., C. Thomas and D. M. Wilson (1973) *St Ninian's Isle and its Treasure*. Aberdeen University Studies 152, 2 vols. Oxford: Oxford University Press.

Smith, B. (2003) Not welcome at all: Vikings and the native population in Orkney and Shetland. In J. Downes and A. Ritchie (eds), *Sea Change: Orkney and Northern Europe in the Later Iron Age AD 300–800*. Balgavies: Pinkfoot Press, 145–50.

Stevenson, R. B. K. (1981) Christian sculpture in Norse Shetland. *Froðskaparrit (Heiðurscrit til Sverra Dahl), Annales Societatis Scientiarum Faeroensis* 28/29 (1981), 283–92.

Thomas, A. C. (1971) *The Early Christian Archaeology of North Britain: The Hunter Marshall lectures delivered at the University of Glasgow in January and February 1968*. London: Oxford University Press for the University of Glasgow.

Thomas, C. (1973) Sculptured stones and crosses from St Ninian's Isle and Papil. In A. Small, C. Thomas and D. M. Wilson (eds), *St Ninian's Isle and its Treasure*. Aberdeen University Studies 152, 2 vols. Oxford: Oxford University Press, 8–44.

Turner, V. (1998) *Ancient Shetland*. London: Batsford.

Part II

Scandinavian Settlement

An explosion of new information made available by an increase in archaeological excavations and environmental recovery techniques in the 1970s and '80s led Graham-Campbell and Batey to describe the picture of Viking and Late Norse period settlement in 1998 as 'altered radically' (1998: 155). *Vikings in Scotland* appeared just as many of these excavations were coming to fruition, and a greater awareness of the complexities in building techniques, economic activity and settlement distribution was beginning to be appreciated. Exploration of multi-period sites, and the identification of earlier, Viking-Age, as well as Late Norse, houses was showing that the Vikings often colonised existing settlement sites and that their buildings did not always conform to the later, bow-sided longhouses seen at Jarlshof and other such 'type sites'.

Twenty years later, many more newly excavated and reassessed settlement sites have come to publication, including those reported on in this volume. This has been matched by an increase in Norse place-name studies, and both have resulted in new interpretations of Scandinavian settlement and the forms it took (see also Part III).

The papers in this section aptly demonstrate the complexity of Scandinavian settlement between areas and centuries. At Bornais in South Uist in the Western Isles (Sharples, this section), the exceptional quality of preservation seen in the excavation of three high-status houses spanning the late 9th to early 14th centuries has enabled a study of the social position of female slaves through artefact distributions and building layout on the site. To the north, in Unst, Shetland, where a uniquely high number of longhouses have been identified through survey, the excavations at Hamar and Underhoull (Bond and Dockrill, this section), have revealed that a longer, and far more complex, settlement history is present than previously thought. In contrast, the excavation of the remains of a farm founded in the 10th century at Machair Bharabhais, Lewis, discovered that it was abandoned by the end of the 13th century at a time of great political turmoil in the Hebrides (MacLeod Rivett and Cowie, this section).

New scientific techniques are aiding greatly in the study of the spread of Scandinavian settlement since *Vikings in Scotland* and highlight the differences between different areas. Scientific analysis by Forster and Jones (this section) of steatite artefacts demonstrates the potential for identifying *landnám* populations, distribution routes, and understanding when and how new arrivals began to discover and utilise local resources as they settled the landscape. Place-name work reflects this complex picture: Macniven (next section), for instance, suggests that rather than hybridity, the Norse were free to claim the best land for settlement following a period of disconnection with their Gaelic predecessors at the outset of Viking-Age settlement in Islay, whereas in contrast, the highest-status farms in Mull had Gaelic names in 15th-century sources, while lower-status farms retained their Old Norse names (Whyte, next section).

Chapter 5

The Use of Space in Norse Houses: Some Observations from the Hebrides

Niall Sharples

In this short chapter, I intend to briefly discuss the results of the recent excavation at the settlement of Bornais on the island of South Uist in the Western Isles of Scotland (Sharples 2005, 2012, 2020a and 2020b). The settlement at Bornais is located on the machair plain (a thick deposit of shell sand created by glacial activity) of the west coast of the island and is an unusually large settlement that covers approximately 4,625m² and comprises five discrete settlement mounds. The principal focus for the settlement is Mound 2, the largest settlement mound, in which excavation revealed a sequence of three large high-status houses (Figure 5.1). Houses 1 and 2 were bow-walled longhouses characteristic of the Norse settlement of the North Atlantic. House 3, in contrast, was a rectangular house which was short and wide in comparison to the earlier houses.

The chronology of this mound has been determined by the acquisition of a large number of radiocarbon dates (Marshall et al. in Sharples 2020a) and large quantities of material culture including dateable items, such as coinage. These indicate that House 1 was built in the late 9th or early 10th century and was used until the middle of the 11th century (Sharples 2020a: 94). House 2 was built in the second half of the 11th century and was abandoned early in the 12th century (Sharples 2020a: 137). House 3 was constructed in the middle of the 13th century and was abandoned possibly as late as the early 14th century (Sharples 2020a: 383). It was constructed after a long period when there appears to be no high-status residence present on Mound 2.

The Early Norse houses

House 1 is approximately 23m long, but only small areas at the east and west end of this house were explored by our excavation, so understanding of this house is strictly limited (Sharples 2020a: 57). The east end was paved and an entrance was visible in the gable end. The west end, in contrast, had a charcoal-rich floor layer, and there was just enough

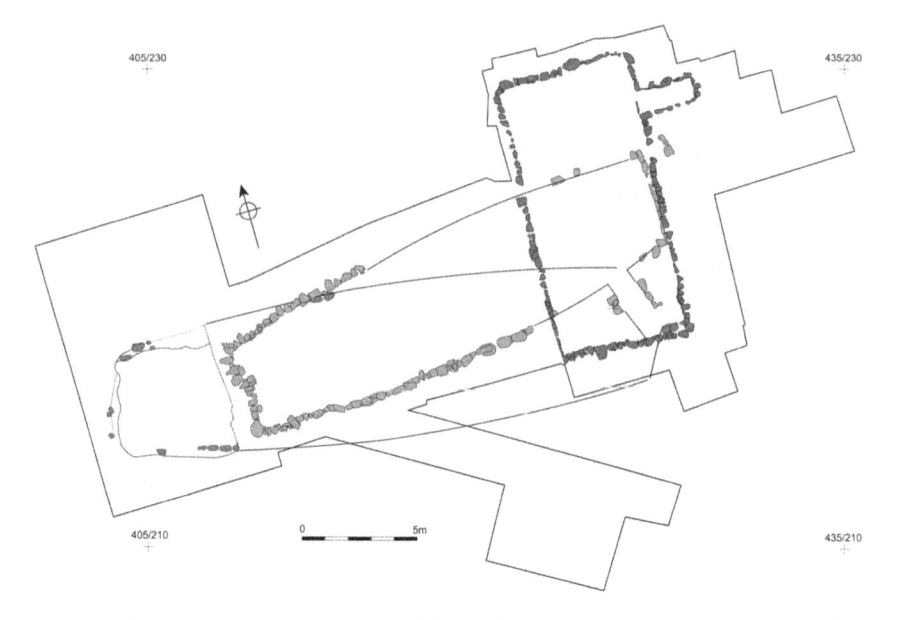

Figure 5.1 The sequence of large houses on Mound 2. Amended by David Battley.

excavated to reveal the presence of a central hearth area defined by thick deposits of peat ash. The floor contained a range of interesting finds, including a cluster of sherds from broken steatite vessels, imported from Scandinavia, and a large ceramic vessel, made on the island. Large amounts of timber appear to have been used in the construction of this house and a range of pits was found underneath the floor layer.

House 2 is just under 20m long and up to 5.8m wide and is defined by stone walls that survive in the west half of the house up to 1.3m in height (Sharples 2020a: 145). The entrance was placed on the south side close to the east gable wall and reused the original gable end of House 1. The house would have been largely subterranean, with perhaps only the gable ends and the roof showing above ground level.

The floor deposits (Figure 5.2) suggested the interior was divided into three aisles, though no significant structural postholes were observed. The central aisle was distinguished by an accumulation of multiple thin layers of orange, yellow and pink ash, which derive from the burning of peat and indicate the repeated raking out of the hearth deposits. This created a compact surface on which people could move through the interior of the house.

The stone walls of the house are well built and impressive and use substantial slabs that are otherwise rarely used in Viking and Norse houses. They probably came from the robbing of indigenous Iron-Age structures on the machair plain. This would be a socially significant as well as a functionally effective way of sourcing good building stone.

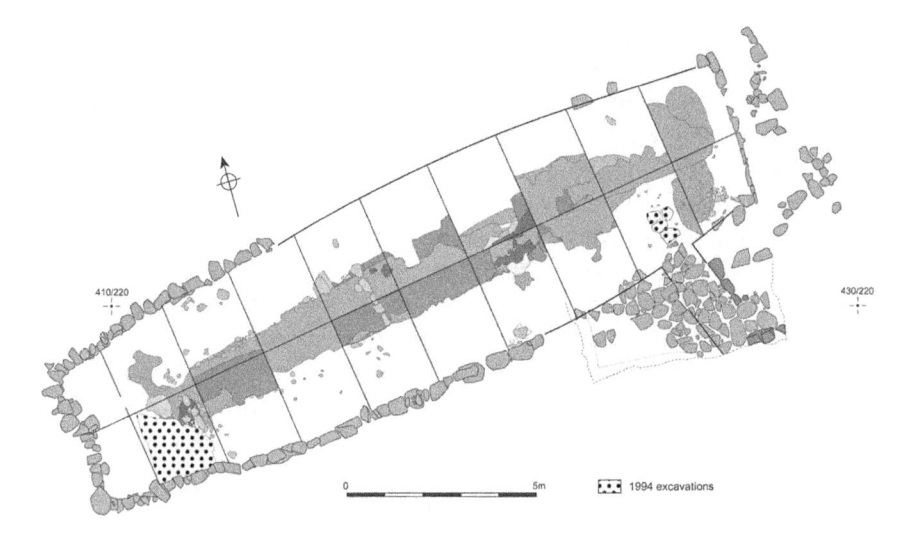

Figure 5.2 A plan of the interior of House 2 showing the ash deposits covering the central aisle of the house and the paved area at the entrance. Amended by David Battley.

The finds assemblage recovered from the floor of House 2 was substantial (Sharples, Pannett, Smith and Taylor in Sharples 2020a: 193); it included 689 small finds, over 2,953 potsherds and 1,957 identified animal bones. Almost all of the objects in these assemblages can be accurately located in the house. The highlights include:

- an antler cylinder decorated with a Ringerike-style animal
- a collection of unusual antler tine handles possibly associated with ritually charged feasting and drinking
- numerous exotic trinkets, including a fragment of green porphyry, the arm from an amber cross, clipped coins of Æthelræd II and Olaf Kyrre, eight glass beads, a lead pendant, a pearl and a small fragment of gold strip
- the comb assemblage was substantial, with sixty-six fragments, and could be classed as classic Irish Sea assemblage with a few relics, such as a fragment of a large Ambrosiani A comb, which could have been made over a hundred years earlier
- an assemblage of forty-eight bone, copper alloy and iron stick pins, almost half of which were complete
- a wide range of tools, including significant assemblages of knives, whetstones, spindle whorls and needles.

The ceramic assemblage was substantial and included many largely complete vessels which appear to have been smashed in situ at the west end of the house. Most of the vessels were crudely made straight or slightly bow-sided bowls with sagging bases. There was very little evidence for ceramic platters being used in this house.

All the floor layers were bagged and floated, and a quantified proportion of the residues from these samples was sorted down to 2mm, providing large assemblages of materials rarely found on archaeological sites, including eggshell, crabshell, small mammal bones and worm casts. We have exceptionally complete assemblages of carbonised plant remains and animal, bird and fish bones. Barley dominated the assemblage of carbonised grain, but oats, rye and flax were all present and there were very large concentrations of wild seeds from the goosefoot family (*Chenopodiaceae*) and dock (*Rumex/Polygonum* spp.; Summers and Bond in Sharples 2020a: 221). The principal animal species present were young cattle, a prime source of meat, sheep/goat, pig and deer (Powell, Best, Mulville and Sharples in Sharples 2020a: 226); and fish, largely herring, were also present (Ingrem in Sharples 2020a: 230). It is clear that this was a well-provisioned household and the inhabitants had a rich and varied diet.

A detailed examination of the spatial patterning of the assemblages from House 2 suggests the house can essentially be divided into three to four rooms (Sharples in Sharples 2020a: 235):

1. the west end, which appears to be the principal cooking space defined by the large quantities of pottery and the presence of numerous pits
2. the west central area is the principal social space where indoor activities were undertaken and is characterised by large quantities of small finds
3. the east central area where distinctive activity is difficult to identify, but it could possibly be for storage and/or sleeping
4. the east end was an area where rubbish such as shellfish, fish and animal bones were allowed to accumulate.

The artefacts in the west central area give us a good indication of the types of activities that were undertaken inside this house. These included:

- drinking and the consumption of food
- the care and maintenance of the body
- spinning and sewing (but not weaving?)
- the use and maintenance of iron knives
- the systematic dismantling of antler combs
- the breaking-up of sheet iron vessel(s).

Many of these artefacts come in clusters that suggest they were deposited by individuals who had their own seating area within the living space at the west end of House 2 (Sharples 2020a: figs. 159–67). The large quantity of objects present is also worthy of consideration. Many of the objects appear to have been discarded when they were still functionally useful: most of the pins were whole, for example. This was not a single abandonment deposit as the different objects were found within several separate layers that accumulated during the life of the house. It indicates a wasteful society that was content to throw away materials in a very casual manner.

Comparisons

There are very few sites that we can compare Bornais to as the quality of the preservation and stratigraphy of this site is exceptional. The best parallels are in Iceland, and it is instructive to look at the spatial organisation of two settlements, Granastaðir and Aðalstræti.

The settlement at Granastaðir lies in Eyjafjarðardalur in northern Iceland and was excavated by Einarsson (1995). The main house was a bow-walled longhouse oriented north–south, with internal dimensions of 14.7m long and up to 5.4m wide. There are three entrances: an entrance on the west side towards the north gable; a subsidiary entrance opposite this in the north-east corner; and an entrance in the centre of the southern gable wall. This house was accompanied by another large building and a couple of detached subsidiary structures. Einarsson interpreted the main house as being divided into three rooms and follows Myhre's interpretation of the Oma house in Norway (Myhre 1982):

- Room I in the north gable was identified as a kitchen, and work area, with a possible religious role
- Room II/III was a large central living room for work, leisure, recreation and consumption
- Room IV was in the south gable and was a storage or drying room
- an annex was added to the south end and this contained a kitchen and had a separate entrance
- a smoke house was added onto the east side of the house, but it was not directly accessible from the house.

Aðalstræti is one of the earliest known settlements in Iceland (Vésteinsson et al. 2006) and is located in the centre of Reykjavík in the south-west corner of the island. The house was oriented north–south and has internal dimensions of 16.7m by 5.8m. The principal or public entrance lies at the north end of the long east wall and has a porch projecting from the entrance; there is a subsidiary, or private, entrance in the south-west corner. The occupation of the house was thoroughly explored by Milek (2006).

This house has a symmetrical arrangement of internal space similar to that noted at Granastaðir. On coming through the main public entrance, one entered a vestibule which led into a transitional space at the north end of the central aisle. This was surrounded by numerous small rooms which could be for storage, or provide toilet facilities and animal stalling. The large central room had a distinctive stone-kerbed hearth area with a raised platform to the west, possibly with a timber floor, and a layer of 'grass bedding' covered a similar sized space to the east. At the south end was another transitional space surrounded by small rooms; one of these was for textile production and included a loom, and another may have been for washing/dyeing wool.

One of the important distinctions between these Icelandic houses and the houses in the Western Isles appears to be the location of the cooking area. At Bornais, both House 1 and House 2 appear to have the cooking area located at the west end, as far from the single eastern entrance as it was possible to be. This was also the case in the contemporary houses at Cille Pheadair (Parker Pearson et al. 2018) and Drimore (MacLaren 1974), also on South Uist.

At Granastaðir, it was suggested the hearth at the north end, close to the entrance, was for ceremonial or religious cooking (Einarsson 1995: 135), while the main kitchen was at the south end, where a subsidiary entrance was located. Similarly, at Aðalstræti there was no evidence for cooking at the south end of the house and the distribution of burnt bone was argued to indicate cooking was located at the north end of the central hearth, near the entrance (Milek 2006: 202). It is important to note that in both these houses there is a main entrance and a subsidiary entrance at the opposite end of the house, and that subsidiary entrances are a feature of many Icelandic houses (Milek 2006: 109), but not as far as we can see in the Hebridean houses.

These differences appear to mark a major social distinction in the use of space in the Hebrides and Iceland, which is worth thinking about. It seems clear from the historical record that cooking was primarily a female activity in Viking societies (Einarsson 1995: 135; Jochens 1995: 129) and therefore we might expect the cooking area to be the principal nexus of female activity within the house. In Iceland, this appears to be taking place in a public location visible to any individual entering the house, and this contrasts significantly with the situation in the Hebrides where the cooking area appears to be in the most inaccessible part of the house. These patterns suggest that women had a much more powerful and independent role in Icelandic society, at least in some households.

It is possible that this deep space at the west end of House 2 at Bornais was occupied by disenfranchised indigenous slaves. The presence of substantial quantities of pottery of distinctive Hebridean form in this location may be related to the presence of local women, as it has been argued that the production of Norse ceramics indicates the continuity of local traditions of ceramic production (Sharples 2020b: 462). A desire to control the individuals occupying this part of the Hebridean houses might also explain the lack of a subsidiary entrance in this area.

The Norse or Scottish house

These patterns can also be expanded upon if we consider the changes that take place in the 13th century at Bornais. On Mound 2, House 3 was built towards the beginning of the 13th century and is a completely different type of house from the bow-walled longhouses of Houses 1 and 2. House 3 had a distinctive playing-card shape and proportions, and was turf-walled with an internal timber frame that supported the roof (Sharples 2020a: 304). However, there was a single entrance at the north end of the long east wall, which is reminiscent of the earlier entrance arrangements. It is unclear whether the changes in the form of the house reflect increasing Scottish influence in the islands or indicate a local evolution of the Viking longhouse. Unfortunately, the numbers of excavated medieval buildings in Argyll and western Scotland are very limited and do not provide a clear delineation of the architectural traditions of the region.

The house had at least two separate floor layers (Figure 5.3). In the earliest floor, two hearths were present, located in the centre and south end of the house, but in the latest floor there was a central hearth and

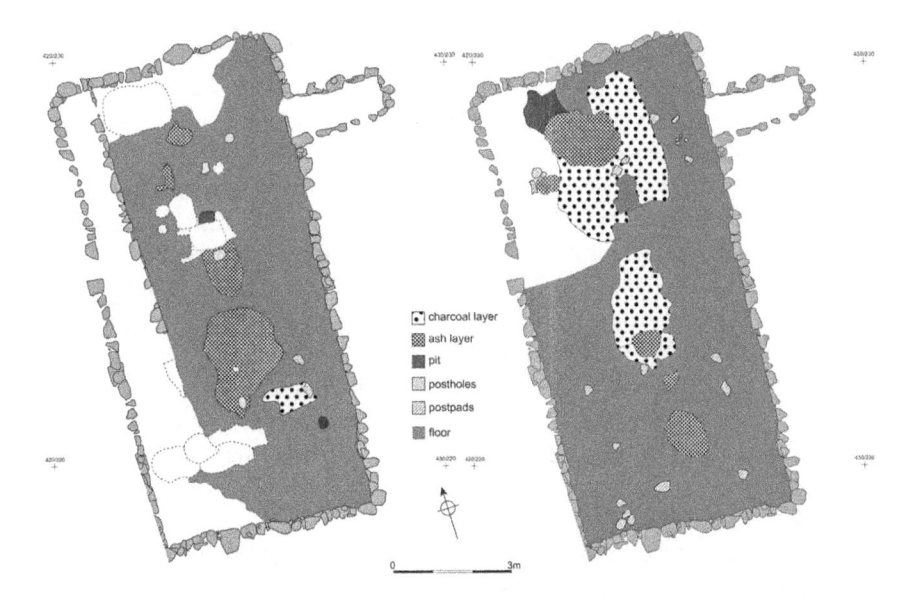

Figure 5.3 The floor layers inside House 3. The earliest floor is on the left and the latest floor on the right. Amended by David Battley.

a hearth opposite the entrance; it was the latter hearth that seemed the most important. The defined oval spreads of ash that characterise these later hearths are very different to the earlier longhouse hearths that were long rectangular spreads of ash.

This change in the shape and location of the hearth is also visible in the lower-status houses, which are smaller, roughly 8m by 4m, but have the same shape. The last house at Cille Pheadair (Parker Pearson et al. 2018: 212), which dates to the middle of the 12th century, has a long rectangular hearth. This contrasts markedly with the small rectangular hearth located opposite the entrance within the final house on Bornais Mound 3 (Sharples 2005: 53), which dates to the 14th century.

Another significant difference between the late rectangular houses and the early longhouses is the quantities of finds present in the house floors. The conspicuous consumption that was visible in the longhouses is noticeably absent in House 3 and the other excavated 13th- and 14th-century houses. Very few finds were recovered from the various floor layers of House 3 (Sharples 2020a: figs. 249 and 262) and those that were found can mostly be explained as accidental losses and damaged waste. The distribution of food waste suggests that in the later houses most of the cooking activities were taking place around the hearth and close to the entrance. The deep space seems to be relatively underused and may have been a sleeping area.

The development of the small rectangular houses in the 13th century is associated with the appearance of ancillary buildings, which seem to serve particular specialist tasks. On Bornais Mound 3, the ancillary building was used for agricultural processing and included an external kiln and space for winnowing and crop storage (Sharples 2005: 86). On Mound 2A, one of the ancillary structures was a comb-maker's workshop (Sharples 2020a: 451).

This fracturing of the domestic space into either separate buildings or separate rooms which served specialist functions can be observed across the North Atlantic in the 13th and 14th centuries. In Orkney and Caithness (Fenton 1978a), the tendency is for these spaces to be arranged end to end to create exceptionally long houses, whereas in Shetland (Tait 2012) and the Isle of Lewis (Fenton 1978b) they are often arranged side by side. In Iceland, the arrangement of spaces around a corridor creates a very distinctive structure known as the 'passage house'. This is the period when the architectural elements that define the recent historical record emerge and develop their distinctive regional characteristics.

All of these developments seem to be an attempt to remove messy activities from the main domestic space, which becomes increasingly cleansed of artefacts. They also isolate particular activities in their own distinctive spaces. The spatial arrangement of these functional-distinct buildings is regionally distinctive, but it is part of a general trend which is occurring all across the Scandinavian territories of the North Atlantic at this time.

Conclusion

In this chapter, I have argued that, despite the overall similarity between the longhouses in the Scandinavian territories of the North Atlantic, there are significant differences which highlight the different social position of females in the households of Iceland and the Hebrides. These differences are highlighted by the location of the cooking areas in the longhouses and how this is positioned in relation to the access to the house. In the Hebrides, cooking areas are embedded as far away from the entrance as possible. In Iceland, the cooking locations are often in public locations next to doors that provide immediate access to the outside. The degree of freedom available to the females undertaking cooking in the Hebrides seems to be constrained and suggests they could be slaves.

The spatial relationship of the hearth and the entrance change as the Scandinavian longhouses evolved during the 13th and 14th centuries in the Hebrides. New smaller, more formal, defined hearths are located in the middle of the house in front of the entrance and this becomes the focal point for cooking and food consumption. If one accepts that the hearth and cooking had a specific gendered significance, then this move suggests a major change in the social significance of women in these houses. A female located directly opposite the entrance would effectively control access to the house and all the internal space. Furthermore, most of the messy male activities related to craft and agricultural activities appear to have been moved to external buildings. This could be seen to indicate a decline in the social importance of the house, and it is noticeable that prestige objects related to competitive male activities were no longer found scattered around the interior of these later houses.

References

Einarsson, B. F. (1995) *The Settlement of Iceland: A Critical Approach*. Granastaðir and the Ecological Heritage. Reykjavík: Íslenska Bókmenntafélag.
Fenton, A. (1978a) *The Northern Isles: Orkney and Shetland*. Edinburgh: John Donald.
Fenton, A. (1978b) *The Island Blackhouse*. Edinburgh: Historic Scotland.
Jochens, J. (1995) *Women in Old Norse Society*. Ithaca: Cornell University Press.
MacLaren, A. (1974) A Norse house on Drimore machair, South Uist. *Glasgow Archaeological Journal* 3(1), 9–18.
Milek, K. B. (2016) *Houses and Households in Early Icelandic Society: Geoarchaeology and the Interpretation of Social Space*. Unpublished PhD thesis, University of Cambridge.

Myhre, B. (1982) Bolighusets utvikling fra jernalder til middelalder i sørvest-Norge. In B. Myhre, S. Stoklund and P. Gjærder (eds), *Vestnordisk Byggeskikk Gjennom to Tusen År: tradisjon og forandring fra romertid til det 19. århundre. AmS-Skrifter 7*. Stavanger: Arkeologisk Museum i Stavanger, 195–217.

Parker Pearson, M., M. Brennand, J. Mulville and H. Smith (2018) *Cille Pheadair: A Norse Farmstead and Pictish Burial Cairn in South Uist*. Oxford: Oxbow Books.

Sharples, N. (2005) *A Norse Farmstead in the Outer Hebrides: Excavations at Mound 3, Bornais, South Uist*. Oxford: Oxbow Books.

Sharples, N. (2012) *A Late Iron Age Farmstead in the Outer Hebrides: Excavations at Mound 1, Bornais, South Uist*. Oxford: Oxbow Books.

Sharples, N. (2020a) *A Norse Settlement in the Outer Hebrides: Excavations at Mounds 2 and 2A, Bornais, South Uist*. Oxford: Oxbow Books.

Sharples, N. (2020b) *The Economy of a Norse Settlement in the Outer Hebrides: Excavations on Mounds 2 and 2A, Bornais, South Uist*. Oxford: Oxbow Books.

Tait, I. (2012) *Shetland Vernacular Buildings 1600–1900*. Lerwick: The Shetland Times Ltd.

Vésteinsson, O., H. Þorláksson and A. Einarsson (2006) *Reykjavík 871 ± 2. Landnámssýningin. The Settlement Exhibition*. Reykjavík: Reykjavík City Museum.

Chapter 6

Hamar and Underhoull, Unst: Settlement in Northernmost Scotland
Julie M. Bond and Stephen J. Dockrill

The island of Unst has a large number of recorded longhouses of apparently Viking or Norse date (Dyer et al. 2013). Unst is unique in that sites like this are found in a density and state of preservation unseen elsewhere in Britain, and it was this that led Shetland Amenity Trust to propose the 'Viking Unst Project' to investigate some of these sites and display them as a means of encouraging archaeological tourism to the island (Turner et al. 2013). In research terms, the unusual nature of the Unst settlement pattern demanded investigation. Previous survey and excavation (for example, Stumman-Hansen 1995, 2000) had suggested the sites were largely single-period with no evidence of earlier occupation. Many are on or above the 30m contour, which at this northern extremity of the British Isles today makes for environmentally precarious conditions. Just 20m above the site of Hamar House 2, for example, is the Keen of Hamar, where solifluction stripes caused by freeze-thaw action, and subarctic plant species, can be seen.

A settlement pattern of Viking-period farms with no pre-Viking activity, such as the Unst data suggested, is largely absent elsewhere in the Northern Isles, where Norse settlement is usually identified as a phase within multi-period sites located on good agricultural land (Dockrill and Bond, this volume). These deeply stratified sites, such as Jarlshof and Old Scatness in southern Shetland, often represent several millennia of occupation, of which the Viking-Age/Late Norse periods are late in the sequence (Hamilton 1956; Dockrill et al. 2010).

The main aim of the excavations at Hamar and Underhoull was to investigate this unusual settlement pattern, to test the presumed date of the houses and the theory that they were single-period settlements. Hamar was chosen as one of the sites because previous investigation had suggested it was early in date (Stummann-Hansen 2000) and it appeared remarkably well preserved with defined wall lines. Upper House, Underhoull, with its proximity to both Underhoull broch and

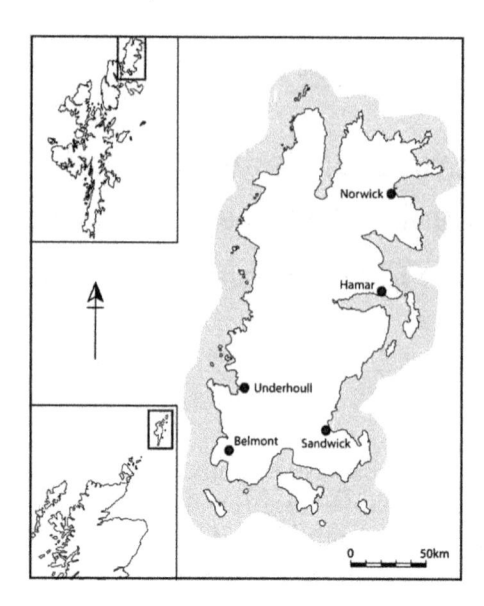

Figure 6.1 Map of Unst, Shetland, showing the main Norse sites mentioned in the text. L. D. Brown, used with permission.

Small's excavations at the Norse site nearby, seemed likely to increase our understanding of the settlement pattern there (Small 1966).

Hamar

The site of Hamar consists of two single longhouses on the south-facing slope below the Keen of Hamar above Baltasound, Unst (Figure 6.1). The structure now called House 1 is aligned down slope on a slight platform, while House 2 is tucked into the hill where the slope changes in steepness, approximately 85m above House 1 and lying across the slope. The outlines of both houses were very clear before excavation and can be seen on the Ordnance Survey First Edition map of 1880, though not on subsequent versions. The modern house of Hamar, after which the site is named, is lower down the slope to the west and closer to the shores of the voe.

Hamar was surveyed and described by Stummann Hansen, who also excavated a test trench across the upper part of the interior (Stummann Hansen 1995, 2000). He described it as a single longhouse almost 24m long, with no associated outhouses. Stummann Hansen's small trench, 0.6m wide, revealed a feature that was interpreted as the setting for a bench running parallel to the outer wall. A floor surface was also identified at a depth of approximately 0.75m below the level of the topsoil. A fragment of steatite was recovered from the floor surface, which 'confirmed the dating of the structure to the Scandinavian period' (Stummann Hansen 2000: 90–1). It is now known that the floor surface belonged to an earlier pit house and the 'bench' was its wall.

House 1, the main focus of excavation, sits on a platform on the hillside backed by a steep slope leading up to the Keen of Hamar. It has a panoramic view of Balta Sound, much of the coastline south and north, and much of the sea behind Balta Isle (which guards the entrance to Balta Sound), making this a very good position from which to monitor sea traffic along the east coast of Shetland and also vessels wishing to enter Balta Sound. The second house further upslope (now published as Hamar House 2; Turner et al. 2013) was known from at least the 19th century but had been assumed to be post-medieval in date. Survey and test excavation showed there was also a Late Norse phase to this house.

Excavation showed extensive rabbit damage around and within the walls, as well as through the deposits within the upper room of the structure. There was very little in the way of later deposits, including collapse from the walls. The clearly visible wall lines suggest the whole site has been disturbed at some point in the past, perhaps scalped for turf to fertilise another area. No midden deposits were found around the house area, which is also suggestive of the removal of turf and topsoil.

Previous investigations could not determine if the long walls were actually curved or if this was an illusion caused by collapse. Excavation showed that the curvature was a deliberate feature. A change in alignment on the lower part of the walls suggests that the building had been rebuilt, possibly shortened, at this point. The walls were composed of inner and outer faces with a core of rubble and earth. The basal interior courses were carefully made of large boulders split to give a straight face. The walls were quite thick (approximately 1m wide), which could suggest that the superstructure had originally been of turf walls on a stone foundation, also suggested by the uniform level of the surviving wall heads and perhaps by the general lack of tumbled rubble, although this could be due to later robbing.

Hamar 1 appeared to be a longhouse with a single division into an upper and lower room, aligned roughly north to south down the slope. There was a small doorway between the two rooms and a doorway in the lower short wall, as well as three openings in the long walls (Figure 6.2).

Excavation revealed that the earliest structure on the site was not in fact this two-roomed longhouse but a sunken-floored building which lay under the cross wall between the rooms. The later longhouse was on the same alignment and excavation showed that the cuts into the bedrock assumed by Stummann Hansen (2000) to be bench features in the longhouse were actually the west and east sides of this structure. It was c. 3m x 4m, with cuts for post-pads at the centre of the north and south edges and evidence of possible post cuts at the corners. The floor was

Figure 6.2 Hamar, House 1; the pit house is visible as the negative feature beneath the walls of the upper room of the later longhouse, built on the same orientation. Photo: J. M. Bond.

covered in a layer of black ash and there were indications of a possible oven or hearth in the south-east part of the building. An annular blue glass bead was found on this floor surface; Colleen Batey has identified a close parallel from York (Batey 2013a). Other finds included a steatite line sinker, fragments of copper alloy and an imported Eidsborg schist whetstone (Batey 2013a).

An archaeomagnetic date was obtained from the hearth suggesting a last use of 1065–1250 AD. Radiocarbon dates from barley grains in the series of black and orange ashy floors produced calibrated dates of 1040–1210 and 1040–1220 cal AD (see Table 6.1 for details).

The pit house was deliberately infilled with a series of ash-rich layers which have produced two further radiocarbon dates from charred barley grains: 1025–1220 cal AD and 1040–1220 cal AD.

The Hamar pit house bears a close resemblance to pit houses found in Norway from the 9th century onwards (Mortensen 1997) and to Icelandic structures (Simpson et al. 1999; Milek 2006) but no comparable sunken-featured building has yet been found elsewhere in Shetland or Orkney.

Although Hamar House 1 was well known and recorded as a single-period settlement, in excavation there was evidence that a series of structures had been built on the site. Possibly the earliest of these

Table 6.1 Radiocarbon and archaeomagnetic dates from the sites of Hamar and Underhoull ('AM' dates are archaeomagnetic dates). University of Bradford Archaeomagnetic Research Laboratory.

Site	Phase	Description	Uncalibrated date (BP)	Calibrated date (95% probability)	Sample/lab number
Hamar	Pit house	Occupation surface/ earliest fill	950 +/-30	1025–1220AD	SUERC-188 61 (GU-16692)
Hamar	Pit house	Floor	900 +/-30	1040–1210AD	SUERC-239 55
Hamar	Pit house	Floor	890 +/-30	1040–1220AD	SUERC-342 78
Hamar	Pit house	Hearth	N/A	1065–1250AD	AM177
Hamar	Pit house infill	Lower midden infill	880 +/-30	1040–1220AD	SUERC-249 42 (GU-19318)
Hamar	Long hearth	Fill	900 +/-30	1040–1210AD	SUERC-177 34
Hamar	Upper room	Central hearth	910 +/-30	1040–1220AD	SUERC 24943
Hamar	Upper room	Secondary hearth on west side	910 +/-30	1035–1220AD	SUERC-249 44
Hamar	Upper room	Secondary hearth on west side	N/A	1100–1330AD	AM154
Hamar	Lower room	Abandonment layer	945 +/-30	1020–1160AD	GU-16693
Hamar House 2	Long room interior	Ashy midden infill	365 +/-30	1485–1650AD	SUERC-188 63
Hamar House 2	Long room interior	Ashy midden infill	365 +/-30	1450–1635AD	SUERC-188 64
Underhoull	Central room	Hearth deposit	765 +/-30	1220–1280AD	SUERC-249 45
Underhoull	Upper room	Floor deposits	849 +/-37	1045–1265AD	SUERC-341 12
Underhoull	West annexe	Black layer in west annexe	856+/-37	1045–1265AD	SUERC-341 11
Underhoull	East annexe	Hearth in east annexe	N/A	1155–1365 AD (combined date)	AM149 and AM150
Underhoull	East annexe	Hearth in east annexe	866+/- 35	1045–1260AD	SUERC-341 08

(contemporary with or later than the pit house) was represented by a feature originally thought to be a byre drain for the lower room, as it appeared to be cut into the bedrock and to run out through the opening in the lower wall. When excavated this feature proved to be wider than the lower doorway and sealed by the end wall of the surviving house. The feature was filled with rubble and ashy deposits including a fragment of pumice and a schist whetstone and fragments of worked steatite. At the base of the feature a concentration of ash and charcoal sealed heat-cracked flags and it seemed that the feature was a long hearth, the depression formed by repeated cracking of the serpentine bedrock by the heat. Fragments of schist and steatite bake plates and vessels were recovered from this feature. A calibrated radiocarbon date of 1040–1210 cal AD was obtained from charred barley grains.

It is unclear whether the long hearth belonged to an earlier phase of House 1 which had extended further south almost to the edge of the rock platform before being shortened, or to an entirely different house on the same alignment. The only other possible feature related to an earlier house was a posthole sealed by the inner face of the west wall. There was a fragment of steatite bake plate at the bottom of the posthole and as it was not cracked by the weight of a post, it is possible it was inserted before the hole was infilled in some kind of closure event.

The fill of the long hearth was paved over with flags before the current end wall was built over them. It is possible that the two current side walls and the long hearth were remnants of an earlier building and that the side walls were shortened and the new end wall added over the original hearth (the build and alignment of the lower part of both side walls is slightly different). A new small hearth was constructed further to the north in this shorter building and later an annexe with a wall hearth was added to the west side of the house. A wall stub suggests an annexe may also have been added to the east side wall; unfortunately, the two openings in the west and east walls have been widened and partially demolished, making interpretation difficult. Later the cross wall with a central doorway was constructed over the filled-in area of the pit house, giving the new longhouse two rooms. This house had a rounded north wall and a rock-cut drainage ditch or gulley surrounded the upper end of the building and continued part way down both side walls, presumably to conduct hillwash away from the house. The gulley had become completely filled with colluvium which had also built up against the back wall of the house, showing the extent of soil movement down the hillside in the last millennium.

Rabbit damage in the upper room meant that only patches of occupation surface remained but there was enough to recognise a central hearth, a small secondary hearth by the west wall and several phases of ashy floor surface, the earliest lying directly over bedrock. The finds from this floor surface included fragments of a pot with a gritty texture, a schist hone stone and fragments of steatite bake plate. A calibrated radiocarbon date of 1040–1220 cal AD was obtained from the central hearth and one of 1035–1210 cal AD from the secondary hearth as well as an archaeomagnetic date of 1100–1330 AD.

The lower room of this phase of the house contained a uniform brown silty deposit containing very little cultural material sealing bedrock. It also sealed the infilled long hearth, a small hearth in the northern part of the room and three rock-cut post settings; one by the west wall and two parallel to the east wall. It seems likely that occupation layers had been removed down to bedrock and the lower room converted to a byre, with the disused long hearth acting as a soakaway. Thin section micromorphology samples supported this suggestion and showed fragments of peat and features related to animal dung and similarities with known byre floors. The upper levels of the long hearth contained evidence of peat, turf, charcoal and degraded fish bone, possibly indicating what the floor deposits may have been like before removal (Hamlet and Simpson 2013). A radiocarbon date was obtained from charred barley grains from the fill of the lower room of 1020–1160 cal AD.

The house suffered a further fall from status with an even smaller room being constructed within the upper room, with evidence of an informal hearth which scorched the stones of the west wall. It is probable that the two large diagonally opposed openings in the west and east walls were formed at this time, perhaps because of a change in function to a byre. The structure to the north (Hamar House 2) may have taken over as the main dwelling and House 1 demoted to a farm building. A similar alteration of a longhouse to a small upper room, a small opening in the short end wall and larger diagonal doorways, can be seen in House 29 at Pool, Orkney (Hunter et al. 2007). That house too has similar dates.

House 2, lying across the slope and further up the hill, was thought to be post-medieval but underlying that building were features which suggested an earlier structure of similar proportions to House 1. It appeared to have an earth bank surrounding a small yard and there is a spring or well downslope. It was only possible to excavate a small assessment trench across this structure, in order to understand House 1 in its landscape context. This confirmed there was a building with an interior only 3m across (compared to Hamar 1's 5m-wide interior) filled with ashy midden with heavy carbon flecking. Artefacts recovered included worked pumice, steatite vessel fragments (including ones from square-sided vessels) and fragments of schist whetstones. The assemblage suggests a late Norse date for the abandonment phase (Batey 2013a). These deposits also contained large amounts of charred barley and oats, giving dates of 1450–1635 cal AD and 1485–1650 cal AD. The surprising thing about this apparent end-date for the second longhouse at Hamar is that cereals of such quality were being grown and processed in the most northerly island of the British Isles in what was a time of climate deterioration.

Underhoull

The site of Underhoull was excavated by Alan Small in the 1960s (Small 1966), but the site of Upper House, Underhoull, close to Underhoull broch and situated 230m north-east of Small's site up a very steep gradient, had not previously been explored though it was recorded in 1969 by the Ordnance Survey (CANMORE ID: 32).

The house site was visible before excavation as low earthworks, with its two long walls aligned roughly west to east across the slope of the hill. On excavation the house had three zones, an upper, central and lower room, with two annexes flanking a flagged entrance passage leading into the longhouse midway along the south wall, facing the sea and a lower doorway on the same side, much as with Hamar 1 (Figure 6.3). At the back of the house on the hillward side, a stone-filled gulley or soakaway ran parallel to the long wall. The gulley would have collected runoff from the hill above, as with the Hamar gulley.

The longhouse had a curious composite construction. The long wall facing the sea was stone built at its base, as were the annexes, while the wall on the hill side appeared to be constructed of turf. It is likely that the main part of all the walls was turf built but the stone base to the front wall and annexes would have provided an impressive frontage for

Figure 6.3 Upper House, Underhoull. The curved wall of the small upper room is at the bottom of the photograph, the turf back wall with drainage gulley to the left and the annexes and path to the right. The stone ledge and sunken surface for the wooden floor of the middle room are visible above the nearest baulk. Photo: S. J. Dockrill.

any visitor climbing the hill from the bay below, while the turf-built rear wall of the building would not have been visible. The gable end of the upper room was rounded and built of coursed stone with orthostats.

The construction of the lower gable end of the building was less clear, with banks of rubble and a gravel and soil matrix, suggesting perhaps a turf and timber construction with a central doorway.

The two annexes flanked a flagged entrance passage that led into the middle room of the longhouse. The evidence suggested that this middle room had a sprung timber floor and was possibly also lined with timber. There was an internal ledge against the long-walls and on both sides this ledge was sealed by a line of small set flags which butted against the interior of both the long-walls and were carefully set to line the ledge. These ledges and stones were interpreted as level supports for wooden beams, from which a dry wooden floor could be created over a void. The beams may also have supported an inner planked wall to this central living zone. A similar form of construction was observed in a 10th- to 11th- century building excavated by the authors at Undir Junkarinsfløtti, Sandoy, Faroe Islands (unpublished), and later examples are known from other areas of Scandinavia, such as traditional turf buildings in Iceland (Bond and Dockrill 2013: fig. 8.38). Timber for such a house would have to be imported to Shetland (and to the Faroes) as there is no local source, the nearest being Norway or northern Scotland.

In the central part of the building the internal deposits sloped quite steeply down from the flagged sides into the middle of the structure. The deposits in this hollow contained numerous steatite fragments and sealed patches of fine charcoal and red ash. These patches were in the place a long hearth may have been expected but there was no evidence of heating on the bedrock below, suggesting this may have been material that had filtered down from a suspended floor. Magnetic susceptibility values across the central room supported this theory. A radiocarbon date from this material was initially calibrated as 1220–1280 cal AD. Finds from this central room included a steatite line sinker, loom weights and a spindle whorl.

The upper end room was accessed via the central room and it was here that the best-preserved deposits were found and by far the greatest number of artefacts. The floor was formed partly by the exposed bedrock and partly of flags to give a level surface sealed by occupation deposits containing steatite and pottery. Some artefacts were almost complete, including an unfinished oval steatite vessel (Batey 2013b). A radiocarbon date of 1045–1265 cal AD was obtained.

The lower room contained a layer of dark grey deposit with very few finds. There was another doorway into this lower part of the house, again from the seaward side, as well as an entrance through the lower gable end.

The two annexes were both stone built with a hearth and paving. The west annexe had a flagged floor sealed by a black silty deposit. An archaeomagnetic date of 840–1140 AD was obtained from the hearth and a radiocarbon date of 1045–1265 cal AD from the black layer. The east annexe was a U-shaped structure with walls over 1m wide and a flagged floor and hearth which contained the charred remains of complete heads of barley. Samples from the hearth gave a combined archaeomagnetic date of 1155–1365 AD. Grain from this hearth also yielded a radiocarbon date of 1045–1260 cal AD.

After going out of use, the east annexe became covered over by an extensive spread of small rubble which contained steatite vessel fragments, a broken loom weight and a small steatite figurine. Carved from a soft fine-grained soapstone, this object is roughly 90mm long with a shape which suggests it had been carved from a line sinker (Figure 6.4). The top of the head is broken but appears to have had some kind of hat or helmet, possibly conical. The face has been carved by using two vertical cuts to produce a nose, giving the appearance of deeply grooved cheeks with eyes and mouth formed by conical hollows. Two similar conical hollows on either side of the head may represent ears or be for

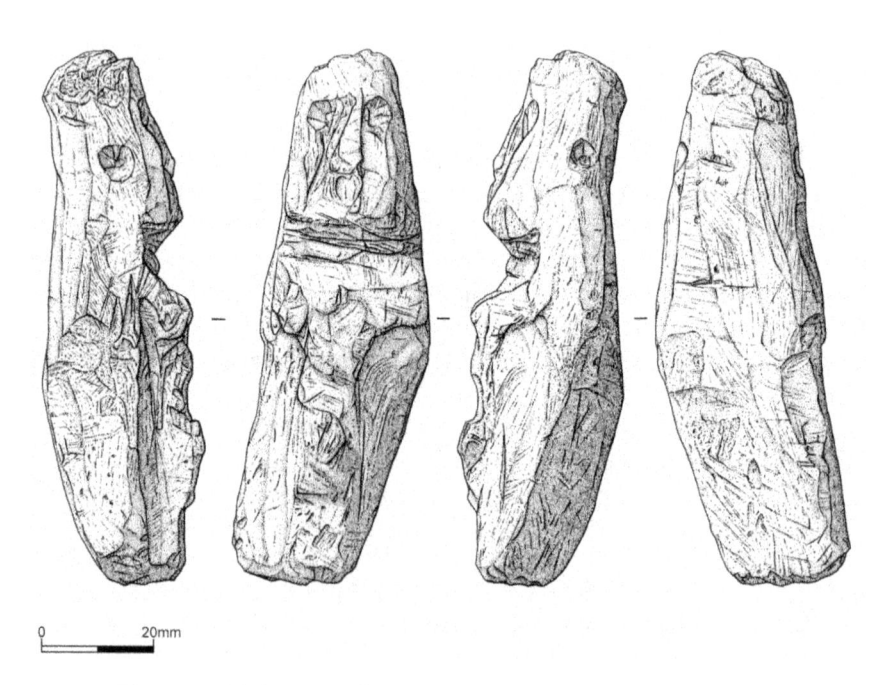

Figure 6.4 The carved steatite (soapstone) figurine from Upper House, Underhoull. Turner et al. 2013. © J. M. Bond/Shetland Amenity Trust.

suspension. A T-shape carved in relief on the front of the figure gives the appearance of short arms clasped in front.

It is difficult to interpret this figure but there are similarities with the figures proposed as 'pocket deities' (Perkins 2001; Graham-Campbell 2021: 156). Perkins has suggested, for example, that the seated figure found on the Eyrarland Icelandic farm site represents Thor. This figure has a conical hat or helmet and hands in front of his chest, clutching his beard. Most such figures are seated but some are standing. The Underhoull figure, with its clasped arms, round 'blowing' mouth and likely conical headdress, has many similarities. Furthermore, being carved from a line sinker suggests associations with fishing, the sea and the wind, all aspects associated with Thor.

Graham-Campbell suggests the Eyrarland figure is no earlier than c. 1000 and may be from the first half of the 11th century. The date for the last use of the east annexe where the Underhoull figurine was found is suggested by Swindles et al. (2019) to be the 12th or 13th century, but the context suggests the figure may have been in the rafters or roof which later collapsed, so it may have been deposited earlier than this date.

The date of the Underhoull occupation and abandonment has recently been recalibrated using Bayesian analysis (Swindles et al. 2019). This study suggests the Underhoull longhouse was constructed between *805–1050 cal* AD and most probably between *880–1000 cal* AD (68 per cent probability). The new analysis suggests the house was in use for probably *295–485* years. Activity at the site probably ended between *1260–1380 cal* AD (68 per cent probability).

The Underhoull and Hamar excavations show that these were not single-phase sites but settlements with long and complex histories of development and decline. Finds from both sites, such as the vessel glass fragments of 6th- to 10th-century type, show unexpected sophistication (Campbell 2013), while the Hamar pit house is so far unique in Scottish archaeology while showing many similarities in construction, use and date with similar features in Iceland. The end-dates for both sites suggest the kind of settlement contraction seen across the North Atlantic as the climate deteriorated, while the charred grain from Hamar House 2 hints at a more varied and complex response to climate change.

References

Batey, C. E. (2013a) Selected finds from Hamar, Unst. In V. E. Turner, J. M. Bond and A.-C. Larsen, *Viking Unst: Excavation and Survey in Northern Shetland 2006–2010*. Lerwick: Shetland Heritage Publications, 140–4.

Batey, C. E. (2013b) Selected finds from Underhoull, Upper House, Unst. In V. E. Turner, J. M. Bond and A.-C. Larsen, *Viking Unst: Excavation and Survey in Northern Shetland 2006–2010*. Lerwick: Shetland Heritage Publications, 166–8.

Bond, J. M. and S. J. Dockrill (2013) Excavations at Upper House, Underhoull. In V. E. Turner, J. M. Bond and A.-C. Larsen, *Viking Unst: Excavation and Survey in Northern Shetland 2006–2010*. Lerwick: Shetland Heritage Publications, 156–65.

Campbell, E. (2013) Glass vessel fragments from Hamar House 2. In V. E. Turner, J. M. Bond and A.-C. Larsen, *Viking Unst: Excavation and Survey in Northern Shetland 2006–2010*. Lerwick: Shetland Heritage Publications, 145.

Dockrill, S. .J, J. M. Bond, V. E. Turner, L. D. Brown, D. J. Bashford, J. Cussans and R. A. Nicholson (2010) *Excavations at Old Scatness, Shetland Volume 1: The Pictish Village and Viking Settlement*. Lerwick: Shetland Heritage Publications.

Dyer, C., J. Outram and V. E. Turner (2013) Gazetteer of longhouses in Unst. In V. E. Turner, J. M. Bond and A.-C. Larsen, *Viking Unst: Excavation and Survey in Northern Shetland 2006–2010*. Lerwick: Shetland Heritage Publications, 109–21.

Graham-Campbell, J. (2021) *Viking Art*. London: Thames and Hudson Ltd.

Hamilton, J. R. C. (1956) *Excavations at Jarlshof, Shetland*. London: HMSO.

Hamlet, L. E. and I. A. Simpson (2013) Thin section micromorphology at Hamar houses 1 and 2. In V. E. Turner, J. M. Bond and A.-C. Larsen, *Viking Unst: Excavation and Survey in Northern Shetland 2006–2010*. Lerwick: Shetland Heritage Publications, 148–53.

Hunter, J. R., J. M. Bond and A. N. Smith (2007) *Investigations in Sanday, Orkney. Vol 1. Excavations at Pool, Sanday, a Multi-period Settlement from Neolithic to Late Norse Times*. Kirkwall: The Orcadian/Historic Scotland.

Milek, K. (2006) *Houses and Households in Early Icelandic Society: Geoarchaeology and the Interpretation of Social Space*. Unpublished PhD thesis, University of Cambridge.

Mortensen, M. (1997) For women only? Reflections on a Viking Age settlement at Stedje, Sogndal in Western Norway. *Studien zur Sachsenforschung* 10, 196–206.

Perkins, R. (2001) *Thor the Wind-raiser and the Eyrarland Image*. London: Viking Society for Northern Research Vol. XV, University College London.

Simpson, I. A., K. B. Milek and G. Guðmundsson (1999) A reinterpretation of the Great Pit at Hofstaðir, Iceland using sediment thin section micromorphology. *Geoarchaeology* 14(6), 511–30.

Small, A. (1966) Excavations at Underhoull, Unst, Shetland. *Proceedings of the Society of Antiquaries of Scotland* 98, 225–48.

Stummann Hansen, S. (1995) *Scandinavian Settlement in Shetland in the Viking and Late Norse Period. Final Report on Surveys and Trial Excavations Carried Out in Unst*. Copenhagen: Report for Shetland Amenity Trust, May 1995.

Stummann Hansen, S. (2000) Viking settlement in Shetland. *Acta Archaeologica* 71, 87–103.

Swindles, G. T., Z. Outram, C. M. Batt, W. D. Hamilton, M. J. Church, J. M. Bond, E. J. Watson, G. T. Cook, T. J. Sim, A. J. Newton and A. J. Dugmore (2019) Vikings, peat formation and settlement abandonment: A multi-method chronological approach from Shetland. *Quaternary Science Reviews* 210, 211–25.

Turner, V. E., J. M. Bond and A.-C. Larsen (2013) *Viking Unst: Excavation and Survey in Northern Shetland 2006–2010*. Lerwick: Shetland Heritage Publications.

Viking Unst Project. Excavations at Hamar and the Upper House, Underhoull: Field season 2007. Interim Report No. 2 (Data Structure Report). (https://www.nabohome.org/publications/fieldreports/Hamar_Underhoull_ShetlandDSRNo22007.pdf) [Last viewed: 1 June 2021].

The interim reports for Hamar and Underhoull can be found online at: Viking Unst Project. Excavations at Hamar: field season 2006. Interim Report No. 1 (Data Structure Report) (https://www.nabohome.org/publications/fieldreports/Hamar_ShetlandDSRNo12006.pdf) [Last viewed: 1 June 2021].

Chapter 7

Investigating the Origins of Steatite Vessels across the Viking Diaspora
Amanda K. Forster and Richard E. Jones

Soapstone, or steatite, is one of the more iconic identifiers of Viking material culture within the North Atlantic region. The stone was used to manufacture many essential and everyday items which accompanied the Norwegian migrants of the *landnám*. It is no coincidence that a distribution map of recorded soapstone finds shadows closely the areas settled by Norse pioneers across the North Atlantic region (see Figure 7.1, below). The Viking diaspora has been described by Jesch as having origins in the migrations which characterise the period but transcending them in time '. . . through linguistic and cultural contacts assiduously maintained throughout the Viking world for centuries after the migration' (2015: 81). Artefacts carved from soapstone remain an ongoing characteristic of the region throughout the period of settlement and the centuries that followed. As a stone with limited provenance and excellent odds for archaeological survival, soapstone artefacts provide a useful tool for the study of migration, settlement and contact across the diaspora.

Following initial migrations and settlement, locally available outcrops of this useful stone, known as *kleber* in Norse tongue, became known and were in use in Shetland by at least the 9th century. This was not the first time Shetland's soapstone resource was utilised for the manufacture of vessels and other objects; examples of use are recorded from the Neolithic and into the later Iron Age (see Forster and Turner 2009). At the time of Viking settlement, the use of soapstone by the local population was limited to smaller portable objects, such as lamps, beads and whorls (Forster 2009: 48), and lacked the larger vessels which the Norwegian incomers brought with them. Viking pioneers would have encountered evidence of quarrying at soapstone outcrops, perhaps including spoil heaps and manufacturing debris created over centuries of use. The use of those same outcrops throughout Viking and Norse periods in Shetland has most likely obliterated any evidence of earlier activity. Place-name evidence linked to the word *kleber* and variant terms attests to a comprehensive knowledge of the location of outcrops across the archipelago (see Brooke-Freeman 2009: 18).

The earliest dated examples of Viking period and Shetland-manufactured vessels were recorded at Norwick, Shetland, dated to 690–750 (Ballin Smith 2013: 229), although the early date was viewed as controversial by some (Turner 2013: 234). Examples from Old Scatness, Shetland, do not date to earlier than 890–935 (Dockrill et al. 2010: 368) and the earliest examples so far recorded in Orkney date to the mid-10th century (from Pool, Sanday: Smith and Forster 2007: 412). The Norse settlement of Greenland in the late 10th century provides a similar model of discovery and use of local soapstone attested in the archaeological record (Arneborg 1984). Soon after the pioneering settlements were established and steatite sources utilised, regional variations in artefacts develop, providing new chronologically and spatially sensitive typologies (Forster 2004a). At the same time, vessels which carried all the attributes of Norwegian-manufactured products are still visible in the archaeological record throughout the Viking diaspora, well beyond the initial period of settlement and across the full extent of the settled region.

In this context, the ability to identify different source regions or quarry sites of steatite artefacts recovered from the diaspora offers the potential to address key questions during the settlement period and beyond (Forster and Jones 2017). For example, material dating from the years of the *landnám* could help pinpoint the home region of migrating groups and, for those dating to the years following settlement, provenanced finds could help articulate the nature of ongoing contact and interconnectedness between the homeland and the diaspora. The unique qualities of both individual finds and recovered assemblages have the potential to help us look beyond the attributes of the artefacts themselves to understand more about everyday life and domestic culture, while considering wider questions of migration, adaptation and contact.

Over the past twenty years, two independent paths of study, one concerning the morphology/typology of soapstone artefacts (Forster 2004a), the other applying analytical techniques to determine provenance (see Clelland et al. 2009), have combined into a single project, *Homeland to Home* (Forster and Jones 2017). Based particularly on displaced artefacts found across the Viking diaspora, the main attributes of seven typological classes have been identified, allowing hypotheses to be proposed about the likely source and chronological currency of each class (Forster 2004a). Some of these hypotheses have been tested by ICP-MS analysis (for rare earth elements) and to a lesser extent by portable XRF for semiquantitative analysis of major, minor and trace elements. Our results for several quarries on Shetland and in south-east Norway, as well as artefacts from Shetland (Sandwick, Unst), York, Orkney (Quoygrew, Westray), Kaupang and the Faroes (see Forster and Jones 2017), have demonstrated the potential for this analytical approach to address the big questions posed above.

But for several reasons, including the still limited size of our quarry chemical database collated by various studies to date (including those in both Norway and Shetland), positive assignments of origin to individual artefacts remain difficult to propose based on chemical composition alone. However, through associating groups of artefacts which display similar compositional characteristics with their typological membership and wider archaeological narrative, some progress is possible. This summary paper sets out where the research is in 2021, publishing new results from Orkney (Tuquoy), Iceland (Hrísheimar í Mývatnssveit, Sveigakot í Mývatnssveit, Aðalstræti í Reykjavík) and Greenland (Igaliku), and outlining our ambition to widen the search further.

Morphology, maps and meaning

During the 9th and 10th centuries, the North Atlantic region was transformed into an inland sea within a predominantly Norwegian sphere of interest (Larsen and Stummann-Hansen 2001: 115). Where a common Norse ancestry provided a persistent cultural bond within the Viking diaspora (Jesch 2015: 55), the experience of everyday life diverged as pioneering family groups adapted to available resources within their new landscapes. Barrett (2012: 6) describes the island settlements of the North Atlantic as insular societies, 'physically removed from centres of consumption yet potentially interconnected by the sea'. Comparisons of artefact assemblages recovered from contemporary settlement sites within these North Atlantic island groups suggest the emergence of differences in material culture throughout the Viking and later periods, for example, between Greenland and Iceland (Kendall 2014: 111) and between the Northern and Western Isles of Scotland (Sharples 2021: 448f).

Detailed analysis of steatite artefacts provides an excellent case study illustrating this variability. Evidence from steatite vessels supports the proposal of a staged model of production, distribution and use spanning 750–1500 (Forster 2004a). Across the North Atlantic region, steatite outcrops can be found in Norway, Shetland and Greenland (Figure 7.1). Artefacts are frequently recorded beyond those areas, with a distribution during the Viking period which correlates closely with areas of Norse settlement (see Forster 2005: 55). Limited availability combined with wide distribution implies movement of raw material and/or finished goods, often taken to indicate long-distance trade networks operating across the North Atlantic (for example, Crawford 1987: 152). However, a close study of soapstone vessel types concluded that the distribution of *displaced* artefacts (for example, those transported, Needham 1993: 162) suggested a complex story of migration, adaptation, resource control and contact throughout the Viking and later Norse periods (see Forster 2005; 2009).

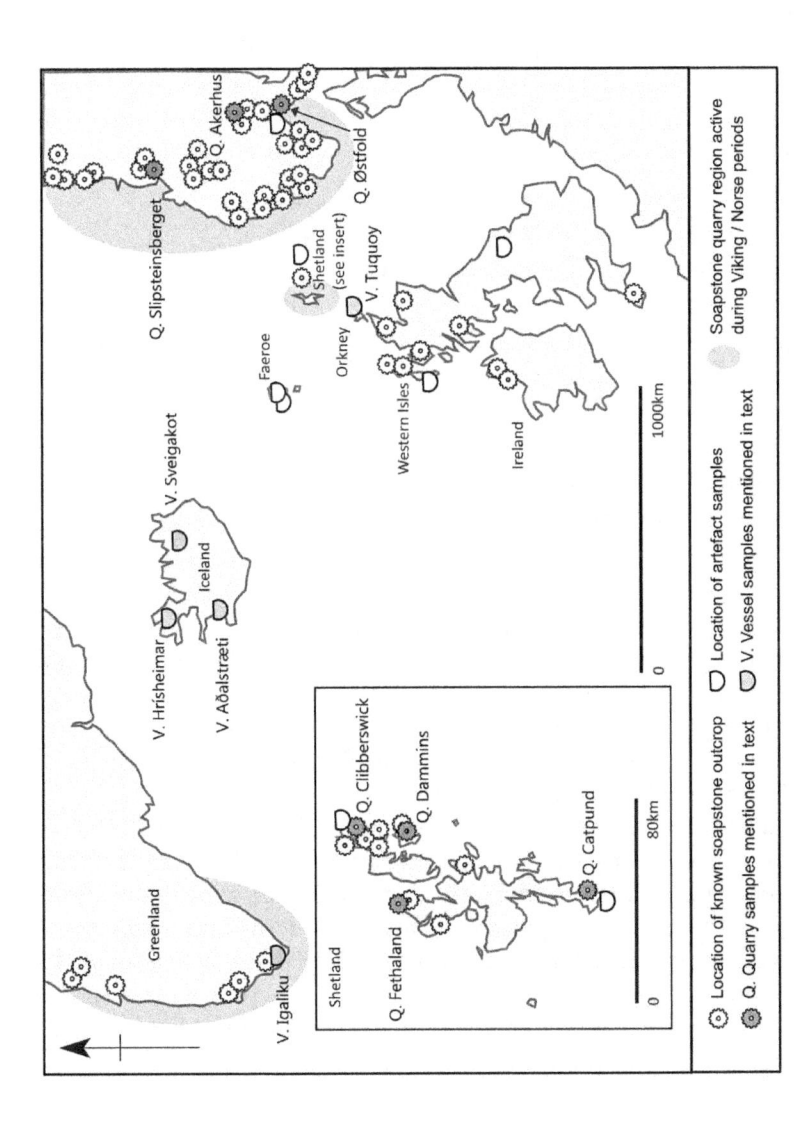

Figure 7.1 Location of steatite quarries and archaeological sites, with samples included in this paper named. © A. K. Forster and R. E. Jones.

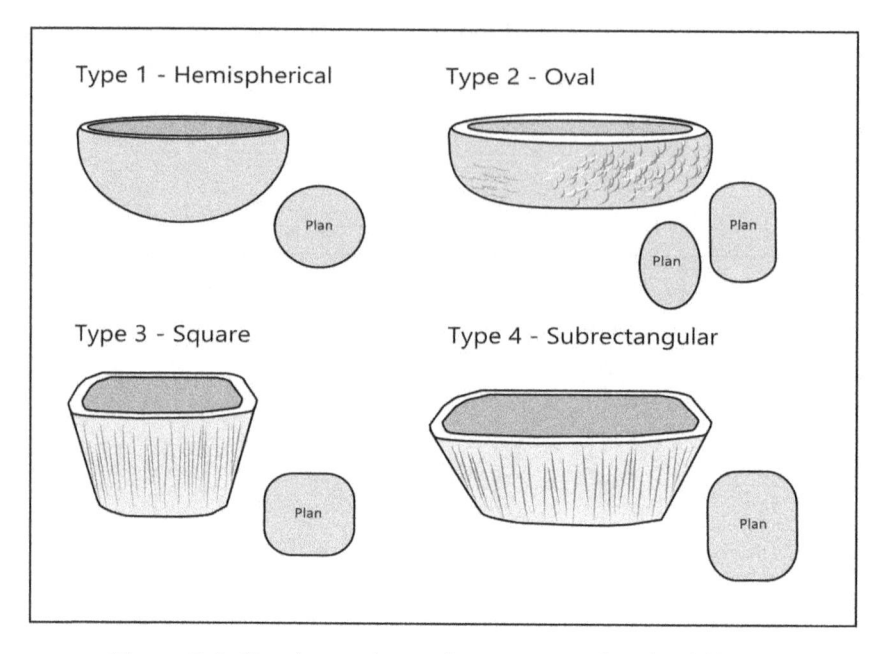

Figure 7.2 Simple typology of steatite vessels. The full typological series is published in Forster and Jones 2017. © A. K. Forster.

By amalgamating regional type series developed through morphological study, Forster developed a series of reference sheets for the assessment of displaced soapstone artefacts (Forster 2004b: figs 5.1 and 5.2; Forster and Jones 2017: figs 2–4). The typological series comprises seven key forms of soapstone vessel showing either or both temporal and regional characteristics (see Forster and Jones 2017 for discussion). Using the main reference types summarised here in Figure 7.2, soapstone assemblages recovered from sites across the region were able to be assessed, characterised and compared as a group. This analysis facilitated interpretation of soapstone vessel assemblages which considered the mechanisms behind displacement activities across the region as a whole (see Figure 7.3; also Forster 2004a; 2005; Forster and Jones 2017 for discussion). In postulating how soapstone vessels may have been distributed, a hypothesis was then established which could be tested with targeted science-based analysis.

Science-based analysis of North Atlantic soapstone vessels

Analysis of quarry samples from Shetland (Catpund, Fethaland, both Mainland; Dammins, Fetlar; and Clibberswick, Unst) and Norway (Slipsteinsberget, Nord-Trøndelag; Pigåssen and Folvelseter, Akerhus;

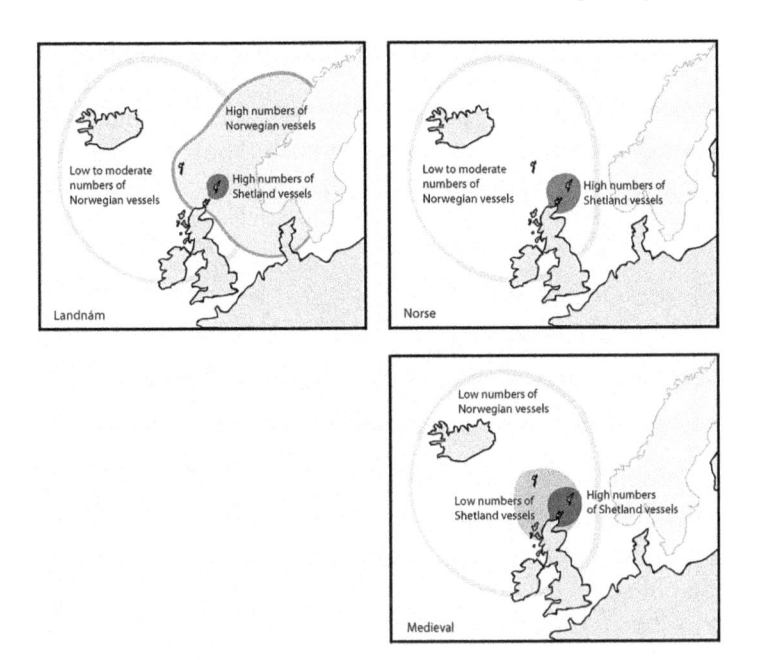

Figure 7.3 Changing trends in the use of Norwegian and Shetland vessels in the North Atlantic. Model based on Forster 2004, first published in Forster 2005. © A. K. Forster.

Solerudberget and Fluetjern, Østfold) have been made through determination of the soapstone's rare earth element (REE) composition by ICP-MS, coupled in a more limited, exploratory manner of the major (Fe, Mg), minor (K, Ti, Ca) and trace (Cr, Mn, Sc, V) element contents with portable XRF (pXRF) (see Forster and Jones 2017: 234–6). While limited in scope, the analysis of quarry sites has demonstrated that positive assignments of origin to an individual site in either Norway or Shetland would prove difficult to make, although it should be possible to exclude sources. Working with associations rather than assignments of origin provides a sensible way forward, and artefacts having similar compositions may be regarded as having a similar origin even where that origin is unknown.

From an archaeological perspective, being able, at least in principle, to positively associate artefacts and to exclude quarry locations for groups of finds from different sites and periods is a significant step forward. In practice, however, the recognition of overlap of REE compositions representing certain soapstone sources in Shetland and Norway is constraining that ability. In this paper we begin to address this issue in the course of making a preliminary presentation of the contrasting results obtained from Tuquoy (Orkney) and various sites in Iceland, and from Greenland.

The project's previous work (Forster and Jones 2017) considered vessel fragments recovered from York, Orkney (Quoygrew) and the Faroe Islands (Inni á Tvørgarði, Uppistovubeitið and Toftanes), and, since 2017, vessel fragments from excavations in Orkney (Pool, Snusgar as well as Tuquoy), Shetland (Norwick and Milla Skerra, Sandwick), Iceland, Greenland and the Western Isles (Bornais, South Uist) have been analysed.

Tuquoy, Orkney

Situated on the south-west shore of Westray, the archaeological site of Tuquoy was discovered in 1981 when signs of structures were noticed eroding from the shore near to the 12th-century church of Crosskirk (Owen 2005: 197). Subsequent excavations recorded a multi-phased complex dating from the 10th to 14th centuries and including a rectilinear hall and a deep waterlogged pit (Owen 2005: 206). Recent analysis and re-evaluation of the project archive has afforded this project team the opportunity to include a number of steatite vessel samples from Tuquoy in the *Homeland to Home* study (Table 7.1). Examination of the REE patterns formed from all fifteen rare earth elements in twenty typologically identified examples indicated the presence of at least two groups. This preliminary approach requires elaboration from an alternative graphical visualisation using particular element ratios; one such example appears in Figure 7.4a, in which the results are colour coded with the proposed vessel types (see Table 7.1):

Group A – 3, 4, 7, 9, 12, 15, 16, 18, 19 and 20
Group B – 1, 2, 5, 6, 8, 11, 14 and 17
Group C – 10 and 13

Of these, Group B is dominated by Type 2 vessels, and Group A encompasses examples of Types 1–4. While the presence of **4, 7, 18** and **19** in Group A, all of Type 4, seems to match the expectation of a Shetland source (and perhaps the same could be said of **16** and **20** which are Type 3), the potential Norwegian imports (Type 1) – **3, 9, 14, 15** and **17** – are scattered across Groups A and B. Drawing on the data for three quarries on Shetland in Figure 7.4b – Catpund, Clibberswick and Cleberswick (Fethaland) – it is evident that first they can be differentiated, especially in the case of Cleberswick which has high Dy/Yb and very low La/Yb values, in keeping with its significantly different REE pattern (Forster and Jones 2017: fig. 7a); second, Group A overlaps with Catpund, and Group B partly with Clibberswick. Furthermore, but not shown on Figure 7.4b, some of the Viking artefacts from Milla Skerra, Sandwick on Unst (Forster and Jones, in Ballin Smith et al. 2019: 91–4) share similarity in composition with Group C (but not with **10** and **13**).

Table 7.1 Tuquoy samples.

Tuquoy sample	SF	Vessel type	Possible region (morphology)	Provenance group
1	719	2	Shetland / Norway	B
2	1262	2	Shetland / Norway	B
3	n/a	1	Norway	A
4	986	4	Shetland	A
5	851	2	Norway	B
6	n/a	2	Shetland / Norway	B
7	1047	4	Shetland	A
8	1273	2	Shetland / Norway	B
9	1209	1	Norway	A
10	839	2	Shetland / Norway	C
11	730	2	Shetland / Norway	B
12	7021.2	2	Shetland / Norway	A
13	1263	1	Norway	C
14	988	1	Norway	B
15	801	1	Norway	A
16	5	3	Shetland	A
17	1034	1	Norway	B
18	1050	4	Shetland	A
19	840	4	Shetland	A
20	921	3	Shetland	A

For all three groups, therefore, there is a measure of ambiguity between the sources based on vessel morphology and chemistry; more precisely, some Norwegian sources have similar or overlapping REE patterns with those on Shetland. Group C members, **10** and **13**, which are probably not from the same source in Norway, are unlikely to be from the Kaupang area (Forster and Jones 2017: 237, fig. 8).

Introducing the results for the eight samples from Iceland (Table 7.2) into Figure 7.4a, **59, 59B** and **200** (all Type 1) seem to associate with Tuquoy **10** and **13** in Group C. These pieces share the feature of consistently higher Cr and lower Mn contents than the members of Groups A and B, as determined by pXRF. **134** (Type 1 or 2) falls between Groups B and C. The three samples assigned to Group B, **42, 56** and **735**, lie outside the Shetland ranges, while the presence of Type 1 examples **48** and **199** in Group A again raises the prospect of overlap of one or more Norwegian sources with Catpund.

106   *Amanda K. Forster and Richard E. Jones*

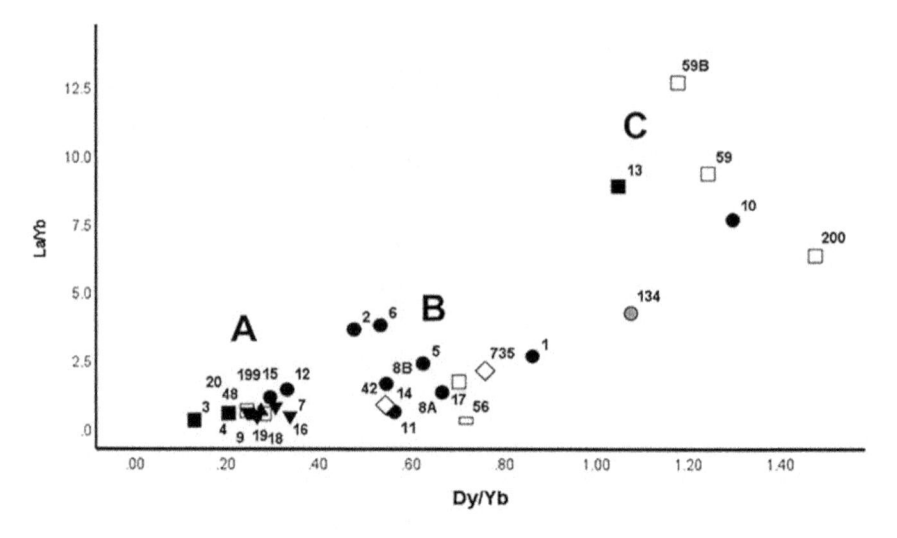

Figure 7.4a La/Yb vs Dy/Yb plot of the samples from Tuquoy and Iceland (black and white symbols respectively). Vessel types (Tables 1 and 2): 1 square, 2 circle, 3 triangle, 4 inverted triangle, 6 rectangle, 1 or 2 grey, and unknown or n/a diamond.

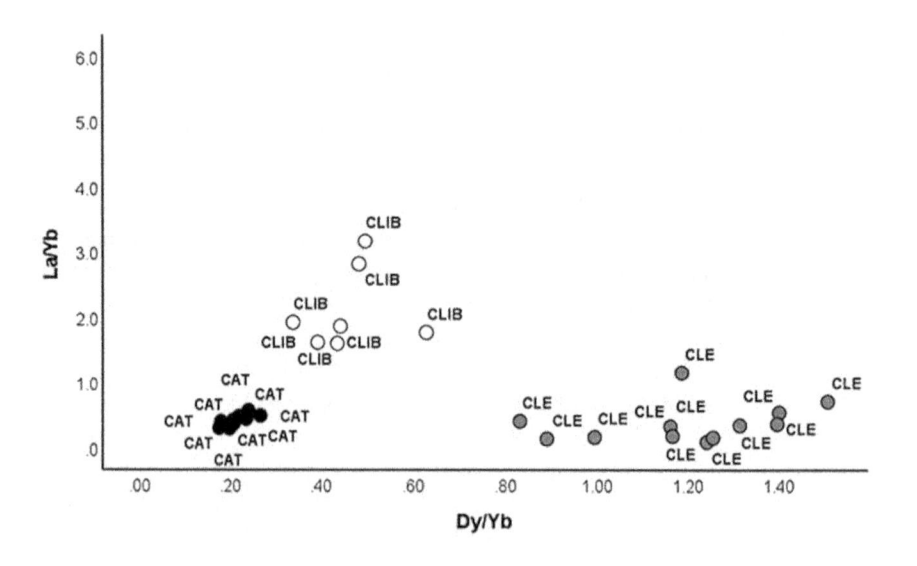

Figure 7.4b La/Yb vs Dy/Yb plot of the quarry samples on Shetland: Catpund (CAT, black), Clibberswick (CLIB white) and Cleberswick (Fethaland) (CLE grey).

Table 7.2 Iceland samples.

Site	SF	Vessel type	Possible region (morphology)	Provenance group
Hrísheimar	04–59	Type 1	Norway	C
Hrísheimar	04–199	Type 1	Norway	A
Hrísheimar	05–200	Type 1	Norway	C
Hrísheimar	06–042	n/a	-	B
Hrísheimar	03–134	Type 1 or 2	Norway	B or C
Sveigakot	03–048	Type 1	Norway	A
Sveigakot	01–56	Type 6	Norway	B
Aðalstræti	01–735	Unknown	-	B

From the 12th-century Norse settlement at Igaliku (Vésteinsson 2014) at the southern tip of Greenland are four artefacts (**987, 998, 1051** and **1057**) which are taken *a priori* to be of 'local' soapstone. Encouragingly, their REE patterns differ from those obtained by the same method (at the Geological Survey of Denmark and Greenland) of geological soapstone from the Nuuk area, Kangerlussuaq and Upernavik along the west coast of Greenland (M. Poulsen and N. Keulen, pers. comm.).

Discussion

Science-based analysis has tested the use of traditional criteria to identify the origin of soapstone vessels. The outcome of the analysis undertaken to date has been reasonably positive: similarity of REE signature may be used to associate artefacts, whether or not from the same findspots, to a common origin, but defining that origin tends to be in the form of a negative rather than a positive statement. The validity of both techniques is confirmed to some extent although, importantly, it is the combination of both the science-based and traditional approaches which offers the most potential to answer key challenges about the Viking and later Norse periods.

In the data presented above, we can see the complications of overlapping data, specifically in the REE compositions representing certain soapstone sources in Shetland and Norway. This is not unexpected and demonstrates the difficulty in providing a clear picture from scientific analysis alone. Despite the complex and seemingly confusing data, there remain interesting implications. For Tuquoy, the Type 4 vessel distribution seen in Figure 7.4a complies well with the Catpund quarry group. This not only offers a potentially positive association but, at the very least, suggests that the source of this vessel type is tightly grouped and perhaps an individual quarry. The group of Norwegian vessels (based on morphology alone) shows a far more scattered pattern, difficult to associate with a source region and not displaying the same tight grouping as seen with the Type 4 vessels. This suggests these vessels are not from the same quarry site and, although we cannot conclude how the objects were distributed, it is interesting to note the variation. The Icelandic samples offer a simpler story; for the majority at least, the finds are clearly not from Shetland. By implication, this suggests they are from Norway, but additional work needs to be done to make a firm association.

Although much remains to be done to expand the reference data for quarries throughout the North Atlantic region as well as to integrate the corresponding data from other techniques of analysis, it is already apparent that the combination of relatively small inter-source composition differences and sometimes significant variations within a quarry and even within a (large) artefact will always limit the quality of assignment of origin to individual soapstone artefacts. For the moment at least, the way forward is to formulate modest aims for the science-based effort. Based on the semi-quantitative pXRF data accumulated so far, it certainly provides a valuable, broad characterisation, but the REE composition seems to be the more informative.

The results provided here and in previous reports (Forster and Jones 2017) have been encouraging. Scientific analysis of soapstone artefacts as a sole technique is potentially time consuming and expensive, and comprehensive analysis of a single site assemblage unlikely to yield impactful results. Where informed by morphological assessment and applied within the context of a wider study, the technique can be used more effectively. Assessment and classification of objects through traditional means can apply a confidence against Type and Origin. This will help target both samples and questions where science-based testing will prove most valuable. At the same time, a first step towards establishing comparability with data obtained by other institutions has very recently been achieved and with satisfactory results; this exercise took the form of ICP-MS analysis at SUERC of samples from a quarry near Bergen, originally analysed at the Earth Science Department at Bergen University, which supplied the data used by Hansen et al. (2017) in their major provenance study of soapstone from the Hordaland region and the town of Bergen. On completion of current analysis (in 2021), the present authors propose to undertake a more ambitious phase of research, increasing the number of samples for both artefacts and quarries to improve the resolution of the science-based provenance results.

The research will focus on the following steps:

Step 1 Review morphological analysis of the recovered assemblage, applying a confidence rating to the assignment of both Type and Origin.

Step 2 Increase the resolution of results through the continued analysis of samples from North Atlantic quarry sites (Shetland, Norway and Greenland) and Types assigned with a high confidence rating.

Step 3 Widen analysis of artefact samples through targeted analysis of archaeological artefacts recovered from well-stratified and scientifically dated sites.

Step 4 Evaluate the success of the combined methodology to determine the origin of soapstone vessels recovered from across the North Atlantic.

Step 5 Review of production/distribution model (Forster 2004a, 2005; Forster and Jones 2017) and comparison with other Viking/Norse artefact groups.

While links to individual quarry sites are currently beyond the capability of techniques used, due to intra-source (and even intra-artefact) variation in composition, associations between artefacts from across the North Atlantic region can provide tangible results. The implications of those results are exciting: through determining the origins of soapstone vessels linked to *landnám* settlement sites, we can map the origins of Norwegian pioneer groups across the region. Interrogation of data spanning the Viking through to the later Norse period will add detail to our understanding of ongoing interactions between the Norwegian homeland and the Viking diaspora.

Acknowledgements

This ongoing research has benefited from the support and advice from a diverse range of people and organisations. The *Homeland to Home* project was initially funded as part of NABO project Comparative Island Ecodynamics in the North Atlantic Project, with support from the US National Science Foundation. Analysis of the Tuquoy material was supported by Historic Environment Scotland. Finally, we thank the reviewers for their comments.

References

Arneborg, J. (1984) *De Norrøne bebyggelser i Nipaitsoq og Niaquusat: material Kultur, udenslandsforbinderelser, kulturet særpræg, kronologi og ophør – bylyst især ud fra oldsagerne udgravet 1976–1977, med en vurdening af, hvad en samlet undersøgelse af oldsagerne fra ogsåde øvnge bebyggelser I Vestbyden vil kunne sige om de naertnte spørgsmål for vesterbyggen som helhed.* (The Norse settlements in Nipaitsoq and Niaquusat: material culture and connection, chronology and cessation – based on archaeological excavations 1976–1977). Unpublished PhD thesis, University of Århus.

Ballin Smith, B. (2013) Norwick – Shetland's earliest Viking settlement? In V. Turner, J. Bond and A.-C. Larsen, *Viking Unst*. Lerwick: Shetland Heritage Publications, 217–33.

Ballin Smith, B., T. Ballin, A. Clarke, A. Forster, M. Goldberg, F. Hunter, R. Jones, O. Lelong, D. McLaren and A. Newton (2019) Craftwork at Milla Skerra, metalworking and bone, stone and iron tools. In O. Lelong, *Excavations at Milla Skerra Sandwick, Unst: Rhythms of Life in Iron Age Shetland*. Oxford: Oxbow Books, 84–111.

Barrett, J. H. (ed.) (2012) *Being an Islander: Production and Identity at Quoygrew, Orkney AD 900–1600*. Cambridge: MacDonald Institute Monographs.

Brooke-Freeman, E. (2009) Locating Shetland steatite using place name evidence. In A. K. Forster and V. E. Turner (eds), *Kleber: Shetland's Oldest Industry: Shetland Soapstone since Prehistory*. Lerwick: Shetland Amenity Trust, 18–26.

Clelland, S. J., C. M. Batt, B. Stern and R. E. Jones (2009) Scientific analysis of steatite: Recent results. In A. K. Forster and V. E. Turner (eds), *Kleber: Shetland's Oldest Industry: Shetland Soapstone since Prehistory*. Lerwick: Shetland Amenity Trust, 106–17.

Crawford, B. E. (1987) *Scandinavian Scotland*. Studies in the Early History of Britain: Scotland in the Early Middle Ages, Volume 2. Leicester: Leicester University Press.

Dockrill, S. J., J. M. Bond, V. E. Turner, L. D. Brown, D. J. Bashford, J. E. Cussans and R. A. Nicholson (2010) *Excavations at Old Scatness, Shetland, Vol 1: the Pictish Village and Viking Settlement*. Lerwick: Shetland Heritage Publications.

Forster, A. K. (2004a) *Shetland and the Trade of Steatite Goods in the North Atlantic Region during the Viking and Early Medieval Period: An Investigation into Trade and Exchange Networks in the Norse North Atlantic and the Extent to which Steatite Goods Manufactured in Shetland were Included in Such Networks*. Unpublished PhD thesis, University of Bradford.

Forster, A. K. (2004b) The soapstone trade in the North Atlantic: Preliminary research of Viking and Norse period soapstone imports in Iceland. In G. Guðmundsson (ed.), *Current Issues in Nordic Archaeology*. Reykjavík: Society of Icelandic Archaeologists, 17–21.

Forster, A. K. (2005) Steatite, resource control and the Orkney Earldom. In O. Owen (ed.), *The World of Orkneyinga Saga: The Broad-Cloth Viking Trip*. Kirkwall: Orkney Islands Council, 55–74.

Forster, A. K. (2009) Steatite use in the Middle and Later Iron Age: c. 500 BC to AD 800. In A. K. Forster and V. E. Turner (eds), *Kleber: Shetland's First Industry. Shetland Soapstone since Prehistory*. Lerwick: Shetland Amenity Trust, 48–57.

Forster, A. K. and R. E. Jones (2017) From homeland to home: Using soapstone to map migration and settlement in the North Atlantic. In G. Hansen and P. Storemyr (eds), *Soapstone in the North: Quarries, Products and People 7000 BC–AD 1700*. Universitetet i Bergens arkeologiske serier UBAS 9. Bergen: University of Bergen, 225–48.

Forster, A. K. and V. E. Turner (eds) (2009) *Kleber: Shetland's Oldest Industry: Shetland Soapstone since Prehistory*. Lerwick: Shetland Amenity Trust.

Hansen, G., O. J. Jansen and T. Heldal (2017) Soapstone Vessels from Town and Country in Viking age and early medieval western Norway. A Study of Provenance. In G. Hansen and P. Storemyr (eds), *Soapstone in the North: Quarries, Products and People 7000 BC–AD 1700*. Universitetet i Bergens arkeologiske serier UBAS 9. Bergen: University of Bergen, 249–328.

Jesch, J. (2015) *The Viking Diaspora*. Medieval World Series. London: Routledge.

Kendall, A. (2014) Material culture and North Atlantic trade in Iceland and Greenland. In R. Harrison and R. Maher, *Human Dynamics in the North Atlantic: A Collaborative Model of Humans and Nature Through Space and Time*. London: Lexington Books, 101–16.

Larsen, A.-C. and S. Stummann Hansen (2001) Viking Ireland and the Scandinavian communities in the North Atlantic. In A.-C. Larsen (ed.), *The Vikings in Ireland*. Roskilde: The Viking Ship Museum, 115–26.

Needham, S. (1993) Displacement and exchange in archaeological methodology. In C. Scarre and F. Healy (eds), *Trade and Exchange in Prehistoric Europe*. Oxbow Monograph 33. Oxford: Oxbow Books, 161–9.

Owen, O. (ed.) (2005) *The World of Orkneyinga Saga: The Broad-Cloth Viking Trip*. Kirkwall: Orkney Islands Council.

Sharples, N. (ed.) (2021) *The Economy of the Norse Settlement in the Outer Hebrides; Excavations at Mounds 2 and 2A, Bornais, South Uist*. Oxford: Oxbow Books.

Smith, A. N. and A. K. Forster (2007) Steatite. In J. R. Hunter, *Investigations in Sanday. Volume 1: Excavations at Pool, Sanday. A Multi-period Settlement Site from Neolithic to Late Norse Times*. Kirkwall: The Orcadian in association with Historic Scotland, 412–32.

Turner, V. (2013) The Legacy of the Viking Unst Project. In V. Turner, J. Bond and A.-C. Larsen, *Viking Unst*. Lerwick: Shetland Heritage Publications, 234–52.

Vésteinsson, O. (2014) *Archaeological Investigations in Igaliku: Excavations in the Meadow 2012-2013*. Unpublished report. Reykjavík: Fornleifastofnun Íslands.

Chapter 8

Machair Bharabhais, Leòdhas: A Scandinavian Settlement in its Context

Mary MacLeod Rivett and Trevor Cowie

In 1978, a rapid survey was carried out under the direction of Trevor Cowie to assess the impact of marine and aeolian erosion on archaeological sites around the coastline of Lewis and Harris. On Lewis, the whole of the exposed Atlantic coastline was walked from Mealista in Uig on the west coast to the Butt of Lewis in the extreme north of the island. In the course of this work, which focused particularly on the machair landscapes of the island, numerous new archaeological sites were located, with most at that time undergoing at least some active erosion. Among these previously unrecorded sites was a weathered spread of eroding midden deposits and partially exposed walling on the floor of a deflation hollow in an area of high dunes on the northern part of the machair system at *Barabhas* (Barvas), the largest such area in Lewis (Ritchie and Mather 1970; Cowie and MacLeod Rivett 2015; this paper, Figure 8.1). Among the surface collection of pottery from the site were some diagnostic sherds of Norse pottery, particularly the distinctive Hebridean platter ware which had at that time recently been characterised as a result of Alan Lane's doctoral research on the massive assemblages of Dark-Age and Viking-Age ceramics recovered during the late Iain Crawford's long-running excavations at *An Udail* (The Udal) in North Uist (Lane 1983). As few Viking-Age or Norse sites were then known in the Outer Hebrides, and almost none in Lewis, the site at Barabhas was prioritised for evaluation. Accordingly, in 1979, limited excavation was undertaken (by Cowie) to assess the extent and survival of the settlement. Unfortunately, the suite of high dunes within which the site lay was subsequently quarried for sand without further intervention and the site is now presumed to have been lost.

The intention of the evaluation was to map the extent of the site and assess the quality of the survival of the structural remains. Surface finds collection and an auger survey were followed by the opening of a 6m x 15m area across the structures and the excavation of a series of four 1m² test pits (Figure 8.2). These revealed that the eroded surfaces masked

Machair Bharabhais, Leòdhas 113

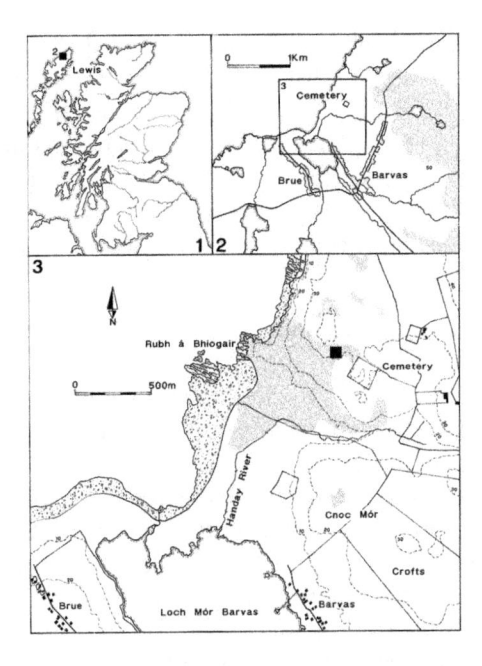

Figure 8.1 Machair Bharabhais: location map. The Norse site (■) lay in a deflation hollow in an area of high dunes to the west of the cemetery.

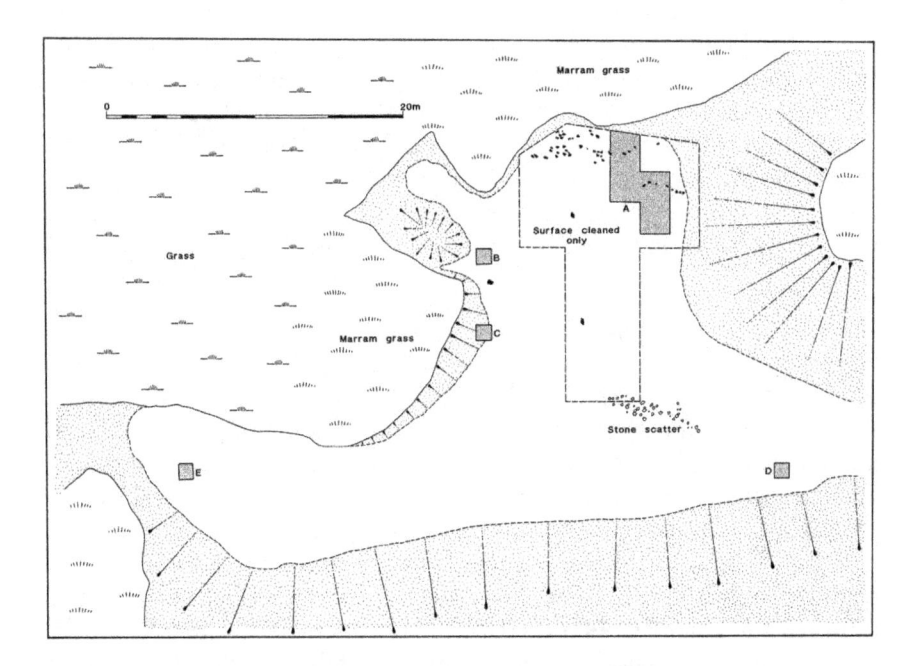

Figure 8.2 Plan of Norse site prior to excavation, showing location of test pits and excavation area.

a substantial settlement mound with stratified deposits up to 1.2m in depth. Despite the limited nature of this initial assessment of the site, the information gathered from it was sufficient to shed light on the probable nature of the settlement and its date range, and understanding of the site has been further clarified in the years since its excavation, particularly as more information on the wider context of Viking-Age and Norse settlement in the Hebrides has become available.

The landscape context

The Norse site was located on the higher, northern edge of the machair system to the west of the Barabhas cemetery and the location of the medieval parish church of St Mary. To the south of this, down the south-facing slope, erosion has revealed extensive remains of the prehistoric landscape, including traces of houses, midden, field systems, burials and ritual monuments, dating from the Chalcolithic/Early Bronze Age to the Late Iron Age (Cowie and MacLeod Rivett 2015; MacLeod Rivett 2018). Recent careful management of this area has subsequently allowed the machair surface to stabilise, protecting what remains of this landscape. At the bottom of this slope, the *Abhainn Shanndaigh* (Handay River) flows out to the shore, and on the southern side of the river, a low hill is covered by the exposed remains of a probable medieval and early modern field system. On the other side of this, near the shore of *Loch Mòr Bharabhais* is the now mostly submerged location of further later prehistoric settlement (ibid.; Ponting and Ponting 1979: 46–7).

The prehistoric settlement landscape is focused on the lower, south-facing slopes of the machair, on what would have been the optimal agricultural land. Fringing this, the areas of higher ground are occupied by traces of the medieval and post-medieval settlement pattern associated with the surrounding townships.

The excavation

The lowest deposits within the test pits showed that the earliest recorded construction at the Norse site was founded on the basal, slightly sandy mineral soil; in places this soil appeared to incorporate traces of midden material, suggesting it may have been cultivated. At the base of the deepest test pit, a layer of paving was laid directly on this soil and a sample of red deer metatarsal bone from midden material directly above the paving provided a calibrated date range of AD 972–1041 at one sigma (1021±26 BP; SUERC-44268/GU29438). This is the earliest date from the site and it falls within what is conventionally considered the Viking Age, rather than the Norse period.

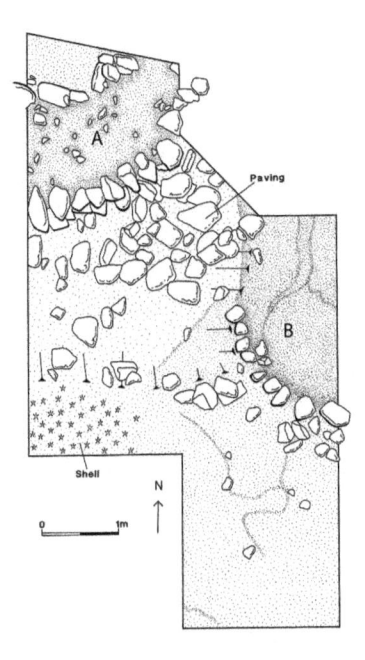

Figure 8.3 Plan of main excavation area showing location of structures A and B.

In the larger excavation area, removal of blown sand exposed the adjacent corners of two buildings, one built with stone-faced walls, with a fill of midden, probable turf and small stones (Structure A), while the other was apparently walled in turf and midden, with an external stone face (Structure B) (Figure 8.3). The gap between the walls of the two buildings had filled with accumulated midden.

Only very limited excavation took place within the buildings; however, a spit was excavated across the top of the wall-fill of Structure A. Pottery from this context included sagging bases and platter ware now seen to be characteristic of Norse assemblages (Lane 2014), while a sample of a carbonised grain of barley (*Hordeum vulgare* (hulled)) also from this context gave a calibrated date range of AD 1164–1265 (824±30 BP; SUERC-43881/GU29070). The wall-core of the building was constructed using soil or turves from a midden on the site itself, and it demonstrates that the construction of the building dated to after platter ware became common.

The latest layers of accumulated midden between the buildings lay over the top of the wall of Structure B, indicating that it went out of use before Structure A did. However, layers of blown sand and midden below this respected both buildings, indicating that they were contemporary in their use. Owing to the limits of the excavation, it is not clear whether they were constructed at the same time. A sample of a carbonised grain of hulled barley (*Hordeum vulgare* from the uppermost midden layer gave an overall calibrated date range of AD 1262–1388 (698±30 BP; SUERC-43765/GU29069). This provides the latest reliable *terminus ante quem* date for the occupation sequence. A 13th- to 14th-century date for this phase of use, culturally Late Norse in character, is reinforced by three similar dates from underlying midden deposits in this area.

The eventual inundation of the site by the dunes is likely to have occurred during the post-medieval period, but lenses and layers of blown sand revealed in the excavation suggest that the area was prone to episodes of erosion during the lifetime of the settlement. Plough marks cut into the surface of the uppermost deposits demonstrated that the site was cultivated at the end of its use, but these were not directly dateable, and given the mobility of the blown-sand landscape, they could have been created considerably later than the abandonment of the buildings.

Although the ceramic assemblage from the site is relatively small by Hebridean standards, Barabhas is a significant addition to the inventory of sites from the region producing pottery of the period. Otherwise, artefacts were few in number and mostly not closely dateable, apart from a fragment of a single-sided copper-riveted composite comb of Late Norse type and a biconical blue glass bead found during surface collection.

By contrast, analysis of the faunal, fish and plant remains has shed valuable light on the subsistence economy of the site. The mammal bone assemblage was dominated by cattle, analysis of which indicated an economy in which dairying was an important element, while sheep were kept for both wool and meat (Harman in Cowie and MacLeod Rivett 2010; Serjeantson in Cowie and MacLeod Rivett 2010; Serjeantson 2013). Red deer, pig and horse were also present as minor elements of the assemblage, which also included the bones of a terrier-sized dog. No evidence of antler processing was found. Although small bones may admittedly have been missed, extensive sieving resulted in the recovery of a substantial assemblage of fish bone, consisting predominantly of larger gadids, especially cod and ling (Colley in Cowie and MacLeod Rivett 2010). Large quantities of limpets and periwinkles were present throughout the midden deposits, probably gathered both for bait and as food.

Carbonised remains of barley, oats and flax were all recovered and the linseed would appear to have been cleaned for eating. No evidence of malting was found (Dickson and Dickson 2000; Dickson in Cowie and MacLeod Rivett 2010).

Discussion

Bearing in mind the limitations of what was only a brief evaluation, what is it possible to determine from the results of the excavation?

The settlement appears to have been constructed on previously cultivated ground towards the end of the Viking Age in the late 10th century at the earliest. By the end of the life of the settlement, at around the end of the 13th century, it consisted of at least two rectilinear buildings, possibly built using different techniques. One of the buildings may have been of higher status than the other, reflected in the use of stone for both the inside and outside faces of the wall, though it is possible that the apparent differences are an artefact of the limited excavation. On the basis of the evidence from the associated midden deposits, the two buildings served a mixed farm cultivating barley and oats and raising cattle and sheep; wild resources, particularly fish, formed a significant part of the diet.

The farm was built on an area which had apparently not formed part of the Iron-Age infield. No residual Iron-Age finds were discovered in the test pits, and the settlement was constructed to the north and overlooking the prehistoric landscapes to its south. The separation of high-status prehistoric and Viking-Age settlement is characteristic of the Outer Hebrides (Raven and MacLeod Rivett 2021); in contrast, there is evidence from Driomor (MacLaren 1974) and Bostadh (Neighbour, pers. comm.) for continuity from Iron-Age through to Viking-Age occupation on less prestigious settlements. However, there is no evidence that this was a particularly high-status site, so the lack of continuity from Iron-Age settlement and relatively late dates of occupation suggest that it resulted from settlement expansion onto less desirable agricultural ground.

In many ways, this small farm appears to have been similar to the settlement at *Cille Pheadair* (Kilpheder) in South Uist (Parker Pearson et al. 2018), which was also built on cultivated land in the second half of the 10th century (Parker Pearson et al. 2018: 42–64) and went out of use probably in the late 12th to early 13th century. The later phases of the Cille Pheadair farm also had more than one building, with distinct functions (Parker Pearson et al. 2018: 597–601), and the finds assemblage from Barabhas, although limited, is similar.

The available evidence suggests that the site at *Machair Bharabhais* (Barvas machair) was a small, secondary, late Viking-Age farm, established on cultivated ground in the second half of the 10th century. The need for such settlements, both in South Uist and in Lewis, suggests the possibility of rising populations at this time in the islands. It is noticeable, however, that this farm and that at Cille Pheadair both fell out of use between around 1200 and 1400 and were not reoccupied. This was a period of great political turbulence, climatic deterioration and epidemics, including the Black Death (Oram 2014: 223–44). In the Outer Hebrides, the islands shifted from the Crown of Norway to the Crown of Scotland with the Treaty of Perth in 1266 (Crawford and Parker Pearson 2018: 586). We have very little understanding as yet of the impacts of these various social, political and environmental changes and upheavals in the Outer Hebrides, but looking at Barabhas in its context, the evidence hints at a significant medieval landscape reorganisation. Whether this was due to population decline or political change, or both, is as yet unclear.

Acknowledgements

We are grateful to Colleen Batey, Tom Horne, Elizabeth Pierce and Rachel Barrowman for the opportunity to submit this summary account in advance of our final report. The excavation and the coastal erosion survey which preceded it were undertaken while Trevor Cowie was a member of the Central Excavation Unit within the Ancient Monuments Branch of what was then the Scottish Development Department, and post-excavation analysis has been funded by Historic Environment Scotland. This summary paper draws on the results of specialist reports prepared by Sarah Colley, Mary Harman, Alan Lane, Dale Serjeantsen and the late Camilla Dickson. Radiocarbon dating was undertaken by Gordon Cook and his colleagues at Scottish Universities Environmental Research Centre (SUERC), Glasgow. Finally, thanks are due to Alan Braby for preparing the illustrations.

References

Cowie, T. and M. MacLeod Rivett (2010) *Barabhas 2: Data Structure Report. A Norse/Medieval settlement at Barvas (Barabhas) Machair, Isle of Lewis*. Unpublished report commissioned by Historic Scotland. https://www.academia.edu/7827570/BARABHAS_2_DATA_STRUCTURE_REPORT_A_Norse_Mediaeval_Site_on_Barabhas_Machair_Lewis

Cowie, T. and M. MacLeod Rivett (2015) Machair Bharabhais: a landscape through time. *Journal of the North Atlantic* Special Volume 9, 99–107.

Crawford, B. E. and M. Parker Pearson (2018) The Cille Pheadair farmstead in its context. In M. Parker Pearson, M. Brennand, J. Mulville and H. Smith, *Cille Pheadair: A Norse Farmstead and Pictish Burial Cairn in South Uist*. Oxford and Philadelphia: Oxbow Books, 580–604.

Dickson, C. and J. Dickson (2000) *Plants and People in Ancient Scotland*. Stroud: Tempus.

Lane, A. (1983) *Dark Age and Viking Age Pottery in the Hebrides*. Unpublished PhD thesis, University of London.

Lane, A. (2014) Ceramic and cultural change in the Hebrides AD 500–1300. In J. V. Sigurðsson and T. Bolton (eds), *Celtic–Norse Relationships in the Irish Sea in the Middle Ages 800–1200*. The Northern World 65. Leiden, Boston: Brill, 119–49.

MacLaren, A. (1974) A Norse House on Drimore Machair, South Uist. *Glasgow Archaeological Journal* 3, 9–18.

MacLeod Rivett, M. (2018) *Barabhas Machair: Surveys of an Eroding Sandscape*, SAIR 76. http://journals.socantscot.org/index.php/sair/article/view/3194

Oram, R. (2014) 'The Worst Disaster Suffered by the People of Scotland in Recorded History': Climate change, dearth and pathogens in the Long Fourteenth Century. *Proceedings of the Society of Antiquaries of Scotland* 144, 223–44.

Parker Pearson, M., M. Brennand, J. Mulville and H. Smith (2018) *Cille Pheadair: A Norse Farmstead and Pictish Burial Cairn in South Uist*. Oxford and Philadelphia: Oxbow Books.

Ponting, G. and M. Ponting (1979) Loch Mor Barbas [sic] (Barvas p). *Discovery and Excavation in Scotland 1979*, 46–7.

Raven, J. and M. MacLeod Rivett (2021) morentur in Domino libere et in pace: Cultural identity and the remembered past in the medieval Outer Hebrides. In S. Stoddart, E. D. Aines and C. Malone (eds), *Gardening Time: Monuments and Landscape from Sardinia, Scotland and Central Europe in the very long Iron Age*. Cambridge: McDonald Institute for Archaeological Research, 175–83.

Ritchie, W. and A. S. Mather (1970) *The Beaches of Lewis and Harris*. Aberdeen: Department of Geography, University of Aberdeen.

Serjeantson, D. (2013) *Farming and Fishing in the Outer Hebrides AD 600 to 1700: The Udal, North Uist*. Southampton Monographs in Archaeology New Series No. 2. Southampton: The Highfield Press.

Part III

Place-names: Interactions with the Landscape

Vikings in Scotland's interdisciplinary strength is particularly apparent in its incorporation of linguistics, such as documentary evidence and place-names, which it noted were 'of the greatest value', despite the then-uneven research foci (1998: 37). That said, Graham-Campbell and Batey advised caution in attempting to make hard and fast assumptions about sequences of settlement from this evidence, something especially true for the Hebrides.

Since at least the 19th century (Macniven, this section), scholars have attempted to understand Scandinavian settlement in the Hebrides amid the fog of a post-Viking-Age resurgence and northern expansion of Gaelic over areas with an Old Norse (ON)-speaking interlude. Key questions centre on the linguistic border of Gaelic and Pictish before ON speakers settled (as is generally considered) in the first half of the 9th century; how extensive the settlement of ON speakers was; and whether this settlement weakened from the northern and western (particularly the Western Isles and Skye) to the southern and eastern Hebrides, creating distinct north-western and south-eastern sociolinguistic regions.

Where *Vikings in Scotland* described the then-accepted model of this north to south (and Outer to Inner Hebrides) change (1998: 41, 72), Macniven (this section) suggests we rethink assumptions about weak(er) *landnám* in the southern Hebrides, and on Islay in particular: given prominent ON nature generics (like *dalr*), the survival of ON place-names on prime land throughout Islay and the virtual absence of a pre-ON onomastic stratum, Macniven argues that 'the initial impact of Viking settlement in the south was very similar to that in the north. The defining difference was what happened next'.

Taking a somewhat different tack, Clancy (this section) describes the Hebridean church encountered by the Vikings as inhabiting a 'particular sociolinguistic domain' that provided a measure of continuity into the Viking Age and beyond, expanding upon ideas expressed in *Vikings in Scotland* (1998: 39) about the survival of indigenous communities potentially helping to maintain Celtic Christianity, languages and place-names. For Clancy, Gaelic was considered by all communities as a high-status language due to its links to the Christianity Scandinavians in the Hebrides were adopting (potentially as early as the initial *landnám*), with some island names indicating early Scandinavian settlers added Gaelic saints to their pantheon.

Clancy agrees with Whyte (this section), who argues for a move away from models that separate ON- and Gaelic-speaking (southern Hebridean) communities and whole islands in favour of interdisciplinary ones that, as on Mull, allow for a 'more nuanced' view that is 'more alive to the human nature of linguistic and cultural change'.

Chapter 9

Norse Settlement in the Southern Hebrides: The Place-name Evidence from Islay

Alan Macniven

There can be little doubt that the Hebrides were among the first parts of the British Isles to witness the Viking expansion. A location along the sea road from Norway to Ireland means that through traffic, at the very least, was a certainty. Beyond that, however, the extent of raiding and land-taking is not immediately obvious. While the Irish annals report a series of attacks on Iona,[1] contemporary accounts are otherwise vague. For this reason, the Hebridean Viking experience can only be gauged by a process of jigsaw identification using a variety of different sources. The most ubiquitous are the names of places. From the late 19th century, scholars focused on the ratio of Old Norse (ON) to Gaelic material. Early assessments of 4:1 for Lewis, 3:2 for North Uist and Skye, 1:2 for Islay, 1:4 for Kintyre and 1:8 for Arran (MacBain 1893–4: 218; Scott 1954: 189–90) helped embed the idea of a dichotomy in Scottish Viking studies, with 'extirpation' in the north giving way to integration in the south (Thomas 1874–6: 503). For the islands closest to Ireland, the concept of 'hybridity', albeit in a loosely defined sense, became a keystone of interpretational models. More recently, however, attempts to unpack the place-name evidence have sought to take account of demographic, linguistic and onomastic change in the centuries separating the earliest records from the height of the Viking Age. For the southern Hebrides, the island which has attracted the most attention is that of Islay (Figure 9.1). Lying within sight of both the Irish mainland and the Kintyre peninsula, Islay controls the strategically important North Channel, and with it, access to the Irish Sea. By geological coincidence, Islay's large expanses of limestone bedrock also provide the basis for a relatively fertile agricultural landscape, explaining why it became known in later times by the Gaelic epithet *Bannrigh*, or 'Queen' of the Hebrides. If any part of this region was fated to attract or repel the flood of Scandinavian colonists sweeping across the North Atlantic, Islay would surely have been near the top of the list.

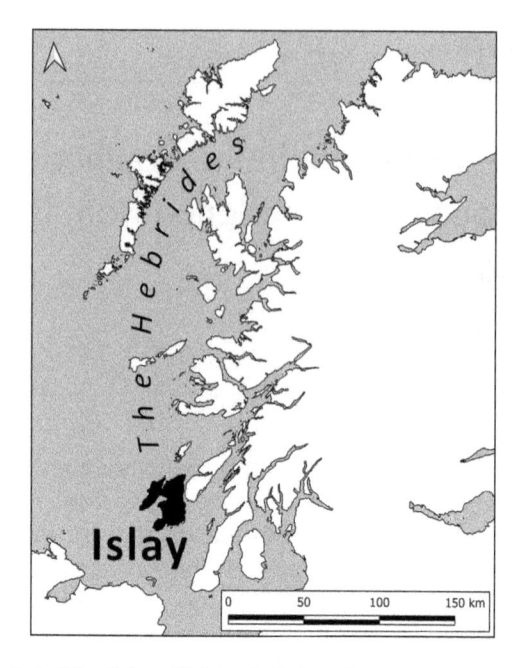

Figure 9.1 The Isle of Islay. A. Macniven.

In traditional accounts, Islay's Viking legacy is minimal. The local heritage language, for example, is not Norn but Scottish Gaelic. This was the case in 1791, when the Reverend George McLeish noted, '[t]he Gaelic is the general language of the common people' (Sinclair 1983: XI 287), a situation seemingly unchanged since the heyday of the Islay-based Lords of the Isles in the later Middle Ages, the kindred of Oengus in the 7th century, and the legendary Fergus mor MacErc in the 5th. On closer inspection, this apparent chain of continuity is not as secure as it first seems. Following the report of an earthquake in Islay in *AU* 740.3, there are no references to the island until Manx king Godred Crovan is said to have died there in the *Chronicle of the Kings of Man and the Isles* for 1095 (Broderick 2004: §23), a period encompassing the Viking Age. On emerging from this historical hiatus, the political settlement in Islay is, moreover, radically different. Gone are the *Cenél nÓenguso* and their estates measured in *tech*, or 'houses'. Indeed, the whole notion of the kingdom of *Dál Riata* had disappeared without trace. Instead, the region had been reconceptualised in the Irish annals as *Innse Gall*, 'The Islands of the Strangers', in contradistinction to mainland Argyll, from OIr *Airer Goídel*, 'The Coast or Border of the Gaels' (Woolf 2004). Hints at what or who might have precipitated these changes can be found in the archaeological record.

Thus far, the only material remains dated to Islay's Viking Age reflect diagnostically Scandinavian practice. Sites include a pagan graveyard with seven or more burials at Ballinaby (CANMORE ID: 37407, 37408, 37409, 37410 and 37395), a further burial near Newton Cottage (37757), a 10th-century coin hoard from Machrie (37593), along with an 11th-century stone cross with Ringerike-style interlace at *Doid Mhairi* (37540), and several part-excavated or suspected Scandinavian structures at *Rubha Buidhe* (106776), *An Sìthean* (37374), *Àird Thòrr-innis* (37411) and Nave Island (37473). The close association of these finds with high-quality farmland, combined with their gender balance and two-century span, points to an established, landowning class with Scandinavian cultural aspirations, signalling their ownership of the area and its resources.

A degree of cultural disjuncture can also be found in the forms of Gaelic language attested in the Hebrides after the Viking Age. Their divergence from those of Ireland is marked by a small but culturally significant portion of ON vocabulary, some of which can be explained as retention of core vocabulary by native speakers of ON learning Gaelic, as opposed to borrowing by Gaelic-speaking communities (Stewart 2004: 402–6). Linguistic interference can also be found in aspects of pronunciation, such as supradentalisation and probably pre-aspiration (Gammeltoft 2004: 55–9).[2] In an Islay context, traditional pronunciation of the word *cat*, 'cat' as [kö[h]t] (Grannd 2000: 45), appears to reflect that of ON *köttr*, 'cat'. Taken together, these relics point to a large and socially influential Viking presence, which probably adopted the Gaelic language following their conversion to (Celtic) Christianity and increasing involvement in regional power politics.

The most significant traces of Old Norse and its elevated status can be found fossilised in the traditional names of places. More than six thousand features of the natural and built environment are named in the Ordnance Survey Object Name Books for Islay, from the highest hills to individually numbered houses on given streets. Around two-fifths are newer names coined in Scots or standard English. The remainder can be considered Gaelic in the sense that they were created or preserved in a Gaelic language environment. In a small but important portion of these names, however, there are elements which can only be convincingly explained in terms of Scandinavian place-name typology. This in turn can be linked to Viking settlement. In the pre-map-making era of the Viking Age, local names would not have taken root had the name-givers been itinerant and not remained in place to reinforce usage. The survival of this material through the medium of Gaelic language can be explained in terms of place-name mechanics. While names can be coined with clear appellative meaning, they only have to be understood as address labels to work. This means they can survive as sequences of phonemes without lexical meaning, enduring even language shift (Macniven 2015: 11–12). Not all names are equally resilient. A basic distinction can be drawn between what Olsen (1934: 10–12) calls 'Names of the Farm' and 'Names of the District'. The key factor is the scale and stability of their respective 'User Groups'. The former would typically include minor topographical and cultural features known only to the inhabitants of an individual holding, and therefore vulnerable to loss with developments as minor as a change in tenancy. The latter, on the other hand, would include the names of the wider farm-districts and most prominent topographical features. As their user groups are much bigger, they are more likely to become entrenched in the regional toponymy, but still not immune to loss or replacement.

While the place-name records for Islay are among the most venerable in the Hebrides, they are nevertheless extremely limited before the very end of the 15th century, and far from exhaustive until the work of the Ordnance Survey in the late 1800s. In the centuries which separate these collections from the Viking Age, there are known to have been several waves of significant demographic change with the potential to erode the ON toponymy. These include the immigration of prestigious Gaelic-speakers from Argyll in the 12th century, the north of Ireland in the 16th, the resettlement of farm-workers from Nairnshire in the 17th century, the population expansion following the agricultural innovations of the 18th century and the settlement retraction and reorganisation resulting from the clearances and introduction of planned villages, such as Bowmore, in the 19th century (Macniven 2015: 55–60, 93, 26, 368 n. 51).

In 1881–2, Thomas famously set the ratio of ON to Gaelic place-names in Islay at 1:2. Coupled with the misconception that ON names with nature generics were only indicative of seasonal exploitation (Nicolaisen 2001: 122–4 but cf. Kruse 2004: 102–3), this fuelled the assumption that Scandinavian settlement was either temporary or piecemeal, and restricted to defensive enclaves or less productive land. It should be noted, however, that Thomas derived his ratio from the Islay material in the Valuation Rolls for Argyllshire for 1872–3, the settlement patterns, taxonomies and even name-material of which represent quite a departure from earlier times. Furthermore, with no consideration given to the relative settlement-historical importance of these names, the scope for retrospective distortion is rather large (Macniven 2015: 27–32). To minimise interference from post-Norse developments, it makes more sense to begin with names of the same type, encountered in the oldest possible source material. For Islay, the best candidates by far are the names of traditional farm-districts pre-dating the Agricultural Revolution. The Rosetta Stone which allows us to unlock their historical significance is Stephen McDougall's *Map of the Island of Islay* from 1749–51 (Figure 9.2).

Norse Settlement in the Southern Hebrides 127

Figure 9.2 Stephen MacDougall's (1749–51) *Map of the Island of Islay*. Smith 1895: 552–3.

McDougall's map is the first document to show the names, relative locations and boundaries of Islay's traditional farm-districts across the whole island, enabling the easy compartmentalisation and analysis of associated geomorphological and cultural data. Taking this as the basis for the study, the proportion of primary settlement names with ON origins accounts for 87 of the 162 linguistically certain, non-Scots and non-contrasted names, or 54 per cent of the total. More importantly, it is clear

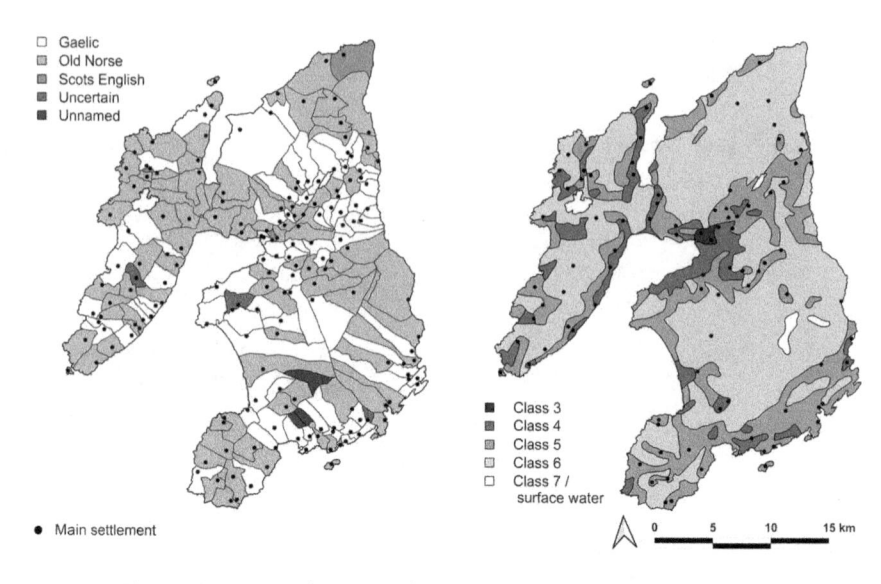

Figure 9.3 Distribution of Islay farm-names by language background and ON farm-names and 'Land Capability for Agriculture'. After Brown et al. 1982, Macniven 2015: 46, 54.

that these names are not restricted to enclaves or lower-quality land, but can be found on every landform, across every part of the island, with concentrations on the best land, whether coastal or far from the sea (Figure 9.3) (Macniven 2015: 51–3).

The ON settlement names on the map include around twenty nature generics, potentially indicative of the earliest stages of land-taking, the most common being *dalr*, 'Valley' (12), e.g. Ardenistle, and Glenegedale, from **Askdalr*, 'Ash-Tree Valley', and **Eikadalr*, 'Oak-Tree Valley'; *vík*, 'bay' (6), e.g. Port Askaig and Proaig, from **Askvík*, 'Ash-Tree Bay', and **Breiðvík*, 'Broad Bay'; and *á*, 'river' (4), e.g. Avinlussa, from **Laxá*, or 'Salmon River' (Laxan 1541, Avinluska 1631 [Macniven 2015: 193]). They also contain around eleven cultural generics, often associated with the division of larger estates, or differentiation in farm-types. The most common is *bólstaðr* (18), usually with the typical Islay ending *-bus*, e.g. Asabus and Kinnabus, from **Ássabólstaðr*, 'Ridge Farm', and **Kinna(r)bólstaðr*, 'Farm on the Cheek (of Land)'; *staðir* (11), e.g. Grimsay and Kelsay, from **Grímsstaðir*, 'Grim's Steading', and **Kelsstaðir*, 'Ke(ti)ll's Steading'; and *býr* (3), including Consiby, from *Konungsbýr*, which local tradition links to Manx king Godred Crovan (Maceacharna 1976: 90 fn12).

There are areas with lower concentrations of ON names, but these coincide with rugged uplands and boggy terrain with few settlements of any kind, or areas associated with the incoming Lords of the Isles and their office-bearers in the later Middle Ages (Macniven 2015: 55–60).

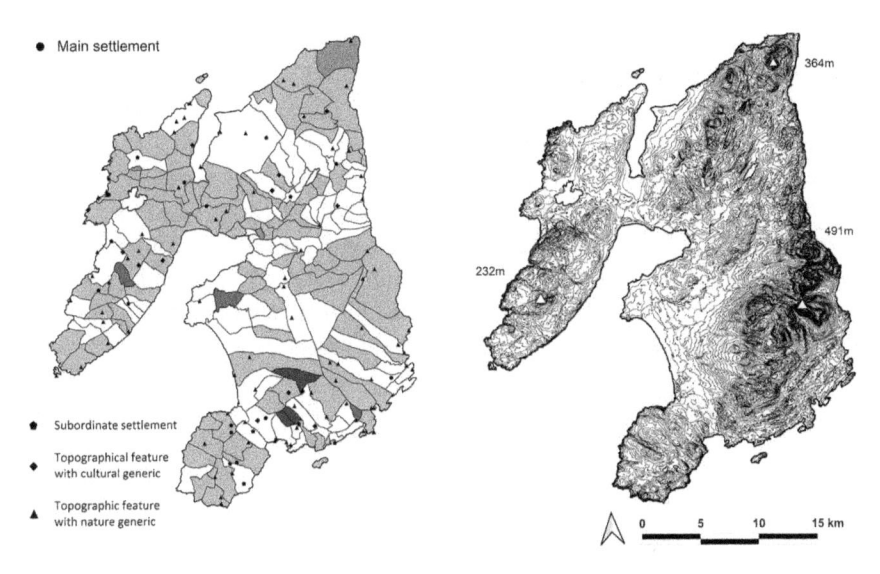

Figure 9.4 Distribution of other ON place-names and topography (10m contours). Macniven 2015: 46.

Significantly, however, even these parts of the island contain Norse names for topographical features and subordinate settlements (Figure 9.4), e.g. Eas forsa, from ON *Forsá*, 'Waterfall River', in G (Gaelic) Carnbeg; Cornabus, from *Kornabólstaðr*, 'Corn Farm', in G Kilnaughton; and Cnoc Creagascail, from *Krákaskáli*, 'Kraki's Shieling' or 'Crow Shieling', in G Kilbride. The most straightforward interpretation of these distribution patterns is that Old Norse was once the island's prestige language.

At the same time, there is little evidence for onomastic continuity from the previous period. In Islay, as elsewhere in the Hebrides, there are examples of phonological adaptation, whereby pre-Norse names have been adapted to fit the typologies and sounds of a Scandinavian linguistic environment (Gammeltoft 2007: 479–95). But these are limited to the names of larger islands, like Islay itself, i.e. ON *Ílarey* cf. the *Ilea insula* of Admonán (Broderick 2013: 11–12), which would have been essential aides to navigation in the early stages of exploration and settlement. By way of contrast, it has not been possible to identify any pre-Norse settlement names, adapted or otherwise, suggesting they were neither learned nor remembered by the colonists.

Conversely, many of Islay's recorded Gaelic names appear to be later medieval innovations. *Baile*, meaning 'enclosure, farm', is found in fifteen of the seventy-five independent Gaelic names on MacDougall's map. While the word itself is ancient, its use as a place-name element was not common until the later Middle Ages, when it appears to have been repurposed as a standard term in the emerging documentation of landownership

(Price 1963). The term *cill*, 'church, chapel', although later also 'burial place', appears fourteen times, and seems to have proliferated around the same time, as a result of the systematic introduction of the parish network (Macniven 2015: 67–9). It may be significant in this respect that each of Islay's three medieval Rectories contains six farm-districts with a *cill*-name. Another indication of the re-Gaelicisation of Islay's namescape is the appearance of linguistically phrasal names in the later Middle Ages (Watson 1904: xl–xli), e.g. *Àirigh nam Beast*, 'Animal Shieling', and the inclusion of personal names, particularly those which have come from ON tradition, e.g. Balulive and Àirigh Ghuaidhre, from ON Ulfr and Guðrøðr.

Assumptions of 'hybridity' can also be challenged. Names like Port Bhoraraic, of which there are dozens of examples, do indeed contain word material from both languages, i.e. G *port*, 'bay' + ON **Borgarvík*, 'Fortbay'. But they are far from hybrid in a strict linguistic sense. On the contrary, what they show is not the early fusing of different cultures but an initial period of disjuncture, where pre-existing Gaelic names were ignored by Viking settlers in favour of their own creations, followed at a much later date by the appendage of an explanatory prefix, after language shift and the inevitable fall of their original meaning into obscurity. While these two-part names can be considered formally Gaelic, the epexegetic onomastic units they contain would once have functioned as ON names. Crucially, there are no convincing examples of ON names containing epexegetic onomastic units in Gaelic.

Further scrutiny of Islay records reveals what appear to be the ON names for several districts and administrative units: for example, the Oa peninsula, from ON **Höfuð*, 'Head'; the historical Herries in central Islay from **Herað*, 'Administrative District'; the *Lanndaidh* once associated with the south-east coast from **Landeyjar*, 'Islands of (Arable) Land'; and possibly also the central watershed known as The Glen, from G *An Gleann*, but arguably adapted from an earlier ON **Dalr*, 'Valley' (Macniven 2015: 93–4). In addition to this, there are hints of Þing or assembly-names, in Sunderland, whose pronunciation suggests derivation from **Sjóvarþing*, 'Assembly Place by the Lake', or **Sunnarrþing*, the 'More Southerly Assembly Place'; Grulin with possible derivation from **Grjótþing*, 'Assembly Place by the Cairn' (Whyte 2014); and Loch Leòdamais, from **Ljóðanes*, 'Assembly point'.

While there have been several attempts to trace the continuity of the assumed Dál Riatan districts of the *Senchus fer n'Alban* into the Early Modern period, the arguments made are difficult to sustain (for example, Lamont 1966, but cf. Macniven 2015: 81–6). Working from later sources, the island's apparent subdivision into six early parishes, and three Rectories/Feudal Ward Divisions, finds close parallels in the *séttungr*, or 'sixth', and *þriðjungr*, or 'third' divisions familiar from the

Manx 'Sheadings' and Yorkshire 'Ridings'. The 1617 *Tenandry of Lossit*, with its *reddendo* to provide annually 'a boat with fourteen oars' (Smith 1895: 353), raises the possibility that Islay's first parishes developed from units of ship service akin to the Norwegian *skipreiða*.

Attempts have also been made to link the enigmatic Islay extents to reconstructed Dál Riatan norms. McKerral (1943–4: 45–7), for example, posited the Islay Quarterland of 33s 4d as one-quarter of an undocumented and unusually large *bailebiataigh* denomination. Given its late appearance, however, and absence from the place-name record as the G element *Cearramh*, 'quarter', it is more convincingly explained as a new term for a standard large landholding, probably imported with other 'strange and foreign laws' by unpopular Irish tacksmen in the late 16th and early 17th centuries (Smith 1895: 153–5). On review of the early charters, the most common large unit is the five-Merk extent, with the same rental value as two Quarterlands. As the equivalent of twenty Islay Cowlands, another late and poorly attested denomination, the five-Merk extent is also directly comparable in terms of composition and relative value to the Ounceland-Pennyland tradition of Insular Norse practice in other parts of the Hebrides (Macniven 2015: 89–94).

For Viking chieftains relocating families and followers from Norway to the Hebrides, there was no 'free' land to claim. On the contrary, native traditions of landownership and status (for example, Gerriets 1983; Kelly 1997) would have made the acquisition and retention of landed property extremely difficult without the support of overwhelming force. It is now accepted that a period of undocumented but inevitable requisitioning and raiding in the Isles allowed Scandinavians to take control without encountering substantial resistance, possibly by 847 (Nelson 1991: 65; Woolf 2007: 100). With Viking fleets of a hundred and more ships active in the Irish Sea (for example, *AU* 849.6, 852.3, 871.2), the logistics of such an occupation would have posed little difficulty. In fact, the fractured seascapes of the Hebrides, which had been pivotal for regional connectivity and political cohesion, would also have hastened their downfall. With the final eradication of the local warrior class (Macniven 2015: 114–15) and the removal of a significant portion of the wider population as slaves (cf. Holm 1986; Hudson 1999), the leading settlers were free to claim the best land and divide the rest between their followers. Parallels are likely with the elite-driven land-taking witnessed in Iceland from the 870s, inspired by the need for mid-ranking nobles to maintain status and privilege in the face of political centralisation by the emerging Norwegian monarchy (Helle 1993: 10). This kind of predatory migration might now be considered unusual in other parts of medieval Europe, where it has been possible to explain developments in terms of modern 'cost benefit analysis', with its emphasis on individual economic perspective and personal agency (Heather 2009).

But it is worth considering that the rural Viking economy was not monetary but socially embedded, with an emphasis on hierarchy. In reality, the majority of migrants would have had little say in their movements. When assessing their societal outlook, comparisons can be drawn with the large-scale Norwegian migration to the Midwest of the USA in the 19th century. While personal experiences may have varied, the tendency of Norwegian immigrant communities to be conspicuously conservative and inward-looking has been explained as an attempt to maintain cultural stability in a time of societal flux (Munch 1949: 780–1). The terms of Norse settlement may have differed in other parts of western Scotland (for example, Clancy 2008; Jennings and Kruse 2009). However, the evidence emerging from Tiree (Holliday 2016) and elsewhere in the Hebrides suggests that the initial impact of Viking settlement in the south was very similar to that in the north. The defining difference was what happened next.

Notes

1. *The Annals of Innisfallen (AI)* 795.2; *The Annals of Ulster (AU)* 802.9, 806.8, 825.17, 878.9, 986.3. For the assumed attack on Skye in *AU* 795.3, see Downham (2000).
2. Iosad (2020: 219) makes a case for native pre-aspiration in OIr, which rests heavily on its appearance in Ulster Gaelic. No account is taken, however, of the five hundred years when high-status warrior-aristocrats from Innse Gall, including the MacDonalds of Dunyvaig and the Glens, and various Gallowglass kindred, plundered, settled and dominated political life in the region.

References

Broderick, G. (ed.) (2004) *Chronica Regum Manniae et Insularum, Chronicles of the Kings of Man and the Isles*. Douglas: Manx National Heritage.
Broderick, G. (2013) Some island names in the former 'Kingdom of the Isles': A reappraisal. *Journal of Scottish Name Studies* 7, 1–28.
Brown, C. J., B. M. Shipley and J. J. Bibby (1982) *Soil and Land Capability for Agriculture: South-Western Scotland*. Handbook to accompany the 1:250,000 scale Soil and Land Capability for Agriculture maps, Sheet 6. Aberdeen: The Macaulay Institute for Soil Research.
Clancy, T. C. (2008) The Gall-Ghàidheil and Galloway. *Journal of Scottish Name Studies* 2, 19–50.
Downham, C. (2000) An imaginary Viking raid on Skye in 795? *Scottish Gaelic Studies* 20, 192–6.
Gammeltoft, P. (2004) Scandinavian–Gaelic contacts: Can place-names and place-name elements be used as a source for contact-linguistic research? *Nowele* 44 (March), 51–90.
Gammeltoft, P. (2007) Scandinavian naming-systems in the Hebrides – a way of understanding how Scandinavians were in contact with Gaels and Picts? In

B. Ballin Smith, S. Taylor and G. Williams (eds), *West Over the Sea: Studies in Scandinavian Sea-Borne Expansion and Settlement Before 1300*. Leiden: Brill, 479–95.

Gerriets, M. (1983) Economy and society: Clientship according to the Irish laws. *Cambridge Medieval Celtic Studies* 6, 42–61.

Grannd, S. (2000) *The Gaelic of Islay: A Comparative Study*. Aberdeen: Department of Celtic, University of Aberdeen.

Heather, P. (2009) *Empires and Barbarians*. London: Pan Books.

Helle, K. (1993) Norway, 800–1200. In A. Faulkes and R. Perkins (eds), *Viking Revaluations*. Birmingham: Viking Society for Northern Research, 1–14.

Holliday, J. (2016) *Longships on the Sand*. Scarinish, Isle of Tiree: An Iodhlann Press.

Holm, P. (1986) The slave trade of Dublin, ninth to twelfth centuries. *Peritia* 5, 317–45.

Hudson, B. (1999) The changing economy of the Irish Sea province: AD 900–1300. In B. Smith (ed.), *Britain and Ireland, 900–1300: Insular Responses to Medieval European Change*. Cambridge: Cambridge University Press, 39–66.

Iosad, P. (2020) The life cycle of preaspiration in the Gaelic languages. In J. Kopaczyk and R. McColl Millar (eds), *Language on the Move across Domains and Communities*. Aberdeen: FRLSU, 200–30.

Jennings, A. and A. Kruse (2009) From Dál Riata to the Gall-Ghàidheil. *Viking and Medieval Scandinavia* 5, 123–49.

Kelly, F. (1997) *Early Irish Farming: A Study Based Mainly on the Law-texts of the 7th and 8th Centuries AD*. Dublin: Dublin Institute for Advanced Studies.

Kruse, A. (2004) Norse topographical settlement names on the western littoral of Scotland. In J. Adams and K. Holman (eds), *Scandinavia and Europe 800–1350: Contact, Conflict and Coexistence*. Turnhout: Brepols, 99–109.

Lamont, W. D. (1966) *The Early History of Islay (500–1726)*. Glasgow: Lamont, W. D.

MacBain, A. (1893–4) The Norse element in the topography of the Highlands and Islands. *Transactions of the Gaelic Society of Inverness* 19, 217–45.

Maceacherna, D. (1976) *The Lands of the Lordship: The Romance of Islay's Names*. Port Charlotte: Argyll Reproductions.

McKerral, A. (1943–4) Ancient denominations of agricultural land in Scotland: A summary of recorded opinions, with some notes, observations and references. *Proceedings of the Society of Antiquaries of Scotland* 78, 39–80.

Macniven, A. (2015) *The Vikings in Islay: The Place of Names in Hebridean Settlement History*. Edinburgh: John Donald.

Munch, P. A. (1949) Social adjustment among Wisconsin Norwegians. *American Sociological Review* 14(6) (December), 780–7.

Nelson, J. (1991) *The Annals of St-Bertin*. Manchester: Manchester University Press.

Nicolaisen, W. F. H. (2001) *Scottish Place-names: Their Study and Significance* (revised edn). Edinburgh: John Donald.

Olsen, M. (1934) *Hvad våre stedsnavn lærer oss*. Oslo: Stenersen.

Price, L. (1963) A note on the use of the word *Baile* in place-names. *Celtica* 6, 119–26.

Scott, L. (1954) The Norse in the Hebrides. In W. D. Simpson (ed.), *The Viking Congress*. Edinburgh and London: Oliver and Boyd, 189–215.

Sinclair, J. (1983) *The Statistical Account of Scotland 1791–1799*. Wakefield: EP Publishing.

Smith, G. G. (1895) *The Book of Islay: Documents Illustrating the History of the Island*. Edinburgh: Privately published.

Stewart, T. W. (2004) Lexical Imposition: Old Norse vocabulary in Scottish Gaelic. *Diachronica* 21(2), 393–420.

Thomas, F. W. L. (1874–6) Did the Norsemen extirpate the inhabitants of the Hebrides in the Ninth Century? *Proceedings of the Society of Antiquaries of Scotland* 11, 472–507.

Thomas, F. W. L. (1881–2) On Islay place-names. *Proceedings of the Society of Antiquaries of Scotland* 16, 241–76.

Watson, W. J. (1904) *Place Names of Ross and Cromarty*. Inverness: Northern Counties Printing and Publishing.

Whyte, A. C. (2014) Gruline, Mull, and other Inner Hebridean *Things*. *Journal of Scottish Name Studies* 8, 115–52.

Woolf, A. (2004) The age of Sea-Kings: 900–1300. In D. Omand (ed.), *The Argyll Book*. Edinburgh: Birlinn, 94–9.

Woolf, A. (2007) *From Pictland to Alba 789–1070*. Edinburgh: University of Edinburgh Press.

Chapter 10

Understanding the Norse Period through Place-name Evidence: A Case Study from the Island of Mull

Alasdair C. Whyte

As tools for understanding Scotland's Norse period, place-names are invaluable. The place-name evidence, especially when considered alongside local archaeological and historical evidence, suggests that we need to be more circumspect about the dates we use to define Scotland's Norse period. This chapter focuses on the place-names of a relatively small area within one of the islands off Scotland's west coast – the island of Mull – which has major implications for our understanding of the Norse period in the Hebrides and the wider North Atlantic.

Many of Scotland's place-names were coined between 500 and 1000 (Taylor 1998: 1). Place-names are therefore key artefacts for at least part of Mull's Norse period, if not this period in its entirety. In terms of dating the beginning of Mull's Norse period, 795 is a reliable watershed. This is the year in which an entry in a contemporary year-by-year chronicle – *The Annals of Inisfallen* – records pagans plundering the monastery of Mull's neighbouring island of Iona, which had been established in the 6th century (*AI* 795.2). The native language of these pagans was Old Norse. From at least as early as 795 then, speakers of Old Norse were active in the vicinity of Mull and the implication is that at least some of Mull's Old Norse place-names may have been established from around this date.

The very fact that Old Norse place-names exist in Mull at all provides evidence of resident Old Norse-speakers on the island, although this was not always the prevailing view among scholars (see, for example, Nicolaisen 1992; but see Kruse 2004; Rixson 2010; Whyte 2017: 77). Moreover, the fact that these Old Norse place-names survive long enough to be recorded among Mull's settlement-names when they first appear en masse in textual sources in the 15th century provides evidence of some degree of continuity and stability in the resident population from the Norse period into the subsequent period – a period in which Gaelic was the predominant language of the island. In other words, the shift from Old Norse being the predominant language used to create new place-names in at least some parts of Mull to Gaelic being the predominant language used in local place-naming did not involve Gaelic-speakers exterminating

Old Norse-speakers. Instead, this language shift happened within family groups and communities. Place-names were passed down through the generations. Without this continuity and stability, it is highly unlikely that our 15th-century sources would contain Old Norse place-names. These names would have been replaced by names of Gaelic origin. Gaelic had also been the predominant language in Mull for at least two hundred years before 795, as place-names, personal names and other evidence in contemporary local sources, such as year-by-year chronicles and the *Life of St Columba*, clearly indicate (see, for example, Clancy 2011a: 381). This makes local place-name research challenging given that it is often very difficult to identify whether any given Gaelic place-name in Mull pre-dates or post-dates 795. In the body of this chapter, we will consider two Gaelic place-names in Mull, Laggan and Moy, alongside local archaeological and historical evidence, and consider the implications of their likely pre-Norse origins for answering perhaps the most controversial question of all regarding the Norse period in the Hebrides: Was there continuity and stability within the resident local population from the pre-Norse period into the Norse period and beyond?

The geographical focus of our case study is the area around the head of Loch Buie: a major sea-loch in south-east Mull (NGR: NM598229) (Figure 10.1). Firstly, it is striking that the most valuable settlements (landholdings) of this area in our earliest textual sources have names of Gaelic origin. Had Old Norse names ever been established for these settlements, we would expect them to survive long enough to be recorded in our 15th-century sources, as indeed they do elsewhere in Mull. We will return to Old Norse names elsewhere in Mull. However, focusing firstly on the Loch Buie area, the most valuable settlement of the seventeen settlements recorded within the local historical district of Moloros in a royal charter (legal document) of 1494 is Laggan (recorded in the source as *lagan*) (*ALI* no. A42; *RMS* ii no. 2200). At two pennylands, it is twice the value of the next most valuable settlement, this value being a measure of the agricultural capability of its lands. The name of the modern farm here is Laggan Farm (NM628238; OS2015, Sheet Number 375). It is possible that the name Laggan is from the Gaelic word *lagan* meaning 'a small hollow' – a productive element in Scottish place-names. However, there is strong place-name, archaeological and historical evidence for this place-name instead being derived from the Old Gaelic word *locán* meaning 'a Christian site', or perhaps more precisely 'a monastery' (eDIL; Clancy 2016: 31–43), and for it being a place-name of pre-Norse origin. The first piece of archaeological evidence for a pre-Norse Christian site in the vicinity of Laggan comes in the form of a cross-incised stone built into the porch of the nearby 19th-century episcopal church which lies around 2km north-west of Laggan Farm (CANMORE ID: 22396). This yellow sandstone slab bears an outline ringed cross and is one of

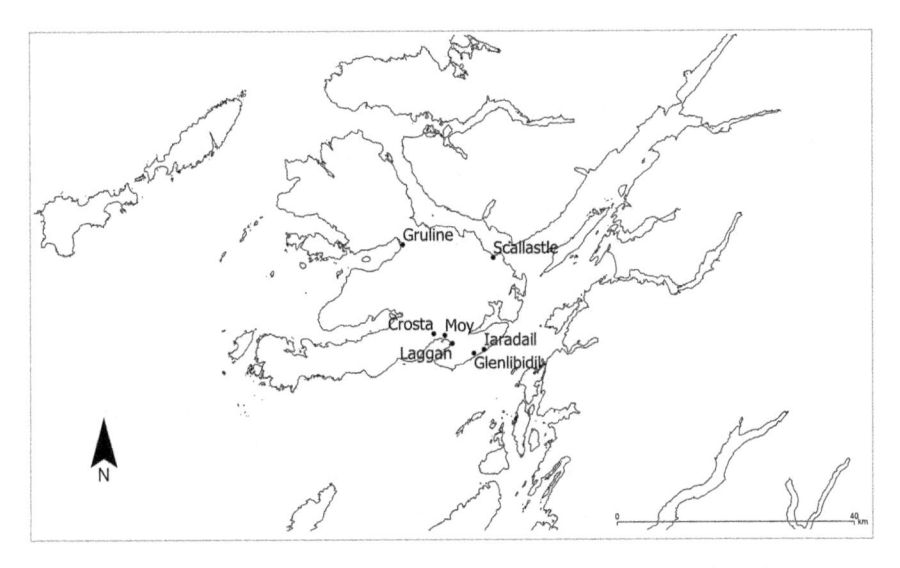

Figure 10.1 Places in south-east Mull mentioned in this chapter. A. Whyte.

a corpus of ringed crosses identified as having been influenced by freestanding crosses, therefore suggesting an origin in the second half of the 8th century (Fisher 2001: 38). Considering this Early Christian sculpture, it is significant that a nearby chapel (NGR: NM626236), identified as a medieval parish church (Thomas 2008: 115, 141, fig. 30), is dedicated to St Coinneach, a saint typically known as St Kenneth within an English-speaking context (Hannan 1926: 194). The name of this chapel – Caibeal Mheomhair meaning 'chapel of remembrance' – and its present condition owe much to 19th-century restoration but its south window has the appearance of 12th-century work and the window may well be in secondary use (CANMORE ID: 22395). The chapel lies around 350m south-west of Laggan Farm. There is more evidence for local veneration of St Coinneach: a 1509 document which records lands near Laggan being bequeathed to the church of St Coinneach (NRS E38/339; ER xiii 212–13) and the nearby shieling-name Àirigh Choinnich (NM663240) which, considering the evidence, is likely best translated as 'St Coinneach's shieling'. It is likely that this shieling formed part of the lands of a local church-estate with a church dedicated to St Coinneach at its core (Whyte 2017: 136–9). This is hugely significant considering the correlation between dedications to St Coinneach and known pre-Norse church sites elsewhere in Argyll and the southern Hebrides. There is Early Christian sculpture at three church sites in Argyll where St Coinneach is commemorated: Cill Chainnich in Iona, Cill Choinnich in Tiree and Kilchenzie in Kintyre (Butter 2007: i 128; LSS: 369; Whyte 2017: 30). It has, subsequently, been suggested that commemorations of St Coinneach in South Uist in the Outer Hebrides pre-date the Norse Age (Clancy and Evemalm 2019; Clancy 2021: 35).

To summarise, place-names and archaeology provide strong evidence that Laggan originally referred to a pre-Norse Christian site at the head of Loch Buie. The implication is of a degree of continuity and stability from the pre-Norse period into the Norse period and beyond.

There is further support for continuity and stability in the name of Laggan's neighbouring settlement to the north-west, Moy (NM616247). The 1494 charter which provides our earliest known form of Laggan records this settlement-name as *moy* and its value as one pennyland: half the value of neighbouring Laggan. The name Moy derives from the Old Gaelic term *mag* which, at a basic level, means 'a plain'. The place-name's anglicised form, Moy, is also found nearby in the name Moy Castle (NM616247), a late-medieval secular power centre and seat of Maclean (later Maclaine) of Lochbuie. There is no evidence for the castle having been built on the site of an earlier secular power centre (Thomas 2008: 115; CANMORE ID: 22392) but Moy is precisely the place-name we would expect to find at the heart of a pre-Norse early medieval Gaelic polity. As comparative place-name evidence tells us, the Old Gaelic term *mag* was applied in place-names to areas of well-cultivated land which formed the core of *túatha* (small kingdoms) in the early medieval Gaelic-speaking world (Charles-Edwards 2000: 13; Mac Mathúna 2004: 156). Importantly, contemporary sources such as the *Life of Saint Columba* tell us that the term was productive in the Hebrides in the pre-Norse period (*VC* I 30; Sharpe 1995: 21). To summarise, Laggan and Moy are precisely the place-names that we would expect to find in a pre-Norse Gaelic namescape in the Hebrides, based on comparative place-name evidence from the contemporary Gaelic-speaking world. They provide compelling evidence for continuity and stability in the local namescape and, therefore, the local population from the pre-Norse period into the Norse period and beyond.

In order to fully understand this continuity and stability and begin to reconstruct an historical narrative for the Norse period in this part of Mull, we must also consider the place-names of Old Norse origin which are recorded in the vicinity of Laggan and Moy in the royal charter of 1494. As we have seen, these Old Norse place-names provide us with unequivocal evidence that Old Norse was spoken in this area long enough for local place-names in this language to become established. As we will see, analysis of the agricultural capability of these settlements bearing Old Norse names, as well as individual words within the place-names, can significantly improve our understanding of the Norse period in this area. Firstly, the settlements bearing Old Norse names are of relatively low value when compared to Laggan and Moy. There are three names of certain Old Norse origin within 5.5km of Laggan, and each of them applies to a settlement valued at a quarter of Laggan's value: Iaradail

(NM679234) from Old Norse *Jǫrfadal* meaning 'gravel-dale'; Dibadil (NM667223; now Glenlibidil) from Old Norse *Djúpadal* meaning 'deep dale'; and Crosta (NM593247; now Gortenasroine) from Old Norse *Krossstaði* meaning 'cross-stead' or 'cross-farm' (Whyte 2017). The last of these names is particularly significant given that the Old Norse term *kross* which makes up the first part of the name almost certainly refers to a Christian monument (Whyte 2017: 197–202; see also Gammeltoft 2001: 110). The implication of the name Crosta and of other local evidence, such as a well dedicated to Calum Cille (St Columba) whose cult can be shown to have been appropriated by Hebridean Norse (Whyte 2017: 65–6), is of a resident Christian population in this place when this name was established by local people speaking Old Norse. We should consider the possibility that these residents were in fact Old Norse-speaking Christians (Whyte 2017: 142–3).

To summarise, the Old Norse place-names of the Loch Buie area tell a story of Old Norse-speakers inhabiting places of relatively poor agricultural capability and, in Crosta, of a possible resident population of Old Norse-speaking Christians. This raises new questions. When did these Old Norse-speakers establish names such as Crosta? To whom were the inhabitants of places like Crosta subject when these names were established? We should consider the possibility that the Old Norse place-names of the Loch Buie area were not, in fact, established in the immediate aftermath of 795 but at a later date.

Before we try to answer these questions in more detail, we must consider the fact that some Old Norse place-names in Mull refer to the most valuable settlements recorded in their respective districts. In the old district of Forsa to the north of Loch Buie in central eastern Mull, the most valuable settlements in the 1494 charter bear Old Norse names: Gruline (NM547398), likely derived from Old Norse *Grjýting* meaning 'stones-place' (Whyte 2017: 243–5; see also Whyte 2014), and Scallastle (NM699381) from Old Norse *Skál-stǫðul* meaning 'milking-place at the hollow' (Whyte 2017: 296–303). The implication of this place-name evidence is that Old Norse was the predominant language of the inhabitants of the two most valuable settlements in the medieval district of Forsa long enough for these place-names to become established. The district-name Forsa is itself a place-name of Old Norse origin from *Forsá* meaning 'waterfall-river'.

The Norse period in Mull is clearly complex. The island's place-names tell us of an Old Norse-speaking elite in places like Gruline and Scallastle but of a seemingly lower-class Old Norse-speaking population in places like Iaradail, Dibadil and Crosta in an area of Mull where the evidence suggests that the Church may have remained strong and retained possession of the most valuable local lands. If we accept the compelling evidence that Laggan and Moy are place-name survivals from the pre-Norse period, we should perhaps see the name Crosta, for example, as evidence of a local Gaelic-speaking Christian elite facilitating the local settlement of Old Norse-speakers, perhaps patronising the local church of St Coinneach. As Lesley Abrams has suggested, we should envisage a situation in some parts of the Hebrides in which landholders had to fit into existing Christian frameworks, advantages being available for some in joining the Christian establishment (Abrams 2007: 173). In this way, the continued strength of the Church locally would provide an incentive for Norse settlers to emulate local culture, including adoption of the Gaelic language, which would have facilitated communication with church people and a Gaelic-speaking elite in neighbouring areas. It is noteworthy that areas of the mainland adjacent to Mull retained their pre-Norse Gaelic districtnames into the medieval period and beyond – for example, Lorn, from *Cenél Loairn* meaning 'kindred of Loarn' (*CPNS*, 121) and Kinelvadon (*OPS* II i: 188–90), from *Cenél mBáetáin* meaning 'kindred of Báetán', a name understood to have applied to the district later known as Morvern (*CPNS*, 122–3; Fraser 2009: 245). Mull and Morvern are separated by little more than a mile of sea in places. In relation to the church, we should consider the proposed pre-Norse origins of Laggan, Moy and a local dedication to St Coinneach within the context of the survival of the pre-Norse name Iona and a local dedication to St Columba on that island off the south-west tip of Mull. There is strong evidence that Iona's pre-Norse prominence was undiminished in the Norse period (Clancy 1996, 2004, 2011b) and perhaps we should envisage the same at Laggan.

We should conclude by returning to the main question posed above: When did Old Norse-speakers establish names such as Crosta in Mull? We would be naive to assume that the names Gruline and Crosta, for example, were established at a single moment in time. While we might envisage a situation in which an Old Norse-speaking elite settled in places like Gruline and Scallastle and facilitated the settlement of Old Norsespeakers of lower status in the Loch Buie area, it is tempting to envisage Old Norse names such as Crosta being established by a later wave of Old Norse-speaking Christian settlers from elsewhere. The expulsion of pagan Norse from Dublin in 902, for example, or events like it, might be seen as an avenue by way of which some Old Norse-speakers came to settle in Mull within pre-existing Christian frameworks, as has been proposed for Norse settlement elsewhere (Dodgson 1957: 309). In light of close analysis of the place-name evidence, commentaries which propose pan-Hebridean models (Macniven 2013) or neat linear divisions of the Hebrides into outer and inner zones of Norse settlement (Jennings and Kruse 2009: 135, fig. 2) are overly simplistic. The placename evidence demands us to take a more critical view of traditional narratives which pit Norse-speakers against Gaelic-speakers and Norse culture against Gaelic culture across centuries. The reality of the Norse period is likely to have been more nuanced, more fluid, more dynamic. We need to be more alive to the human nature of linguistic and cultural change; for change occurring at faster and slower rates depending on local circumstances. Comprehensive local place-name surveys and more thorough analysis of place-names alongside archaeology and historical sources have the potential to significantly improve our understanding of the Norse period in places like Mull and across the North Atlantic.

References

Abrams, L. (2007) Conversion and the Church in the Hebrides in the Viking Age: 'A Very Difficult Thing Indeed'. In B. Ballin Smith, S. Taylor and G. Williams (eds), *West Over Sea: Studies in Scandinavian Sea-Borne Expansion and Settlement Before 1300, A Festschrift in Honour of Dr Barbara E. Crawford*. Leiden: Brill, 169–93.
AI Mac Airt, S. (ed.) (1951) *The Annals of Inisfallen*. Dublin: DIAS.
ALI Munro, J. and R. W. Munro (eds) (1986) *Acts of the Lords of the Isles, 1336–1493*. Edinburgh: Scottish History Society.
Butter, R. (2007) Butter, R. (2007) Cill-*names and Saints in Argyll: A Way towards Understanding the Early Church in Dal Riata?*, 2 vols. Unpublished PhD thesis, University of Glasgow.
Charles-Edwards, T. M. (2000) *Early Christian Ireland*. Cambridge: Cambridge University Press.
Clancy, T. O. (1996) Iona, Scotland, and the Céli Dé. In B. E. Crawford (ed.), *Scotland in Dark Age Britain*. St John's House Papers No. 6. St Andrews: Scottish Cultural Press, 111–30.
Clancy, T. O. (2004) Diarmait sapientissimus: The career of Diarmait dalta Daigre, Abbot of Iona. *Peritia* 17–18, 215–32.
Clancy, T. O. (2011a) Gaelic in Medieval Scotland: Advent and expansion. *Proceedings of the British Academy* 167 (2009 Lectures), 349–92.
Clancy, T. O. (2011b) Iona v. Kells: Succession, jurisdiction and politics in the Columban Familia in the later tenth century. In F. Edmonds and P. Russell (eds), *Tome: Studies in Medieval Celtic History and Law in Honour of Thomas Charles-Edwards*. Studies in Celtic History 31. Woodbridge: Boydell Press, 89–101.
Clancy, T. O. (2016) Logie: An ecclesiastical place-name element in eastern Scotland. *The Journal of Scottish Name Studies* 10, 25–88.
Clancy, T. O. (2021) The church and the domains of Gaelic in early medieval Scotland. In W. McLeod, A. Gunderloch, and R. Dunbar (eds), *Cànan & Cultar / Language & Culture. Rannsachadh na Gàidhlig 10*. Aberdeen: Aberdeen University Press, 19–46.
Clancy, T. O. and S. Evemalm (2019) Eòlas nan Naomh / Early Christianity in Uist. uistsaints.co.uk
CPNS Watson, W. J. (1926) *The History of the Celtic Place-Names of Scotland*. Reprinted Edinburgh, 2011. Edinburgh and London: Birlinn.
Dodgson, J. M. (1957) The background of Brunanburh. *Saga Book of the Viking Society* 14, 303–16.
eDIL (1976) Dictionary of the Irish Language based mainly on Old and Middle Irish examples. Dublin: Royal Irish Academy. Electronic version at edil.qub.ac.uk [Last viewed: 2 August 2021].

ER Stuart, J. et al. (eds) 1878–1908. *The Exchequer Rolls of Scotland*, Edinburgh.
Fisher, I. (2001) *Early Medieval Sculpture in the West Highlands and Islands*. Monograph Series 1. Edinburgh: Royal Commission on the Ancient and Historical Monuments of Scotland and the Society of Antiquaries of Scotland.
Fraser, J. E. (2009) *From Caledonia to Pictland: Scotland to 795*. Edinburgh: Edinburgh University Press.
Gammeltoft, P. (2001) *The Place-name Element* bólstaðr *in the North Atlantic Area*. Copenhagen: C. A. Reitzels Forlag A/S.
Hannan, T. (1926) *The Beautiful Isle of Mull with Iona and the Isle of Saints*. Edinburgh: R. Grant and Son.
Jennings, A. and A. Kruse (2009) From Dál Riata to the Gall-Ghàidheil. *Viking and Medieval Scandinavia* 5, 123–49.
Kruse, A. (2004) Norse topographical settlement names on the western littoral of Scotland. In J. Adams and K. Holman (eds), *Scandinavia and Europe 800–1350: Contact, Conflict and Coexistence*. Turnhout: Brepols, 109–19.
LSS Macquarrie, A. with R. Butter and contributions by S. Taylor and G. Márkus (eds) (2012) *Legends of Scottish Saints: Readings, Hymns and Prayers for the Commemorations of Scottish Saints in the Aberdeen Breviary*. Dublin: Four Courts Press.
Mac Mathúna, L. (2004) Continuity and change in early Irish words for 'plain': Exploring narrative text and place-name divergence. *Ériu* 54, 149–70.
Macniven, A. (2013) Modelling Viking migration to the Inner Hebrides. *Journal of the North Atlantic* Special Volume 4, 3–18.
Nicolaisen, W. F. H. (1992) Arran place names – A fresh look. *Northern Studies* 28, 1–13.
NRS E38/339 National Records of Scotland, unpublished source in Exchequer Records: Exchequer Rolls, 'Ballivi ad extra', June 1509.
OPS 1854 *Origines Parochiales Scotiae: The Antiquities Ecclesiastical and Territorial of the Parishes of Scotland*. 2 vols, vol. II in two parts. Edinburgh: Bannatyne Club.
Rixson, D. (2010) The shadow of 'onomastic graffiti'. *The Journal of Scottish Name Studies* 4, 131–58.
RMS *Registrum Magni Sigilli Regum Scottorum*. John Maitland Thomson et al. (eds). Edinburgh 1882–1914.
Sharpe, R. (ed.) (1995) *Adomnán of Iona: Life of St Columba*. London: Penguin.
Taylor, S. (1998) Introduction. In S. Taylor (ed.), *The Uses of Place-Names*. Edinburgh: Scottish Cultural Press, 1–11.
Thomas, S. E. (2008) *From Rome to 'the Ends of the Habitable World': The Provision of Clergy and Church Buildings in the Hebrides, circa 1266 to circa 1472*. Unpublished PhD thesis, University of Glasgow.
VC Anderson, A. O. and M. O. Anderson (eds) (1991) *Adomnán's Life of Columba*. Oxford: Clarendon Press.
Whyte, A. C. (2014) Gruline, Mull, and other Inner Hebridean *Things*. *The Journal of Scottish Name Studies* 8, 115–52.
Whyte, A. C. (2017) *Settlement-names and Society: Analysis of the Medieval Districts of Forsa and Moloros in the Parish of Torosay, Mull*. Unpublished PhD thesis, University of Glasgow.

Chapter 11

The Church and Gaelic–Norse Contact in the Hebrides

Thomas Owen Clancy

The two chief difficulties facing historians of the Hebrides in the Viking Age remain the extent to which Scandinavian settlement displaced the previous inhabitants on the islands and their language(s); and the pace and nature of the conversion of Scandinavians to Christianity. This short contribution considers the nexus between these two problems and proposes some potential solutions.

The linguistic problem has been much reviewed and remains inconclusive (the best recent review remains Jennings and Kruse 2009; see also Crawford 1981; Barrett 2004; Jennings and Kruse 2005; Kruse 2005; Clancy 2010; Macniven 2013, 2015; Whyte 2016; 2017; see also the wider contextual review in Woolf 2007: 275–311). Our key source of evidence is toponymy: the rich harvest of place-names of Old Norse derivation throughout the Hebrides assures us that Scandinavian presence was deep, long-term and linguistically influential. However, the fact that the Hebrides emerge into the historically better-attested period of the later Middle Ages as a strongly Gaelic-speaking region poses some searching questions. Did Norse completely replace Gaelic in the Hebrides for some of the period between c. 800 and c. 1300, and if so, for how long? Or was there some continuity from the pre-Viking period? If Gaelic was completely displaced, how then did it come to dominate in the later Middle Ages?

Although often forgotten, it is crucial to note that in linguistic terms the Hebrides prior to 800 were not evidently a homogenous region (see Jennings and Kruse 2005; 2009). While Gaelic was certainly the language of the region south of Ardnamurchan (historically the kingdom of Dál Riata), and we can demonstrate Gaelic dominance in islands such as Islay and Tiree, matters are more difficult north of Ardnamurchan. The presumption, based on art-historical proxy evidence, is that this northern region prior to 800 had been predominantly Pictish-speaking. There is good reason to suspect the spread of Gaelic-speaking ruling kindreds, and churches, into this northern region across the later 7th and through the 8th century (see Fraser 2004; Jennings and Kruse 2009; Clancy forthcoming), but to what extent, if at all, this led to the northern region adopting Gaelic as a language is unknowable. A point I will return to below is that Gaelic may well have been the main language of the church, whatever the nature of the wider speech-community in the northern Hebrides was (on this, see further Clancy 2021). The importance of this point is that, if Gaelic was not the community language of the northern part of this zone before 800, then 'continuity' of Gaelic either is a chimera or needs to be sought in a different sociolinguistic context.

The reason for drawing this distinction for understanding the linguistic impact of Scandinavian settlement is that that settlement was in two different zones. In the northern zone, Norse-speakers were most likely coming into contact with Pictish, a language which would be, as far as we can tell, extinct even in eastern Scotland by the 11th century, and hence a language increasingly without wider status or nearby speech community. In the southern zone, on the other hand, Norse was encountering Gaelic, a language with a very extensive wider community of speakers in immediately neighbouring regions: in Ireland, to which the Hebrides were still closely connected, and in eastern Scotland, where it was a language on the ascendancy, and from c. 900 the overt language of the kings of Alba. We might expect different results from these different underlying situations.

Even in this southern zone, however, recent commentators have seen the linguistic effect of Scandinavian settlement as creating a *tabula rasa*. Alan Macniven (2015, and this volume) in particular has argued forcefully that there is no clear evidence of the survival of Gaelic place-names from the pre-Norse period in Islay, the southernmost of the Inner Hebrides. While Macniven's demonstration of Scandinavian influence on Islay is commanding, the extent to which the Gaelic side of his case is proven is less clear (see Whyte 2016). A different, more balanced view of Scandinavian settlement in the southern Hebrides is to be found in Alasdair Whyte's doctoral thesis on the settlement names of Torosay parish, Mull, which envisages a patchwork of localities on Mull in which either Scandinavian dominance or Gaelic continuity can be differently discerned (Whyte 2017, and this volume). John Holliday's recent review of the evidence for Tiree is also more nuanced, envisaging the possibility of some linguistic continuity (drawing on the work of Richard Cox elsewhere) but admitting the lack of clear evidence (Holliday 2016: 145–9; cf. Cox 2007, 2009).

One of the key issues is that, aside from some major island names, it is difficult to point to a clear class of Gaelic place-names or name-types which can be demonstrated to have pre-dated Scandinavian settlement. Even for those names which have been suggested as being pre-Scandinavian, we lack a clear explanation for how such names would have been preserved, given the otherwise strong evidence in much of the Hebrides for very extensive, if not complete, Scandinavian domination. A potential

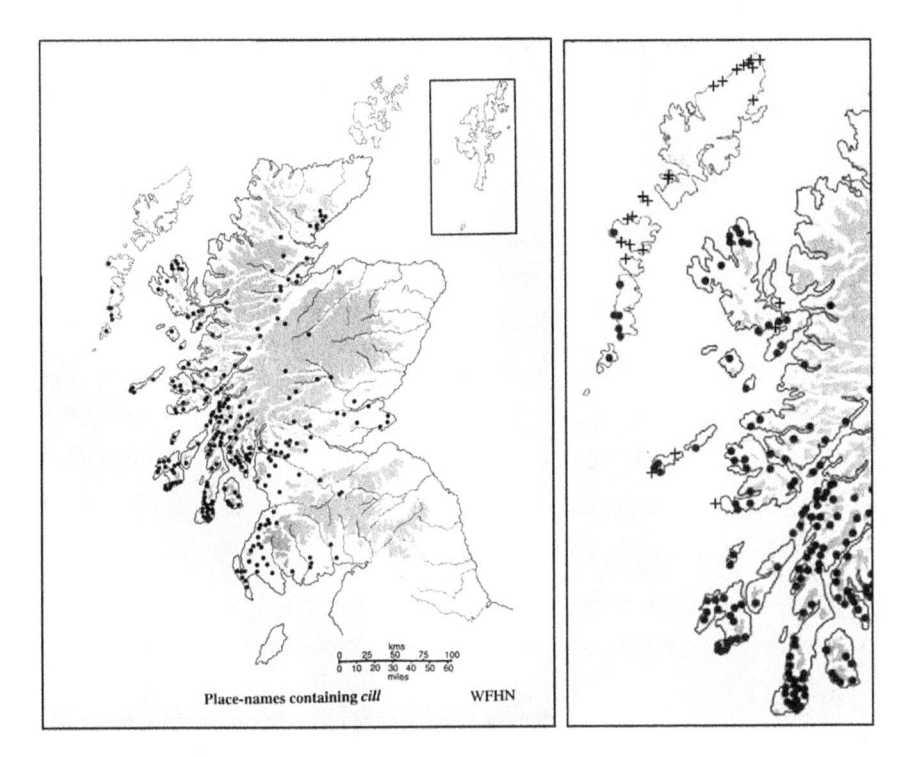

Figure 11.1 Map by W. F. H. Nicolaisen of place-names containing *cill* in Scotland; with detail of Hebrides, to which place-names in *teampull* have been added by the author, marked with +. Data on *teampull* is taken from the Saints in Scottish Place-Names web resource (saintsplaces.gla.ac.uk). Neither map should be treated as completely comprehensive, pending detailed surveys of the Hebrides. The map is reproduced with permission of the Trustees of the Scottish Medievalists: The Society for Scottish Medieval and Renaissance Studies. It was originally published in P. McNeill and H. MacQueen (eds), *Atlas of Scottish History to 1707*. Edinburgh: The Scottish Medievalists, 1996: 59.

exception, remarked on by commentators such as Whyte (2016, 2017) and Holliday (2016: 69–70), are ecclesiastical names, particularly those employing the Gaelic element *cill* (Figure 11.1), originally *cell* 'a church' followed by a saint's name (reviews of this category of names can be found in Macdonald 1979; Butter 2007; Clancy 2014). These are plentiful throughout the Hebrides aside from Lewis and Harris where, however, there is some possibility of generic substitution having occurred in names which contain *teampull* (for example, Teampull Mholuaidh), masking names which had earlier contained *cill*, a phenomenon demonstrably found elsewhere (see Clancy and Evemalm-Graham 2019, s.n. Teampull

Chaluim Chille; Macdonald 1979: 14; and for Lewis chapel sites, Barrowman 2020; for Teampull Mholuaidh, 13–19). While we lack Viking-Age or earlier church buildings at these sites, a number have early medieval sculptural evidence, encouraging the possibility of continuity of usage (for example, Figure 11.2).

We lack full studies of these names from throughout the region, but a number of corpora from among them have been examined. Holliday (2016: 69–70), for instance, envisages the possibility that the *cill*-names on Tiree could pre-date Scandinavian settlement. The saints commemorated here (for instance, Cainnech and Moluag) are not easily explained as later introductions of the high Middle Ages, nor does the pattern of sites where *cill*-names are found conform easily to later medieval ecclesiastical structures. Some Scandinavian names on Tiree, such as Circnis ('church promontory': Holliday 2016: 305–7), imply the presence of churches there during the period of Norse speech, churches which themselves otherwise have Gaelic names, commemorating for the most part Gaelic saints (for further discussion of the evidence from Tiree, see now McNamara 2021: ch. 6). With Sofia Evemalm-Graham, I have recently reviewed the evidence for the Uists and Benbecula (see Clancy and Evemalm-Graham 2019). While there was some evidence for the creation of churches dedicated to saints from the Scandinavian period, such as St Olaf (d. 1029), and while many saints, such as Peter, are highly ambiguous in terms of when churches might have been commemorating them (ibid., s.nn. Olaf, Peter), nonetheless, our conclusion was that on the whole the pattern and nature of the saints' dedication on the Uists was best explained as partly a creation of the pre-Viking Age (ibid., Project Introduction). It seems likely that close examination of patterns of *cill*-names elsewhere, in particular on Islay, Mull and Skye, would suggest something similar.

One thing that can be said for certain: despite all the Norse place-names of the Hebrides, there is not a single name preserved which employs an Old Norse ecclesiastical term as a generic, in a form which would reflect a Norse original like **Olafskirkja* or **Peterskirkja*, although we have *kirkja* preserved as a specific element in many names, such as *Circnis* 'church promontory' or *Circeabost* 'church settlement' (Holliday 2016: 304–7; Clancy and Evemalm-Graham 2019, s.nn. Kirkidale, *Kirkibost). There is, in fact, one record of such a name in Norse saga, as *Kólumkilla kirkju inni litlu* 'the little Colum Cille's church' (Jónsson 1893: 245), referring to a church on Iona, probably St Columba's shrine chapel (on which, see Campbell and Maldonado 2020: 63–6), but this seems exceptional, and also does not certainly reflect local usage (see Gammeltoft 2007: 484, though his identification of the church in question is incorrect). Given the intensity of the preservation of Norse place-names otherwise throughout the Hebrides, and the fact that Hebridean Scandinavians were likely largely Christian by the 11th or 12th centuries, this seems a significant and suggestive absence.

Figure 11.2 Early medieval cross from the graveyard at Kilmuir, North Uist. See Clancy and Evemalm-Graham 2019, s.n. 'Kilmuir'. See Fisher 2001: 43 for discussion. Photo by the author.

How and why would Gaelic names for churches be marked by continuity across a period of such displacement otherwise in terms of language and settlement? I have recently suggested that one way to understand this is by reference to the church as a particular sociolinguistic domain, one where, by the 8th century, Gaelic was the language of status, and the main language used by the professionals who staffed the churches, not only in the Gaelic-speaking regions of Ireland and Dál Riata, but elsewhere as well, such as Pictland (Clancy 2021). As such, even during the period of Scandinavian settlement, the church is likely to have remained a Gaelic-speaking sociolinguistic domain, and hence church settlements would have been Gaelic-speaking enclaves. What slim evidence we have of church personnel in the Hebrides between 800 and 1200 reveals a solidly Gaelic personal-name stock.

To propose this, then, is also to propose that there was some continuity of the church across the Viking Age. Here, we enter that other difficult topic mentioned at the start, the pace and nature of the conversion of Scandinavians to Christianity. The best and clearest review for the Hebrides remains that by Lesley Abrams (2007), which the present study at best supplements. The problem is fundamentally one of evidence – it is difficult to make the various dots join up. How clear can we be about the nature of the paganism of early Norse settlement, and the attitude of settlers towards the religion of the locals? The primary evidence for paganism is in the form of burials, but as has been much emphasised, the period of overtly pagan burials in the Hebrides may be less than a century (Graham-Campbell and Batey 1998: 152–4), leaving much of the time period uncertain in terms of religious practice (and see Márkus 2017: 242 on the religious ambiguity of some burials).

Any argument for an anti-Christian element to Norse paganism is of course largely driven by the early records of destruction of monasteries. This needs to be offset by the observation that Christians also raided and destroyed monasteries, in Ireland and elsewhere, during the same period (see Lucas 1967). That the early Scandinavian settlers in the Hebrides were pagan need not mean that they were intrinsically intolerant of other religionists. There is some limited evidence of the preservation of saints' cults within Old Norse island names, for instance Barra and Taransay (see, for example, comments of Jennings 1998: 51). While Christianity is hard-wired to exclude the culting of other gods, polytheistic paganism should not necessarily be averse to the incorporation of new gods, or new powerful sacred figures such as saints. As Jón Víðar Sigurðsson (2014: 230) notes, 'It also has to be underlined that the Old Norse religion was a tolerant religion, respecting other beliefs and adopting Christian elements. It was not "one" religion, as the term "Old Norse religion" indirectly implies; rather, it was an ethnic religion with strong local variations that made it more difficult to withstand the pressure of Christianity.' Sigurðsson further notes the suggestion of Torstein Jørgensen that, since 'the Old Norse religion was an ethnic religion and its gods were linked to regions in the north', it might have been perceived that 'they could not protect the Vikings when travelling abroad', and hence new supernatural protectors linked to the new country needed to be acquired (ibid.: 228, citing Jørgensen 1996; see further, Abram 2014). There might then be good reason to imagine a context in which Scandinavian settlers respected and accommodated the churches and church personnel of the islands on which they settled, once they lived in those islands and were no longer merely seasonal raiders. The presence of saints in island-names such as Barra and Taransay may lend some credence to this idea; as also perhaps the presence of *papar* names in the northern zone (Crawford et al. 2005). A parallel might be sought in the area around Dublin where, Fiona Edmonds notes, 'the relatively prolific local churches of pre-Viking Ireland seem to have survived and thrived in Scandinavia-settled areas' (Edmonds 2019: 133). David Wilson's recent reflections on the accommodation of Christianity by Scandinavians in the Isle of Man – as well as the clear signs of mixing with Gaels – afforded by sculpture and inscriptions on Man is well worth bringing into the argument, as it has the potential to allow us to look at the Hebridean evidence with fresh eyes (Wilson 2014).

Two of the better evidenced churches of the Hebrides suggest that this model is one worth pursuing. Both Iona and Eigg seem to demonstrate, through sculptural and textual evidence, some continuity of use as going Christian concerns throughout the Viking Age, even, in the case of Iona, perhaps a thriving centre. There is not the space here to examine these case studies in detail, but Andrew Jennings (1998) has reviewed the case of Iona, and recent archaeological work has underlined his main thesis (see Campbell et al. 2019; Maldonado et al., 2021); while I explore the situation of Eigg in a number of places (Clancy 2015; 2021, forthcoming). The church presents us, then, with a possible way of understanding the mixed signals of disruption and continuity – linguistic, cultural and religious – in the Hebrides during the Viking Age. This is not a full solution to the problems of the period, but it has the potential to contribute some nuance to the ongoing scholarly argument.

Acknowledgements

I would like to thank Alex Woolf and Lesley Abrams for supply of articles and ideas in the preparation of this piece. They bear no responsibility for the contents.

References

Abram, C. (2014) The two 'modes of religiosity' in conversion-era Scandinavia. In I. Garipzanov (ed.), *Conversion and Identity in the Viking Age*. Turnhout: Brepols, 21–48.

Abrams, L. (2007) Conversion and the Church in the Hebrides in the Viking Age: 'A Very Difficult Thing Indeed'. In B. Ballin Smith, S. Taylor and G. Williams (eds), *West Over Sea: Studies in Scandinavian Sea-Borne Expansion and Settlement before 1300. A Festschrift in honour of Dr Barbara E. Crawford*. Leiden: Brill, 169–93.

Barrowman, R. C. (2020) Chapel-sites on the Isle of Lewis: Results of the Lewis Coastal Chapel-sites Survey. Society of Antiquaries of Scotland: *Scottish Archaeological Internet Reports* 88: https://doi.org/10.9750/issn.2056-7421.2020.88

Barrett, J. H. (2004) Beyond war or peace? The study of culture contact in Viking-age Scotland. In J. Hines, A. Lane and M. Redknap (eds), *Land, Sea and Home: Proceedings of a Conference on Viking-period Settlement at Cardiff, July 2001*. Society for Medieval Archaeology monograph 20. Leeds: Society for Medieval Archaeology, 207–18.

Butter, R. (2007) Cill- *names and Saints in Argyll: A Way Towards Understanding the Early Church in Dál Riata?*. Unpublished PhD thesis, University of Glasgow.

Campbell, E., C. E. Batey, G. Murray and C. Thickpenny (2019) Furnishing an Early Medieval monastery: New evidence from Iona. *Medieval Archaeology* 63(2), 298–337.

Campbell, E. and A. Maldonado (2020) A new Jerusalem 'at the ends of the earth': Interpreting Charles Thomas's excavations at Iona Abbey 1956–63. *The Antiquaries Journal* 100, 374–407.

Clancy, T. O. (2010) Gaelic in Medieval Scotland: Advent and expansion (Sir John Rhys Memorial lecture, 2009). *Proceedings of the British Academy* 167, 349–92.

Clancy, T. O. (2014) Saints in the Scottish landscape. *Proceedings of the Harvard Celtic Colloquium, vol. xxxiii, 2013*, 1–34.

Clancy, T. O. (2015) *St Donnan of Eigg: Context and Cult*. Eigg History Society: http://www.spanglefish.com/eigghistorysociety/index.asp?pageid=616291

Clancy, T. O. (2021) The church and the domains of Gaelic in early medieval Scotland. In W. McLeod, A. Gunderloch and R. Dunbar (eds), *Cànan is Cultar/Language and Culture: Rannsachadh na Gàidhlig 10*. Aberdeen: Aberdeen University Press, 19–46.

Clancy, T. O. (Forthcoming) St Donnan of Eigg: Martyrdom, monastery and cult.

Clancy, T. O. and S. Evemalm-Graham (2019) *Eòlas nan Naomh. Early Christianity in Uist*. Website: uistsaints.co.uk

Cox, R. A. V. (2007) Notes on the Norse impact upon Hebridean place-names. *Journal of Scottish Name Studies* 1, 139–44.

Cox, R. A. V. (2009) Towards a taxonomy of contact onomastics: Norse place-names in Scottish Gaelic. *Journal of Scottish Name Studies* 3, 15–29.

Crawford, B., I. Simpson and B. Ballin Smith (2005) *The Papar Project: The Hebrides*. Website: http://www.paparproject.org.uk/hebrides.html

Crawford, I. A. (1981) War or peace – Viking colonisation in the Northern and Western Isles of Scotland. In H. Bekker-Nielsen, P. G. Foote and O. Olsen (eds), *Proceedings of the Eighth Viking Congress*. Odense: Odense University Press, 259–69.

Edmonds, F. (2019) *Gaelic Influence in the Northumbrian Kingdom: The Golden Age and the Viking Age*. Woodbridge: Boydell Press.

Fisher, I. (2001) *Early Medieval Sculpture in the West Highlands and Islands*. Royal Commission on the Ancient and Historical Monuments of Scotland and Society of Antiquaries of Scotland monograph series 1. Edinburgh: Royal Commission on the Ancient and Historical Monuments of Scotland.

Fraser, J. E. (2004) The Iona Chronicle, the descendants of Áedán mac Gabráin, and the 'Principal Kindreds of Dál Riata'. *Northern Studies* 38, 77–96.

Gammeltoft, P. (2007) Scandinavian naming-systems in the Hebrides – a way of understanding how the Scandinavians were in contact with Gaels and Picts? In B. Ballin Smith, S. Taylor and G. Williams (eds), *West Over Sea: Studies in Scandinavian Sea-Borne Expansion and Settlement before 1300. A Festschrift in honour of Dr Barbara E. Crawford*. Leiden: Brill, 479–96.

Graham-Campbell, J. and C. E. Batey (1998) *Vikings in Scotland: An Archaeological Survey*. Edinburgh: Edinburgh University Press.

Holliday, J. (2016) *Longships on the Sand. Scandinavian and Medieval Settlement on the Island of Tiree: A Place-name Study*. Scarinish, Tiree: An Iodhlann Press.

Jennings, A. (1998) Iona and the Vikings: Survival and continuity. *Northern Studies* 33, 37–54.

Jennings, A. and A. Kruse (2005) An ethnic enigma – Norse, Pict and Gael in the Western Isles. In A. Mortensen (ed.), *Viking and Norse in the North Atlantic: Select Papers from the Proceedings of the Fourteenth Viking Congress,*

Tórshavn, 19–30 July 2001. Tórshavn: Foroya Fródskaparfelag (The Faroese Academy of Sciences) in collaboration with Foroya Fornminnissavn (Historical Museum of the Faroe Islands), 251–63.
Jennings, A. and A. Kruse (2009) One coast – Three peoples: Names and ethnicity in the Scottish West during the Early Viking Period. In A. Woolf (ed.), *Scandinavian Scotland – Twenty Years After*. St Andrews: University of St Andrews Committee for Dark Age Studies, 75–102.
Jónsson, F. (1893) *Snorri Sturluson, Heimskringla: Nóregs Konunga Sögur*. Copenhagen.
Jørgensen, T. (1996) Mision fra vest. In I. Montgomery and D. Thorkildsen (eds), *Kristninga av Norge: rapport fra etterutdanningskurs for lærere 20–21. November 1995: det Teologiske Facultet*. Oslo: University of Oslo, 12.
Kruse, A. (2005) Explorers, raiders and settlers. The Norse impact upon Hebridean place-names. In P. Gammeltoft, C. Hough and D. Waugh (eds), *Cultural Contacts in the North Atlantic Region: The Evidence of Names*. Lerwick: NORNA, Scottish Place-Name Society and Society for Name Studies in Britain and Ireland, 141–56.
Lucas, A. T. (1967) The plundering and burning of churches in Ireland, seventh to sixteenth centuries. In E. Rynne (ed.), *North Munster Studies*. Limerick: Thomond Archaeological Society, 172–229.
MacDonald, A. (1979) Gaelic *Cill (Kil(l)-)*. In Scottish Place-Names, *Bulletin of the Ulster Place-name Society*, series 2, vol. 2, 9–22.
McNamara, C. (2021) *Tracing the Community of Comgall across the North Channel: An Interdisciplinary Investigation of Early Medieval Monasteries at Bangor, Applecross, Lismore and Tiree*. Unpublished PhD thesis, University of Glasgow.
Macniven, A. (2013) Modelling Viking migration to the Inner Hebrides. *Journal of the North Atlantic* Special Volume 4, 3–18.
Macniven, A. (2015) *The Vikings in Islay: The Place of Names in Hebridean Settlement History*. Edinburgh: John Donald.
Maldonado, A., E. Campbell, T. O. Clancy and K. Forsyth (2021) Iona in the Viking Age: laying a 'zombie' narrative to rest. *Current Archaeology* 381 (27 October 2021), 18–25. https://the-past.com/feature/iona-in-the-viking-age-laying-a-zombie-narrative-to-rest-new/.
Márkus, G. (2017) *Conceiving a Nation: Scotland to AD 900*. Edinburgh: Edinburgh University Press.
Sigurðsson, J. V. (2014) Conversion and identity in the Viking-Age North: Some afterthoughts. In I. Garipzanov (ed.), *Conversion and Identity in the Viking Age*. Turnhout: Brepols, 225–44.
Whyte, A. (2016) Review of Alan Macniven, *The Vikings in Islay*. *Journal of Scottish Name Studies* 10, 213–18.
Whyte, A. (2017) *Settlement-names and Society: Analysis of the Medieval Districts of Forsa and Moloros in the Parish of Torosay, Mull*. Unpublished PhD thesis, University of Glasgow.
Wilson, D. M. (2014) The conversion of the Viking settlers in the Isle of Man. In I. Garipzanov (ed.), *Conversion and Identity in the Viking Age*. Turnhout: Brepols, 117–38.
Woolf, A. (2007) *From Pictland to Alba, 789–1070*. Edinburgh: Edinburgh University Press.

Part IV

Environmental Impact and Land Use

When Scandinavians arrived in Scotland, they brought with them subsistence practices from their homelands: animal husbandry, dairying, grain cultivation, an infield-outfield system and the intensified exploitation of marine resources (for example, Barrett and Richards 2017), and their impacts on the environment can be seen in the botanical and faunal material. These include the probable introduction of flax cultivation in Orkney (Bond and Hunter 1987), the practice of manuring crops and possibly hunting red deer to extinction in the Western Isles (Jones, this section). However, much of this evidence was previously overlooked; Graham-Campbell and Batey (1998: 50) noted that the original Jarlshof excavation publication (Hamilton 1956) had devoted only one page to environmental evidence, whereas by the late 1990s it was routine to recover environmental samples during excavation.

Since 1998, further developments in stable isotope analysis and aDNA, plus new approaches to studying older collections from sites such as Earl's Bu (Orphir, Orkney), are allowing researchers to learn not just which species were present on a site, but how they were used and the social implications of that management (see Jones and Mainland, both this section). Food production is now seen as part of a more complex social system which included gifting and displays of wealth, such as feasts hosted by the local Earls. Although attested to in written sources such as the *Orkneyinga Saga*, feasting is now convincingly identified in the archaeological record in Viking-Age Scotland, with evidence for the slaughter of animals for meat at a prime age and large-scale consumption causing farms to become increasingly specialised in the Late Norse period.

Scandinavians would have had to adapt their farming practices to suit the landscapes and soils of Scotland, and it appears that cultural contact between Scandinavians and native groups took place on the farm. Cattle were important to all groups during the Viking Age. Foster (this section) argues that the separation of milk cows from other cattle in shielings rather than grazing them all together, may have been a practice learnt by the Norse from the native inhabitants, as seen in the place-name elements of Gaelic *ærgi* and Old Norse *sætr*.

Since *Vikings in Scotland*, the continued development of environmental archaeological research using old and new collections, as well as a greater emphasis on the landscape rather than just specific sites, has resulted in exciting inroads into the study of the effect of the Norse on the wider rural landscape, economy and population of Scotland.

References

Barrett, J. and M. Richards (2017) Identity, gender, religion and economy: New isotope and radiocarbon evidence for marine resource intensification in Early Historic Orkney, Scotland, UK. *European Journal of Archaeology* 7(3), 249–71.

Bond, J. M. and J. R. Hunter (1987) Flax-growing in Orkney from the Norse period to the 18th century. *Proceedings of the Society of Antiquaries of Scotland* 117, 175–81.

Hamilton, J. R. C. (1956) *Excavations at Jarlshof, Shetland*. Edinburgh: HMSO.

Chapter 12

Isotope Zooarchaeology in Viking Scotland: Previous Research, Possibilities and Future Directions

Jennifer R. Jones

Over the last twenty years there have been huge advances in stable isotope archaeology, allowing the exploration of bone assemblages on a biomolecular level (Britton 2017). Specifically, isotope zooarchaeology has revolutionised our understanding of animal management and wider economies in a way that was not possible using solely traditional zooarchaeological methods (Makarewicz 2016). Stable isotope zooarchaeology can inform on changing land use strategies, control over the landscape, birth seasonality and the use of unusual fodder (Towers et al. 2011; Jones and Mulville 2016), all of which are central to understanding Viking interactions with the environment that they encountered during their diaspora to Scotland.

On arrival in Scotland, the Vikings needed to adapt to new and often quite challenging conditions. Many key Scottish Norse settlement sites are found in the insular locations of Orkney, Shetland and the Western Isles, representing a range of site types including farmsteads (for example, Bornais and Cille Pheadair [both South Uist], Quoygrew [Orkney]), Earl's palaces (like Earl's Bu, Orkney) and settlements (such as the Brough of Birsay, Orkney). Such insular locations can present unique challenges in terms of agriculture and pastoralism due to the fragile soils, saline conditions and geographical constraints. Regarding domestic stock, providing sufficient fodder for overwintering and locating fruitful pastures would have presented challenges to the populations inhabiting these insular locations. Populations settling in these regions would have been required to quickly adapt in order to survive and then thrive as Norse populations.

Successful economic strategies in Scotland during the Norse period were fundamental for several reasons. Firstly, large increases in populations in Scottish insular and coastal locations (Graham-Campbell and Batey 1998) meant that sufficient resources were needed to feed these larger volumes of people. Secondly, commensality and feasting were fundamental aspects of shaping identities, demonstrating power and asserting authority within the

Norse Earldoms (Mainland and Batey 2018), and required production of surplus resources and specialist products. Finally, the ability to contribute to emergent market economies was also fundamental to success in Norse Scotland, amid a changing world of centralised authorities, power and control (Barrett et al. 2000; Barrett et al. 2001). Resource production was a crucial political tool, as well as being essential for survival; for example, Viking-Age special animal deposits relating to sacrifices and feasting have been viewed as a way of legitimising political power, religion and identity (Lucas and McGovern 2007). The ability to rear domesticated animals for both meat and secondary products successfully, while protecting crops growing in fragile environments, was crucial to success for the Vikings and their subsequent Norse descendants.

This chapter summarises the current state of play of Norse isotope zooarchaeology in Scotland, with a focus on insular locations, where bone preservation and intensive excavation campaigns in recent years have allowed detailed isotopic investigations to be conducted. Key themes and research findings are outlined, before exploring future directions and areas for research to further enhance our understanding of Norse adaptations to the environments that they lived in.

State of play: Norse isotope zooarchaeology in Scotland

Baseline shifts and manuring of crops

Stable isotope values can be affected by a range of geographical and environmental factors, and baselines are crucial for determining expected values for a given location. Baseline changes, achieved through cross-period comparative studies of local wild and domestic fauna, can inform on human activities such as the introduction of manure to plants and crops (Bogaard et al. 2007; Fraser et al. 2011). The analysis of wild species alongside domesticates provides the most effective proxies for understanding natural isotopic signatures versus anthropogenically modified ones.

Within insular Scotland, baselines for Orkney and the Western Isles during prehistoric and Norse periods of occupation of the islands were constructed using large-scale analysis of wild and domestic species (Jones et al. 2012). A shift in the baseline $\delta^{15}N$ values between Orkney and the Western Isles during the Norse period, in comparison to the preceding prehistoric times, suggests that crops may have begun to be manured in the Norse period (Jones et al. 2012). Manuring is a valuable way of maximising the yield of crops, particularly when considering the fragile and nutrient-poor soils of the Western Isles, which reduces their suitability for agriculture (Smith 2012). The possibility of manuring having been practised is further supported by the presence of species such as flax and barley at sites such as Bornais (Summers and Bond 2020), which produce the best yields when provided with enriched soils (Dockrill 2007). Direct $\delta^{15}N$ analysis of plant remains themselves can help to explore manuring practises further, such as the duration of manuring and types of plants being manured (for example, Bogaard et al. 2007; Fraser et al. 2011). Stable isotope analysis of plant and animal remains from different contexts and phases of sites will allow more precise insights into when this practice first starts to be used. Nevertheless, current evidence of manuring suggests an innovation in Norse agricultural practices not seen in prehistoric periods of occupation in the islands.

Animal management in the wider landscape

Management and control of animals in the landscape would have been critical in ensuring that herbivores had access to sufficient grazing material without destroying precious arable land and crops. The challenges of agriculture in locations where nutrient-poor soils, saline environments and heavy wind erosion are experienced, such as the Outer Hebrides (Smith 2012), adds pressure to agriculturalists. Additionally, in insular locations good-quality arable land is at a premium due to geographical restrictions such as mountains and coastlines.

Bone collagen analysis, which reflects the long-term average diet of individuals, has informed on how Norse farmers tackled the challenges of both growing crops and herding animals (Mulville et al. 2009; Mainland et al. 2016; Jones and Mulville 2018; Jones et al. 2020). The majority of Norse herbivores analysed from the Outer Hebrides, Shetland and Orkney have $\delta^{13}C$ values that are not influenced by the 'sea spray effect' (Figure 12.1), suggesting that they were being kept in the interior zones of the islands, away from coastal settlements and agricultural land, indicative of a high level of control and management of animals in the wider landscape (Jones and Mulville 2018). Norse animal management contrasts with prehistoric animal management strategies, where shorefront grazing was practised across the Atlantic island groups, and where animals were more free to roam the landscape in a less controlled way (Jones and Mulville 2016). Micro-abrasions on teeth and incremental $\delta^{13}C$ and $\delta^{18}O$ analysis from Norse cattle at Earl's Bu did not yield evidence of coastal grazing, again supporting the hypothesis of careful, inland management of herbivores (Mainland et al. 2016). Several cattle from Jarlshof have outlying $\delta^{13}C$ values, apparently influenced by the sea spray or coastal effect (Figure 12.1) and could suggest individuals were being kept closer to settlements, perhaps for milking (Jones and Mulville 2018). The relationship between domestic herbivores (cattle/sheep) and the wild deer in the Outer Hebrides (Figure 12.1) shows that there was

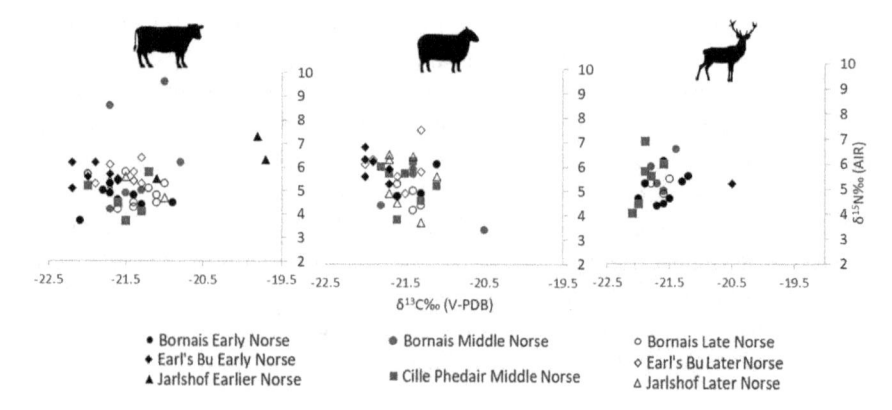

Figure 12.1 The Bone collagen $\delta^{13}C$ and $\delta^{15}N$ values from isotope evidence of cows (left), sheep (centre) and red deer (right) from the sites of Bornais, Cille Pheadair (both Outer Hebrides), Earl's Bu (Orkney) and Jarlshof (Shetland). Data taken from Mulville et al. 2009; Jones and Mulville 2018; Jones et al. 2020.

little difference in the niches of these species, and suggests that domestic stock were being reared further from the coastal settlements and more inland. This is supported by the zooarchaeological record, with a scarcity of adult cattle remains in settlement sites such as Bornais, particularly in the Middle Norse phases, indicating that older animals were being kept away from the main settlement to graze elsewhere (Ingrem 2020).

The overlap between the ecological niches of cattle, sheep and red deer in the Outer Hebrides could suggest habitat or niche competition between wild and domestic fauna, which may have contributed to the eventual extirpation of red deer at the end of the Norse period there. Current evidence suggests that the Norse occupants of the Scottish islands, regardless of the type of site, were carefully managing their domestic stock, likely as a way of protecting agricultural crops to enhance economic success.

Seasonality of birth and winter foddering

Bone collagen can be useful for understanding the long-term or average diet of herbivores. Fine-grained approaches are also required to achieve a more nuanced understanding of animal management during the Norse era. Sequential $\delta^{18}O$ and $\delta^{13}C$ analysis of bioapatite from tooth enamel is a recognised technique for exploring the seasonal diets of domestic animals (for example, Balasse et al. 2019) and birthing season (Towers et al. 2011; Buchan et al. 2016), which can inform on distinctive animal management strategies practised by past populations. In a similar way, incremental analysis of $\delta^{13}C$ and $\delta^{15}N$ from collagen in dentine can also provide information on the diet of animals during the time when the tooth was growing, informing on finer-scale seasonal diet eaten by individuals. These methods have been successfully applied to Scottish Norse assemblages, analysing cattle and sheep at both Earl's Bu (Mainland et al. 2016) and Bornais (Griffiths and Mulville 2020) to understand animal foddering and birthing seasonality.

At Earl's Bu in Orkney, results showed that cattle were living in the same localised area (Mainland et al. 2016), which is consistent with the bone collagen evidence, suggesting that the same tracts of land were being used in the management of these animals in each phase of the site. The low inter-individual ranges in the sheep support this trend of a lower level of movement of domesticates in the landscape (Mainland et al. 2016). The seasonal dietary evidence suggested that, in the winter months, these animals were grazing on foods with elevated $\delta^{13}C$ values, such as hay, straw or grains, supported by dental microwear analysis (Mainland et al. 2016).

At Bornais in the Outer Hebrides, the birth season of three individuals was established to be the autumn, which has important implications for sheltering newborn animals during the winter and providing sufficient fodder (Griffiths and Mulville 2020). This is contra to the natural springtime birthing seasons of cows, when fresh grass and warmer conditions facilitate the survival of mothers and their offspring, but has the important bonus of providing milk as a protein source to the inhabitants of Bornais to see them through the autumn and winter months (Griffiths and Mulville 2020). Early weaning of three Middle Norse cattle, as identified from the incremental tooth dentine $\delta^{15}N$ values (Griffiths and Mulville 2020), also suggests the importance of dairying, as supported by the presence of milk residues in Norse pottery from Bornais (Cramp et al. 2014). The limited numbers of samples studied in this way have yielded interesting results regarding foddering strategies and birthing seasonality of cattle. Research such as this highlights the importance of studying animals both as individuals and as a large population to understand animal husbandry on a variety of scales.

Pig keeping and site function: household production versus feasting

Pig bone collagen $\delta^{13}C$ and $\delta^{15}N$ values can vary depending on how animals are treated. If being kept by individual households, pigs fed on scraps from the human table can exhibit large ranges in values, reflecting food sources available to humans (Madgwick et al. 2013). Pigs managed more centrally may exhibit less variation in the values observed and may reflect broader economic strategies linked to site function. To date, adult

160 Jennifer R. Jones

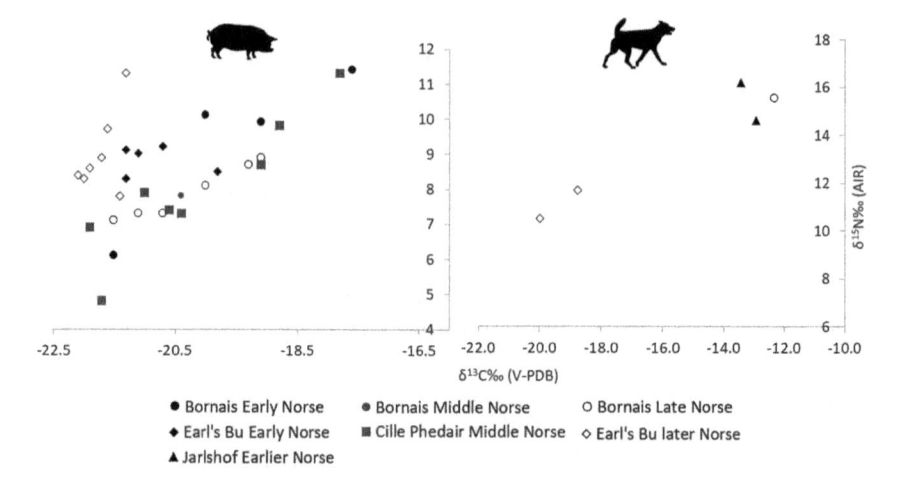

Figure 12.2 Bone collagen $\delta^{13}C$ and $\delta^{15}N$ values from pigs (left) and dogs (right) from the sites of Bornais, Cille Pheadair (both Outer Hebrides), Earl's Bu (Orkney) and Jarlshof (Shetland). Note that the scale of both axes is different for the two species. Data taken from Mulville et al. 2009; Jones and Mulville 2018.

Norse pigs sampled from different settlement types across the Scottish islands provide evidence of both management strategies (Figure 12.2).

The pigs from the manorial estate of Earl's Bu exhibited little interindividual variation within each of the phases analysed, with all individuals having a diet that included terrestrial protein as reflected in their elevated $\delta^{15}N$ relative to the herbivores and no evidence of marine protein consumption (Figure 12.2). A shift in the management of the species is seen between the earlier and later phases of occupation observable in the lower $\delta^{13}C$ values of the later Norse individuals. The shift in diet of the pigs between the earlier and later phases may be due to a change in pig husbandry and fodder provision between two phases of occupation (Jones and Mulville 2018). The Earl's Bu specimens appear to be reflecting centralised management of animals. Pigs and their wild counterparts (boar) can be very disruptive to agricultural land with their rooting behaviour (Ballari and Barrios-García 2014). The isotopic values of the Earl's Bu indicate careful control of this species, potentially to keep them away from crops. The pigs may also have been carefully and centrally managed due to their importance in the feasting process. Pigs, found in large quantities in zooarchaeological assemblages in Scandinavian urban sites between the 8th and 11th centuries, were an important resource for Norse populations (Barrett et al. 2007; O'Connor 2010). Large proportions of pigs in the Earl's Bu assemblage, with an overrepresentation of high-meat-bearing bones (upper and lower limbs), are consistent with them being a feasting resource and reflect a continuation of practices from Viking countries of origin (Mainland and Batey 2018). Feasting was a crucial political activity, used by the Orkney Earls to reaffirm alliances and establish control (Mainland and Batey 2018), and the production of pigs for feasting may explain why they were a centrally managed resource at Earl's Bu.

Conversely, the South Uist pigs from Bornais and Cille Pheadair show greater inter-individual variability in terms of protein consumed in comparison to the site of Earl's Bu, with varying degrees of marine protein (for example, fish) in some individuals, as seen by the elevated δ^{13}C and δ^{15}N values (Figure 12.2). This dietary variability suggests management of pigs on a local or household scale, representing more ad hoc feeding strategies (Jones and Mulville 2018). Pigs were likely being kept in pens or sties as a way of protecting crops (Ingrem 2020) and the dietary isotope analysis supports this possibility. The household-scale management of this species may also have been an effort to keep pigs away from arable land, with pigs potentially being reared near domestic dwellings to prevent them from roaming and causing destruction to valuable crops, again showing levels of control of these animals but in a different way to the Earl's Bu manorial estate. The inclusion of marine protein in the South Uist pigs appears to reflect wider economic trends of intensive fishing during the Norse period, with processing waste potentially being fed to pigs.

Dogs as a proxy for Norse diet in Scotland

A further area of Norse stable isotope research explores the diet of domestic dogs. Dogs can be used cautiously as a proxy for contemporaneous human diet, as they are typically fed scraps from the human table and are particularly useful when human remains are not available to study (Guiry 2013). That said, it is acknowledged that dogs may not fully reflect the social and demographic complexities of human diet within archaeological populations (Perri et al. 2019). Stable isotope analysis of dogs can also reflect treatment of this species, with diversity in the diets of dogs potentially differentiating between working animals and household pets (Jones et al. 2019).

In the case of the Scottish islands, particularly the Western Isles, Norse burials are not especially common, meaning that dogs can help to inform on human diet and wider economic practices when human remains are not available. Dogs analysed from Jarlshof (Shetland) and Bornais (South Uist) have isotopic signatures consistent with the consumption of large quantities of marine protein (Figure 12.2). Conversely, the two dogs from Earl's Bu (Orkney) had diets of almost exclusively terrestrial protein (Figure 12.2), despite icthyological remains being plentiful in the zooarchaeological record at Earl's Bu (Harland 2006). This may reflect differences in the function of the sites, with dogs from the farmstead-style settlements of Jarlshof and Bornais reflecting human diet, potentially eating fish-processing waste, and the Earl's Bu specimens representing animals that were kept for herding on the wider manorial estate, rather than household pets. The implication of this is that dogs may be reflecting wider economic practices linked to the role of the site.

Future directions

Comparisons to other parts of Scotland and to the wider Norse world

Isotope zooarchaeology research to date is exclusively related to the Scottish islands, in part due to the exceptional bone preservation in the islands, the excavation focus in these regions, and the presence of large settlement sites with rich faunal assemblages available for study. Insular locations have distinctive challenges regarding agriculture and animal husbandry, and future comparisons to mainland Scotland would enhance our understanding of how the Vikings adapted to new environments during their diaspora. This of course relies on there being large, well-preserved assemblages available in mainland Scotland, which to date are limited. Comparing and contrasting patterns of food production and animal management observed in Scotland with other Viking-Age diasporic regions such as Iceland, Ireland, Anglesey and the mainland UK, as well as Viking home countries, would enable connectivity across the Norse world to be explored as well as the specific adaptations used by Viking populations when settling in new regions. While some faunal isotope studies exist from sites within some regions (see Nelson et al. 2012; Sayle et al. 2013; Ascough et al. 2014), there is a need for a more systematic and comparative approach towards exploring these questions.

Exploring animal management and provisioning in different types of settlements

The differences in the treatment of animals observed between the manorial estate of Earl's Bu and the farmstead sites of Cille Pheadair and Bornais demonstrate how stable isotope techniques can inform on animal management strategies in relation to the role and function of sites. This allows insights into wider societal organisation, production chains and the contribution of animal resources to the wider economy. Comparisons between different phases of sites using multi-isotope techniques would enable diachronic changes in animal management strategies and land use throughout the period of occupation of these sites. Larger sample sizes from Early, Middle and Late Norse phases from a variety of different types of sites are needed in order to do this. The incorporation of greater numbers of juvenile bones for bone collagen $\delta^{13}C$ and $\delta^{15}N$ analysis can be invaluable in determining the treatment of pregnant animals (Schulting et al. 2017), which may inform on more sophisticated animal management strategies, especially during the harsh winter months. Greater exploration of the treatment of animals in a variety of different types of sites across insular and mainland Scotland, and indeed the wider Norse world, would also be beneficial to determine how site role or function affected food production and agricultural strategies. A major focus of research previously has been the trade and exchange of fish products, particularly in reference to Viking identity, and their importance in the emergent market economies (Barrett et al. 1999; Barrett and Richards 2004; Perdikaris et al. 2007; Locker et al. 2009). There is a need to shift the focus more to domestic stock and animal products to understand how they contributed to these dramatic cultural, social, religious and economic changes that occurred throughout the Norse period.

Greater integration of different biomolecular and zooarchaeological methodologies

Integration of zooarchaeological and isotopic approaches with the wider suite of scientific archaeological techniques is fundamental in being able to answer questions that cannot be addressed using each method independently (Makarewicz 2016). The application of microwear analysis, with toothwear ageing and incremental tooth $\delta^{13}C$ and $\delta^{18}O$ isotope sampling, has demonstrated the value of multi-evidential approaches towards understanding foddering strategies and animal management (Mainland et al. 2016), which could be applied to larger assemblages across the Norse world. A rigorous and extensive study of both cattle and sheep tooth incremental $\delta^{13}C$ and $\delta^{18}O$ analysis would enhance understanding of the manipulation of birthing seasonality in a variety of different sites to explore more nuanced animal management strategies being practised.

Strontium analysis of faunal teeth can inform on the movement of past populations of humans and animals, sometimes showing faunal movements over long distances (Evans et al. 2019; Madgwick et al. 2019), but to date has not been applied to Norse insular animal populations. Strontium studies of Norse humans have explored the Norse diaspora: humans interred at Cnip in the Outer Hebrides showed that these people were indigenous to the islands (Montgomery et al. 2003), whereas further studies at Westness in Orkney show that three individuals from Orkney were not native (Montgomery et al. 2014).

Regarding fauna, the situation is more complex. Zooarchaeological evidence from the site of Bornais suggests that cattle were born and bred in the locality of the settlement (Ingrem 2020), being indicative of small-scale animal movements, if any. In the Scottish islands, the similarity in strontium signatures within individual island groups and to their respective adjacent mainland (Evans et al. 2010) means that recognising the animal movements happening over shorter distance on an intra-island basis, or even from the local mainland to replenish breeding stock, may not be possible to determine. The application of this method for exploring possible trade and exchange over larger distances could potentially identify animals brought as start-up stock to settlements, although robust sampling strategies of early Viking deposits to address such questions would need to be in place to warrant this form of destructive analysis.

Sulphur isotopes have been successfully used to explore marine protein consumption and the movement of animals in Viking Iceland (Sayle et al. 2013) and may help to explore these themes further in the Scottish islands, particularly in relation to the management of pigs and the possibility of control of herbivores on specific tracts of land. Existing collagen extracted could be used to explore this to avoid further destruction of bone specimens, although in insular locations the constant proximity to the sea may mask patterns in $\delta^{34}S$ values (see review by Nehlich 2015).

The use of aDNA and toothwear analysis to provide valuable ageing and sexing information of cattle has provided insights into cull rates and milking economies in Bronze- Age and Norse period assemblages from the Western Isles (McGrory et al. 2012). Combining such approaches with further stable isotope studies would help to determine the treatment of animals, such as keeping females closer to settlements, with the rest of the herd being kept in the wider landscape, which has been hypothesised from previous studies (Jones and Mulville 2018) and is suggested by the wider zooarchaeological record (Ingrem 2020). This would help to explore further how dairying and secondary products were used in the islands, and the importance of these products in the wider economy.

The possibility of manuring in the Norse period has been suggested by faunal bone collagen $\delta^{13}C$ and $\delta^{15}N$ studies (Jones et al. 2012). Further research analysing plant stable isotope values directly, from well-defined contexts within different phases of Norse activity for the characteristic elevated $\delta^{15}N$ associated with manuring (Bogaard et al. 2007), would allow insights into the exact chronologies of when manuring was taking place in the islands. Similarly, incremental tooth analysis of $\delta^{13}C$ and $\delta^{15}N$ may be able to further inform on the foddering of animals on manured crops. Finally, greater engagement with the archaeobotanical record will allow more integration of pastoral and agricultural strategies used, enabling a more holistic understanding of the economy. This is particularly important given the highly politicised nature of fodder in parts of the Norse world (Amorosi et al. 2014).

Ultimately, the most powerful studies are those that apply multiple isotopes (for example, $\delta^{13}C$, $\delta^{15}N$, $\delta^{34}S$, $^{87/86}Sr$, $\delta^{18}O$) from different bodily tissues which reflect a variety of timescales to understand nuances in animal management and movement, such as those successfully employed in other parts of the UK (for example, Madgwick et al. 2019). Combining these multi-isotope studies with techniques including aDNA, archaeobotany and traditional zooarchaeology using high-resolution sampling (on an inter- and intra-site level) will enable enhanced understanding of Viking agricultural and pastoral adaptations to Scottish environments.

Conclusions

To date, Norse isotope zooarchaeology in Scotland, predominantly focused on insular locations, has provided valuable insights into the use of the landscape, crop manuring, animal birthing seasons and control of animals in the landscape. It has also helped to highlight differences in the treatment of animals relating to site type, such as the strict management of pigs used for feasting at manorial estates compared to ad hoc management of pigs at farmstead settlements.

There is a need for systematic and integrated analysis of faunal assemblages using a suite of scientific methodologies with traditional zooarchaeological methods and archaeobotanical evidence in order to gain a more comprehensive and nuanced understanding of how pastoralism related to the wider economy. Further expansion of these isotope archaeological approaches to mainland Scotland, other parts of the UK and the wider Norse world will help to contextualise how the Vikings adapted to environments in Scotland, and the similarities and differences in economic strategies used between diaspora regions. Greater exploration of changes during different phases of occupation will inform further on adaptation and acculturation of Viking settlers in Scotland. It is crucial to note that the application of stable isotope zooarchaeology relies on successful collaborations between museums, curators and researchers to ensure that robust research design and coherent sampling strategies maximise knowledge gained from an assemblage, while limiting damage to a finite archaeological resource.

As more Viking-Age sites in Scotland are unearthed, the scientific approaches used to date can be expanded to explore new regions and site types in order to understand Viking adaptations to the different environments they encountered in Scotland, and how the Vikings expressed religion, identity and power in the regions they occupied.

References

Amorosi, T., P. C. Buckland, K. J. Edwards, I. Mainland, T. H. McGovern, J. P. Sadler and P. Skidmore (2014) They did not live by grass alone: The politics and palaeoecology of animal fodder in the North Atlantic region. *Environmental Archaeology* 1(1), 41–54.

Ascough, P. L., M. J. Church, G. T. Cook, Á. Einarsson, T. H. McGovern, A. J. Dugmore and K. J. Edwards (2014) Stable isotopic (δ 13 C and δ 15 N) characterization of key faunal resources from Norse period settlements in North Iceland. *Journal of the North Atlantic* Special Volume 7, 25–42.

Balasse, M., A. Tresset, G. Obein, D. Fiorillo and H. Gandois (2019) Seaweed-eating sheep and the adaptation of husbandry in Neolithic Orkney: New insights from Skara Brae. *Antiquity* 93(370), 919–32.

Ballari, S. A. and M. N. Barrios-García (2014) A review of wild boar *Sus scrofa* diet and factors affecting food selection in native and introduced ranges. *Mammal Review* 44(2), 124–34.

Barrett, J. H., R. A. Nicholson and R. Cerón-Carrasco (1999) Archaeo-ichthyological evidence for long-term socioeconomic trends in Northern Scotland: 3500 BC to AD 1500. *Journal of Archaeological Science* 26(4), 353–88.

Barrett, J. H., R. Beukens, I. Simpson, P. Ashmore, S. Poaps and J. Huntley (2000) What was the Viking Age and when did it happen? A view from Orkney. *Norwegian Archaeological Review* 33(1), 1–39.

Barrett, J. H., R. P. Beukens and R. A. Nicholson (2001) Diet and ethnicity during the Viking colonization of Northern Scotland: Evidence from fish bones and stable carbon isotopes. *Antiquity* 75(287), 145–54.

Barrett, J. H. and M. P. Richards (2004) Identity, gender, religion and economy: New isotope and radiocarbon evidence for marine resource intensification in early historic Orkney, Scotland, UK. *European Journal of Archaeology* 7(3), 249–71.

Barrett, J. H., A. R. Hall, C. Johnstone, H. Kenward, T. O'Connor and S. Ashby (2007) Interpreting the plant and animal remains from Viking-age Kaupang. In Dagfinn Skre (ed.), *Kaupang in Skiringssal. Kaupang Excavation Project Publication Series*. Århus: Århus University Press, 283–319.

Bogaard, A., T. H. E. Heaton, P. Poulton and I. Merbach (2007) The impact of manuring on nitrogen isotope ratios in cereals: Archaeological implications for reconstruction of diet and crop management practices. *Journal of Archaeological Science* 34(3), 335–43.

Britton, K. (2017) A stable relationship: Isotopes and bioarchaeology are in it for the long haul. *Antiquity* 91(358), 853–64.

Buchan, M., G. Müldner, A. Ervynck and K. Britton (2016) Season of birth and sheep husbandry in late Roman and Medieval coastal Flanders: A pilot study using tooth enamel δ18O analysis. *Environmental Archaeology* 21(3), 260–70.

Cramp, L. J. E., J. Jones, A. Sheridan, J. Smyth, H. Whelton, J. Mulville, N. Sharples and R. P. Evershed (2014) Immediate replacement of fishing with dairying by the earliest farmers of the Northeast Atlantic archipelagos. *Proceedings. Biological Sciences* 281(1780), 20132372.

Dockrill, S. J. (2007) *Investigations in Sanday, Orkney. Vol. 2, Tofts Ness, Sanday: An Island Landscape through 3000 years of Prehistory*. Kirkwall: The Orcadian Ltd.

Evans, J., M. Parker Pearson, R. Madgwick, H. Sloane and U. Albarella (2019) Strontium and oxygen isotope evidence for the origin and movement of cattle at Late Neolithic Durrington Walls, UK. *Archaeological and Anthropological Sciences* 11(10), 5181–97.

Evans, J. A., J. Montgomery, G. Wildman, N. Boulton (2010) Spatial variations in biosphere 87Sr/86Sr in Britain. *Journal of the Geological Society* 167(1), 1–4.

Fraser, R. A., A. Bogaard, T. Heaton, M. Charles, G. Jones, B. T. Christensen, P. Halstead, I. Merbach, P. R. Poulton, D. Sparkes and A. K. Styring (2011) Manuring and stable nitrogen isotope ratios in cereals and pulses: Towards a new archaeobotanical approach to the inference of land use and dietary practices. *Journal of Archaeological Science* 38(10), 2790–804.

Graham-Campbell, J. and C. E. Batey (1998) *Vikings in Scotland: An Archaeological Survey*. Edinburgh: Edinburgh University Press.

Griffiths, J. and J. Mulville (2020) A sequential multi-isotopic analysis of Norse cattle teeth. In N. Sharples (ed.), *The Economy of a Norse Settlement in the Outer Hebrides: Excavations at Mounds 2 and 2A, Bornais, South Uist*. Oxford: Oxbow, 367–81.

Guiry, E. J. (2013) A canine surrogacy approach to human paleodietary bone chemistry: Past development and future directions. *Archaeological and Anthropological Sciences* 5(3), 275–86.

Harland, J. F. (2006) *Zooarchaeology in the Viking Age to Medieval Northern Isles, Scotland: An Investigation of Spatial and Temporal Patterning*. Unpublished PhD thesis, University of York.

Ingrem, C. (2020) Animal management. In N. Sharples (ed.), *The Economy of a Norse Settlement in the Outer Hebrides: Excavations at Mounds 2 and 2a, Bornais, South Uist, Vol. 4*. Oxford: Oxbow, 350–61.

Jones, J. R., J. A. Mulville, R. A. R. McGill and R. P. Evershed (2012) Palaeoenvironmental modelling of δ 13C and δ 15N values in the North Atlantic Islands: Understanding past marine resource use. *Rapid Communications in Mass Spectrometry* 26(20), 2399–406.

Jones, J. R. and J. Mulville (2016) Isotopic and zooarchaeological approaches towards understanding aquatic resource use in human economies and animal management in the prehistoric Scottish North Atlantic islands. *Journal of Archaeological Science: Reports* 6, 665–77.

Jones, J. R. and J. A. Mulville (2018) Norse animal husbandry in liminal environments: Stable isotope evidence from the Scottish North Atlantic islands. *Environmental Archaeology* 23(4), 338–51.

Jones, J. R., C. V. Maeso, E. C. Ballestero, L. V. Martín, M. Eugenía, D. Arceo and A. B. Marín-Arroyo (2019) Investigating prehistoric diet and lifeways of early farmers in central northern Spain (3000–1500 CAL BC) using stable isotope techniques. *Archaeological and Anthropological Sciences* 11, 3979–94.

Jones, J. R., R. Madgwick and J. A. Mulville (2020) Animal management and marine resource use: the stable isotope evidence. In N. Sharples (ed.),

The Economy of a Norse Settlement in the Outer Hebrides Excavations at Mounds 2 and 2A, Bornais, South Uist. Oxford: Oxbow, 361–7.

Locker, A. M., C. M. Roberts and J. H. Barrett (2009) 'Dark Age Economics' revisited: The English fish-bone evidence, 600–1600. In L. Sicking and D. Abreu-Ferreira (eds), *Beyond the Catch: Fisheries of the North Atlantic, the North Sea and the Baltic, 900–1850*. The Northern World Series. Leiden and Boston: Brill, 29–60.

Lucas, G. and T. McGovern (2007) Bloody slaughter: Ritual decapitation and display at the Viking settlement of Hofstaðir, Iceland. *European Journal of Archaeology* 10(1), 7–30.

Madgwick, R., A. L. Lamb, H. Sloane, A. J. Nederbragt, U. Albarella, M. Parker Pearson and J. A. Evans (2019) Multi-isotope analysis reveals that feasts in the Stonehenge environs and across Wessex drew people and animals from throughout Britain. *Science Advances* 5(3). doi: 10.1126/sciadv.aau6078.

Madgwick, R., J. Mulville and R. E. Stevens (2013) Diversity in foddering strategy and herd management in late Bronze Age Britain: An isotopic investigation of pigs and other fauna from two midden sites. *Environmental Archaeology* 17(2), 126–40.

Mainland, I., J. Towers, V. Evans, G. Davis, J. Montgomery, C. Batey, N. Card and J. Downes (2016) Toiling with teeth: An integrated dental analysis of sheep and cattle dentition in Iron Age and Viking-Late Norse Orkney. *Journal of Archaeological Science: Reports* 6, 837–55.

Mainland, I. and C. Batey (2018) The nature of the feast: Commensality and the politics of consumption in Viking Age and Early Medieval Northern Europe. *World Archaeology* 50(5), 781–803.

Makarewicz, C. A. (2016) Toward an integrated isotope zooarchaeology. In G. Grupe and G. McGlynn (eds), *Isotopic Landscapes in Bioarchaeology*. Berlin, Heidelberg: Springer Berlin Heidelberg, 189–209.

McGrory, S., E. M. Svensson, A. Götherström, J. Mulville, A. J. Powell, M. J. Collins and T. P. O'Connor (2012) A novel method for integrated age and sex determination from archaeological cattle mandibles. *Journal of Archaeological Science* 39(10), 3324–30.

Montgomery, J., J. A. Evans and T. Neighbour (2003) Sr isotope evidence for population movement within the Hebridean Norse community of NW Scotland. *Journal of the Geological Society* 160(5), 649–53.

Montgomery, J., V. Grimes, J. Buckberry, J. A. Evans, M. P. Richards and J. H. Barrett (2014) Finding Vikings with isotope analysis: The view from wet and windy islands. *Journal of the North Atlantic* Special Volume 7, 54–70.

Mulville, J., R. Madgwick, R. Stevens, T. O'Connell, O. Craig, A. Powell, N. Sharples, N. MacPherson and M. Parker Pearson (2009) Isotopic analysis of faunal material from South Uist, Western Isles, Scotland. *Journal of the North Atlantic* 2(1), 51–9.

Nehlich, O. (2015) The application of sulphur isotope analyses in archaeological research: A review. *Earth-Science Reviews* 142, 1–17.

Nelson, D. E., J. Heinemeier, J. Møhl and J. Arneborg (2012) Isotopic analyses of the domestic animals of Norse Greenland. *Journal of the North Atlantic* Special Volume 3, 77–92.

O'Connor, T. (2010) Livestock and deadstock in early medieval Europe from the North Sea to the Baltic. *Environmental Archaeology* 15(1), 1–15.

Perdikaris, S., G. Hambrecht, S. Brewington and T. H. McGovern (2007) Across the fish event horizon: A comparative approach. In H. Plogmann (ed.), *The Role of Fish in Ancient Time, Proceedings of the 13th Meeting of the ICAZ Fish Remains Working Group, August 2005, Basel*. Rahden: Leidorf, 38–52.

Perri, A. R., J. M. Koster, E. Otárola-Castillo, J. L. Burns and C. G. Cooper (2019) Dietary variation among indigenous Nicaraguan horticulturalists and their dogs: An ethnoarchaeological application of the Canine Surrogacy Approach. *Journal of Anthropological Archaeology* 55, 101066.

Sayle, K. L., G. T. Cook, P. L. Ascough, H. R. Hastie, Á. Einarsson, T. H. McGovern, M. T. Hicks, Á. Edwald and A. Friðriksson (2013) Application of 34S analysis for elucidating terrestrial, marine and freshwater ecosystems: Evidence of animal movement/husbandry practices in an early Viking community around Lake Mývatn, Iceland. *Geochimica et Cosmochimica Acta* 120, 531–44.

Schulting, R. J., P. Vaiglova, R. Crozier and P. J. Reimer (2017) Further isotopic evidence for seaweed-eating sheep from Neolithic Orkney. *Journal of Archaeological Science: Reports* 11, 463–70.

Smith, H. (2012) An ethnohistory of Hebridean agriculture. In M. Parker Pearson (ed.), *From Machair to Mountains: Archaeological Survey and Excavation in South Uist*. Oxford: Oxbow, 379–400.

Summers, J. and J. Bond (2020) The carbonised plant remains. In N. Sharples (ed.), *The Economy of a Norse Settlement in the Outer Hebrides Excavations at Mounds 2 and 2A, Bornais, South Uist*. Oxford: Oxbow, 381–6.

Towers, J., M. Jay, I. Mainland, O. Nehlich and J. Montgomery (2011) A calf for all seasons? The potential of stable isotope analysis to investigate prehistoric husbandry practices. *Journal of Archaeological Science* 38(8), 1858–68.

Chapter 13

Feasts, Food and Fodder: Viking and Late Norse Farming Systems in Scotland
Ingrid Mainland

When *Vikings in Scotland* was first published, consideration of human–animal interactions was largely focused on agricultural interpretations. Since the late 1980s, there has been a shift in zooarchaeology away from purely economic interpretations towards perspectives encompassing the materiality of animals, animals in identity, ritual and so on. At the same time there has been an expansion in the application of scientific approaches within archaeology – most notably palaeodietary techniques, but also increasingly aDNA. The last thirty years have also witnessed new excavations of significant Viking and Late Norse settlements not only in Scotland but across the North Atlantic, providing many new insights into farming practices and other human–animal interactions across the Viking 'diaspora'. This chapter explores how some of these diverse sources of evidence have transformed our understanding of the agricultural economy and the role of animals in Viking and Late Norse society within Scotland, situating this within the wider context of Scandinavian North Atlantic settlement during the end of the 1st and early 2nd millennium AD.

Data sets and approaches to human–animal interactions in Viking and Late Norse Scotland

The animal faunas arising from Viking and Late Norse Orkney and Shetland has generated considerable archaeological interest over the last forty years, with major environmental archaeology programmes undertaken on earldom sites featured in the *Orkneyinga Saga* (*OS*), including residences of the Orkney Earls on the Brough of Birsay (Morris, this volume) and at the Earl's Bu in Orphir (Batey, this volume), those of their chieftains, or *goðing*, at Tuquoy in Westray (Owen, this volume) and Skaill in Deerness, and increasingly at other locations across the islands: Pool (Sanday), Quoygrew (Westray), Old Scatness (Shetland), Snusgar (Sandwick) and Skaill (Rousay). The preceding Late Iron-Age or 'Pictish' settlements have been less systematically targeted but have benefited from the multi-period nature of many of the Orcadian sites, which afford insight into the transition between Pictish and Viking at several locations, including the Birsay Bay area and Deerness on the Mainland of Orkney, Pool, Westness/Swandro in Rousay and Old Scatness. There has been less sustained interest in human–animal interactions in the areas of Viking settlement on the mainland of Scotland, with few sites additional to those summarised in *Vikings in Scotland*; however, the publication of large faunal assemblages from Bornais (Sharples 2020) and Cille Phedair (Mulville et al. 2018) have added significantly to our understanding of Viking farming in the Western Isles. Moreover, the long-running NABO programme of environmental archaeology research in Greenland, Iceland and the Faroe Islands has produced extensive faunal data sets, providing a wider context of human–animal interactions in the 'Viking' diaspora of the North Atlantic islands for these Scottish assemblages (Dugmore et al. 2012; Smiarowski et al. 2017).

This increased volume of zooarchaeological data is beginning to facilitate regional syntheses exploring the nature and organisation of Viking and Late Norse farming practices across Scotland, as well as identification of intra-site variation in husbandry practices and economic focus at sites of differing status, size or type, albeit with a focus on the Northern Isles (Mainland et al. 2016; Mainland and Batey 2018; Mainland forthcoming a, b). In addition, these faunal assemblages are increasingly being drawn on to provide more detailed insights into Viking and Late Norse husbandry practices using new scientific approaches. Examples include stable isotope analysis of foddering and grazing strategies (Mainland et al. 2016; Jones and Mulville 2018; Jones, this volume) and birthing season (Towers et al. 2017), analyses of body size and stature as an indicator of health, nutrition and 'breed' (Cussans 2013), developmental stresses in dentition to explore weaning age and meat versus dairy production in sheep (Ewens 2010; Mainland et al. 2016), and more recently, studies of genetic diversity and ancestry in modern and ancient livestock (Mullin 2018). aDNA studies have also been undertaken or are in progress on other mammals from Viking contexts in Scotland, including mice (Jones et al. 2012), cats (Jamieson 2021) and cetaceans (Kitchiner et al. 2021). In contrast with Scandinavian Viking archaeology (such as Jennbert 2011; Toplak 2019), social zooarchaeology approaches are still less widely adopted in a Scottish context, notable exceptions being Cooke's (2017) analyses of liminality and hunting of wildfowl and red deer in Viking Scotland and of the role of cats and horse as expressions of social identity (Cooke 2016, 2017). Likewise, Mainland and Batey (2018) have argued that societal drivers such as social obligation, power and identity may have been key factors underpinning farming and food production in Viking Scotland rather than calorific, economic or environmental factors per se.

Livestock farming and other human–animal interactions in Viking and Late Norse Scotland: An overview

Viking and Late Norse settlements in the Northern Isles and across the North Atlantic were fundamentally agricultural societies (Fitzhugh and Ward 2000; Brink and Price 2012). Livestock husbandry was based on the rearing of cattle and sheep with some pigs (Rackham 1986; Bond 2007; Cussans and Bond 2010; Harland 2012; Dugmore et al. 2012; Mulville et al. 2018; Mainland et al. 2019; Sharples 2020; Mainland and Harland 2021; Mainland forthcoming b). Although cereal cultivation was more limited in the other North Atlantic islands, arable farming was possible in Scotland where it was focused on barley and oats, intended as both human food and for fodder in the form of grains and straw (Adams et al. 2012; Alldritt 2019). Other fodder sources will have included hay and potentially seaweed, though this appears to have been less commonly used than in prehistory (Barrett and Richards 2012; Jones and Mulville 2018; Jones, this volume). Flax was also grown and is thought to have been introduced from Scandinavia by the incoming settlers (Bond and Hunter 1987; Adams et al. 2012), likely for linen production but also as a potential human food. An expansion of arable agriculture between the Late Iron Age and into the Viking period is suggested from weed floras indicative of sandy soils (Bond 2007). This has been attributed to cultivation of oats as fodder and an increasing intensification of animal husbandry (Bond 2007; Mainland et al 2016; Jones and Mulville 2018; Alldritt 2019). Oats are, however, also widely used in human food – and indeed were the main dietary staple in Scotland up until the early 20th century (Fenton 1978). Intensification of arable practices into the Late Norse period is further indicated by enhanced soil erosion and the development of plaggen-type soils (Simpson 1997).

Cattle, sheep and pigs, cats, dogs and horses, together with chickens, domestic geese and ducks, were the species of the household (Mainland forthcoming a). Beef and mutton comprised the bulk of the meat consumed, a situation paralleled across the North Atlantic and in Scandinavia (Jennbert 2011; Dugmore et al 2012; Zori et al. 2013; Gotfredsen et al. 2015). Variation is seen in relative species frequencies through time and at different settlements, suggesting regional and status-related variations in culinary practices (see regional case studies below).

Inter-site comparisons can be affected by issues of taphonomy specific to individual sites such as recovery methods and soil preservation conditions (Amorosi et al. 1996; Holmes 2014). To avoid some of these biases, in the regional case studies presented below (Table 13.1) only the larger assemblages were included (>300 NISP), and species trends were evaluated using ratios rather than absolute counts. Moreover, while the impact of taphonomy can never be entirely removed, a consistent patterning in species utilisation is apparent at similar types of sites across the Northern Isles (such as at high-status sites, see below), indicating that culinary or economic trends are being observed (see similar arguments in McGovern 1992; O'Connor 2010; Holmes 2014).

Cattle also provided milk and were used to pull ploughs and carts, shown by osteopathological lesions indicative of traction at, for example, Snusgar (Mainland et al. 2019), Pool (Bond 2007), Quoygrew (Harland 2012) and Tuquoy (Smith forthcoming). Specialised milk production, as evidenced by culling patterns which emphasise slaughter of high frequencies of neonatal calves, is found in Norse contexts at Pool (Bond 2007) and during Late Norse phases at Quoygrew (Harland 2012) and Snusgar (Mainland et al. 2019). Sheep were used for wool and may have been milked, although there is less evidence for this than elsewhere in the North Atlantic (Ewens 2010). Similarly, the intense focus on wool production evident in Icelandic sites from the 11th century onwards does not seem to be a feature of Scottish Late Norse farming strategies (Mainland forthcoming a).

Goats are very rarely found in Scottish contexts, and most sheep/goat bones recovered from Viking/Norse contexts will be the former species. The use of goat leather is attested to at Tuquoy, perhaps indicating imports (Smith forthcoming; Mainland forthcoming a) from sites such as Bergen or Hedeby where dumps of goat horn cores suggest manufacturing processes involving this species (Salvagno and Albarella 2019).

During summer, cattle and sheep are likely to have been grazed away from the settlement, beyond the tunship dykes or at shieling sites (Jones and Mulville 2018; Jones, this volume). Very little research has been done to characterise and identify shielings and other grazing areas within the wider landscape, and further research is needed here to bring together the landscape and place-name evidence with the faunas (Foster 2018; Mainland and Harland 2021; Foster, this volume; Jones, this volume). Based on the extensive evidence of stalled byre structures in Viking and Late Norse Scotland (for example, Jarlshof, Snusgar, Pool and so forth), it can be assumed that cattle were housed inside during winter. Some sheep may also have been taken inside; dental microwear at the Earl's Bu, for example, suggests indoor feeding (Mainland et al. 2016), a practice which is known from Icelandic sagas and continues there today. Again, research linking faunal and architecture/structural evidence is lacking, and there is much potential to apply, for example, the integrative approaches used in Greenland and Iceland (for example, McGovern 1992, Brown et al. 2012, Ascough et al. 2014 and Kupiec et al. 2016) to Scottish contexts.

The cattle were small, standing on average 104cm at shoulder height, comparable with modern breeds such as the Dexter (Cussans 2013; Mainland et al. 2019). Sheep were also small and slight, similar to the modern North Ronaldsays in stature (Cussans, Bond and O'Connor 2007; Cussans 2013). Cussans (2013) has explored how skeletal stature (bone breadth, depth and length) in domestic cattle and sheep varies across the Norse North Atlantic, including at Scottish sites in the Northern and Western Isles, reflecting impacts of nutrition, husbandry, environment and breed. Pigs too were small and long-snouted, likely resembling the small, black hairy pigs found in the Northern Isles up until the early 20th century (Fenton 1978; Mainland et al. 2019). Morphologically and in stature, Viking and Norse livestock in Scotland are comparable with their predecessors in the Late Iron Age, and most researchers have assumed a continuity of livestock across the Pictish/Viking interface (for example, Cussans 2013). DNA analysis of modern short-tailed sheep breeds in the North Atlantic, Scotland, northern England and Scandinavia points to a common ancestry for these breeds, potentially indicating importation of sheep from Scandinavia, as well as the movement of animals between Scotland and the western and eastern North Atlantic islands (Chessa et al. 2009; Bowles et al. 2014). North Atlantic cattle and horses also share genetic affinities with Scandinavian breeds (Edwards et al. 2011; Petersen et al. 2013). However, until ongoing aDNA studies (for example, Mullin 2018; Pálsdóttir nd) are published, the precise direction of travel and when this occurred remains unclear. As livestock are known to have been moved from Norway to Iceland and Greenland, it seems probable that some animals were also being brought into the Northern Isles to continue bloodlines for species which were linked with identity or status.

Horses were small, c. 11 hands in height, more properly classified as ponies (Mainland forthcoming a). Published metrical data for cats and dogs is scant, but for the latter anecdotal evidence suggests the presence of both large and small breeds, the former likely hunting and/or working dogs for livestock. At the Earl's Bu, the presence of lapdogs has been suggested from finds of very small canid bones (Mainland forthcoming b). These smaller breeds of dog are also found elsewhere in the North Atlantic. The association with the Earl's Bu indicates that the keeping of these smaller breeds in the Northern Isles was status-related, perhaps as lapdogs. More research is however needed on biometrics in Scottish Norse dogs to confirm these hypotheses. aDNA would also add to our understanding of origins for these smaller breeds. Cats were likely working animals, keeping down mice and other vermin, but in earlier contexts may also have had a religious function through their association with Freya (Cooke 2017; Toplak 2019). Animal bone groups involving cats are found at several sites, including Snusgar where a pair of cat burials was found on the threshold between the byre and the hall (Mainland et al.

2019). Similar deposits are also recovered from Pool (Bond 2007). By the Late Norse period, the prevalence of cut marks on cat bones at sites such as the Earl's Bu (Cooke 2017; Mainland forthcoming b) indicates that this species may have been utilised for its fur – a trend also found elsewhere in the Norse world (Hatting 1990; Poole 2015). aDNA analysis is pointing to diverse origins for the Viking and Norse cats in Orkney (Jamieson 2021). Butchery marks are also found on some dog and horse bones, for example, at Snusgar and Quoygrew, and could indicate the occasional consumption of these species or the use of their skins and hides (Harland 2012; Mainland et al. 2019). Consumption of carnivores and otherwise 'taboo' species such as horse was known to occur during sacrificial consumption events in Scandinavia (Magnell and Iregen 2010; Poole 2013; Godfredsen et al. 2015), and at least some examples of butchery marks in the Scottish isles may relate to such practices (Mainland and Batey 2018).

Wild bird fowling is a further feature of Norse settlements in Scotland, particularly in the earlier Viking periods (Serjeantson 2014: 281). A wide variety of seabirds were exploited for food but also likely for feathers and eggs (Best and Mulville 2016). Gannet, cormorant/shag and guillemot were the most common species hunted. Exploitation of these was not straightforward and involved a degree of danger, from the scaling of sea cliffs to long sea voyages to access gannetries on remote stacks. Cooke (2017: 147), observing an association between gannet frequencies and higher-status sites, such as Snusgar and Bornais, has argued that exploitation of this species was controlled by the elite, with its hunting potentially even acting as a rite of passage for those involved. If so, the large assemblage of butchered gannet humeri at Snusgar (Mainland et al. 2019) may suggest a small-scale feasting event associated with such an activity. Other species hunted by the Norse were red deer, seal, otter and potentially cetacean, although the latter may also reflect judicious exploitation of strandings. Red deer were likely close to extinction in Orkney if not absent by the time of the initial Viking settlements, but the *OS* records hunting expeditions to mainland Scotland. Red deer were present in the Western Isles and were exploited by the Norse, both for meat and as sources of antler for artefact production (Mulville and Powell 2018; Sharples 2020). Whalebone was also widely used in artefact production (Szabo 2008). Otters and seals provided furs but may also have been consumed (Mainland forthcoming a).

Regional variations in Late Iron-Age, Viking and Late Norse husbandry practices: A case study from the Northern Isles

In the Northern Isles, the last forty years has seen publication or analysis of nineteen faunal assemblages dating to Late Iron-Age and Norse contexts, enabling new insights into chronological and intra-site variability in livestock husbandry (Mainland et al. 2016; Mainland and Batey 2018; Mainland forthcoming). A shift in strategy can be identified from the Late Iron Age to Late Norse in both husbandry and diet, potentially reflecting a move from subsistence farming to a system geared towards the production of specific products. For the Late Iron-Age sites (n=11), a mixed herding strategy emphasising cattle and sheep/goat is apparent with little evidence for specialisation on any one species (Figures 13.1 and 13.2, Tables 13.1 and 13.2a&b). In the Norse assemblages (Viking, n=8; Late Norse, n=6; Viking/Late Norse, n=4), sheep/goat and cattle also predominate, indicating some continuity in species selection at the Pictish and Viking interface (Bond 2007). More focused herding strategies are however apparent at several Norse sites, suggesting a shift had occurred in the goals of economic production (Figures 13.1 and 13.2). Sheep/goat are emphasised at Viking Pool and Late Norse Beachview, Birsay, while cattle are the dominant species at Old Scatness (Viking and Late Norse) and Quoygrew (Late Norse). Although always a minority species, pig frequency shows distinct intra-site variability and is associated in particular with some of the higher-status Earldom sites, the residences and/or estates of the Earls of Orkney: The Earl's Bu (Late Norse), the Brough of Birsay (Viking)

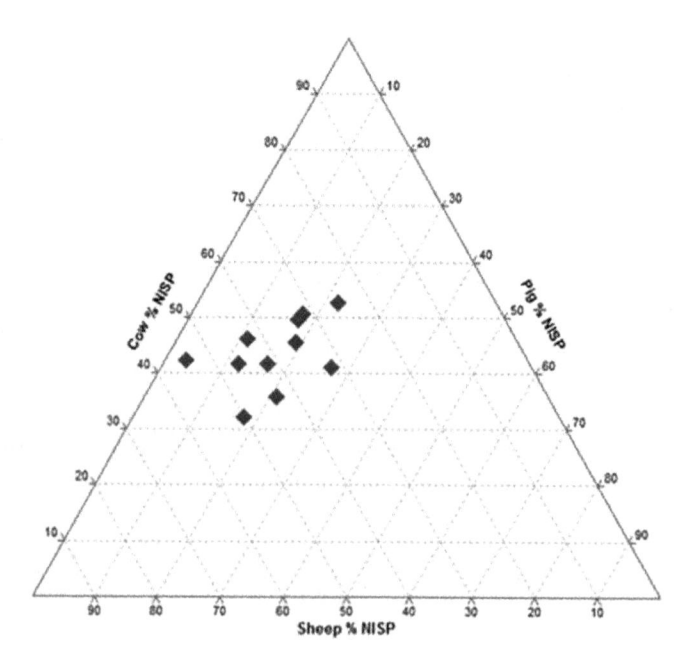

Figure 13.1a Relative frequency (%NISP) of cow, sheep/goat and pig in Late Iron-Age Northern Isles. For data values, see Table 13.1.

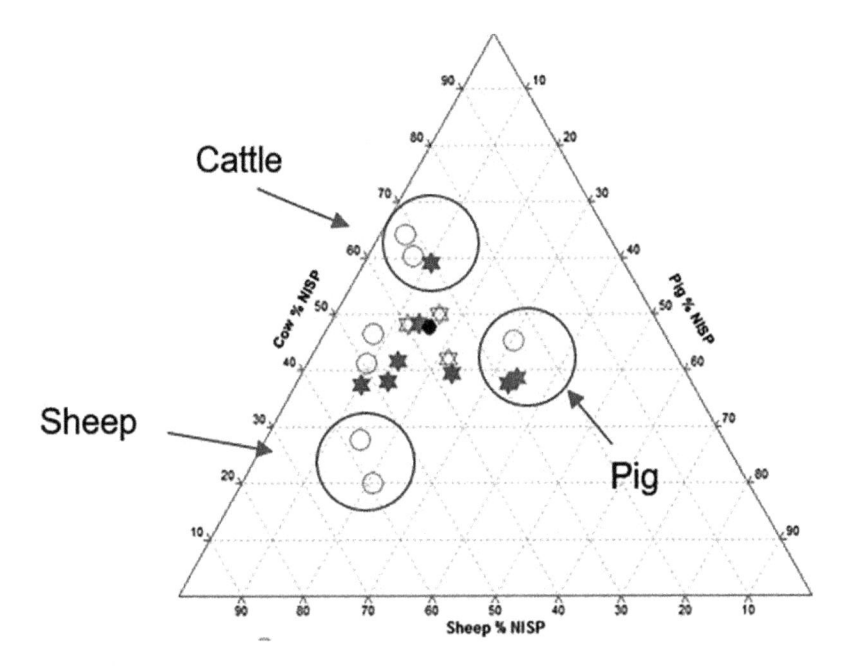

Figure 13.1b Relative frequency (%NISP) of cow, sheep/goat and pig in Viking (solid star), Late Norse (open circle) and Medieval (black circle) faunal assemblages from the Northern Isles. Open stars indicate Norse sites for which chronological subdivision into earlier and later periods is not possible. For data values, see Table 13.1.

and Brough Road, Birsay (Viking). Mainland and Batey (2018) have equated this with elite consumption patterns (explored further below). In medieval England, a preference for pigs at high-status sites has been attributed to their ideal role as food rent/tribute animals, as they can be raised cheaply without loss of more valuable livestock such as cattle (for example, Sykes 2007). For Viking Scotland, Scandinavian food traditions and social practices surrounding gift-giving and commensal activities are likely also to have contributed to dietary choices made by the Earls and their households (Mainland and Batey 2018).

By the Late Norse period, the overall impression is of a structured, potentially hierarchical farming system in which specific farmsteads are focusing on particular pastoral products (Figure 13.2). At Skaill (Deerness), Scatness and possibly Saevar Howe, there is an emphasis on older sheep from the Viking period onwards, suggestive of wool production. For Earl's Bu and the Birsay Bay sites, the prevalence of individuals at a prime-meat age (c. 2–4 years) suggests cattle and sheep raised for meat. At Pool and Snusgar, culling patterns show a high number of neonatal cattle deaths, indicative of specialised dairy production. This is in

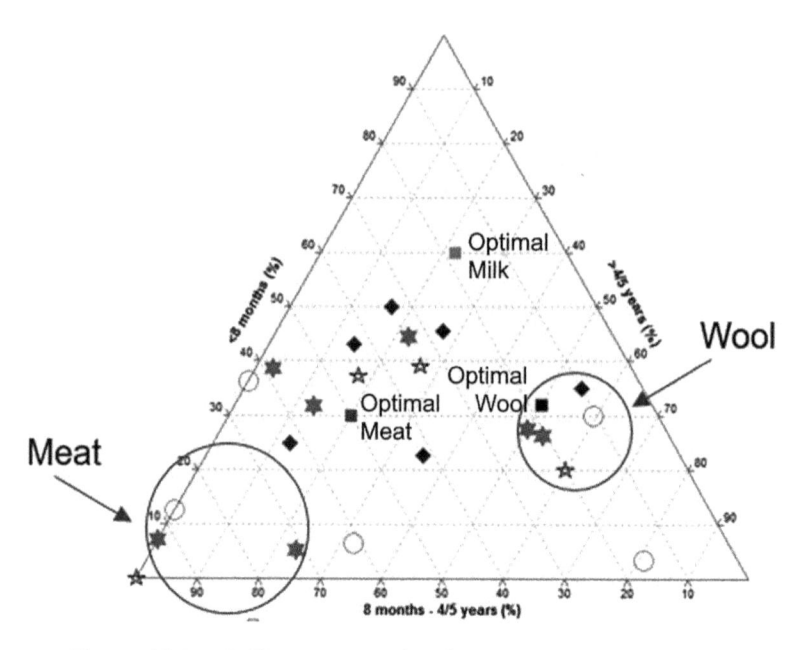

Figure 13.2a Culling strategy for sheep in Late Iron-Age, Viking and Late Norse Orkney (diamond = Late Iron Age; solid star = Viking; open star = Norse; open circle = Late Norse) (squares show expected % for optimised production strategies, after Payne [1973]). For data values, see Table 13.2a.

contrast with the Late Iron Age, where a more mixed-subsistence-style farming economy is represented: sheep were being used for all products, cattle for dairy and with little variation between sites. There are currently too few well-dated sites with large faunal assemblages from the Late Iron Age, Pictish/Viking interface and earlier Viking period (from c. 600 to 1000) to say whether this shift towards more specialised farming economies is a consequence of new approaches to farming and estate management brought in with initial settlement of the islands or a consequence of estate reorganisation as the earldom was established.

The power and politics of Norse farming practices: Feasting, commensality and identity

The significant role that feasting played in Norse society as a form of gift-giving, facilitating social interactions between host and recipients, is demonstrated by the many vivid depictions of such events and their consequences in the Icelandic sagas (Zori et al. 2013), including in the *Orkneyinga Saga* (Mainland and Batey 2018). Zooarchaeological data is

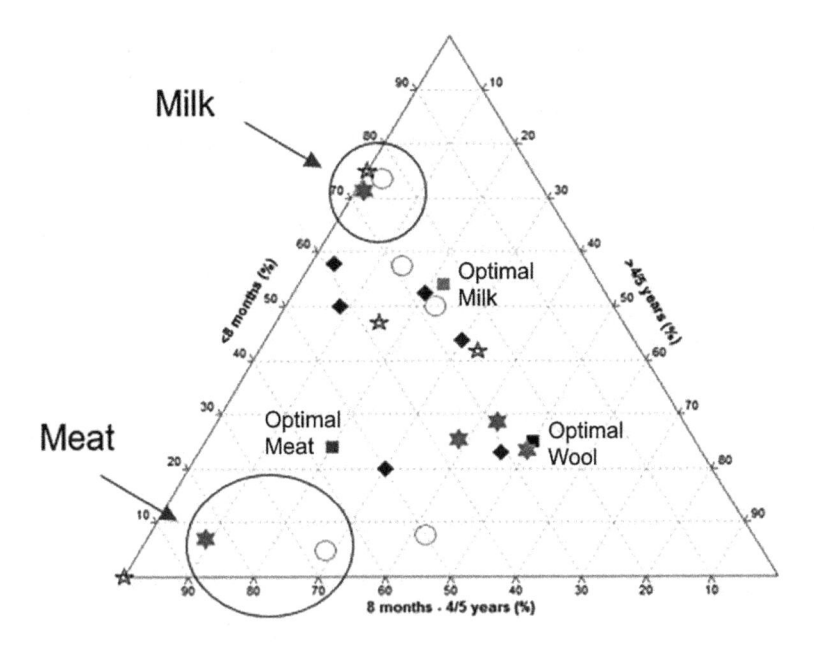

Figure 13.2b Culling strategy for cattle in Late Iron-Age, Viking and Late Norse Orkney (diamond = Late Iron Age; solid star = Viking; open star = Norse; open circle = Late Norse) (squares show expected % for optimised production strategies, after Halstead [1985]). For data values, see Table 13.2b.

now being used to flesh out these literary accounts. Following on from Zori et al.'s (2013) research on feasting practices in Iceland, Mainland and Batey (2018) demonstrate how a detailed contextual analysis of middens at the Earl's Bu in Orphir provides insight into the nature of consumption at a high-status residence in Viking and Late Norse Orkney (Batey, this volume). Pigs and cattle were the main species consumed, with evidence for redistribution of pork joints pointing to movement of meat and/or meat products. Similar patterns of consumption are evident at other higher-status sites likely associated with the Orkney Earls or their chieftains, for example, Birsay, Tuquoy (Mainland forthcoming a) and Skaill, Deerness and Snusgar (Mainland and Batey 2018; Mainland et al. 2019). The preference for pork at these higher-status sites may be evidence for a continuation of Scandinavian culinary and potentially religious traditions (Magnell and Iregen 2010; Gräslund 2012; Gotfredsen et al. 2015). Alternatively, pre-Viking elite dietary traditions from the Northern Isles may be indicated, pig consumption being higher at presumed high-status Late Iron-Age sites such as Howe and Scatness (Figure 13.1). Either way, elite culinary traditions in the Northern Isles contrast with elsewhere in the

180 Ingrid Mainland

Table 13.1 Relative frequency of cattle, sheep/goat and pig (% NISP) at Late Iron-Age (LIA), Viking (V), Norse (N) and Late Norse (LN) sites in the Northern Isles. Chronologies are as follows: Late Iron Age = AD 300/400–800; Viking = end 8th century to 1050; Late Norse = 1050 to c. mid-15th century; Medieval = mid-15th to 16th century.

Site	Cow	Sheep/goat	Pig	Period
Beachview (Rackham 1986)	27.75	57.28	14.96	LN
Earl's Bu (Mainland in prep)	42.08	36.35	21.57	N
Pool (Bond 2007)	41.36	49.46	9.17	N
Saevar Howe (Rowley-Conwy 1983)	50	33.76	16.24	N
Skaill (Noddle 1997)	48.18	39.63	12.19	N
Brough Road A1&2 (Rackham 1989)	37.61	29.17	33.21	V
Buckquoy (Noddle 1978)	41.78	44.27	13.95	V
Pool (Bond 2007)	37.47	52.16	10.37	V
Broch of Birsay (Seller 1986)	38.61	27.14	34.24	V
Earl's Bu (Mainland in prep)	39.45	37.05	23.5	V
Quoygrew (Harland 2012)	38.03	47.7	14.27	V
Scatness (Cussans and Bond 2010)	59.02	30.39	10.59	V
Snusgar (Mainland et al. 2019)	48.43	37.66	13.91	V
Broch of Birsay (Seller 1986)	46.54	45.82	7.63	LN
Earl's Bu (Mainland in prep)	45.29	24.34	30.38	LN
Quoygrew (Harland 2012)	64.19	31.86	3.95	LN
Scatness (Cussans and Bond 2007)	60.28	32.62	7.09	LN
Snusgar (Mainland et al. 2019)	45.24	40.51	14.25	LN
Snusgar (Mainland et al. 2019)	47.75	36.52	15.73	M
Pool (Smith 1994)	41.67	46.28	12.05	LIA
Skaill (Noddle 1997)	46.25	42.68	11.08	LIA
Howe (Smith 1994)	35.9	43.31	20.79	LIA
Scalloway (Sharples et al. 1998)	49.6	33.15	17.25	LIA
Brettanness (Serjeantson pers comm)	32.24	50.12	17.64	LIA
Broch of Birsay (Sellar 1986)	42.36	54.33	3.31	LIA
Brough Road A1&2 (Rackham 1989)	41.03	32.05	26.92	LIA
Buckquoy (Noddle 1978)	52.54	25.24	22.22	LIA
Cairns (Behrendt 2015)	41.7	41.7	16.6	LIA
Scalloway (Sharples et al. 1998)	45.56	35.52	18.92	LIA
Scatness (Cussans and Bond 2010)	50.66	31.9	17.44	LIA

Table 13.2a Culling profiles for sheep/goat. Age categories are based on grouped Payne (1973) age stages as follows: <1 year = A–D; 1–4 years = D–F; > 4 years = G–I. For references and chronological groupings, see caption Table 13.1. Full mortality profiles for these sites are shown in Mainland and Batey (2018) and Mainland (forthcoming).

Site	< 1 year	1 to 4 years	>4 years	Period
Saevar Howe	20	20	60	N
Skaill	39.02	34.15	26.83	N
Pool	37.25	45.1	17.65	N
Earl's Bu	0	100	0	N
Buckquoy	44.44	33.33	22.22	V
Pool	31.71	55.28	13.01	V
Snusgar	26.25	20.63	53.13	V
Scatness	27.5	22.5	50	V
Quoygrew	38.57	58.57	2.86	V
Broch of Birsay	5.22	71.3	23.48	V
Earl's Bu	7.14	92.86	0	V
Snusgar	29.86	10.63	59.5	LN
Broch of Birsay	3.45	15.52	81.03	LN
Quoygrew	36.19	63.81	0	LN
Earl's Bu	12.5	87.5	0	LN
Beachview	6.45	61.29	32.26	LN
Skaill	22.7	41.84	35.46	LIA
Pool	25	62.5	12.5	LIA
Howe	43.06	43.06	13.89	LIA
Scatness	35	10	55	LIA
Broch of Birsay	0	19.35	80.65	LIA
Buckquoy	45.45	27.27	27.27	LIA
Cairns	50	33.33	16.67	LIA
Meat	30	50	20	Payne 1973
Milk	60	18	22	Payne 1973
Wool	32	18	50	Payne 1973

Table 13.2b Culling profiles for cattle. Age categories are based on grouped Halstead (1982) age stages as follows: <8 months = A–B; 8 months to 4–5 years = 1–4 years = C–F; > 4–5 years = G–I. For references and chronological groupings, see caption Table 13.1. Full mortality profiles for these sites are shown in Mainland and Batey (2018) and Mainland (forthcoming).

Site	Age-at-death <8months	8months to 4–5 years	>4–5 years	Period
Pool	73.53	23.53	2.94	N
Saevar Howe	75	25	0	N
Skaill	47.06	37.25	15.69	N
Buckquoy	41.67	25	33.33	N
Earl's Bu	0	100	0	N
Pool	71.36	27.41	1.23	V
Snusgar	25.38	36.15	38.46	V
Quoygrew	23.33	26.67	50	V
Scatness	28.57	28.57	42.86	V
Earl's Bu	7.14	83.93	8.93	V
Snusgar	50	27.27	22.73	LN
Quoygrew	57.42	28.6	13.98	LN
Earl's Bu	4.76	66.67	28.57	LN
Beachview	7.69	50	42.31	LN
Skaill	43.71	26.35	29.94	LIA
Pool	57.93	38.62	3.45	LIA
Howe	50	41.67	8.33	LIA
Buckquoy	23.08	30.77	46.15	LIA
Cairns	52.5	27.5	20	LIA
Scatness	20	50	30	LIA
Meat	24	56	20	Halstead 1982
Milk	54	24	22	Halstead 1982
Traction	25	25	50	Halstead 1982

Norse North Atlantic diaspora, where Zori et al. (2013) and Lucas and McGovern (2007) have argued cattle underpin feasting economies, and that it is the sacrifice of cattle and consumption of beef which was used to acquire power and status. Here there are hints of variability in adaptation of farming practices across the North Atlantic, reflecting differing trajectories of initial settlement, cultural interactions with indigenous inhabitants, and the limitations placed on farming practices by the environment and climate of these island groups. Exploring further the factors underpinning this variability and its links with identity, as well as environmental factors, is a priority for future research.

Conclusions

Livestock farming in Viking and Norse Scotland emerged as a highly organised system geared towards the production of specific products, particularly in the Late Norse period but perhaps earlier also. In the Northern Isles, the Earls' estate farms were heavily focused on meat production, and at the Earl's Bu, at least, appear to have been the primary resource base supporting the feasting and other commensal activities expected of leading members in what was essentially a warrior-based aristocracy until well into the late 12th/early 13th century. Intensification through time during the Norse period is evident at other, lower-status sites in dairying and possibly wool production. This likely represents production for taxation (wool, butter) to meet the Earls' growing fiscal demands to finance (along with fish and grains) the developing Earldom and participate in growing European trading economies.

References

Adams, C. T., S. L. Poaps and J. P. Huntley (2012) Arable agriculture and gathering: The botanical evidence. In J. Barrett (ed.), *Being an Islander: Production and Identity at Quoygrew, Orkney, AD 900–1600*. Cambridge: McDonald Institute for Archaeological Research, 161–98.

Aldritt, D. (2019) The plant remains. In D. Griffiths, J. Harrison and M. Athanson (eds), *Beside the Ocean: Coastal Landscapes at the Bay of Skaill, Marwick and Birsay Bay, Orkney. Archaeological Research 2003–17*. Oxford: Oxbow, 144–74.

Amorosi, J., J. Woollett, P. Perdikaris and T. McGovern (1996) Regional zooarchaeology and global change: Problems and potentials. *World Archaeology* 28, 126–57.

Ascough, P. L., M. J. Church, G. T. Cook, Á. Einarsson, T. McGovern, A. J. Dugmore and K. J. Edwards (2014) Stable isotopic ($\delta 13C$ and $\delta 15N$) characterization of key faunal resources from Norse period settlements in North Iceland. *Journal of the North Atlantic* Special Volume 7, 25–42.

Barrett, J. H. and M. Richards (2012) Feeding the livestock: The stable isotope evidence. In J. Barrett (ed.), *Being an Islander: Production and Identity at Quoygrew, Orkney, AD 900–1600*. Cambridge: McDonald Institute for Archaeological Research, 199–206.

Best, J. and J. Mulville (2016) Birds from the water: Reconstructing avian resource use and contribution to diet in prehistoric Scottish island environments. *Journal of Archaeological Science* 6, 654–64.

Bond, J. M. (2007) The mammal bone. In J. Hunter (ed.), *Excavations at Pool, Sanday. A Multi-Period Settlement from Neolithic to Late Norse Times*. Kirkwall: The Orcadian, 207–62.

Bond, J. M. and J. R. Hunter (1987) Flax-growing in Orkney from the Norse period to the 18th century. *Proceedings of the Society of Antiquaries Scotland* 117, 175–81.

Bowles, D., A. Carson and P. Isaac (2014) Genetic distinctiveness of the Herdwick sheep breed and two other locally adapted hill breeds of the UK. *PLoS ONE* 9(1), e87823.

Brink, S. and N. Price (2012) *The Viking World* [reprint]. London: Routledge.

Brown, J. L., I. A. Simpson, S. J. L. Morrison, W. P. Adderley, E. Tisdall and O. Vésteinsson (2012) Shieling areas: Historical grazing pressures and landscape responses in Northern Iceland. *Human Ecology* 40, 81–99.

Chessa, B., F. Pereira, F. Arnaud, A. Amorim, F. Goyache, I. Mainland, R. R. Kao, J. M. Pemberton, D. Beraldi, M. J. Stear, A. Alberti, M. Pittau, L. Iannuzzi, M. H. Banabazi, R. R. Kazwala, Y.-P. Zhang, J. J. Arranz, B. A. Ali, Z. Wang, M. Uzun, M. M. Dione, I. Olsaker, L.-E. Holm, U. Saarma, S. Ahmad, N. Marzanov, E. Eythorsdottir, M. J. Holland, P. Ajmone-Marsan, M. W. Bruford, J. Kantanen, T. E. Spencer and M. Palmarini (2009) Revealing the history of sheep domestication using retrovirus integrations. *Science* 324, 532–6.

Cooke, S. (2016) Trading identities: Alternative interpretations of Viking horse remains in Scotland. A Pierowall perspective. *Papers from the Institute of Archaeology* 26, 1–15.

Cooke, S. (2017) *How the Vikings Inhabited Scotland: A Social Zooarchaeological Approach*. Unpublished PhD thesis, University of Aberdeen.

Cussans, J. (2013) *Changes in the Size and Shape of Domestic Mammals across the North Atlantic Region over Time: The Effects of Environment and Economy on Bone Growth of Livestock from the Neolithic to the Post Medieval Period with Particular Reference to the Scandinavian Expansion Westwards*. Unpublished PhD thesis, University of Bradford.

Cussans, J. E. and J. M. Bond (2010) Mammal bone. In S. Dockrill, J. M. Bond, V. E. Turner, L. D. Brown, D. J. Bashford, J. E. Cussans and R. Nicholson (eds), *Excavations at Old Scatness, Shetland Volume 1: The Pictish Village and Viking Settlement*. Lerwick: Shetland Heritage Publications, 132–55.

Cussans, J. E., J. M. Bond and T. O'Connor (2007) Biometry and population change: Metrical analysis of the mammal bone. In J. Hunter (ed.), *Excavations at Pool Sanday*. Kirkwall: The Orcadian Press, 242–62.

Dugmore, A. J., T. H. McGovern, O. Vésteinsson, J. Arneborg, R. Streeter and C. Keller (2012) Cultural adaptation, compounding vulnerabilities and conjunctures in Norse Greenland. *Proceedings of the National Academy of Sciences of the United States of America* 109, 3658–63.

Edwards, C. J., C. Ginja, J. Kantanen, L. Pérez-Pardal and A. Tresset (2011) Dual origins of dairy cattle farming – Evidence from a comprehensive survey of European Y-chromosomal variation. *PLoS ONE* 6(1), e15922.

Ewens, V. (2010) *An Odontological Study of Ovicaprine Herding Strategies in the North Atlantic Islands: The Potential of Dental Enamel Defects for Identifying Secondary Product Utilisation in an Archaeological Context*. Unpublished PhD thesis, University of Bradford.

Fenton, A. (1978) *The Northern Isles*. Edinburgh: John Donald.
Fitzhugh, W. W. and E. I. Ward (2000) *Vikings: The North Atlantic Saga*. Washington, DC: Smithsonian Institution Press.
Foster, M. R. (2018) *Norse Shielings in Scotland: An Interdisciplinary Study of* setr/saetr *and* aergi *Names*. Unpublished PhD thesis, University of Edinburgh.
Gotfredsen, A. B., C. Primeau, K. M. Frei and L. Jørgensen (2015) A ritual site with sacrificial wells from the Viking Age at Trelleborg, Denmark. *Danish Journal of Archaeology* 3(2), 145–63.
Gräslund, A. S. (2012) The material culture of Old Norse religion. In S. Brink and N. Price (eds), *The Viking World*. London: Routledge, 249–56.
Halstead, P. H. (1985) A study of mandibular teeth from Romano-British contexts at Maxey. In F. Pryor (ed.), *Archaeology and Environment in the Lower Welland Valley. Vol. 1* (East Anglian Archaeology Report No. 27). Cambridge: Cambridgeshire Archaeological Committee, 219–24.
Harland, J. (2012) Animal husbandry: The mammal bone. In J. H. Barrett (ed.), *Being an Islander: Production and Identity at Quoygrew, Orkney,* AD *900–1600*. Cambridge: McDonald Institute for Archaeological Research, 135–54.
Hatting, T. (1990) Cats from Viking Age Odense. *Journal of Danish Archaeology* 9(1), 179–93.
Holmes, M. (2014) *Animals in Saxon and Scandinavian England: Backbones of Economy and Society*. Leiden: Sidestone Press.
Kupiec, P., K. Milek, G. A. Gisladóttir and J. Woollett (2016) Elusive *sel* sites: The geoarchaeological quest for Icelandic shielings and the case for Þorvaldsstaðasel, in northeast Iceland. In J. Collis, F. Nicolis and M. Pearce (eds), *Summer Farms: Seasonal Exploitation of the Uplands from Prehistory to the Present*. Sheffield: J. R. Collis Publications, 221–35.
Jamieson, A. (2021) *Rats, Cats and Hares: Exploring Natural and Humanly-Mediated Dispersal through a Genetic Approach*. Unpublished PhD thesis, University of Oxford.
Jennbert, K. (2011) *Animals and Humans: Recurrent Symbiosis in Archaeology and Old Norse Religion*. Lund: Nordic Academic Press.
Jones, E. P., K. Skirnisson, T. H. McGovern, M. T. P. Gilbert, E. Willerslev and J. Searle (2012) Fellow travellers: A concordance of colonization patterns between mice and men in the North Atlantic region. *BMC Evolutionary Biology* 12, 35.
Jones, J. R. and J. A. Mulville (2018) Norse animal husbandry in liminal environments: Stable isotope evidence from the Scottish North Atlantic islands. *Environmental Archaeology* 23(4), 338–51.
Kitchiner, A., V. E. Szabo, M. Buckley, Y. van den Hurk, I. Mainland, M. Carruthers, C. Mackay and B. A. Frasier (2021) First records of grey whale (*Eschrichtius robustus*) from Scotland. *Mammal Communications* 7, 17–28.
Lucas, G. M. and T. McGovern (2007) Bloody slaughter: Ritual decapitation and display at the Viking settlement of Hofstaðir, Iceland. *European Journal of Archaeology* 10(1), 7–30.
McGovern, T. H. (1992) Bones, buildings, and boundaries: Palaeoeconomic approaches to Norse Greenland. In C. D. Morris and J. D. Rackham (eds),

Norse and Later Settlement in the North Atlantic. Glasgow: University of Glasgow, 193–230.

Magnell, O. and F. Iregen (2010) Vestu hév blótu skal? The Old Norse blót in the light of osteological remains from Frösö Church, Jämtland, Sweden. *Current Swedish Archaeology* 18, 223–50.

Mainland, I. (Forthcoming a) Tuquoy: The faunal assemblages. In O. Owen (ed.), *Excavations at Late Norse Tuquoy*.

Mainland, I. (Forthcoming b) Earl's Bu: The mammal and avian assemblages. *The Earl's Bu, Orphir, Orkney: A Norse Economic Hub*.

Mainland, I. and J. Harland (2021) Human impact on North Atlantic biota: Farming and farm animals, fishing, sealing and whaling. In E. Panagiotakopulu and J. Sadler (eds), *North Atlantic Island Biota: Aspects of the Past, Choices for the Future*. Oxford: Routledge, 251–72.

Mainland, I. and C. Batey (2018) The nature of the feast: Commensality and the politics of consumption in Viking Age and Early Medieval Northern Europe. *World Archaeology* 50(5), 781–803.

Mainland, I., V. Ewens and C. Webster (2019) The mammal bones. In D. Griffiths, J. Harrison and M. Athanson (eds), *Beside the Ocean: Coastal Landscapes at the Bay of Skaill, Marwick and Birsay Bay, Orkney. Archaeological Research 2003–17*. Oxford: Oxbow, 175–99.

Mainland, I., J. Towers, V. Ewens, G. Davis, J. Montgomery, C. Batey, N. Card and J. Downes (2016) Toiling with teeth: An integrated dental analysis of sheep and cattle dentition in Iron Age and Viking–Late Norse Orkney. *Journal of Archaeological Science: Reports* 6, 837–55.

Mulville, J. A. Powell, J. Williams, C. Ingrem and J. R. Jones (2018) The faunal remains – mammals. In M. Parker Pearson, M. Brennand, J. Mulville and H. Smith (eds), *Cille Pheadair: A Norse Farmstead and Pictish Burial Cairn in South Uist*. Oxford: Oxbow, 419–65.

Mullin, V. (2018) *Herding Ancient Domesticates: From Bones to Genomes*. Unpublished PhD thesis, University College Dublin.

Noddle, B. A. (1977) Appendix 1. The animal bones from Buckquoy, Orkney. In A. Ritchie (ed.), Excavations of Pictish and Viking-Age farmsteads at Buckquoy, Orkney. *Proceedings of the Society of Antiquaries of Scotland* 108, 174–227.

Noddle, B. (1997) Animal bone. In S. Butuex (ed.), *Settlements at Skaill, Deerness, Orkney*. British Archaeological Reports (British Series) 260. Oxford: BAR, 234–42.

O'Connor, T. (2010) Livestock and deadstock in early medieval Europe from the North Sea to the Baltic. *Environmental Archaeology* 15(1), 1–15.

Pálsdóttir, Albína Hulda (n.d.) https://www.icelandiczooarch.is/ [Last updated 22 September 2019].

Payne, S. (1973) Kill-off patterns in sheep and goats: The mandibles from Aşvan Kale. *Anatolian Studies* 23, 281–303.

Petersen, J. L., J. R. Mickelson, E. G. Cothran, L. S. Andersson, J. Axelsson, E. Bailey, D. Bannasch, M. M. Binns, A. S. Borges, P. Brama, A. da Câmara Machado, O. Distl, M. Felicetti, L. Fox-Clipsham, K. T. Graves, G. Guérin, B. Haase, T. Hasegawa, K. Hemmann, E. W. Hill, T. Leeb, G. Lindgren, H. Lohi, M. S. Lopes, B. A. McGivney, S. Mikko, N. Orr, M. C. T. Penedo, R. J.

Piercy, M. Raekallio, S. Rieder, K. H. Røed, M. Silvestrelli, J. Swinburne, T. Tozaki, M. Vaudin, C. M. Wade and M. E. McCue (2013) Genetic diversity in the modern horse illustrated from genome-wide SNP data. *PLoS ONE* 8(1), e54997.

Poole, K. (2013) Horses for courses? Religious change and dietary shifts in Anglo-Saxon England. *Oxford Journal of Archaeology* 32(3), 319–33.

Poole, K. (2015) The contextual cat: Human–animal relations and social meaning in Anglo-Saxon England. *Journal of Archaeological Method and Theory* 22, 857–82.

Rackham, D. J. (1986) Beachview Birsay: The biological assemblage. In C. D. Morris (ed.), *The Birsay Bay Project Vol 2. Sites in Birsay Village and on the Brough of Birsay, Orkney*. Stroud: Sutton Publishing, 161–86.

Rackham, D. J. (1989) Domestic and wild mammals. In C. D. Morris (ed.), *The Birsay Bay Project Volume 1. Coastal Sites beside the Brough Road, Birsay, Orkney Excavations 1976–82*. Stroud: Sutton Publishing, 232–47.

Rowley-Conwy, P. (1983) The animal and bird bones. In J. Hedges (ed.), Trial excavations on Pictish and Viking settlements at Saevar Howe, Birsay, Orkney. *Glasgow Archaeological Journal* 10, 109–11.

Salvagno, L. and U. Albarella (2019) Was the English medieval goat genuinely rare? A new morphometric approach provides the answer. *Archaeological and Anthropological Science* 11, 5095–132.

Seller, T. J. (1986) Animal bone material. In J. R. Hunter (ed.), *Rescue Excavations on the Brough of Birsay 1974–82*. Society of Antiquaries of Scotland monograph series 4. Edinburgh: Society of Antiquaries of Scotland, 208–16.

Serjeantson, D. (2014) The diverse origins of bird bones from Scottish coastal sites. *International Journal of Osteoarchaeology* 24, 279–88.

Sharples, N. (1998) *Scalloway: A Broch, Late Iron Age Settlement and Medieval Cemetery in Shetland*. Oxford: Oxbow Books.

Sharples, N. (2020) *A Norse Settlement in the Outer Hebrides. Excavation on Mounds 2 and 2a, Bornais, S. Uist*. Oxford: Oxbow Books.

Simpson, I. A. (1997) Relict properties of anthropogenic deep top soils as indicators of infield management in Marwick, West Mainland, Orkney. *Journal of Archaeological Science* 24, 365–80.

Smiarowski, K., R. Harrison, S. Brewington, M. Hicks, F. Feeley, C. Dupont-Herbert, G. Hambrecht, J. Woollett and T. H. McGovern (2017) Zooarchaeology of the Scandinavian settlements in Iceland and Greenland: Diverging pathways. In U. Albarella, M. Rizzetto, H. Russ, K. Vickers and S. Viner-Daniels (eds), *Oxford Handbook of Zooarchaeology*. Oxford: Oxford University Press.

Smith, C. (1994) Animal bone report. In B. Ballin Smith (ed.), *Howe: Four Millennia of Orkney Prehistory, Excavations 1978–1982*. Society of Antiquaries of Scotland monograph series 9. Edinburgh: Society of Antiquaries of Scotland, 139–53.

Smith, C. (Forthcoming) The animal bones from Tuquoy.

Sykes, N. (2007) *The Norman Conquest: A Zooarchaeological Perspective*. BAR International Series 1656. Oxford: Archaeopress.

Sykes, N. (2014) *Beastly Questions: Animal Answers to Archaeological Issues*. London: Bloomsbury.

Szabo, V. (2008) *Monstrous Fishes and the Mead Dark Sea. Whaling in the Medieval North Atlantic*. Leiden: Brill Academic Publishers.

Toplak, M. S. (2019) The warrior and the cat: A re-evaluation of the roles of domestic cats in Viking Age Scandinavia. *Current Swedish Archaeology* 27, 213–45.

Towers, J., I. Mainland, J. Bond and J. Montgomery (2017) Calving seasonality at Pool, Orkney during the first millennium A.D.: An investigation using intra-tooth isotope ratio analysis of cattle molar enamel. *Environmental Archaeology* 22(1), 40–55.

Zori, D., J. Byock, E. Erlendsson, S. Martin, T. Wake and K. J. Edwards (2013) Feasting in Viking Age Iceland: Sustaining a chiefly political economy in a marginal environment. *Antiquity* 87, 150–65.

Chapter 14

Norse Shielings in Scotland: An Example of Cultural Contact

Ryan Foster

Shielings were a characteristic feature of Scandinavian infield-outfield farming from the Iron Age up until relatively recent times. To sustain fertility of the limited arable land in Norway, cattle were stall fed in winter and the manure collected to fertilise the arable land (Zimmermann 1999: 313–16). Shielings are secondary farming units, where livestock were driven to provide summer grazing and allow winter fodder collection. The Norse infield-outfield system involved an integration of arable and pastoral farming. The growing of cereal crops and hay in the infield was directly supported by the addition of nutrients from the outfield, through the input of cattle manure (Øye 2009: 101).

The export of this type of farming system has been suggested through onomastic (place-name) and archaeological evidence in Scandinavian settlements abroad (Fellows-Jensen 1980). What is unusual in Britain and the Faroe Islands was that Scandinavian settlers also adopted *ærgi*, a Gaelic word for a shieling (Fellows-Jensen 1980: 67), alongside the Old Norse (ON) *sætr*. As one of the few Gaelic words adopted into Old Norse, *ærgi* highlights an important area of cultural contact.

Definitions

The two most common names for a shieling in ON were the related terms *setr* and *sætr* (Beito 1949: 11–84). Cleasby and Vigfusson (1874: 525, 619) give the meaning of *setr* n. as: 1. seat, residence, or 2. a mountain pasture or dairy lands; while *sætr* n. was a specific term for a mountain pasture. The two terms are now indistinguishable from each other in the Scottish onomastic corpus (Crawford 1987: 102–3), and for simplicity will be referred to as *sætr* hereafter.

Ærgi (erg) n. has the same definition as *sætr* (Cleasby and Vigfusson 1874: 133), and was adopted from either Scottish Gaelic *àirigh* f.: 1. hill pasture, 2. shieling (MacBain 1911: 10) or Old Irish *áirge* f.: 1. herd of cattle, 2. pasture, 3. herdsman's hut, 4. milk herd (Dineen 1904: 24).

190 Ryan Foster

Contact linguistic theory

For any word to be adopted into another language, there needs to be contact between speakers of the two languages. Weinreich emphasised social indicators in borrowing, with the less prestigious language borrowing from the more prestigious one (1968: 3). The adoption of *ærgi* is unusual as not only was ON the dominant language, but it already had its own word for a shieling. In this situation, Weinreich (1968: 54–6) suggests that there are three possible outcomes: (1) confusion, leading to the abandonment of one of the terms; (2) replacement of the old word with the new foreign term; or (3) the specialisation of usage.

Distribution

ON shielings in Scotland have a complementary distribution: *ærgi* predominate in Sutherland, Uists and Inner Hebrides, while *sætr*-names are concentrated in the Northern Isles, Caithness and Lewis (Figure 14.1). These three regions were believed to be Pictish in the pre-Viking Age (Bannerman 1974: 28) and remained ON-speaking until between the 12th and 16th centuries (Waugh 1993: 125; Clancy 2008: 46). It is also possible that settlement occurred before contact with Gaelic-speakers,

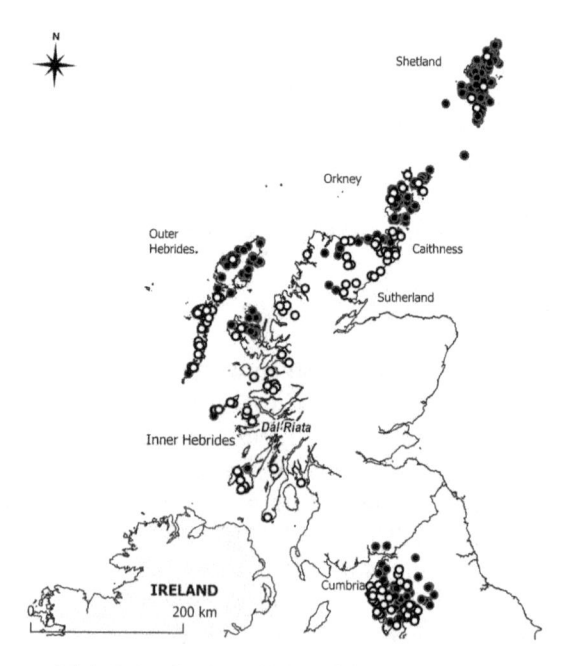

Figure 14.1 Distribution map of Old Norse shieling-names in Britain (*sætr* black centred and *ærgi* white).

or at least before contact developed past the point of a sword (Dumville 2008: 357–8). The long period of ON dominance would also allow *sætr*-names to become cemented into the landscape (Gammeltoft 2007: 481).

In comparison, *ærgi*-names increase with closeness to the heartland of Gaelic Dál Riata, which covered much of modern Argyll (Bannerman 1974: 28). Waugh has suggested that areas with a higher proportion of Gaelic-speakers might have led to *ærgi* simply replacing *sætr* (1993: 123). However, both *sætr* and *ærgi* are present in the later 10th-century settlement of Cumbria, which would suggest that *ærgi* was incorporated within the Norse onomastic lexicon rather than replacing *sætr* (Oram 2000: 248).

Macniven has argued for a comprehensive Scandinavian settlement in Islay (2015: 64) and other parts of the Inner Hebrides, which was later obscured by the length of subsequent Gaelic influence (2015: 120). The relative absence of *sætr*-names in the Inner Hebrides and Uists may link to an early language shift back to Gaelic, which saw many ON names abandoned (Jennings and Kruse 2009: 141). If *sætr* was not replaced by *ærgi*, then either there was specialisation in use, or *ærgi* represented a new concept that *sætr* did not cover (Weinreich 1968: 54–8); in this regard, Gammeltoft (2004: 73–4) makes the point that adopted Gaelic place-names are not topographical, but relate to specialist farming terms.

Discussion

Cattle formed the basis of both Norse and Gaelic farming systems. There are differences, however, which may help explain the adoption of *ærgi*. At the Norwegian market town of Kaupang, most cattle bones excavated were from animals aged between 24 and 30 months (Barrett et al. 2004: 87). Similarly, a three-year-old ox was given for a feast when acknowledging an illegitimate son in the 11th-century Norwegian *Gulathing* Law Code (Larson 1935: 79). The law code also states that a cow's value (*kýrlag*), when offered as compensation, remained constant until eight winters (Larson 1935: 151). However, when a ship's crew slaughtered cattle for food (*Strandhǫgg*), both a cow and a three-year ox were valued at two ǿra (48g of silver, based on the later Scandinavian ǿra, see Brøgger 1921: 82–5), but a full-grown ox at two-and-a-half ǿra (60g of silver) (Larson 1935: 192). This suggests a general pastoral economy, but with an emphasis on meat production. Bjørgo's study of Viking-Age shielings in Inner Sogn also concluded dairying was probably not an important part of the shieling economy, which focused on accessing summer grazing, winter fodder collection and ancillary activities (2005: 225).

One of the few sources for Gaelic farming in pre-Viking Age are Irish laws from the 8th century. What is evident is the importance of dairy farming in

Gaelic society; a *milch* (milking) cow with calf was worth twice that of a 'dry' cow and reached a maximum value (28.349g of silver) at six years old on the birth of a third calf (*bó threlóeg*) (Kelly 1997: 64–5; McCormick 2014: 122–4). A two-year-old bullock (*colpthach firenn*) was only valued at 4.17g of silver, a third less than a dry two-year-old cow (Kelly 1997: 62). Male cattle, other than oxen, were not given a value after three years (McCormick 2014: 122).

References in early Irish sources link *áirge* with a cattle herd (9) or to milking/dairy products (7), giving the impression of a close link with dairying (Foster 2018: 456–8). Archaeological excavations corroborate this emphasis on dairying, with McCormick (2014) finding bone assemblages had a two-stage age-slaughter pattern. There was an initial cull around two years, probably of cattle not needed for dairying or traction, and a second involving animals over seven years old and likely older dairy cows (2014: 122). The Viking-Age bone assemblage from Fishamble Street, Dublin, consisted of these older cattle, hinting at its integration into the Irish dairy system, at least as an outlet for older animals (McCormick 2014: 122).

The only fully excavated *ærgi* site is Argisbrekka in the Faroes, where Mahler (1993: 489–91) found close parallels with Norwegian shielings concerning ancillary activities, including possible hay making. Fodder collection was unknown in Ireland in the pre-Viking Age, with cattle feeding outside all year (Kelly 1997: 45–7). However, it remained an essential aspect of Norse farming across the North Atlantic and throughout the Viking Age (Amorosi et al. 1998: 48–51). This implies that the Norse farming system was tweaked to incorporate *ærgi*, rather than substantially changed.

A key factor in the adoption would seem to be that *ærgi*-names are located on more fertile sites than *sætr*-names (Foster 2018: 381–97, 465–88). This suggests a structured grazing regime with milk cattle separated from dry and beef cattle and sent to the *ærgi* for better-quality grazing, leading to higher- and better-quality milk yields (Hofstetter et al. 2011: 717). In South Uist, a different management strategy has been suggested for dairy and beef cattle, which remained unchanged here throughout the Viking Age. Notably, there is a change in the grazing regime evident in the Northern Isles between the early and later phases (Jones and Mulville 2018: 345–6). This might imply that *ærgi* had been adopted prior to settlement in South Uist, but later than the Northern Isles.

Conclusion

Norse shieling names in Scotland show contact between Gaelic-speakers and Scandinavian settlers occurred on the farm. Though each society was cattle-centric, Norse farming was an integrated arable/pastoral system, whereas Gaelic farming's focus was dairying. Scandinavian settlers in the Irish Sea Region encountered Gaelic-speakers and a new concept: specialised milking shielings. Once adopted, *ærgi* was transferred during secondary migration to new settlements in the Faroes and Cumbria and older ones in the Northern Isles. Overall, I would agree with Mahler's conclusion that the Scandinavian 'decentralised farming system was not just directly transposed to the new homelands, but was itself subject to adaption' (1993: 501) and, as such, highlights a key area of cultural contact.

References

Amorosi, T., P. C. Buckland, K. J. Edwards, I. Mainland, T. H. McGovern, J. P. Sadler and P. Skidmore (1998) They did not live by grass alone: The politics and paleoecology of fodder on the North Atlantic islands. *Environmental Archaeology* 1(1), 41–54.

Bannerman, J. W. M. (1974) *Studies in the History of Dalriada*. Edinburgh: Scottish Academic Press.

Barrett, J. H., A. Hall, C. Johnstone, H. Kenward, T. O'Connor and S. Ashby (2004) *Plant and Animal Remains from Viking Age Deposits at Kaupang, Norway*. Reports from the Centre for Human Paleoecology: University of York.

Beito, O. (1949) *Norske Sæternamn*. Oslo: Aschehoug.

Bjørgo, T. (2005) Iron Age house remains from mountain areas in Inner Sogn, Western Norway. In K. A. Bergsvik and A. Engevik (eds), *Fra funn til samfunn: jernalderstudier tilegnet Bergljot Solberg på 70-årsdagen*. Bergen: Universitetet i Bergen, 209–28.

Brøgger, A. W. (1921) *Ertog og Ore: den gamle norske vegt*. Kristiania: Jacob Dybwad.

Clancy, T. C. (2008) The Gall-Ghàidheil and Galloway. *Journal of Scottish Name Studies* 2, 19–50.

Cleasby, R. and G. Vigfusson (1874) *An Icelandic–English Dictionary*. Oxford: Clarendon.

Crawford, B. E. (1987) *Scandinavian Scotland*. Leicester: Leicester University Press.

Dineen, P. (1904) *Irish–English Dictionary*. Dublin: Irish Text Society.

Dumville, D. N. (2008) Vikings in Insular chronicling. In S. Brink and N. Price (eds), *The Viking World*. Abingdon: Routledge, 350–67.

Fellows-Jensen, G. (1980) Common Gaelic *Aírge*, Old Scandinavian *Ærgi* or *Erg*. *Nomina* 4, 67–74.

Foster, M. R. (2018) *Norse Shielings in Scotland: An Interdisciplinary Study of setr/sætr and ærgi-names*. Unpublished PhD thesis, University of Edinburgh.

Gammeltoft, P. (2004) Scandinavian–Gaelic contacts: Can place-names and place-name elements be used as a source for contact-linguistic research? *NOWELE* 44, 51–90.

Gammeltoft, P. (2007) Scandinavian naming-systems in the Hebrides: A way of understanding how the Scandinavians were in contact with Gaels and Picts. In B. Ballin Smith and S. Taylor (eds), *West over Sea: Studies in Scandinavian Sea-borne Expansion and Settlement before 1300: A festschrift in honour of Dr Barbara E. Crawford*. Leiden: Brill, 479–95.

Hofstetter, P., M. Steiger Burgos, R. Petermann, A. Münger, J. W. Blum, P. Thomet, H. Menzi, S. Kohler and P. Kunz (2011) Does body size of dairy cows, at constant ratio of maintenance to production requirements, affect productivity in a pasture-based production system? *Journal of Animal Physiology and Animal Nutrition* 95(6), 717–29.

Jennings, A. and A. Kruse (2009) From Dál Riata to the Gall-Ghàidheil. *Medieval Scandinavia* 5, 123–49.

Jones, J. R. and J. Mulville (2018) Norse animal husbandry in liminal environments: Stable isotope evidence from the Scottish North Atlantic islands. *Environmental Archaeology* 23(4), 338–51.

Kelly, F. (1997) *Early Irish Farming: A Study Based Mainly on the Law-Texts of the 7th and 8th centuries AD*. Dublin: Dublin Institute for Advanced Studies.

Larson, L. M. (1935) *The Earliest Norwegian Laws, Being the* Gulathing *Law and the* Frostathing *Law*. Menasha: Columbia University Press.

MacBain, A. (1911) *An Etymological Dictionary of the Gaelic Language*. Stirling: Eneas Mackay.

Macniven, A. (2015) *The Vikings in Islay: The Place of Names in Hebridean Settlement History*. Edinburgh: John Donald.

Mahler, D. L. D. (1993) Shielings and their role in the Viking-Age economy. In C. E. Batey, J. Jesch and C. D. Morris (eds), *The Viking Age in Caithness, Orkney and the North Atlantic*. Edinburgh: Edinburgh University Press, 487–505.

McCormick, F. (2014) Agriculture, settlement, and society in Early Medieval Ireland. *Quaternary International* 346, 119–30.

Oram, R. D. (2000) *The Lordship of Galloway*. Edinburgh: John Donald.

Waugh, D. (1993) Caithness: An onomastic frontier zone. In C. E. Batey, J. Jesch and C. D. Morris (eds), *The Viking Age in Caithness, Orkney and the North Atlantic*. Edinburgh: Edinburgh University Press, 120–8.

Weinreich, U. (1968) *Languages in Contact. Findings and Problems*. London: Mouton.

Zimmermann, W. H. (1999) Why was cattle-stalling introduced in prehistory? The significance of byre and stable and of outwintering. In C. Fabech and J. Ringtved (eds), *Settlement and Landscape: Proceedings of a Conference in Århus*. Moesgård: Jutland Archaeological Society, 301–18.

Øye, I. (2009) On the margins of the medieval farm – Norwegian cases. In J. Klápště and P. Sommer (eds), *Medieval Rural Settlement in Marginal Landscapes*. Turnhout: Brepols, 99–107.

Part V

Power and the Political Landscape

In *Vikings in Scotland*, Graham-Campbell and Batey introduced the reader not only to the impact of *landnàm* and settlement on the landscape and power dynamics operating within Scandinavian Scotland (Parts I and II, this volume), but also to research on the subsequent development of *thing* (assembly) sites and architecturally impressive elite power centres, that was then at completed or near-complete publication.

Scandinavian *thing*-sites, where religious debates and legal rulings (and possibly markets: see Sanmark, this section) were held, are preserved in today's place-names such as *Tingwall* (Orkney and Shetland) and *Dingwall* (Ross). Over two decades on, Sanmark adds to their importance beyond the administrative role presumed in the 1990s by articulating how a *thing* also provided a widely accessible arena in the regional landscape for the negotiation of power relations between elites and their community.

Sanmark also explores the regionally specific evolution of *thing*-sites. Scotto-Scandinavian elites, for example, responded to a unique colonial environment in the North Atlantic that, unlike Iceland, for example, contained ancient indigenous mound monuments like barrows and overgrown brochs. Scandinavians in Scotland behaved like elites in the homelands in their use of these venerable mounds to legitimise an 'ancient' right to rule that was rooted in the landscape.

Domination of both the pre-existing and contemporary landscape is also apparent in the site location and wealth demonstrated at the Brough of Birsay, an influential Pictish site that became 'the power centre of the Viking Earldom of Orkney' (Morris, this section) and an important church site. Indeed, as *Vikings in Scotland* demonstrated, the story of Orcadian power evolution and its landscape impact is one of the increasing importance of Christianity.

Beyond church power, secular control in Orkney and the Northern Isles pivoted increasingly to the Norwegian kingdom as the Viking Age moved into the Late Norse period. At the same time, however, regional elites like the Orkney Earls could increase their wealth from the ever-more efficient exploitation of natural resources; this seems to have been the case within Orkney at the Earl's Bu, Orphir with its elite *bu* place-name, sophisticated watermill, and important manufacturing complex at nearby Lavacroon (Batey, this section). This coastal site dominated both the landscape and the seascape, becoming a hub for far-reaching networks and conspicuous consumption. With its highly visible hall and stone church, Earl's Bu exemplifies the impressive architecture of Late Norse elites in the Northern Isles.

As with the elite sites of Earl's Bu and the Brough of Birsay, Tuquoy (Orkney) has greatly benefited from advances to survey and sampling techniques since 1998, notably improving the palaeoenvironmental evidence, refining the image of Tuquoy as a relatively short-lived but architecturally impressive and wealthy complex, perhaps now with a massive Late Norse tower/castle to further dominate the landscape (Owen, this section).

This section concludes by showing how power was also demonstrated non-architecturally, where, as with *thing*-site reuse of monuments, the past was used to legitimise the present: Hall and Caldwell (this section) explore this in the Lewis gaming pieces, elements of which 'helped to recall . . . a Viking past' within the hybridising and politically fraught Gaelic-Norse society of the 12th- and 13th-century Western Isles.

Chapter 15

Thing-sites and the Political Landscape in the North
Alexandra Sanmark

This chapter examines assembly (*thing*, ON *þing*) sites in the Norse settlements in the North Atlantic set within the context of the Viking homelands (for full discussion, see Sanmark 2017a). Particular attention will be paid to the traits and features of Norse assembly-sites in Scotland, Iceland, Greenland and the Faroe Islands. *Things* functioned as both parliaments and courts and were held at outdoor sites and constituted arenas where the elite and the local community met. Assembly-sites existed across Scandinavia, and the people of the Viking Age also brought law and *thing* to all their new homes in the west. These sites were not randomly chosen, but were the outcome of well-planned and well-executed elite strategies, involving all aspects from site selection to the construction and maintenance of features, which were charged with symbolism and meaning. Different combinations of these features are found at *thing*-sites, depending on what message the creators – the elite – wanted to transmit to the population (Sanmark 2017a: 1, 5, 28, 56–7).[1] In general, *thing*-sites were slotted into tiers of administrative territorial units, which, in simplified form, resulted in top-level sites for whole law provinces and local sites for the smaller units often, but not exclusively, referred to as *herað* units (Sanmark 2017a: 37–42, 56–81, 162–240). As will be demonstrated here, *thing*-sites across the North Atlantic share many traits and features with Scandinavian assembly-sites, but there are some striking variations, the reasons for which will be examined in detail. An important difference between the areas under examination and with implications for *thing*-site design is that Scotland had been settled since the Mesolithic period, while Iceland, Greenland and the Faroes were (almost) unpopulated prior to Norse settlement (Sanmark 2017a: ch. 7 and 8).

The overriding characteristic in the selection of assembly-sites was a location on important communication routes. In Scandinavia, sites were often situated at the convergence of land and water routes (Brink 2004; Sanmark 2017a: 122–31). It was in the interest of the ruler and the elite that as many as possible attended the meetings. The larger the number of people who attended and thus approved a decision or verdict, the stronger the position of the ruler. In order to facilitate mass participation, assembly-sites were created at places that could easily be reached at a predetermined time, which would have been widely known (Sanmark 2017a: 43, 117).

In Scandinavia, mounds were a key feature at *thing*-sites, although they do not appear on every location. The sites chosen for assemblies often had a long biography of human use, signified by visible monuments, frequently cemeteries composed of burial mounds of a wide variety of forms and scales (Brink 2004; Sanmark and Semple 2010; Sanmark 2017a: 3, 56–7). Top-level *thing*-sites often had particularly large mounds, such as those which dominate Gamla Uppsala (Uppland), Anundshög (Västmanland) and Söderala (Hälsingland) in Sweden. Such mounds are presumed to contain burials, but as many remain unexcavated this may not always be the case. Whether the mounds were actual burial mounds or not, they were intended to look as though they were (cf. Sanmark and Semple 2010). The importance of mounds is further demonstrated by the *thing*-sites which incorporate the element *hög* ('mound') in their name, such as **Hög* in Högsby parish (Småland) and Anundshög (Brink 1990: 275–6).

In Norse Scotland, integrated study of place-names, archaeology, medieval court records and sagas has identified over thirty potential *thing*-sites (see Table 15.1).[2] The nature of the evidence is varied, partly as a result of the differing cultural and political situations. The most detailed evidence relates to Orkney and Shetland, where Norse rule lasted the longest. Despite becoming part of the kingdom of Scotland in the 15th century, Norse law remained in use here until 1611 (Smith 2009: 39; Imsen 2014: 76–7). In western Scotland, however, the local legal system was replaced by Scottish legal practices with the Treaty of Perth in 1266, when this area was incorporated into Scotland (McDonald 1997: 131; Oliver 1860–62, vol. III, Appendix). An increasing number of potential *thing* place-names have been identified in western Scotland (Márkus 2012; Whyte 2014; Macniven 2015), and further names are likely to be found as research progresses. There is, however, a degree of uncertainty with many of these place-names, especially those that have gone through a transition into Gaelic (cf. Gordon 1963: 90–1).

Just as in Scandinavia, *thing*-sites in Scotland are found by communication routes, mostly water routes, as the sites tend to be close to the sea, often on isthmuses or within fjords. Such isthmuses often have place-names containing ON *eið*, which can be translated as 'portage', i.e. a narrow strip of land across which boats were pulled (Stewart 1987: 80; Waugh 2010: 545–6). In Shetland, several such *thing*-sites have been identified (Sanmark 2013: 102–4), e.g. Lunnasting, derived from *hlunnr-eið*, where ON *hlunnr*

Table 15.1 List of all potential *thing*-sites identified in Scotland. For full discussion of these, see Sanmark 2017a and b.

No.	Name	Location
1	Sand in Sandsting	Shetland Mainland
2	Aith in Aithsting	Shetland Mainland
3	Lunna in Lunnasting	Shetland Mainland
4	Dale in Delting	Shetland Mainland
5	Gardiestaing in *Rauðarþing*	Yell, Shetland
6	*Thing* site in *Þvæitaþing*	Shetland Mainland
7	*Gnipnathing* potentially for Nesting	Shetland Mainland
8	Loch Benston, potentially for Nesting	Shetland Mainland
9	Tingwall	Shetland Mainland
10	Tingwall	Orkney Mainland
11	Dingieshowe	Orkney Mainland
12	Kirkwall	Orkney Mainland
13	Maeshowe	Orkney Mainland
14	Ting	Westray, Orkney
15	Tingly Loup	Sanday, Orkney
16	Hoxa	South Ronaldsay, Orkney
17	Doomy Hill	Eday, Orkney
18	Gruddo	Rousay, Orkney
19	Thingsva	Caithness
20	Sordale Hill	Caithness
21	Dingwall	Ross and Cromarty
22	Tinwald	Dumfries and Galloway
23	Tiongal	Lewis
24	Eileann Thinngartsaigh	Harris
25	Glen Hinnisdal	Skye
26	Gruline	Mull
27	Grulin/Sunderland Farm	Islay
28	Finlaggan	Islay
29	*Edin	Bute
30	Cnoc nan Gall	Colonsay
31	Govan	Glasgow
32	Area by Taoinis/Manal	Tiree

refers to the wood rollers used for dragging boats across land. This is a narrow isthmus recorded as a portage in modern times (Stewart 1987: 80; McCullough 2000: 183–5; Waugh 2010: 545–6; Sanmark 2013: 102–3). Sand in Sandsting was also located on a rather narrow strip of land, possibly a portage, or alternatively, a channel for boats, and Aithsting, named after Æiði farm (derived from *eið*), may be another example (Jakobsen 1936: 125; Stewart 1987: 80, 300; Ballantyne and Smith 1999: 1; Sanmark 2013: 103–4). Further such sites are Dingieshowe on the Orkney Mainland, where the name is most likely derived from *þingeiðshaugr*, 'the mound of the *thing* portage/isthmus', which indeed is a mound located on a very narrow stretch of land (Crawford 1987: 206; Fellows-Jensen 1996: 23; Berit Sandnes, pers. comm.) (Figure 15.1) and Hoxa known in the *Orkneyinga Saga* as Haugaeið, 'isthmus with the mounds'. The *Saga*'s statement that Hoxa was the burial location of Earl Thorfinn 'the Skull-Splitter' in the 10th century (Waugh 2010: 549; *OS* ch. 8) lends further support to this as a *thing*, in view of Scandinavian *thing*-sites, although the association of Viking-Age burials with *thing*-sites in Scotland is not strong.

In western Scotland, there are further examples of *thing*-sites situated on isthmuses, but because of the 13th-century changes to the legal system the evidence here is more ambiguous. One such example is Edin on Bute, recorded as *Atyngar* in 1319 x 1321 and preserved in the names Edinbeg and Edinmore. *Atyngar* has been given two potential *thing* interpretations: either a derivation from ON *alþing* or from ON *eið* + *þing* (Márkus 2012: 8; Sanmark 2017b: 175).[3] Edinbeg and Edinmore are located in the middle of the low-lying isthmus, central to the various parts of the island (Figure 15.2). The portage interpretation is supported by the presence of the St Colman Burn, which on Blaeu's 1654 map is depicted as a major watercourse stretching far across the isthmus (Blaeu Atlas of Scotland). The most conspicuous landscape feature is a mound

Figure 15.1 Dingieshowe on a narrow isthmus on the Orkney Mainland. The broch mound is seen to the right of the white farm building. Photo: Fredrik Sundman.

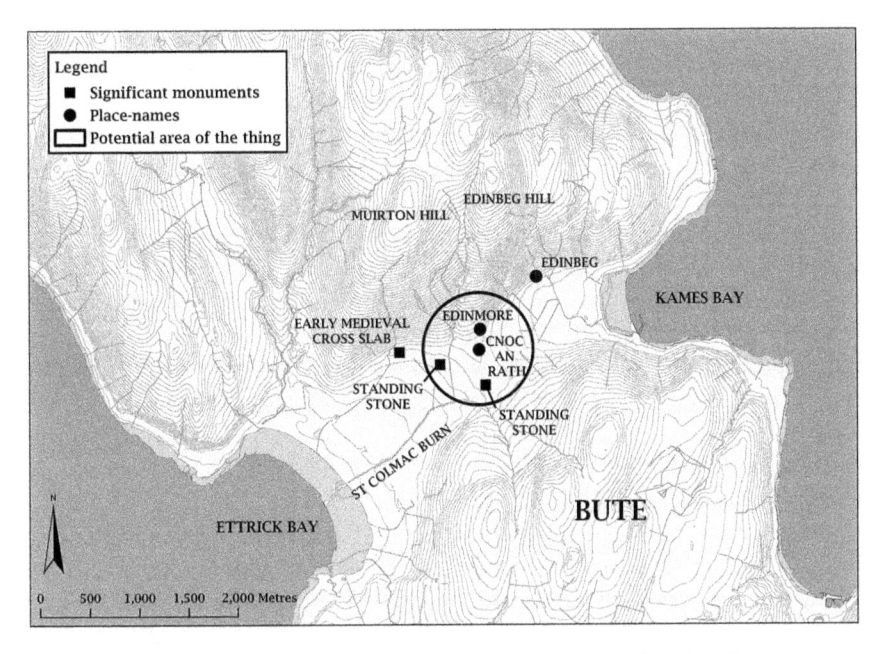

Figure 15.2 The potential *thing*-site at Edin in the Isle of Bute. © Crown Copyright/database right 2011. An Ordnance Survey/ EDINA supplied service. All rights reserved 2010. Map created by Alex Sanmark and Tudor Skinner.

(c. 24m in diameter) named Cnoc an Rath ('Hill of the fort': Márkus 2012) surrounded by a substantial ditch and bank and with good views to the sea on both sides (Sanmark 2017b: 175–6). Excavations have provided calibrated radiocarbon dates of the 8th and 9th centuries (Márkus 2012; Paul Duffy, pers. comm.). Approximately 500m to the west there are standing stones and an early medieval cross-slab, an undated chapel and a burial ground (CANMORE ID: 40317). Altogether, this means that although the place-name is rather uncertain, the location is suggestive of a *thing*-site (Sanmark 2017b: 176).

Another potential assembly-site of this type is Gruline on Mull, arguably derived from ON *grjót* and *þing*, where *grjót* translates as '(rough) stones, stony ground', 'cleared and cultivated ground' (Whyte 2014: 117), but 'chiefly with the notion of *rough stones* or *rubble* in a building, etc' (Cleasby 1874: 216). This could be interpreted in the light of the many Scandinavian *thing*-sites with names referring to cleared or non-agricultural land (Semple and Sanmark 2013: 528–32). In addition, Gruline is situated on an isthmus between the sea and Loch Ba, roughly in the middle of the island (Whyte 2014: 117, 125–6, 133–5; Sanmark 2017b: 176–7). On the isthmus are also two prehistoric cairns and standing stones, which may have had a role in the *thing* proceedings, as suggested for Scandinavia (Brink 2004: 309–12; Whyte 2014: 117). Another possible *thing*-site is found on Tiree by a major isthmus ('The Reef'), allowing a north–south crossing of the island. On Blaeu's map, there is a large inlet here, leaving only a narrow stretch of land to cross (Blaeu Atlas of Scotland). Close to the estuary in the south, on the eastern side of the isthmus, is Eibrig, seemingly derived from *eið* and *bryggja*, 'Landing place of the portage' (Holliday 2016: 330–1). On the opposite, western, side of the portage is a promontory named Taoinis, possibly derived from *Þing-nes* (Holliday 2016: 433–4). John Holliday has suggested that a Tiree *thing* was located 1km from both the isthmus and Taoinis, on the small island in *Loch an Eilein*, the location of the medieval power centre and castle. The loch-name translates as 'loch of the island', suggesting an island-wide function (it is not the island's only loch). The place-name 'the dune of the gallows', 200m to the south, is suggestive of judicial function, although *thing*-sites and gallows are only occasionally linked (Holliday 2016: 94–5, 433–4; Sanmark 2017a: 153). In support of this, parallels can be drawn with other small island *thing*-sites, such as Tingwall in Shetland (Sanmark 2017a: 200–8). It is also interesting to note that 3km to the south is Manal, another striking place-name, seen to be derived from *mannavöllur* ('Field of people'), which may refer to an assembly,[4] although there are no visible assembly features and it is rather inaccessibly situated above the rocky coastline. Altogether, this area of Tiree has many features suggestive of an assembly, but the exact location(s) is difficult to determine with certainty.[5]

As indicated above, another common *thing*-site feature in Scotland is large mounds. Broch mounds, the remains of ruined Iron-Age structures, seem to be the most frequently occurring mound feature, probably with good reason. At the time of the Viking settlement, the broch remains were most likely large turf-covered mounds (O'Grady 2008: 199) and therefore visually similar to the burial mounds at *thing*-sites in Scandinavia. Examples of *thing*-sites focusing on broch mounds are Lunnasting, Tingwall, Dingishowe and Hoxa (MacKie 2002: 116; Ritchie 1997: 94–5; Fellows-Jensen 1996: 23; Crawford 1987: 206–7). Another such example is Thingsva, most likely derived from *þing-svað*, 'assembly slope' (Thorson 1965: 75),[6] situated 3km west of Thurso in Caithness. This mound, c. 35m in diameter and 4m in height, is clearly visible in the rather flat landscape, next to a prehistoric turf-covered cairn. 'Thurso' is seemingly derived from *Þórsá*, 'Thor's river', or *Þórshaugr*, 'Thor's mound', where the latter could refer to the assembly (O'Grady 2008: 200–1; Thorson 1965). This may be a theophoric name denoting the god Thor, but could also be the name of a person. Many of these sites, moreover, have level areas nearby suitable for *thing*-attendees to gather and perhaps camp,

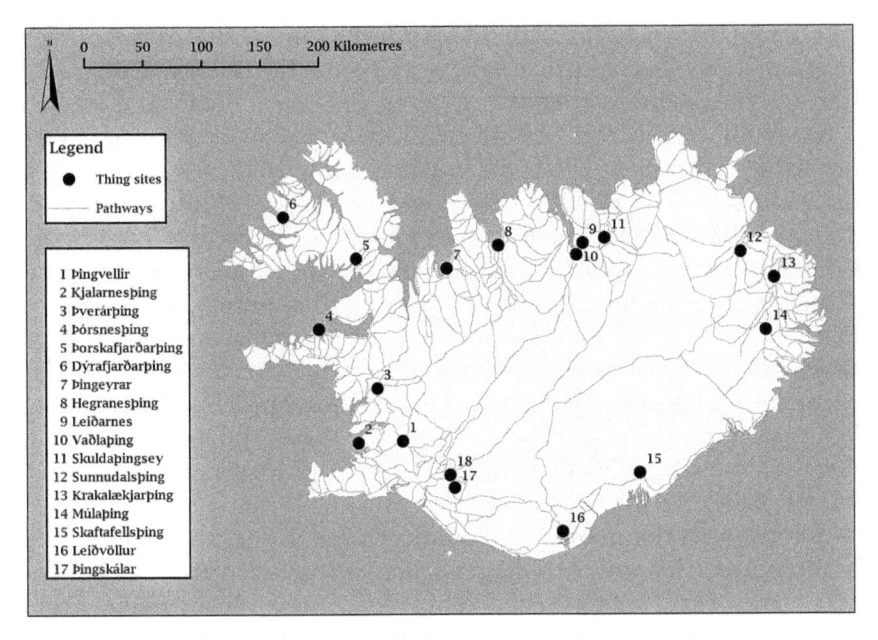

Figure 15.3 The correlation between the Icelandic *thing*-sites, mid-19th-century pathways and taxed farms named in sources from the 17th century and earlier. Very few roads existed in Iceland before the 20th century and the close correlation between these pathways and the farms suggests that they go far back in time. Map by Alex Sanmark and Tudor Skinner, based on data from Alice Whitmore, Gunnlaugsson (1844–8) and Lárusson (1967).

most clearly seen at Tingwall (Orkney), Dingieshowe and Thingsva (Sanmark 2017a: 219–21).

Moving on to Iceland, where a large number of *thing*-sites have been identified, using archaeological evidence, medieval sagas and place-names; a comprehensive survey is provided by Whitmore (2013). The accessibility of the *thing*-sites was a key consideration also here, but a notable difference is that the main means of travel to the *thing* was overland, on horseback or foot. This is seen from the landlocked nature of many assembly-sites and also their strong correlation with bridle paths (Sanmark 2017a: 166) (Figure 15.3). In terms of constructed features, *thing*-sites in Iceland were different from both Scotland and Scandinavia, as they are not associated with mounds or burials (Sanmark 2017a: 163–74) but marked by square or rectangular booths (*búð*, pl. *búðir*) used as temporary dwellings by the assembly attendees. These booths consisted of turf walls, at times with stone inclusions, over which a tent-like roof on a wooden frame was raised. The structures are recorded in the earliest Icelandic law *Grágás*, numerous sagas, as well as excavations. It seems that each year, before the *thing*-meetings had started, the assembly attendees went to their own booth and erected a new roof, which they would take down when the meetings were finished (Friðriksson 1994: 107; Vésteinsson 2013). When needed, the walls were also rebuilt (Vésteinsson et al. 2004; Friðriksson et al. 2005a; 2005b: 32–4). The number of identified structures varies from site to site, from just a few to, in some instances, thirty or forty (for example, Friðriksson 1994: ch. 4). Aerial photography and archaeological surveys show that the booths are very similar in size. In those cases where a floor layer has been identified, short-term but regular occupation of *búðir* is indicated. Little settlement debris has come to light; apart from occasional finds of animal bones and hearth material, there is almost a complete dearth of artefacts (Friðriksson 2004: 9–10, 28–40; 2007: 9–10).

Booths were not needed for comfort as, for this, simple tents would have sufficed. Instead, building booths can be seen as a symbol for being part of the 'booth-owners' of the local assembly district and that the size, number and arrangement of the booths reflected the units of the local administrative district. By counting the number of booths at a local *thing*-site and comparing this to the assembly district, it is suggested that each booth may have represented a local community of 5–15 farms, possibly headed by a *thingman*[7] (Vésteinsson 2013: 118–20).

In Norse Greenland, two possible *thing*-sites have been identified, one at Garðar (Igaliku) and the other at Brattahlíð (Qassiarsuk), both in the Eastern Settlement (Sanmark 2010a). The evidence is scant, consisting of a few written references and archaeological remains of booth structures. According to *The Saga of the Sworn Brothers* and *The Tale of the Greenlanders*, *thing*-meetings were held at Garðar, the episcopal seat supposedly established around 1123 (Clemmensen 1911: 328, 340; Sveinsson and Þórðarson 1935: 245, 273; Hreinsson 1997: II, 376–7, V, 373; Arneborg 2006: 42, 45–59). *Thing*-meetings at Brattahlíð, a chieftain's farm and a probable lawmen's residence, are also inferred from written evidence (Jónsson 1905–12: I, 161; Sveinsson and Þórðarson 1935: 273; Seaver 1996: 62–3). Both sites are situated by the sea with suitable landing places for boats (Sanmark 2010a: 182–3, 186). The booths at Brattahlíð and Garðar were excavated in the early 20th century and were after some debate accepted as *thing*-site remains (Clemmensen 1911; Nørlund 1929; Nørlund and Stenberger 1934). This conclusion seems valid in the light of analysis of the site locations and layout, although the booths may also have been used as accommodation for traders and church visitors (Sanmark 2010a: 187–8).

Figure 15.4 The presumed location of the outdoor assembly site and booths at Tinganes in Tórshavn on Streymoy, Faroe Islands. The modern parliament building is seen in the background. Photo: Fredrik Sundman.

Finally, to the Faroe Islands, where both archaeological and written evidence of *thing*-sites is sparse, but oral traditions have proven useful in the search for assemblies (Thorsteinsson 2012; Sanmark 2017a: 174–83). According to the scant medieval written sources, there was a top-level assembly in Tórshavn known as an *althing*, which in the late 13th or early 14th century was made into a *lawthing*, as well as a local *thing* organisation (Thorsteinsson 2012: 55). According to oral tradition, *thing*-booths existed in the area above Tinganes in Tórshavn, called *Tingunibúð*, derived from *Þingmannabúð* (Barnes 1974: 382–7). Archaeological investigations in some of the most southerly buildings at Tinganes revealed the remains of merchants' buildings, also referred to in post-medieval sources (Arge and Michelsen 2004: 35, 49; Thorsteinsson 1986: 2, 6–7) (Figure 15.4). There is another Faroese booth reference, which is linked to the Suðuroy *thing*-site at Uppi millum Stovur. According to a 19th-century account, assembly participants were 'supposed to have camped there in tents while the assembly was in session, from which the bay Tjaldavik ['Tent bay'] has taken its name' (Hammershaimb 1847: 260, cited in Macgregor 1987). Tjaldavík is located on the coast, c. 2km south-east of the *thing*-site (Thorsteinsson 2012: 35). The potential overlap between *thing*-booths and traders' booths seen in the Faroes, and alluded to in the discussion of Greenland, needs further exploration and discussion.

The contrasting character of *thing*-sites in the Norse Atlantic diaspora raises important questions: Why were mounds such important *thing*-site features in Scotland and Scandinavia and why were booths the defining feature of *thing*-sites in Iceland, Greenland and possibly the Faroes? Mounds were, in practical terms, useful as site markers and as platforms for those speaking to the people gathered. The usefulness of the latter naturally depended on the size of the mound and the general layout of the site. However, detailed study of the written sources reveals that the significance of mounds is more complex (Sanmark 2017a: 83–6). In these sources, mounds feature rather heavily and relate to three main themes: *óðal* land, ancestor cult and kingship claims.

Óðal land denotes 'land that belonged to a family and which could not be sold except when forced by necessity' (Zachrisson 1994). Ownership of *óðal* land was central to power in Old Norse society as this is what defined the freemen and their rights, such as voting and representing themselves at the assembly. *Óðal* land therefore came with judicial and legal implications, and of course status. This is further evidenced in Old Norse poetry, where a kenning for *óðal* man was *sætti manna*, translated as 'conciliator' or 'mediator' or 'chieftain' (Faulkes 1987: 129; Pálsson 2003: 194; Zoëga 1910: 223).

There are strong links between mounds and landownership. A 14th-century Norwegian regulation stated that a person should prove that they owned a particular piece of land by counting the generations back 'to the mound and to pagan times' (*till haughs ok till heiðni*, Keyser and Munch 1849: 121; Zachrisson 1994: 221). Slightly earlier, in the *Law of King Magnus the Lawmender*, it was stated that one-third of items 'found in the ground' should go to the 'man of the odal mound' (*haugóðals-maðr*), which most likely refers to the person whose ancestor was buried in the mound on the farm (Keyser and Munch 1848: 102; Cleasby 1874: 241; Larson 1935: G 310; Zachrisson 1994: 220).

In this sense, ownership of *óðal* land was closely linked to the idea of being the legitimate heir. This is also seen in Snorri's *Edda*, where a person who possessed *óðal* land was described as having 'full status as regards their lineage and all their legal rights' (Faulkes 1987: 129). It has therefore been argued that the common Viking-Age tradition of burying dead relatives on top of the graves of early ancestors aimed to confirm possession of *óðal* land and confirm the *óðal* man's/woman's status in society (Zachrisson 1994). Burial mounds can therefore be seen as legal documents in an oral society. This is interesting in the context of assembly mounds, as the *óðal* concept was applied also to kings and kingship (Sundqvist 2016: 448–52). According to the *Saga of King Olav Tryggvason*, Olav was 'the *óðal* heir to the kingdom' (Zachrisson 1994: 221).

It seems that Norwegian kings saw the kingdom as their *óðal* land and mounds were the 'visible proof' of this. Indeed, ownership of *óðal* land was a prerequisite for becoming king (Rafnsson 1974: 196–7; Zachrisson 1994: 221). The burial mounds on royal farms may have been important in this way, but mounds at *thing*-sites were most likely too, especially for claiming power over a wider area and dispersed people being drawn into new communal identities in the settlement areas.

Mounds were important also in the ancestor cult, which was central to Old Norse religion (Sanmark 2010b). Rituals performed at burial mounds seem to have had at least two different functions: to honour the dead through offerings, or to wake the dead to gain esoteric knowledge. In order to communicate with dead ancestors, a ritual termed 'sitting outside' came into play, which involved sitting on the grave of an ancestor (cf. Brendalsmo and Røthe 1992: 96). In the written sources, the habit of sitting on a mound (*sitja á haugi*) was also strongly connected to the claiming of kingship and royal rule (Sundqvist 2016: 493–4). Snorri Sturlusson, for example, stated that the dog Saur 'sat on a hill, as kings do' (Hollander 1964: 105), and in the Flateyarbok-version of *The Saga of Olav Tryggvason*, the young Björn sat on his father's burial mound when he claimed the throne. This theme appears in legendary sagas too; King Rerir sat on a mound, and King Gautrek who, mourning his dead wife, sat on her burial mound every day (Finch 1965: ch. 2 and 3; Sundqvist 2016: 494).

The sources clearly show that mounds played an important role for legitimate access to *óðal* land and kingdoms. This is presumably one of the reasons why mounds were used as focal points for assembly-sites. Adopting mounds from other peoples seems to have been fully acceptable. To gain access to a mound, and in effect rule from them, may have been a sign of successful settlement, as it was perhaps seen as dangerous to sit on a mound that a person was not entitled to, considering that mounds were seen to be inhabited by ancestors and perhaps other beings too. In Norse Scotland and Scandinavia, where the Norse interacted with existing populations and monuments, the Norse elites created *thing*-sites that related to the distant past, providing them with legitimacy and a perceived right to rule. In the previously (almost) unpopulated areas of Iceland, Greenland and the Faroes, on the other hand, the focus was placed on the present and the recent past. This is demonstrated by the *thing*-booths, which were most likely tied to administrative structures and expressed the relationships between the Icelandic settlers who attended the meetings. This link to the recent past and the beginnings of Icelandic history and community is seen also in the assembly procedures. According to Icelandic tradition, the *Gulathing Law* was brought from Norway and developed into their own law (Grønlie 2006: 4). There were also very specific requirements for the person who should be elected lawspeaker. Ideally, this person should be the 'supreme chieftain' (*allsherjargoði*) descended from Ingólfr Arnarson, allegedly the first Icelandic settler. The strength of the link to these increasingly 'legendary' ancestors is further seen in the placement of the Althing at Þingvellir, located on the border of the land belonging to the family Ingólfr Arnarson. Here, there was no need to link with ancestors far back in time.

In conclusion, *thing*-sites fulfilled an important function in Viking-Age and Norse society, to the extent that they were brought to all their new settlements across the North Atlantic. A clear concept of the key constituent features and functions of assembly-sites clearly existed in the minds of the Norse. Importantly, however, this concept was not static, but was changed and revisited according to circumstances, such as topography, politics and history, in the different geographical areas.

Notes

1. A detailed study of *thing*-sites identified further key features, e.g. isthmuses (portages), small islands, large mounds, prehistoric cemeteries, wetlands, elevations, linear stone/wooden monuments, rune-stones, square or circular wooden/stone features, hearths/cooking pits and marginal land (Sanmark 2017a: 56–8).
2. For a full discussion of the methods used for *thing*-site identification, see Sanmark 2019.
3. A third possible interpretation is simply 'rough face' (derived from *aodann garbh*) (Márkus 2012: 8).
4. This suggestion was put forward by Dr Berit Sandnes: http://www.tireeplacenames.org/mannal/manal/ [Last viewed: 30 July 2021].
5. Other interesting aspects include the Crosabol, containing the element *kross*, possibly referring to a free-standing cross, which could have served as an assembly marker (cf. the Gulathing in Norway, Sanmark 2017a: 76), and the collection of Neolithic/Bronze- Age rock art and a Neolithic standing stone south-west of the loch and further south towards Manal (cf. Orkney, Sanmark 2017a: 218–23).
6. But see Doreen Waugh's (2009: 42) reservations of this interpretation.
7. *Þingmaðr* (ON) ('thingman') – a landowner/freeman older than twelve or fifteen, depending on geographical area, who had the right to attend *thing*-meetings. The term could apply to both men and women.

References

Arge, S. V. and H. Michelsen (2004) Fornfrøðiligar rannsóknir í gomlu havnini. In J. P. A. Nolsøe and K. Jespersen (eds), *Havnar Soga* I. Tórshavn: Nørhaven, 23–52.

Arneborg, J. (2006) *Saga Trails. Brattahlið, Garðar, Hvalsey Fjord's Church and Herjolfsnes: Four Chieftains' Farmsteads in the Norse Settlements of Greenland*. Copenhagen: National Museum.

Ballantyne, J. H. and B. Smith (eds) (1999) *Shetland Documents 1195–1579*. Lerwick: Shetland Islands Council and Shetland Times.
Barnes, M. (1974) Tingsted. Vesterhavsøyene for øvrig. In I. Andersson and J. Granlund (eds) (1956–78), *Kulturhistoriskt lexikon för nordisk medeltid från vikingatid till reformationstid*, 22 vols. Malmö: Allhem, vol. 18, 382–7.
Blaeu Atlas of Scotland, National Library of Scotland, https://maps.nls.uk/atlas/blaeu/atlas_index.html [Last viewed: 30 July 2021].
Brendalsmo, J. and G. Røthe (1992) Haugbrot eller de levendes forhold til de døde – en komparativ analyse. *Meta* 1–2, 84–119.
Brink, S. (1990) *Sockenbildning och sockennamn. Studier i äldre territoriell indelning i Norden, Acta Academiae Regiae Gustavi Adolphi 57*. Stockholm: Almqvist and Wiksell.
Brink, S. (2004) Mytologiska rum och eskatologiska föreställningar i det vikingatida Norden. In A. Andrén, K. Jennbert and C. Raudvere (eds), *Ordning mot kaos: studier av nordisk förkristen kosmologi*. Lund: Nordic Academic Press, 291–316.
Cleasby, R. (1874) *An Icelandic–English Dictionary. Enlarged and Completed by Gudbrand Vigfusson*. Oxford: Clarendon Press. https://archive.org/details/icelandicenglish00cleauoft [Last viewed: 3 November 2020].
Clemmensen, M. (1911) Kirkeruiner fra Nordbotiden m.m. i Julianehaab distrikt. *Meddelelser om Grønland* 47, 285–358.
Crawford, B. E. (1987) *Scandinavian Scotland*. Leicester: Leicester University Press.
Faulkes, A. (ed.) (1987) *Edda*. London: Dent.
Fellows-Jensen, G. (1996) Tingwall: The significance of the name. In D. Waugh (ed.), *Shetland's Northern Links*. Edinburgh: Scottish Society for Northern Studies, 16–29.
Finch, R. G. (ed. and trans.) (1965) *The Saga of the Volsungs*. London: Nelson.
Friðriksson, A. (1994) *Sagas and Popular Antiquarianism in Icelandic Archaeology*. Avebury: Aldershot.
Friðriksson, A. (ed.) (2004) *Þinghald að fornu – Fornleifarannsóknir 2003*. Reykjavík: Fornleifastofnun Íslands.
Friðriksson, A. (ed.) (2007) *Fornleifarannsóknir í Þingeyjarsýslu 2006, FS331*. Reykjavík: Fornleifastofnun Íslands.
Friðriksson, A., H. M. Roberts and G. Guðmundsson (2005a) *Þingstaðarannsóknir 2004*. Reykjavík: Fornleifastofnun Íslands.
Friðriksson, A., H. M. Roberts, G. Guðmundsson, G. A. Gísladóttir, M. Á. Sigurgeirsson and B. Damiata (2005b) *Þingvellir og Þinghald að fornu – Framvinduskýrsla 2005*. Reykjavík: Fornleifastofnun Íslands.
Gordon, B. (1963) Some Norse Place-names in Trotternish, Isle of Skye. *Scottish Gaelic Studies* X, Part I, 82–112.
Grønlie, S. (trans.) (2006) *Íslendingabók, Kristni saga, The Book of the Icelanders, The Story of the Conversion*. Exeter: Viking Society for Northern Research, University College London, Short Run Press Limited.
Gunnlaugsson, B. (1844–8) *Uppdráttr Íslands. Kaupmannahöfn: Reykjavík*. See http://islandskort.is/is/map/show/7;jsessionid=87DDA17ABD3597502A9C8FD58EEECA3C [Last viewed: 18 August 2021].

Hollander, L. M. (ed. and trans.) (1964) *Snorri Sturlusson, Heimskringla. History of the Kings of Norway*. Austin, TX: University of Texas Press.

Holliday, J. (2016) *Longships on the Sand. Scandinavian and Medieval Settlement on the Island of Tiree: A Place-name Study.* Tiree: An Ioadhlann Press.

Hreinsson, V. (ed.) (1997) *The Complete Sagas of the Icelanders including 49 Tales*, vols 1–5. Reykjavík: Leifur Eiríksson Publishing.

Imsen, S. (ed.) (2014) *Rex Insularum: The King of Norway and His 'Skattlands' as a Political System c. 1260–1450*. Bergen: Fagbokforlaget.

Jakobsen, J. (1936) *The Place-Names of Shetland*. London: David Nutt.

Jónsson, F. (ed.) (1905–12) *Rímnasafn. Samling af de ældste islandske rimer*. Samfund til Udgivelse af gammel nordisk Litteratur 35, 2 vols. Copenhagen: Möller.

Keyser, R. and P. A. Munch (eds) (1848) *Norges gamle love indtil 1387. Bd 2, Lovgivningen under Kong Magnus Haakonssöns regjeringstid fra 1263 til 1280, tilligemed et supplement till Bd 1*. Christiania: Chr. Grøndahl.

Keyser, R. and P. A. Munch (eds) (1849) *Norges gamle love indtil 1387, Bd 3, Lovgivningen efter Kong Magnus Haakonssons död 1280 indtil 1387*. Christiania: Chr. Grøndahl.

Larson, L. M. (1935) *The Earliest Norwegian Laws, Being the Gulathing Law and the Frostathing Law*. New York: Columbia University Press.

Lárusson, B. (1967) *The Old Icelandic Land Registers*. W. F. Salisbury (trans.). Lund: Gleerup.

Macgregor, L. (1987) *The Norse Settlement of Shetland and Faroe, c. 800–c. 1500: A Comparative Study*. Unpublished PhD thesis, University of St Andrews.

MacKie, E. W. 2002 *The Roundhouses, Brochs, and Wheelhouses of Atlantic Scotland c. 700 BC–AD 500: Orkney and Shetland Isles Pt. 1: Architecture and Material Culture*. British Archaeological Reports British Series. Oxford: Archaeopress.

Macniven, A. (2015) *The Vikings in Islay*. Edinburgh: John Donald.

Márkus, G. (2012) *The Place-Names of Bute*. Donington: Shaun Tyas.

McCullough, D. A. (2000) *Investigating Portages in the Norse Maritime Landscape of Scotland and the Isles*. Unpublished PhD thesis, University of Glasgow.

McDonald, R. A. (1997) *The Kingdom of the Isles: Scotland's Western Seaboard, c. 1100–c. 1336*. East Linton: Tuckwell Press.

Nørlund, P. (1929) Norse ruins at Garðar. The Episcopal seat of Mediaeval Greenland. *Meddelelser om Grønland* 76, 7–170.

Nørlund, P. and M. Stenberger (1934) Brattahlíð. *Meddelelser om Grønland* 88(1), 7–161.

O'Grady, O. (2008) *The Setting and Practice of Open-air Judicial Assemblies in Medieval Scotland: A Multidisciplinary Study*. Unpublished PhD thesis, University of Glasgow.

Oliver, J. R. (1860–2) *Monumenta de insula Manniae or, a Collection of National Documents Relating to the Isle of Man*. Douglas, Isle of Man: The Manx Society.

OS Pálsson, H. and P. Edwards (trans.) (1978) *Orkneyinga Saga: The History of the Earls of Orkney*. London: Hogarth.

Pálsson, H. (ed.) (2003) *Snorra-Edda*. Reykjavík: Mál og menning.

Rafnsson, S. (1974) *Studier i Landnámabók: kritiska bidrag till den isländska fristatstidens Historia*. Lund: CWK Gleerup.
Ritchie, A. (1997) *Shetland*. Exploring Scotland's Heritage series. Edinburgh: HMSO.
Sanmark, A. (2010a) The case of the Greenlandic assembly sites. *Journal of the North Atlantic* Special Volume 2, 178–92.
Sanmark, A. (2010b) Living on: Ancestors and the soul. In M. Carver, A. Sanmark and S. Semple (eds), *Signals of Belief in Early England: Anglo-Saxon Paganism Revisited*. Oxford: Oxbow, 162–84.
Sanmark, A. (2013) Patterns of assembly: Norse *thing* sites in Shetland. *Journal of the North Atlantic* Special Volume 5, 96–110.
Sanmark, A. (2017a) *Viking Law and Order: Places and Rituals of Assembly in the Medieval North*. Edinburgh: Edinburgh University Press.
Sanmark, A. (2017b) An exploration of *thing* sites in the islands on the Scottish west coast. In C. Cooijmans (ed.), *Traversing the Inner Seas*. Edinburgh: Scottish Society for Northern Studies.
Sanmark, A. (2019) A new methodology for assembly site identification and analysis, *Retrospective Methods Networks Newsletter*.
Sanmark, A. and S. J. Semple (2010) 'Something old, something new': The topography of assembly in Europe with reference to recent field results from Sweden. In H. Lewis and S. J. Semple (eds), *Perspectives in Landscape Archaeology: Papers presented at Oxford 2003–5*. BAR International Series. Oxford: Archaeopress, 107–19.
Seaver, K. A. (1996) *The Frozen Echo: Greenland and the Exploration of North America, ca. AD 1000–1500*. Stanford, CA: Stanford University Press.
Semple S. J. and A. Sanmark (2013) Assembly in North West Europe: Collective concerns for early societies?, *European Journal of Archaeology* 16(3), 518–52.
Smith, B. (2009) On the nature of tings: Shetland's law courts from the Middle Ages until 1611. *New Shetlander* 250, 37–45.
Stewart, J. (1987) *Shetland Place-names*. Lerwick: Shetland Library and Museum.
Sundqvist, O. (2016) *An Arena for Higher Powers: Ceremonial Buildings and Religious Strategies for Rulership in Late Iron Age Scandinavia*. Leiden: Brill.
Sveinsson, E. Ó. and M. Þórðarson (eds) (1935) *Eyrbryggja saga, Groenlendinga sögur*, Íslenzk fornrit IV. Reykjavík: Hið íslenzka fornritafélag.
Thorson, P. (1965) Ancient Thurso, a religious and judicial centre. In B. Niclasen (ed.), *Proceedings of the Fifth Viking Congress, Tórshavn, July 1965*. Tórshavn: Føroya Fródskaparfelag, 71–7.
Thorsteinsson, A. (1986) *Tinganes – Tórshavn. En kort historisk orientering. A Brief Historical Guide*. Tórshavn: Føroya Landsstýri.
Thorsteinsson, A. (2012) *Thing* sites in the Faroes. In O. Owen (ed.), *Things in the Viking World*. Lerwick: The Shetland Amenity Trust, 52–67.
Vésteinsson, O. (2013) What is in a booth? Material symbolism at Icelandic assembly sites. *Journal of the North Atlantic* Special Volume 5, 111–24.
Vésteinsson, O., A. Einarsson and M. A. Sigurgeirsson (2004) A new assembly site in Skuldaþingsey. In G. Guðmundsson (ed.), *Current Issues in Nordic*

Archaeology. Proceedings of the 21st Conference of Nordic Archaeologists. Akureyri, Iceland 6.–9. September 2001. Reykjavík: Society of Icelandic Archaeologists, 171–80.

Waugh, D. (2009) Caithness: Another dip in the Sweerag Well. In A. Woolf (ed.), *Scandinavian Scotland – Twenty Years After. The Proceedings of a Day Conference held on 19th February 2007*. St John's House Papers No. 12. St Andrews: University of St Andrews, 31–48.

Waugh, D. (2010) On *eið*-names in Orkney and other North Atlantic islands. In J. Sheehan and Ó. Corráin (eds), *The Viking Age: Ireland and the West. Papers from the Proceedings of the Fifteenth Viking Congress, Cork, 18–27 August 2005*. Dublin: Four Courts Press, 545–54.

Whitmore A. (2013) *A Landscape Study of Medieval Icelandic Assembly Places*. Unpublished PhD thesis, University of Cambridge.

Whyte, A. C. (2014) Gruline, Mull, and other Inner Hebridean *things*. *The Journal of Scottish Name Studies* 8, 115–52.

Zachrisson, T. (1994) The odal and its manifestation in the landscape. *Current Swedish Archaeology* 2, 219–38.

Zoëga, G. T. A. (1910) *Concise Dictionary of Old Icelandic*. Oxford: Clarendon Press.

Chapter 16

The Brough of Birsay, Orkney
Christopher D. Morris

The Brough of Birsay, Orkney. Investigations 1954–2014 (Morris 2021) is the third, and final, volume of the Birsay Bay Project and the culmination of sixty years of investigations that took place on the site and in the archives. As with Volume 2, much effort has gone into researching the archives in order to provide as comprehensive an account as possible of investigations undertaken by previous excavators, whose work had hitherto not been published. It completes a trilogy of studies of the Brough itself, alongside Cecil Curle's and John Hunter's earlier monographs (Curle 1982; Hunter 1986).

This is therefore an appropriate moment to consider in this paper the historiography of this important site, located on a tidal island at the north-western extremity of the Mainland of Orkney (Figure 16.1), and yet the power centre of the Viking Earldom of Orkney. For a discussion of the significance of the site, and reference to more recent work in Birsay more generally and analyses by scholars such as Sarah Jane Gibbon and Barbara Crawford, the reader is referred to chapter 25 of Morris 2021. At the present time, it is now one of Historic Environment Scotland's key monuments and visitor attractions on the islands.

Here, sheer cliffs up to 45m high face the full force of the Atlantic storms from the west, while the ground then slopes down to cliffs 4–5m high on the eastern face and towards the 'Peerie Brough' ('Little Brough': Marwick 1970: 12). The name 'Brough' comes from the Old Norse *borg* (i.e. fortress or fortified place), possibly referring to the naturally defensive qualities of an island difficult to access. Birsay as a name is a contraction of an early form 'Byrgisey' which Lindsay MacGregor has redefined as 'the island (*-ey*) with a narrow neck of land (*-býrgi*)' (Morris 1989:21).

19th- and early 20th-century investigations

Although there was a well-attested tradition of pilgrimage at this site in Birsay, the Brough buildings were clearly in a parlous state from the end

Figure 16.1 Aerial photograph of Brough of Birsay from the south-east at the Point of Buckquoy, showing the 'Guardianship' site and the south-western cliff-side area up to the 'Peerie Brough' in 2009 (CANMORE archive: DP 059281). © Crown Copyright: Historic Environment Scotland.

of the 18th century (George Low in OSA 1795: 324; NSA 1845: 98). It is entirely due to the activities of Henry Dryden, as a pioneering church archaeologist in 1866 (Dryden 1996), that the site came back to the attention of scholars (see Fawcett 1996: illus. 155–61). His unpublished investigation (Dryden 1870) was used, virtually verbatim, thirty years later by MacGibbon and Ross (1896: 135–41), followed by Dietrichson and Meyer in Norway a decade later (1906: 19–29, 80–3).

In the early 20th century, although individuals such as Hugh Marwick and John Fraser emphasised the importance of the site in Orkney, the state of the church building was still poor: 'The church walls are now, for the most part, almost level with the ground . . . [although the] north wall of the chancel had been altered quite recently' (Marwick 1922: 67). Similarly, despite Dryden's recording of a rectangular enclosure around the church, very little was known of the archaeological features surrounding the church: '. . . There are now few traces of the burial ground that was beside the chapel; on account of the inconvenient situation it probably was never much used . . .' (Fraser 1925: 25).

Work directed by J. S. Richardson, IAM for Scotland, from 1934 to 1939 explored a large proportion of the site. Previously in private

Figure 16.2 Aerial photograph of the Brough of Birsay from the west, showing Area I (church, churchyard and buildings to north), Area II (buildings to east) and Area III (buildings to west, including backfilled excavation areas, and north under excavation) in 1976. Reproduced with permission from Morris 2021, Illus. 0.4.

hands, it had recently been gifted to the care of the State (Marwick 1934), and excavations revealed structures, both ecclesiastical and secular, which could be displayed to the public (Figure 16.2). The excavations in and around the church (as Area I) served to emphasise the importance of the site in the period of Norse Christianity as recorded in the *Orkneyinga Saga*, while indicating also the presence of earlier Christian activity of undefined date (Emery and Morris 1996: 217–25, illus. 162–77). Meanwhile, staff of the Royal Commission on the Ancient and Historical Monuments of Scotland recorded the extant buildings in 1935, describing the church and the building-complex to the north as a 'medieval monastery', and outlining a sequence of four stages in construction (RCAHMS 1946, ii, no. 1, 1–5, figs 52–7).

To the east (Area II), where it had been assumed that there was a broch (e.g. Marwick 1922: 67), there was a great complex of superimposed buildings which Cecil Mowbray [later Curle] excavated (Mowbray 1996). This was described by Richardson in the RCAHMS report (RCAHMS 1946, ii, No. 6 and fig. 65, 7–8) and subsequently internally as 'The Viking House' - although thirteen structures were found – 'of Greenland type'. This followed Jan Petersen's views expressed on a visit to the site from

Norway in 1936, that the buildings were part of 'a lay-out similar to what we know from Iceland and Greenland' (Petersen 1936; compared with Emery and Morris 1996: 226–30). The chronological sequences for Area II were initially outlined by Curle as an introduction to her publication of the artefacts from the site (1982: 15–17, ill. 5), and then more definitively in Volume 2 (Emery and Morris 1996: 226–41, illus. 178–91). These indicated, with deposits rich in artefacts, a continuous occupation of the site from the pre-Norse Pictish period through to the Late Norse (or even later medieval).

The identification of buildings to the west and north (Area III) in excavations by William Henderson indicated the presence of Viking-period domestic secular occupation (Emery and Morris 1996: 243–50, illus. 192–8; Henderson 1996). Some industrial activity in this period has received attention in the more recent investigations by Hunter at Site F/VII (Hunter 1986: ch. 4.2) and the author in Sites IV South and North (ch. 14, 15 and 19).

Although not published for over fifty years, and then in *The Birsay Bay Project Volume 2* (Morris 1996), the 1934 to 1939 excavations were of fundamental importance for the preservation and understanding of the site. All subsequent work has been conditioned by the work undertaken during these years, and in particular by the requirement that the standing remains that had been uncovered should be displayed and consolidated. Inevitably, structures from the later phases of the site's evolution have become prominent, with the result that earlier phases were imperfectly understood.

The Radford-Cruden campaign 1954–64

Archival research has demonstrated that although Richardson intended to continue the work immediately after the War, his superior, Bryan St J. O'Neil, the Chief Inspector of Ancient Monuments at the Ministry of Works in London, effectively prevented this. O'Neil spent several years in discussion with Scandinavian archaeologists and Richardson's successor in Scotland, Stewart Cruden, about the best way to proceed and whom to appoint to lead the work. Eventually, O'Neil visited the site in 1954 with Ralegh Radford, a well-known independent archaeologist, with the clear intention that he should then produce a report on the previous work. There is no such report in existence, but Radford had obviously indicated to O'Neil that he felt there was 'Sufficient evidence... recovered to give an outline picture of the site' but that he would need to undertake specialist study of the buildings, especially the church, in the following June. O'Neil wrote an internal memo in October 1954 stating that 'we should defer further excavation for some years and concentrate upon the publication of the results', and in January 1955, Radford was invited by Cruden 'to go to Birsay on our behalf to write an outline history of the site for publication'.

However, this official intention for publication seems to have been diverted and, in Radford's own words in an unpublished report, he describes the work in response to this commission as follows: 'Two weeks in 1955 were devoted to a careful survey of the visible remains and their collation with the available records *with a view to planning the future operations*' [CDM italics]. Thereafter, apart from producing a 'blue book' site guide (Radford 1959), the focus shifted to excavation, which other than short annual summaries and articles (for example, Radford 1962a; b), remained largely unpublished.

Fifty-six years later, Volume 3 now incorporates as comprehensive account of the work planned and undertaken by Radford and Cruden as is possible, using material from the archives of Historic Environment Scotland and, most particularly, the private archive of Radford (held in the Historic England archives at Swindon) made available after his death, alongside these interim statements (and Cruden 1958; 1965). It is evident that Radford took the lead in deciding areas to investigate, essentially designed to corroborate the sequences he proposed from the visits in 1954 and 1955.

A major focus of his attention was Area II and Richardson's 'Viking House', especially on a partially destroyed longhouse, the so-called 'Sigurd's Hall', and a complex of buildings dubbed 'Thorfinn's Palace' (Chapter 9). A secondary focus was in Area III, at the sites known as Buildings C and D, notable for earlier post-built structures below the turf-and-stone longhouses (Chapter 11). Radford had definite views about the chronology of the church and churchyard and interpretation of buildings to the north (Area 1, Chapters 4, 5 and 7), but there is relatively little evidence of direct intervention here – as against interpretation of work undertaken before. However, tantalisingly, postholes perhaps from an early structure at the west end were uncovered (Chapter 4). The artefacts from the excavations were examined alongside the finds from their 1934–9 work, in Curle's monograph (1982).

Cruden saw his role, as IAM for Scotland, to care for and maintain the monument as a visitor attraction, saying, for instance, to a Viking Congress: '. . . let me say that the Ministry has an urgent and inescapable obligation to preserve and display such sites as this for public enjoyment and instruction, and that total archaeological destruction is consequently out of the question' (Cruden 1965: 22). He also initiated the policy of erecting a concrete sea-wall, 'designed to contain and preserve the structures from collapse *and not to offend the eye of the visitor*' [CDM italics] (Cruden 1958: 162). In promoting the site through participation at successive international Viking Congresses, Cruden was also very well aware that the site was of far more than local and regional importance and significance – a matter which he emphasised in an internal minute in 1956:

> I have completed the first stage of the recommencement of work with Mr Radford. ...We have drastically revised all previous interpretations of the site ...*This is but the beginning of work on one of the most important Viking sites in Europe such as the Scandinavians will envy*... [CDM Italics]

Investigations between 1973 and 2007

Excavations under the direction of the author on the site originated in a small-scale excavation carried out with John Hunter in 'Room 5' of the so-called 'Viking House' in 1973 and 1974. The rationale was that 'evidence from earlier excavations on the island indicated that Room 5 would be stratigraphically representative of the full range of occupation observed elsewhere' (Hunter and Morris 1982: 124). Further, Curle specifically intended to relate artefacts excavated here to types from previous excavations in her forthcoming volume (1982).

However, as it was immediately obvious that much was not understood about the structures and deposits on the site as a whole, discussions with the Inspectorate established that some areas examined in the 1930s should be re-examined in order to maximise information and understanding of the site. This governed the early years of work by both the author from Durham University and John Hunter from Bradford University within Area III. To the west of the churchyard, Morris's team undertook work initially in and around 'Houses' L, N, E and 'S' (Henderson 1996: 246–9); and to the north of the ecclesiastical complex, Hunter's team undertook work on 'Houses' F, P and R, buildings truncated by cliff erosion (Henderson 1996: 250–2).

In the area west of the churchyard, although many structural remains had either been investigated previously or subject to significant later disturbance, nevertheless it was possible to unravel building sequences and structural details and to reveal remnants of earlier phases, including primary wooden structures (Chapters 11–15). This is similar to what has emerged from previous excavations at Radford's 'Houses' C and D and Hunter's Site VII (1986, Site VII, Chapter 2.2). Middens were examined and the ecofactual material analysed in specialist studies. A wide range of artefacts were recovered, and specific studies made (in Chapter 16) of a group of ogham inscriptions including one from this area (deciphered by Katherine Forsyth), and a notable gilt-bronze mount of Insular origin (studied by Olwyn Owen) (Figure 16.3). Also, Gerry McDonnell concluded that specialist ironworking was undertaken here, based on analysis of metallurgical material (Chapter 19).

Radford and Cruden asserted the existence of an early 'Celtic enclosure'. The re-discovery of a plan in the Inspectorate archive of the location of their trenches led to a specific re-examination of this (Chapter 8). The conclusion was that various features which they had identified were not

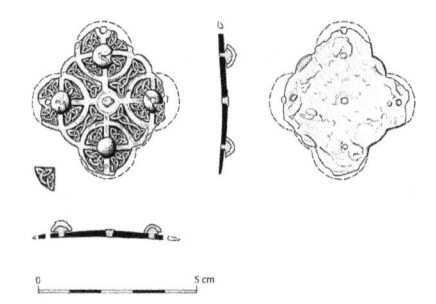

Figure 16.3a Decorated copper alloy mount RF 979. Reproduced with permission from Morris 2021, Illus. 16.2. By K. McBarron and A. Braby.

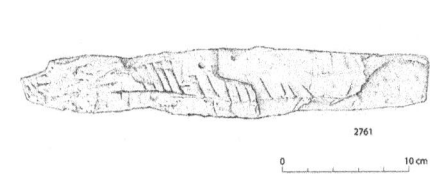

Figure 16.3b Face of stone RF 2761 with detail of ogham inscription shortly after discovery 1980. Reproduced with permission from Morris 2021, Illus. 14.33. By K. McBarron.

contemporary – and indeed unlikely to be from the pre-Viking period. The 'Celtic enclosure' appears to be a chimera.

Further buildings beyond the site boundary to the south had been visible both from the air and on the ground, but they had not attracted official attention or entered the published record. After they were brought to the author's attention by Peter Gelling and Raymond Lamb, work was proposed for the south-western area. Also, walling and building remains appeared to exist right along the cliff-side margins up to and including the 'Peerie Brough' (see Figure 16.1). These were recorded, and a trial trench was opened to follow up where a glass bead had been discovered during this (Towers 1979). At the same time, in the area behind the site museum and store, up to the cliff-edge, Hunter excavated Sites VIII and IX, revealing 'pre-Norse features' including timber buildings implied by gulleys, and also both early and later Viking-Age structures on these sites (Hunter 1986: Chapters 2–4; Chapter 17.3 and 17.4).

Because of the erosion particularly at the south-west extremity, Site V on the 'Peerie Brough', which is connected to the main Brough by a narrow ledge at its east end, and Site VI immediately opposite it, were specifically established to examine a number of building foundations. Although both sites were not completed in excavation, they demonstrated a complexity of building and settlement evidence with occupation in the late Viking Age/Late Norse periods, later activity and also hints of earlier occupation on Site V on the 'Peerie Brough' (Chapters 17.8–17.12 and 18).

This new volume also contains a reassessment of the architecture and dating of the church and related buildings by Fawcett (Chapter 6) and an account of a rescue excavation undertaken in 1993 on the cliff-edge south-west of the churchyard, revealing a sequence of structures and middens adjacent to 'Sigurd's Hall' (Chapter 10). The final piece of fieldwork reported here is a geophysical survey carried out in 2007 by Susan Ovenden on behalf of David Griffiths' landscape project undertaken across the bay (Griffiths et al. 2019) (Chapter 23) as a logical coda to the work of the Birsay Bay Project. A primary aim of the geophysical survey was to determine the extent of the archaeological deposits on the south side of the island, whether the archaeological remains were continuous between the main site area and the 'Peerie Brough', and how far other buried remains might extend (Chapter 21).

An assessment of the different types of artefacts across the excavations as a whole has been undertaken by Colleen Batey in terms of all the individual Areas, the Brough as a whole, and in terms of site status (Chapter 19). Similarly, the author, basing his analysis on the work of James Rackham and colleagues, looked at the sampling procedures employed and the biological assemblage across all areas and genera (Chapter 20). A fundamental piece of work has been re-analysis of the radiocarbon dates from the Brough by Zoe Outram, who then extended this work to a re-examination of the dates from all sites in Birsay Bay (Chapter 22). This work has clearly established groups of both Late Iron-Age/Pictish and Pictish/Viking 'Interface' dates for horizons and structures on the Brough. These are discussed further for their wider implications in Chapter 24 by both Outram and the author. This volume also ties in closely with Griffiths' work in the landscapes of the Bay of Skaill, Marwick and Birsay Bay (Griffiths et al. 2019). Indeed, the final two chapters of this volume put the Brough, as both a Pictish power centre and the hub of the Viking Earldom, in the overall context of Birsay Bay, Viking and Late Norse Orkney, and the wider world, between the Pictish and Late Norse/medieval periods.

Envoi

In bringing to fruition the final volume of the Birsay Bay Project covering sixty years' investigations on the Brough of Birsay, this author's intention is to bring at long last the story up to date. Hopefully it and the preceding volumes will serve as a resource for the future for both professional colleagues and inhabitants of the Birsay area alike – and better inform people about this most amazing site that continues to draw visitors and scholars year after year.

References

Cruden, S. H. (1958) Earl Thorfinn the Mighty and the Brough of Birsay. In K. Eldjárn (ed.), *Þriðji Víkingafundur. Third Viking Congress, Reykjavík 1956 = Árbok hins íslenzka fornleifafélags 1958*. Reykjavík, 156–62.

Cruden, S. H. (1965) Excavations at Birsay, Orkney. In A. Small (ed.), *The Fourth Viking Congress, York, August 1961*. Aberdeen University Studies 149. Edinburgh and London: Oliver and Boyd, 22–31.

Curle, C. L. (1982) *Pictish and Norse Finds from the Brough of Birsay, 1934–1974*. Society of Antiquaries of Scotland Monograph 1. Edinburgh: Society of Antiquaries of Scotland.

Dietrichson, L. and J. Meyer (1906) *Monumenta Orcadica. The Norsemen in the Orkneys and the Monuments they have left*. Kristiania [Oslo], Alb. Cammermeyers Forlag and London: Williams and Norgate.

Dryden, H. E. L. (1870) Ruined Churches in Orkney and Shetland by Sir Henry Dryden, Bart [= papers from *The Orcadian* 1867–70]. Kirkwall (privately produced, hand-paginated copy in Orkney Archives, Kirkwall).

Dryden, H. E. L. (1996) The ruined church on the Brough of Birsay = Appendix 3. In C. D. Morris, *The Birsay Bay Project Volume 2. Sites in Birsay Village and on the Brough of Birsay, Orkney*. University of Durham Department of Archaeology Monograph Series 2. Durham: University of Durham, Department of Archaeology, 267–8.

Emery, N. and C. D. Morris (1996) The excavations on the Brough of Birsay 1934–9. In C. D. Morris, *The Birsay Bay Project Volume 2. Sites in Birsay Village and on the Brough of Birsay, Orkney*. University of Durham Department of Archaeology Monograph Series 2. Durham: University of Durham, Department of Archaeology, 209–55.

Fawcett, R. (1996) The excavation of the church on the Brough by Sir Henry Dryden in 1866. In N. Emery and C. D. Morris, The excavations on the Brough of Birsay 1934–9. In C. D. Morris, *The Birsay Bay Project Volume 2. Sites in Birsay Village and on the Brough of Birsay, Orkney*. University of Durham Department of Archaeology Monograph Series 2. Durham: University of Durham, Department of Archaeology, 210–17.

Fraser, J. (1925) Antiquities of Birsay Parish. *Proceedings of the Orkney Antiquarian Society* III (1924–5), 21–30.

Griffiths, D., J. Harrison and M. Athanson (2019) *Beside the Ocean: Coastal Landscapes at the Bay of Skaill, Marwick and Birsay Bay, Orkney. Archaeological Research 2003–2016*. Oxford and Philadelphia: Oxbow Books.

Henderson, W. (1996) Report on excavations on the Brough of Birsay, 1938–9 = Appendix 5. In C. D. Morris, *The Birsay Bay Project Volume 2. Sites in Birsay Village and on the Brough of Birsay, Orkney*. University of Durham Department of Archaeology Monograph Series 2. Durham: University of Durham, Department of Archaeology, 278–91.

Hunter, J. R. (1986) *Rescue Excavations on the Brough of Birsay 1974–82*. Society of Antiquaries of Scotland Monograph 4. Edinburgh: Society of Antiquaries of Scotland.

Hunter, J. R. and C. D. Morris (1982) Appendix: Excavation of Room 5, Clifftop Settlement, Brough of Birsay 1973–4. In C. L. Curle (1982) *Pictish and Norse Finds from the Brough of Birsay, 1934–1974*. Society of Antiquaries of Scotland Monograph 1. Edinburgh: Society of Antiquaries of Scotland, 124–38.

MacGibbon, D. and T. Ross (1896–7) *The Ecclesiastical Architecture of Scotland*, 3 vols. Edinburgh: David Douglas.

Marwick, H. [M.] (1922) A rune-inscribed stone from Birsay, Orkney. *Proceedings of the Society of Antiquaries of Scotland* 61 (1921–2), 67–71.

Marwick, H. [M.] (1934) Archaeological work in Orkney. Progress during 1934. *Orkney Herald*, 12 September, 8.

Marwick, H. M. (1970) *The Place-Names of Birsay*. Aberdeen: Aberdeen University Press.

Morris, C. D. (1989) *The Birsay Bay Project Volume I. Coastal Sites beside the Brough Road, Birsay, Orkney. Excavations, 1976–1982*. University of Durham Department of Archaeology Monograph Series 1. Durham: Department of Archaeology, University of Durham.

Morris, C. D. (1996) *The Birsay Bay Project Volume 2. Sites in Birsay Village and on the Brough of Birsay, Orkney*. University of Durham, Department of Archaeology Monograph Series 2. Durham: Department of Archaeology, University of Durham.

Morris, C. D. (2021) *The Birsay Bay Project Volume 3. The Brough of Birsay, Orkney Investigations 1954–2014*. Oxford and Philadelphia: Oxbow Books.

Mowbray, C. L. (1996) Report on excavations on the Brough of Birsay, 1936–7 = Appendix 4. In C. D. Morris, *The Birsay Bay Project Volume 2. Sites in Birsay Village and on the Brough of Birsay, Orkney*. University of Durham, Department of Archaeology Monograph Series 2. Durham: Department of Archaeology, University of Durham, 269–77.

NSA (1845) *The New Statistical Account of Scotland*. Edinburgh: Blackwoods.

OSA (1791–9) *The [Old] Statistical Account of Scotland. Drawn up from the Communications of the Ministers of the Different Parishes, compiled by Sir John Sinclair*, 21 vols. Edinburgh: William Creech.

Petersen, J. (1936) Norse Viking houses in the West. *The Orcadian*, 15 October [translated from *Aftenposten*, August 1936].

Radford, C. A. R. (1959) *The Early Christian and Norse Settlements at Birsay*, Official Guide. Edinburgh: HMSO.

Radford, C. A. R. (1962a) The Celtic monastery in Britain. *Archaeologia Cambrensis* CXI, 1–24.

Radford, C. A. R. (1962b) Art and architecture: Celtic and Norse. In F. T. Wainwright (ed.), *The Northern Isles*. Edinburgh and London: Thomas Nelson and Sons, 163–87.

RCAHMS (1946) *Twelfth Report with an Inventory of the Ancient Monuments of Orkney and Shetland*, 3 vols. Edinburgh: HMSO.

Towers, R. (1979) Cliff clues of the blue bead leads to new evidence of the Viking connection. *Glasgow Herald*, 15 September.

Chapter 17

The Earl's Bu, Orphir, Orkney
Colleen E. Batey

Located on the northern shore of Scapa Flow (Figure 17.1), this expansive site has as its focus today the remains of the 12th-century Round Church, dedicated to St Nicholas, and the grass-covered remains of substantial walling commonly identified with the Late Norse Earl's drinking hall. However, the site is considerably larger than traditionally viewed, incorporating industrial activity at Lavacroon to the west, additional dwellings under the current Saga Centre, and a Norse-period horizontal mill with water management system, all complementing the considerable complexity of the visible grass-covered remains in the area under State Care (Guardianship). A Pictish symbol stone was incorporated into these remains, but otherwise it would appear that this site is unusual in being a virgin Viking-Age foundation, lacking immediate estate evidence of the Pictish/Iron-Age periods. There is, however, a growing body of data from the excavations considered here, that there was scattered evidence related to Late Neolithic and Bronze-Age activity, including an earlier discovery of a pecked and decorated stone, flint working and a Bronze-Age burnt mound with ceramics.

There are several entries in the *Orkneyinga Saga* concerning activities at the Earl's Bu (farm) and the church at the site, which add considerable colour to our understanding of the archaeology.

> Earl Paul made preparations for a great Christmas feast at his estate called Orphir, and to it he invited a large number of important guests ... There was a great drinking-hall at Orphir, with a door in the south wall near the eastern gable, and in front of the hall, just a few paces down from it, stood a fine church. On the left as you came into the hall was a large stone slab, with a lot of big ale vats behind it, and opposite the door was the living-room. (Pálsson and Edwards 1978: ch. 66, 112–13)

Within this entry, the main elements of the site are described: the hall in some detail, but the distinctive Round Church is barely described at all. There are various interpretations about the origins for the form of the

224 Colleen E. Batey

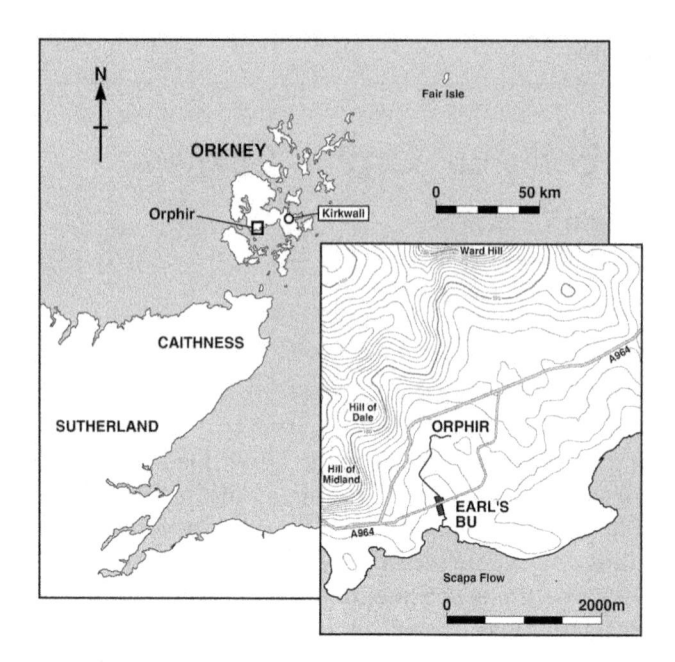

Figure 17.1 Location of Orphir on Scapa Flow, Orkney. Drawn by Walter Newton.

Orphir Church, citing inspiration from the Church of the Holy Sepulchre in Jerusalem as well as southern Scandinavian similarities (summarised in Fisher 1993). The church is described as both 'fine' (Pálsson and Edwards [trans.] 1978: 113) and 'magnificent' (Anderson [trans.] 1938: ch. LXVI, 242), but not as a round building. This is a strange omission, but could perhaps be explained by the extensive building programme of distinctive churches within Late Norse Orkney (such as Kirkwall Cathedral, but more relevant perhaps are the churches of Stenness, Skaill, Deerness and St Magnus, Egilsay, which all share the architectural distinction of having round towers (see Fernie 1988: 153; Fawcett 2021: 67–8). This floruit of architectural distinction may have simply become unremarkable to the recorder, as unlikely as this might seem to us today.

The understanding of the excavated remains over several generations (from c. 1859 to 1939 at the hands of several investigators, discussed in Batey 2003) has been largely dictated by the reading of the saga entries. In Anderson's seminal translation of 1938, his notes include a drawing of his reconstruction of the hall based on his reading of the source (Anderson 1938: note 7, 384–8). This has been reconsidered in some detail by Batey (2003) and it is clear from that reassessment that the visible remains today comprise several phases of activity rather than one single hall-like building. It is also clear from that work that deep midden deposits covered the remains and were discarded in the early investigations; with hindsight, these middens were of considerable significance and relate to the infilling middens of the adjacent horizontal mill excavated 1978–93. Within this evidence lies the key to understanding the nature of activities at this site, where large-scale feasting and consumption was an integral element of kinship bonding and power politics in the Norse Earldom. This is more fully explored elsewhere (Mainland and Batey 2018).

Beyond the immediate boundaries of the Earl's Bu remains, a number of elements have been distinguished. Through geophysical survey (for example, Johnson and Batey 2003) both within the Guardianship area and immediately beyond, further structural elements are suggested, as well as clear indications (that complement ground survey) of modified watercourses to the north that would have fed the horizontal mill. Through fieldwalking, especially at Lavacroon (an industrial site located to the north-west of the Bu), Norse components have been collected in the artefactual assemblage (Batey with Freeman 1986).

However, it was the excavation of the horizontal mill, located immediately to the north of the 'Hall' buildings, which has enabled a much broader understanding of the site in its Late Norse Earldom context and demonstrated the power the Earls had over local, regional and indeed national/international resources (Batey et al. forthcoming). Figure 17.2 shows the excavated elements that make up the horizontal mill structure: an underhouse where the wheel would have been placed, a head race and tail race and a possible pond/sluice. The upperhouse/mill house had been largely dismantled prior to the final infilling and levelling of the site and the stone reused elsewhere. When the mill was built, it cut through a Bronze-Age burnt mound at the west end, and at its east end the outflow or tail race emerged into a watercourse that had been specifically realigned to accommodate this and which resulted in the pre-existing Viking layers being leached out. The life of the mill was relatively short, having been constructed overlying 9th-century middens and infilled in the late 10th to 12th centuries with the richest Late Norse middens that have been excavated to date anywhere in the Northern Earldom. Ongoing refinement of this dating sequence is designed to interrogate this very tight timeframe.

The mill is interpreted as an integral element of the Norse Earls' local power and underlines the consumption nature of the site, with grain brought probably not only from islands such as Sanday, but also perhaps from elsewhere on Mainland. The infilling midden assemblage indicates the management of cattle and sheep resources (Mainland et al. 2016; Jones and Mulville 2018) as well as the importation of fish (discussed elsewhere in the volume by Mainland). This consumption regime is more closely aligned to that from Birsay than from other more recently published sites (Mainland, pers. comm.) such as Snusgar (Griffiths et al. 2019) and Quoygrew (Barrett 2012). The nature of the consumption at the Earl's Bu indicates feasting (Mainland and Batey 2018) and aligns surprisingly

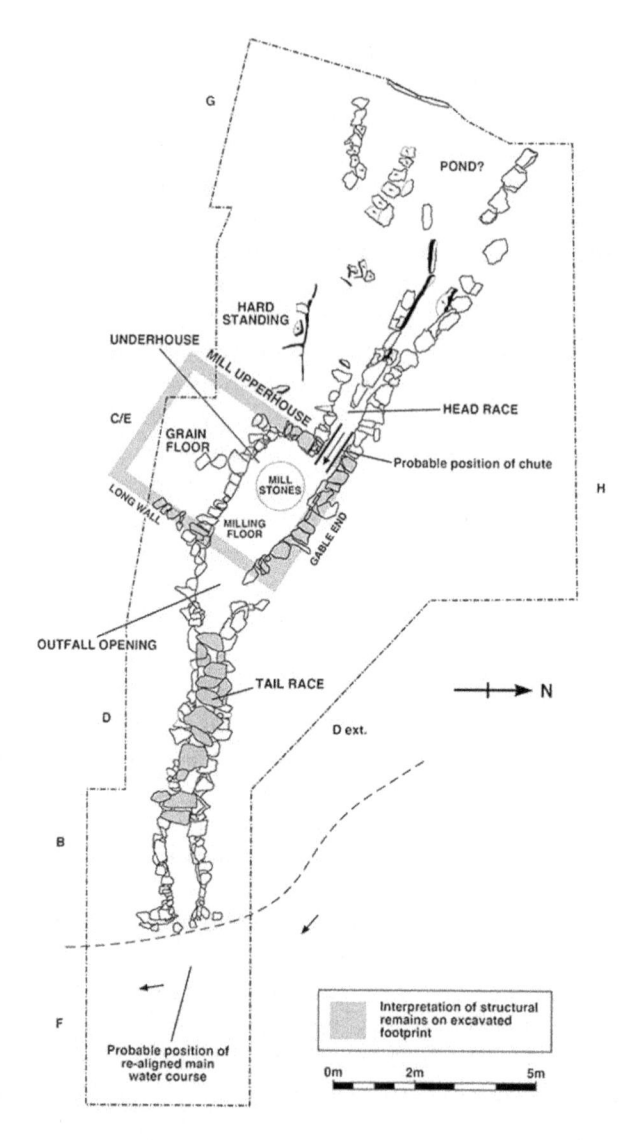

Figure 17.2 Identified structural elements of the horizontal mill. Drawn by Walter Newton.

well with the saga descriptions, where feeding one's potential allies was a recognised form of bribery!

The quantity of the midden debris from the mill site, which was sieved and recorded extensively for as full recovery as possible of ecofactual and artefactual material, is highly significant in the context of this Golden Age of Orkney's past. It has enabled the identification of detailed agricultural management strategies, similar in most ways to that currently practised (Mainland et al. 2016), as well as the recognition of imported commodities. In terms of the artefactual recovery, it has brought to light aspects seldom recovered from a non-urban site, such as the evidence for processing of precious metals, such as crucibles with traces of gold and steatite bar moulds (from both Lavacroon and the Bu, the latter of which was repurposed from a steatite vessel handle) for the forming of silver ingots. Complementing these are significant elements of a bullion (metal-weight) economy at the site (see Horne, this volume), including scraps of hack-gold and a hack-silver segment of silver 'ring money', a type of plain penannular arm-ring that may have functioned as a (rough) currency unit within Scandinavian Scotland between the mid-10th and mid-11th centuries; notably, it is more commonly found in hoards than in settlements. The rare recovery of two copper alloy oblate-spheroid weights (SF 756, weight 7.1g and SF 2705, weight 3.1g) indicates links to the Islamic world via Scandinavia; just one other is known from Orkney (Cleat, Westray; Maleszka 2003: 284), with an unstratified example from Bornais in the Outer Hebrides (Sharples 2020, SF 1445, fig. 388).

Further significant finds include an extensive assemblage of steatite vessel fragments from complete vessels brought to the site. These are mostly concentrated in the layers underlying the mill structure at the east end of the tail race. There is evidence for both Norwegian and Shetland origins for the material, with the greatest number of Norwegian pieces in the pre-mill phase, and although there are Norwegian pieces elsewhere in the sequence, they could be interpreted as pieces which have been redeposited by the upcast from the building of the mill (Forster forthcoming). A collection of eight runic-inscribed bone fragments complements an existing stone runic inscription from the Round Church (Barnes and Page 2006, OR 10 Orphir I; OR 15 Orphir II; OR 19 Orphir III). Despite being somewhat dismissed by these authors, the bone pieces have significance in this context as they indicate that in addition to the potentially more formal literacy of the church runes, there was current a less formal literacy, as would be appropriate for the Earl's retinue and possibly the Earl himself.

Acknowledgements

Many funding bodies have supported this long-running project and this support is very gratefully acknowledged. However, it is the support of Historic Environment Scotland in these later stages of the production of academic papers and the compilation of the final report for publication which requires additional note here.

References

Anderson, A. B. (1938) *The Orkneyinga Saga: A New Translation with Introduction and Notes*. London: Oliver and Boyd.

Barnes, M. P. and R. I. Page (2006) *The Scandinavian Runic Inscriptions of Britain. Runrön. Runologiska bidrag utgivna as Institutionen för nordiska språk vid Uppsala universitet* 19. Uppsala: Uppsala Universitetet.

Barrett, J. (ed.) (2012) *Being an Islander: Production and Identity at Quoygrew, Orkney AD 900–1600*. McDonald Institute Monographs. Cambridge: McDonald Institute for Archaeological Research.

Batey, C. E. (2003) Excavations at the Earl's Bu, Orphir, Orkney, c. 1859–1939. *New Orkney Antiquarian Journal* 3, 29–71.

Batey, C. E. with C. Freeman (1986) Lavacroon, Orphir, Orkney. *Proceedings of the Society of Antiquaries of Scotland* 116, 285–300. Microfiche 5: A5–D9.

Batey, C. E. with R. Barrowman, I. Mainland, J. Harland and J. Huntley (Forthcoming) *The Earl's Bu, Orphir, Orkney: A Norse Economic Hub*.

Fawcett, R. (2021) An architectural analysis of the church and related buildings on the Brough of Birsay. In C. D. Morris, *The Birsay Bay Project Vol 3. The Brough of Birsay, Orkney Investigations 1954–2014*. Oxford and Philadelphia: Oxbow Books, 66–73.

Fernie, E. (1988) The Church of St Magnus, Egilsay. In B. E. Crawford (ed.), *St Magnus Cathedral and Orkney's Twelfth Century Renaissance*. Aberdeen: Aberdeen University Press, 140–61.

Fisher, I. (1993) Orphir Church in its south Scandinavian context. In C. E. Batey, J. Jesch and C. D. Morris (eds), *The Viking Age in Caithness, Orkney and the North Atlantic (Select Papers from the Proceedings of the Eleventh Viking Congress)*. Edinburgh: Edinburgh University Press, 375–80.

Forster, A. (Forthcoming) Steatite: Vessels and other objects. In C. E. Batey, R. Barrowman, I. Mainland, J. Harland and J. Huntley, *The Earl's Bu, Orphir, Orkney: A Norse Economic Hub*.

Griffiths, D., J. Harrison and M. Athanson (2019) *Beside the Ocean: Coastal Landscapes at the Bay of Skaill, Marwick and the Bay of Birsay*. Oxford and Philadelphia: Oxbow Books, 225–37.

Johnson, P. G. and C. E. Batey (2003) Survey at the Earl's Bu, Orphir, Orkney, 1989–91: Geophysical work on a Late Norse estate complex. *Scottish Archaeology Internet Reports* 4.

Jones, J. and J. Mulville (2018) Norse animal husbandry in liminal environments: Stable isotope evidence from the Scottish North Atlantic islands. *Environmental Archaeology* 23(4), 338–51.

Mainland, I. and C. E. Batey (2018) The nature of the feast: Commensality and the politics of consumption in Viking Age and Early Medieval Northern Europe. *World Archaeology* 50(5), 781–803.

Mainland, I., J. Towers, V. Ewens, G. Davis, J. Montgomery, C. Batey, N. Card and J. Downes (2016) Toiling with teeth: An integrated dental analysis of sheep and cattle dentition in Iron Age and Viking-Late Norse Orkney. *Journal of Archaeological Science: Reports* 6, 837–55.

Maleszka, M. (2003) A Viking Age weight from Cleat, Westray, Orkney. *Proceedings of the Society of Antiquaries of Scotland* 133, 283–91.

Pálsson, H. and P. Edwards (trans.) (1978) Orkneyinga Saga: *The History of the Earls of Orkney*. London: Hogarth Press.

Sharples, N. (ed.) (2020) *A Norse Settlement in the Outer Hebrides. Excavations on Mounds 2 and 2A, Bornais, South Uist. Cardiff Studies in Archaeology*. Oxford: Oxbow Books.

Chapter 18

Revisiting Tuquoy – Still Full of Surprises . . .
Olwyn Owen

Tuquoy is not a 'new' Norse site. On the contrary, it was identified some forty years ago by the late Dr Raymond Lamb, then the Orkney Archaeologist, while he was walking the coastline of Papa Westray and Westray in 1981, and amassing sites for inclusion in his latest *List of Archaeological Sites and Monuments* (1983). Adjacent to the remains of Cross Kirk, 'one of the most refined of Orkney's medieval churches' (Lamb 1983: 37, No. 148), Dr Lamb was surprised to find substantial lime-mortared structures erupting from the eroding section (Figure 18.1). With his usual perspicacity, he deduced that this was the high-status Norse settlement originally associated with Cross Kirk and hypothesised that the massive lime-mortared walls were the remains of a 12th-century Norse castle or hall, which he nicknamed 'Haflidi's Hall' in an article for *The Orcadian* (1981). According to *Orkneyinga Saga* (*OS*; Taylor 1938), Haflidi was the son of a 'quarrelsome and overbearing' Norse magnate, Thorkel Flettir (Thorkel 'Flayer'), who played an important part in the story of the usurpation of the Orkney Earldom by Rognvald Kali Kolsson in the 1130s (*OS*, Chapter 56). Dr Lamb immediately wrote to the (then) SDD Ancient Monuments Branch to request an urgent intervention – and so began the Tuquoy project.

Initially, we were tasked with carrying out a 'one-season question-solving session of excavation, with very limited objectives'. In the event, we carried out four discrete episodes of work:

- limited trial excavation centred on the major walls in 1982–3 (by the Department of Archaeology, Durham University);
- fuller assessment of the extent and character of the site through 'tapestry' excavation along a c. 100m stretch of the cliff section in 1988 (by the then Central Excavation Unit, later AOC Archaeology);
- salvage recording of the section following serious storm damage in 1993 (as a one-off exercise by the Inspectorate of Ancient Monuments, Historic Scotland); and

Figure 18.1 Cross Kirk and the site of the Norse settlement from the air (looking approximately west). The settlement lies along the coastal edge in the area immediately beyond the graveyard wall in this photo. © Historic Environment Scotland.

- several discrete and mainly non-invasive episodes of additional fieldwork commissioned in 2017–19 in preparation for final publication (conducted by ORCA, the archaeological unit based in the Institute of Archaeology, Orkney UHI).

The major features observed in the 1980s were:

- the remains of a substantial hall (not fully excavated, but 3.75m wide by at least 6.65m long internally), built of dressed lime-mortared masonry in a style reflecting an essentially Romanesque tradition, and later partitioned (Figure 18.2);
- a substantial specialist craft building, termed a workshop, possibly about 19m long by 5m wide, which was positioned at right angles to the hall and obscured its original entrance; and
- a waterlogged 'pit' containing a wealth of organic material so far unparalleled in the Orkney Earldom, testifying to, among other things, an active domestic woodworking industry taking place on the site.

Figure 18.2 Part of the hall during excavation in 1983. © Historic Environment Scotland.

A suite of post-excavation analyses was undertaken in the late 1980s and early 1990s but stalled after 1992 when I joined the Inspectorate and AOC Archaeology joined the commercial sector. In recent years, work to bring the project to publication restarted in earnest – and has yielded more than a few surprises.

Dating the settlement

One of the first tasks for the renewed post-excavation programme was to improve the dating framework for the site. A total of nineteen radiocarbon dates had been obtained following the 1980s work, but they were a mixed bunch of submissions, some more reliable than others. Bulk samples of seaweed, animal bone, marine shell and plant material were submitted for dating in the 1980s and the early 1990s. In 2017, twenty additional single-entity samples (Ashmore 1999) of animal bone, charred plants, organic silt and wood charcoal were dated by the Scottish Universities Environmental Research Centre (SUERC).

Altogether, therefore, thirty-nine radiocarbon determinations are now available from Tuquoy. Bayesian analysis (by Anthony Krus of SUERC) of all thirty-nine results suggests that the dated activity at Tuquoy began in the 11th century and ended in the 13th to 14th centuries. This is a surprisingly tight dating framework, indicating a rather shorter period of occupation than we had originally proposed, although the artefactual evidence suggests that the settlement may have continued in use into the 15th century.

The radiocarbon dating evidence suggests that activity associated with the hall began around the start of the 12th century, which indicates that it may have been built at the behest of Haflidi's father, or even his grandfather. Analysis of nine dates from the hall and ten from the workshop suggests that the hall ceased to be used as a hall after only a generation or two of use, before it was partly remodelled into an annexe for the workshop. This accords with our original suggestion that the hall, although grand in conception and appearance, was poorly founded and was unlikely to have remained in use for long.

Three major episodes of structural modifications had been identified in the workshop during the 1980s and 1990s work – now termed the 'early', 'middle' and 'late' workshop. It was also clear on stratigraphic grounds that the early workshop was built after the hall. However, the radiocarbon dating results strongly suggest that use of the hall and workshop were broadly contemporaneous – which supports the suggestion that the hall was not in use for long, and that both the hall and the original (early) workshop are very broadly contemporary with the 12th-century Cross Kirk. However, radiocarbon dating evidence indicates that the workshop remained in use for much longer than the hall and that activity associated with the workshop ended in the 13th century (contra the artefactual evidence, which suggests it remained in use for rather longer).

Analysis of fifteen dates from the basal organic layers of the waterlogged 'pit' suggests that activity associated with this feature began around the start of the 11th century and ended around the beginning of the 12th century. Some of the palaeoenvironmental evidence suggests that the organic fills of the 'pit' may have accumulated over a shorter period, but the radiocarbon dates do support our earlier contention that the precious organic material at the base of the 'pit' accumulated most probably before the hall was built.

Perhaps most surprising is the lack of radiocarbon dating evidence for any activity earlier than the 11th century. This has been borne out by updating the specialist artefactual reports: only a handful of finds are likely to date from earlier than about 1000, and there is so far no trace whatsoever of any prehistoric activity at Tuquoy – unlike most other Norse settlements in the Northern Isles, which tend to occur on multi-period sites (as at Pool, Sanday: Hunter et al. 2007; and Jarlshof, Shetland: Hamilton 1956). In short, it seems that Tuquoy was a virgin site when the Norse selected this spot for settlement and began to build – possibly around the turn of the first millennium AD.

Geophysical survey and the extent of the site

In the 1980s we were advised that geophysical survey was unlikely to be successful at Tuquoy and it was not attempted. However, geophysical survey techniques have improved significantly over the last three decades and, by 2017, ORCA (the Orkney-based archaeological unit) had extensive experience of conducting, interpreting and, sometimes, ground-truthing geophysical surveys in Orkney, notably across the World Heritage Area (Brend et al. 2020). A geophysical survey was therefore carried out by ORCA at Tuquoy in early 2017, using a combination of magnetometry and earth resistance. The results were excellent and so the geophysical survey was extended in early 2018.

The magnetometry survey results appear to show densely packed structures and deposits of enhancement material (for example, midden), while a halo of increased magnetic response seems to correspond broadly with the site limits. The surviving 'core' of settlement activity measures around 140m east–west by 50m north–south, extending northwards from the coastal section and westwards from the western wall of the Cross Kirk graveyard. This result more or less correlates with the conclusions of an augur and test-pitting survey carried out in 1988, which confirms that such cost-efficient surveys can accurately assess the extent of sites in similar circumstances.

The structural complexity evident in the coastal section is clearly reflected in the gradiometer data and, while this presents difficulties for detailed interpretation without further excavation, it is clear that a considerable amount of the settlement still survives on the landward side of the coast. Unexpectedly, the survey also picked up indications of a large sub-rectangular enclosure of unknown date and function immediately to the north of the graveyard, which a smattering of snow revealed was also just visible on the ground surface as a slightly raised earthwork.

The targeted earth resistance survey provides a complementary picture, with two definite structures visible and suggestions of other structures and boundaries in the surrounding area. The most surprising, by far, was a building which is completely different in character from the major buildings recorded during excavation (the hall and workshop) (Figure 18.3). This substantial structure is roughly square, measuring about 16.5m north–south by 15m east–west overall, with walls apparently up to 2.6m thick, though undoubtedly including some rubble collapse. Internally, the building measures about 10m by 10m, with an entrance on the east side and a small, curving feature (a stair?) apparently projecting from the building's west side. The clarity of the anomalies suggests that this building is well preserved. Morphologically, the building resembles several examples of Late Norse towers or castles found elsewhere in Orkney, such as The Wirk in Rousay, Cubbie Roo's Castle in Wyre, and

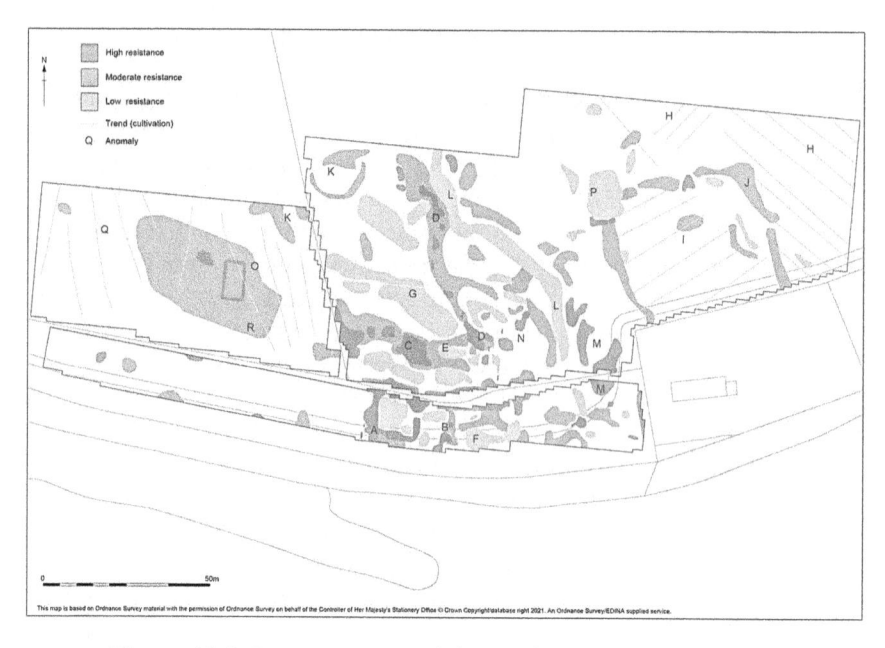

Figure 18.3 Interpretation of the earth resistivity survey results: A = possible tower; B = probably part of the hall. © Historic Environment Scotland/ORCA (UHI Archaeology Institute).

Castle Howe, Holm, which are part of a recognised tradition of grand, high-quality architecture in Orkney during the 12th century (Gibbon 2017). Such towers are also found in association with hall-house buildings, such as that at Tuquoy. If this is a tower, however, the proportions would be somewhat larger than other known examples, even accounting for rubble spread.

To the east of this substantial building, a linear high-resistance anomaly runs north-east–south-west for over 6m from the coastal section before turning 90° and running north-west–south-east for about 4m. It is very likely that this represents the northern end of the hall identified during the 1982–3 excavations.

The earth resistance survey also clearly showed the line of a former stream running roughly north-north-west–south-south-east from the Loch of Tuquoy to the coastal edge, as depicted on the First Edition Ordnance Survey map, and observed in section in the 1980s. The southern end of the watercourse seems to have been amended, possibly in the Late Norse or medieval period, which corresponds with a widening of the area of low resistance seen in the survey data, and the presence of possible linear structures on the west bank. It is tempting to interpret these as evidence for a mill lade and click-mill, perhaps comparable to the remains of the horizontal mill excavated at the Earl's Bu in Orphir (Batey and Morris 1992).

Pollen cores from the former Loch of Tuquoy

Approximately 450m north of the archaeological site at Tuquoy, there is a drained former loch, the Loch of Tuquoy, which is now under pasture, but still prone to waterlogging. This provided an opportunity to obtain a long-term record of vegetation change, soil erosion and palaeo-pollution, and to investigate the environmental impact of the Norse farming and earlier communities in Westray. Two 2.2m cores were retrieved from the loch (by Scott Timpany of ORCA) in 2017, with the aim of reconstructing the palaeoenvironmental history and environmental impact of the settlement. The cores were analysed for pollen, non-pollen palynomorph, microscopic charcoal, geochemistry, loss on ignition and mineral magnetic analyses, and were also sampled for radiocarbon dating. This is the first long-term vegetation study for the northern isles of Orkney, which means that the results will hopefully also be a valuable resource for future archaeological work in Westray and nearby islands.

To summarise the main results, the cores dated from the Late Bronze Age to the post-medieval period and included good coverage of the Late Norse period. Surprisingly, this work clearly identified a phase of previously unknown, early Iron-Age (c. 800–500 BC) agricultural activity in the vicinity, during which barley was the main cultivar in a mixed economy, with evidence for animal grazing. A known settlement mound at Hodgalee (Canmore ID: 2820), located at the head of the Bay of Tuquoy, could be a candidate for the parent farmstead. The presence of *Trichuris* (whipworm) parasite eggs during this phase of occupation is the first recording of this parasite in Orkney and suggests possible pollution of the loch waters.

Agricultural activity began again at around 700, prior to the date of the known lifetime of the Tuquoy settlement, which strongly indicates that Pictish and Viking-Age farmsteads are likely waiting to be discovered in the near vicinity of Tuquoy. Agricultural activity continued throughout the Late Norse period and into the post-medieval period until about 1575. In the later Norse period, during the period of occupation of the Tuquoy farmstead, agriculture placed a greater emphasis on the cultivation of oat/wheat (probably oat) than in the previous Pictish period, alongside the cultivation of barley (probably six-row hulled barley and possibly bere barley) and the keeping of livestock – all of which is corroborated by the results of the 1980s fieldwork. Arboreal pollen values are low during the Late Norse period in the Loch of Tuquoy sequence, but there is a possible signal for the presence of hazel, birch, alder and willow.

Limited evidence for metalworking was picked up in the geochemical record for the site throughout the sequence, with peaks in lead pollution including one in the 12th century (1134). However, the data suggests that metalworking associated with early Iron-Age activity gave a stronger palaeo-pollution signal than that for the Norse farmstead at Tuquoy. The loss on ignition record signalled higher rates of organic content during the Iron-Age and Norse periods, which may relate to increased soil erosion in the catchment from the intensification of agricultural activity at these times.

Artefactual and palaeoenvironmental studies

All of the specialist artefact and palaeoenvironmental reports completed in the 1980s and 1990s have been revisited in recent years, which has yielded some surprising new information.

The metalwork assemblage (analysed by Barbara Ford), for example, includes a range of finds consistent with a working farm and associated household, with various crafts taking place, but some objects also indicate the wealth of the occupants. Among the finest items is a silver gilt annular brooch decorated with twisted cord-like decoration, which was 'rediscovered' in the stored boxes and had not previously been reported on in depth. Raghnall Ó Floinn has identified it as belonging to a type of medieval ring brooch in general use throughout western Europe, but mostly dating to the 13th and 14th centuries. A copper-alloy ringed pin of Hiberno-Scandinavian type, found just outside the hall, is the finest example of the eight kidney-ringed pins on record from Scotland (reports James Graham-Campbell). The Tuquoy pin is closely paralleled by examples from Dublin dating from the late 10th century, or c. 1000, suggesting that it was manufactured probably in Dublin sometime before, or soon after, the millennium, and probably reached Orkney in the 11th century. The unworn condition of its decoration indicates that it was lost before it had been put to any great use.

Other dress accessories include a fragment of goat skin shoe, antler hair combs, bone hair pins, bone toggles (possible dress or shoe fasteners) and a walrus ivory pendant or amulet. A bone mount and copper alloy mounts (one gilded) may also have been fittings from clothing or belts, or they may have decorated boxes or chests. A number of locks and keys indicate the use of boxes or chests for storing valuables or locking gates and doors – demonstrating that the occupants had valuable possessions that needed securing. Parts of at least six copper alloy vessels, including a cauldron, bowls or plates, and possibly caskets, were recovered, and provided clear evidence of vessel repair taking place on site, while the fragmentary remains of a horse curry comb testify to the presence and care of horses.

The organic basal fills of the waterlogged 'pit' yielded a wealth of rare information (summarised previously in Owen 1993, 2005), with the plentiful evidence for the large-scale import of wood and

Figure 18.4a The waterlogged 'pit' during excavation in 1988.
© Historic Environment Scotland.

Figure 18.4b Some of the worked wood from the waterlogged 'pit'.
© Historic Environment Scotland.

a domestic woodworking industry being especially notable (examined by Anne Crone) (Figure 18.4). The trunks had been trimmed to squared cross-sections or planks for ease of transport, probably in Norway. Woodworking offcuts and chips (mainly pine) comprised 60 per cent of the assemblage, and produced evidence for use of a range of tools: knives, spoon-bits, axes, adzes and planes; while the artefacts included handles, spatulas, spoons, pins, pegs, twine, a roll of birch bark and boat fixings.

A summary of just one of the palaeoenvironmental reports gives a flavour of the potential of this organic material. Eva Panagiotakopulu has recently revisited the Diptera assemblage (originally studied by the late Peter Skidmore): the samples produced over 11,000 specimens of flies – one of the richest assemblages Eva has ever seen. There is an equally abundant assemblage of insects, which Paul Buckland reports is markedly similar to the faunas recovered from Viking York. The combined reports on this organic material (including flies, insects, parasites, waterlogged plant remains, macroplant, palynology and sedimentology) indicate that animal dung and litter from the byres, together with some domestic debris, was regularly being dumped into this waterlogged feature – which we now believe may have been a natural hollow, rather than a man-made pit, perhaps the result of dune slack.

Tuquoy is clearly a very special site and would richly reward larger-scale investigation. If ever this becomes possible, this singular settlement will undoubtedly yield further surprises.

References

Ashmore, P. J. (1999) Radiocarbon dating: avoiding errors by avoiding mixed samples. *Antiquity* 73, 124–30.

Batey, C. E. and C. D. Morris (1992) Earl's Bu, Orphir, Orkney: Excavation of a Norse horizontal mill. In C. D. Morris and D. J. Rackham (eds), *Norse and*

Later Settlement and Subsistence in the North Atlantic. Glasgow: University of Glasgow Department of Archaeology Occasional Paper Series 1, 33–42.

Brend, A., N. Card, J. Downes, M. Edmonds and J. Moore (2020) *Landscapes Revealed: Geophysical Survey in the Heart of Neolithic Orkney World Heritage Area 2002–2011*. Oxford: Oxbow Books.

Gibbon, S. J. (2017) A survey of Norse castles in Orkney. In P. Martin (ed.) *Castles and Galleys*. Laxay, Isle of Lewis: Islands Book Trust, 226–48.

Hamilton, J. R. C. (1956) *Excavations at Jarlshof, Shetland*. Edinburgh: HMSO.

Hunter, J., with J. M. Bond and A. N. Smith (2007) *Investigations in Sanday, Orkney, Volume 1: Excavations at Pool, Sanday. A Multi-period Settlement from Neolithic to Late Norse Times*. Kirkwall: The Orcadian Ltd.

Lamb, R. G. (1981) The hall of Haflidi. *The Orcadian*, 23 July.

Lamb, R. G. (1983) *The Archaeological Sites and Monuments of Scotland, 19: Papa Westray and Westray (with adjacent small islands), Orkney Islands Area*. Edinburgh: RCAHMS.

Owen, O. (1993) Tuquoy. Westray, Orkney: A challenge for the future? In C. E. Batey, J. Jesch and C. D. Morris (eds), *The Viking Age in Caithness, Orkney and The North Atlantic*. Edinburgh: Edinburgh University Press, 318–39.

Owen, O. (2005) History, archaeology and *Orkneyinga Saga*: the case of Tuquoy. In O. Owen (ed.), *The World of* Orkneyinga Saga: *The Broad-Cloth Viking Trip*. Kirkwall: The Orcadian Ltd, 192–212.

Taylor, A. B. (trans.) (1938) *The* Orkneyinga Saga: *A New Translation with Introduction and Notes*. Edinburgh: Oliver and Boyd.

Chapter 19

The Lewis Hoard of Gaming Pieces – Evoking and Reassembling a Viking Past?

Mark A. Hall and David H. Caldwell

The aim of this contribution is to briefly summarise the work on the Lewis Hoard of gaming pieces that has taken place since the publication of *Vikings in Scotland*. From that base, the argument is that the gaming pieces, or chessmen if you prefer, are not Viking; they post-date the Viking Age by at least a century. They are not a guide to the Viking economy, but viewed as a performance mechanism we can perhaps suggest that the Lewis Hoard helped to recall or reassemble a Viking Past, updated within newer political and social realities.

This helps to signal a reframing of the discussion of the hoard in the context of the assembly and reassembly of objects – concepts borrowed from, but not exclusive to, ethnographic and colonial studies (for example, Elsner and Cardinal 1994; Harrison, Byrne and Clarke 2013; Hamilakis and Jones 2017; Wingfield 2017 and with the key impetus for the approach, Latour 2005) – which help to emphasise both the affective, material qualities of things and their symbolic, representational ones. It underlies one of the key objectives in reassessing the Lewis Hoard: to raise awareness of it as an act, or rather several acts, of assembly or accumulation, with temporal depth both in its accumulation (probably through gift-giving episodes) and in its heirloom capacity to store and pass on generational knowledge (its later reassembly through its discovery, dissemination and affective influence on cultural practice will not be dealt with here, but see, for example, Caldwell and Hall 2018). This heirloom reflex around gaming pieces can be seen on a grander, institutional scale in Continental church treasuries and fittings (Kluge-Pinsker 1991: 34–5; Hall, Graham-Campbell and Petts, forthcoming). The assembly of the Lewis Hoard may have taken place in what came to be a Gaelic cultural milieu, one which hybridised Scandinavian cultural elements through generational inheritance and through adoption (for example, see Hall 2017). The affective, tangible agency of such pieces (including heraldry and colour) is discussed in Tate et al. 2014, Hall 2014 and Forsyth and Hall 2020.

Vikings in Scotland

'Earls and Bishops' is the final, thirteenth, chapter of Graham-Campbell and Batey's *Vikings in Scotland: An Archaeological Survey* and concludes with a coda (pp. 263–4) on the Lewis chessmen (Figure 19.1) in which they accepted the long-standing view that the pieces were a merchant's stock of the second half of the 12th century. As the products, possibly, of a workshop in Trondheim, they are not directly Viking but are tangible archaeological evidence for continuing links between Norway and Scandinavian Scotland.

New approaches

Prior to the re-evaluation which the authors of this paper led, the dominant line on the understanding of the hoard was held constantly through the British Museum publications from 1978 to 2004 – with Robinson 2004 notably extending the discussion out into the gaming context and the walrus context – that the hoard was an unexplainable loss by a merchant. Contrary to this view, the authors of this paper put forward, in 2009, the premise that the hoard was where it was because it was meant to be there, a position which opened up the hitherto ignored context of the Kingdom of the Isles and a broad range of contacts across the North Sea world. We also explored a range of cultural contexts around gaming, production and legacy, in a range of publications, a conference and an exhibition between 2009 and 2018 (Caldwell, Hall and Wilkinson 2009, 2010; Caldwell and Hall 2014; 2018).

Figure 19.1 Some of the Lewis Hoard laid out for chess. © and courtesy The British Museum.

In terms of the local context, we broadened discussion out from Uig on Lewis to a place further down the coast at Mealasta; this place is mentioned in some of the earlier accounts of discovery and has had various bits of archaeology recorded there over the years, including a stone, souterrain-like chamber and more recently contemporary 12th- to 13th-century material culture. The broader political and cultural context for Lewis in the 12th and 13th centuries is Scandinavian. The local context is the Kingdom of the Isles (Caldwell 2014: 71–94), with a dynasty of kings based in the Isle of Man. Norse was perhaps the main language spoken in Lewis as late as the mid-13th century. Whether speaking Norse or Gaelic, the leaders of local society in the 12th and 13th centuries belonged to the Scandinavian world. The immediate church authority for Lewis was the bishopric of Sodor, centred on the Isle of Man from the 1230s. Prior to that the bishops were itinerant. From 1153, they were under the authority of the archbishops of Nidaros (Trondheim). As remote as Lewis can seem today, during the medieval period it was well connected on the North Sea super highway, with strong links to the rest of Scotland, to Ireland and to the rest of the Scandinavian world. Indeed, as has been long recognised, the Lewis Hoard probably journeyed there from Trondheim, Norway. Among several possibilities spanning the North Sea world, the most plausible theory on the place of manufacture of the hoard's pieces remains Trondheim. There is a strong suite of artistic parallels there and we found no stronger evidence for any other place. Caroline Wilkinson undertook the forensic analysis of the faces of the figurative gaming pieces and suggested a series of related traits that suggested the hands of five craftsmen at work; a sizeable workshop. The workshop also had continuity through time, given the chronological range of several of the features of the gaming pieces, including mitres, thrones and weaponry. This suggested to us sets of gaming pieces made during c. 1150–c. 1230.

Lewis Chessmen: New Perspectives (2014) further explored and extended this range of contexts. It includes a clutch of papers revealing a dynamic, changing cultural context in which the hoard is best understood, including Nedoma (2014) on the nature of chess terminology, which was predominantly central and south European and clearly accompanied the arrival of chess pieces; Hall on the use of colour and heraldry, use as heirlooms and the range of games represented including the overlap between *hnefatafl* and chess; and Teichert on Norse-Icelandic fiction and its coverage of board games.

'Vikingness' and hybrid identities

These aspects all feed into the final discussion point about the hoard and its Viking pedigree, which we develop from the *New Perspectives* volume, beginning with Price's contribution around the hoard's depiction of berserkers. Of course, there is a popular perception that the Lewis Hoard does somehow represent the Vikings. Price does not accept this easy equation, raising instead the intriguing possibility that all twelve warders or rooks may represent berserks, suggesting their militant poses are a close enough link and inferable from the four shield-biting warders. These four in particular (Figure 19.2) are conventionally regarded as berserks, and certainly they are the earliest depictions we have of the shield-biting attribute of berserks, pre-dating the fullest description of berserks in Snorri Sturlusson's *Heimskringla, Ynglingasaga* 6 (translated by Price 2014: 32). Price's analysis certainly persuaded one of the authors (MH) that his scepticism on (but not the humour of) berserker representation was misplaced.

Figures 19.2a–2d The four 'berserkir' pieces from the Lewis Hoard. 2a–2c © and courtesy The British Museum, 2d © and courtesy National Museums Scotland.

In the context of the *hnefatafl* to chess transition and the heraldic devices of the shield-biters, perhaps the berserkers can be seen as a reference to militant paganism and so may be recalling that pagan past as one absorbed by Christianity (cf. the Christianising of the Roman pagan past, something that scholars such as Snorri Sturlusson would have been aware of). On the chessboard the warder is a middle-ranking piece, subservient to several others and more readily sacrificed; on the *hnefatafl* board they are perhaps a nostalgic reference to fighting prowess in defence of or attacking a king. The 13th-century *Hervarar saga ok Heiðreks*, which draws on earlier material, includes a riddle, the answer to which is *hnefatafl* and which refers to shield-maidens defending their king, and one side being fair and the other dark (for English translations, see Tolkien 1960; Tunstall 2005).

The whole question of berserkers was revisited recently by Roderick Dale in his 2014 PhD thesis. This introduces some fresh nuances that move us away from a historical-literal evocation of the Viking past. Dale (pp. 300–2) interprets the Lewis pieces as a later medieval depiction of the idea of *berserkir*, especially in the sagas; in *Grettir's Saga*, for example, the shields as described are very like those of the Lewis berserkers.

He goes on to identify, from a small group of Norwegian sagas, a category of Christian or Christianised berserkers who retain elements of the heathen warrior but without the pagan stigma. They fight for the Christian God and are equated to champions, perhaps partly influenced by Crusading ethics. In translations of French romances into Old Norse, the word 'champion' becomes 'berserkr' and contextually is clearly meant to mean someone who fights on behalf of someone else (Dale 2014: 183–4).

Nedoma's contribution (pp. 243–60) to *New Perspectives* is a very close study of the philological background of chess terminology. Nedoma adduces that the linguistic evidence points to a transfer of chess and its terminology to Scandinavia via central Europe, probably in the 11th or first half of the 12th century, with a key mechanism the journeys of travellers to and back from southern and central Europe.

Teichert's paper in the *New Perspectives* volume (pp. 307–20) explores some of the evidence for the depiction of board games in medieval West Nordic narratives. This includes both narratives containing historical and fictitious information and mainly around the game of chess. The fictitious elements are culturally significant and again help to signal the European introduction of the game while also fusing it to a sense of a Scandinavian past.

The gaming pieces could be used across more than one game. *Króka-Refs Saga* describes how a double-sided gaming board was presented to King Harald Sigurdarson. Likely first recorded in the late 14th century, the earliest completely preserved version of the saga is dated to the late

15th century. The tale is set around 1000, as it refers to the conversion of Scandinavia to Christianity:

> The next summer Bard fitted out his ship for Norway and Gunnar gave him gifts . . . three valuable possessions [for] King Harald . . . The second was a board game skilfully made of walrus ivory . . . The third was a walrus skull . . . Bard put out to sea and his voyage went well. He came to the ports he would have chosen to visit. He brought many excellent Greenland wares to King Harald. One day, Bard came before the king and said, 'Here is a board game which the most honourable man in Greenland sent you. His name is Gunnar and he wants no money for it; rather he wants your friendship. I spent two years with him and he was a good fellow to me. He is very eager to be your friend.' The board game was both for the old game with one king and the new game with two. The king examined the set for a time and ordered him to thank the one who sent him such a gift: 'We certainly must reciprocate with our friendship.' (Trans. G. Clark 2001: 612–13)

This is evidently a gaming board fit for a king, made from the luxurious material, walrus ivory. Critical for us is that it is a double-sided board, '. . . for the old game with one king and the new game with two', almost certainly a reference to *hnefatafl* and chess. We know double-sided boards were used in the Viking Age – we have at least two examples in wood, neither as luxurious as Gunnar's gift to Harald but both combining *hnefatafl* with nine men's morris (when they were made and used, chess had not reached northern Europe). One is a fragment from the 9th-century Gokstad ship-burial (Nicolaysen 1882: 46–7; Hall 2016: table 1); and the second, half of a 10th-century, handled board from Toftanes, Faroes (Rosedahl and Wilson [eds] 1992: cat. 321, p. 311).

This Viking-Age tradition continues into the 12th century; there are fragments of two such wooden, double-sided boards (again combining *hnefatafl* and tables): one certain but incomplete, one indefinite and fragmentary, excavated in Trondheim, and again not luxurious but valued enough to be repaired (McLees 1990: 80–3, plates 11 and 12). All these examples are of the *hnefatafl*/merels combination. Where they differ from Gunnar's board, other than in their materiality, is that Gunnar's board was for a different combination. Reflecting game popularity in later medieval times, this board combines chess and *hnefatafl*, whereas the archaeological examples reflect the reality of when they were made and used, either before chess was known in northern Europe (Gokstad and Toftanes) or from when chess was still becoming popular (Trondheim).

The Lewis Hoard also encapsulates something like the start of this transition. The plain and abstract pawns are equally usable as *hnefatafl* pieces or chess pieces, and there is no inherent reason why some of the pieces could not have been used in both games and their variations. The interoperability of the Lewis pieces across more than one game is reinforced by the ivory discs in the Lewis Hoard. These are always classified as tablesmen – and tables is a group of games, not just the one we think of from its modern survival as backgammon – but they could equally have been used in a game of merels or mill (a position-and-capture game, the simplest version of which is noughts and crosses and the most complex twelve men's morris).

Conclusion

The aim of this short paper has been to outline the wealth of research that has taken place into the Lewis Hoard of gaming pieces in the years since the publication of *Vikings in Scotland*, and to focus that summary on what has until now been a diffuse line of enquiry, the assembly of the hoard across the 12th and 13th centuries. In particular, the paper seeks to explore what might be the sociocultural implications of that act, or series of acts, of assembly in creating a cross-generational network of knowledge, in part sustained by the gaming pieces as a collection and as heirlooms. In a hybridising context, in which Scandinavian and Gaelic sociocultural practices were being woven together, we can begin to think about how the hoard facilitated a looking back at the past and created new meanings and reconciliations from that understanding around individual and social identity, memory, belief and politics. There are surely further research rewards to come.

References

Caldwell, D. H. (2014) The Kingdom of the Isles. In D. H. Caldwell and M. A. Hall (eds), *The Lewis Chessmen: New Perspectives*. Edinburgh: NMS Publishing, 71–94.

Caldwell, D. H. and M. A. Hall (eds) (2014) *The Lewis Chessmen: New Perspectives*. Edinburgh: NMS Publishing.

Caldwell, D. H., M. A. Hall and C. Wilkinson (2009) The Lewis Hoard of gaming pieces: A re-examination of their context, meanings, discovery and manufacture. *Medieval Archaeology* 53, 155–204.

Caldwell, D. H., M. A. Hall and C. Wilkinson (2010) *The Lewis Chessmen Unmasked*. Edinburgh: NMS Publishing.

Caldwell, D. H. and M. A. Hall (2018) The hoard of gaming pieces from Lewis, Scotland: Their context and meaning. In A. Stempin (ed.), *The Cultural Role of Chess in Medieval and Modern Times 50th Anniversary Jubilee of the Sandomierz Chess Discovery*. Poznan: Muzeum Archaeologiczne w Poznaniu (= Bibliotheca Fontes Archaeologici Posnanienses 21), 97–108.

Clark, G. (trans.) (2001) The Saga of Ref the Sly. In *The Sagas of the Icelanders: A Selection*. London: Penguin Books, 595–625.

Dale, R. T. D. (2014) *Berserkir: A Re-examination of the Phenomenon in Literature and Life*. Unpublished PhD thesis, University of Nottingham.

Elsner, J. and R. Cardinal (eds) (1994) *The Cultures of Collecting*. London: Reaktion Books Ltd.

Forsyth, K. and M. A. Hall (2020) Rhetoric and reality in the visual culture of medieval Celtic board games: Literary and archaeological evidence combined. In E. Lapina and V. Kopp (eds), *Games and Visual Culture in the Middle Ages and the Renaissance*. Turnhout: Brepols, 33–76.

Graham-Campbell, J. and C. E. Batey (1998) *Vikings in Scotland: An Archaeological Survey*. Edinburgh: Edinburgh University Press.

Hall, M. A. (2014) 'To you he left ... his brown ivory chessmen': Cultural value in the Lewis hoard of gaming pieces. In D. H. Caldwell and M. A. Hall (eds), *The Lewis Chessmen: New Perspectives*. Edinburgh: NMS Publishing, 221–42.

Hall, M. A. (2016) Board games in boat burials: Play in the performance of migration and Viking Age mortuary practice. *European Journal of Archaeology* 19(3), 439–55.

Hall, M. A. (2017) Gaming, material culture and hybridity: The Kingdom of the Isles at play. In C. Cooijmans (ed.), *Traversing the Inner Seas: Contact and Continuity in and around Scotland, the Hebrides and the North of Ireland*. Edinburgh: Scottish Society for Northern Studies, 51–84.

Hall, M. A. and K. Forsyth (2011) Roman rules? The introduction of board games to Britain and Ireland. *Antiquity* 85, 1325–38.

Hall, M. A., J. Graham-Campbell and D. Petts (Forthcoming) Dress pins, bosses and pegged playing pieces: Changing identities of some late Iron Age and early medieval glass objects.

Hamilakis, Y. and A. M. Jones (2017) Archaeology and assemblages. *Cambridge Archaeological Journal* 27(1), 77–84.

Kluge-Pinsker, A. (1991) *Schach und Trictrac Zeugnisse Mittelalterlicher Spielfreude in Salischer Zeit*. Sigmaringen: Jan Thorbecke.

Latour, B. (2005) *Reassembling the Social. An Introduction to Actor-Network Theory*. Oxford: Oxford University Press.

McLees, C. (1990) *Games People Played, Gaming-Pieces, Boards and Dice in the Medieval Town of Trondheim, Norway*. Trondheim: Riksantikvaren, Utgravningskontoret for Trondheim (= Meddelelser Nr. 24).

Nedoma, R. (2014) Old West Norse chess terminology and the introduction of chess into Scandinavia. In D. H. Caldwell and M. A. Hall (eds), *The Lewis Chessmen: New Perspectives*. Edinburgh: NMS Publishing, 243–60.

Nicolaysen, N. (1882) *The Viking-Ship Discovered at Gokstad in Norway/Langskibet Fra Gokstad Ved Sandefjord*. Oslo: Alb. Cammermeyer.

Price, N. (2014) The Lewis 'berserkers': Identification and analogy in the shield-biting warriors. In D. H. Caldwell and M. A. Hall (eds), *The Lewis Chessmen: New Perspectives*. Edinburgh: NMS Publishing, 29–44.

Robinson, J. (2004) *The Lewis Chessmen*. London: British Museum Press.

Rosedahl, E. and D. M. Wilson (eds) (1992) *From Viking to Crusader: The Scandinavians and Europe 800–1200*. Copenhagen: Rizzoli International Publications/Council of Europe.

Snorri Sturluson Heimskringla: Nóregs konunga sogur af Snorri Sturlusson, 4 vols, F. Jónsson (ed.) (1893–1901). København: Samfundet til udgivelse af gammel nordisk litteratur 23:1–4 [with *Ynglingasaga*].

Stratford, N. (1997) *The Lewis Chessmen and the Enigma of the Hoard*. London: British Museum Press.

Tate, J., I. Reiche and F. Pinzari (2014) The Lewis chessmen: What can examination of the surfaces tell us? In D. H. Caldwell and M. A. Hall (eds), *The Lewis Chessmen: New Perspectives*. Edinburgh: NMS Publishing, 11–28.

Taylor, M. (1978) *The Lewis Chessmen*. London: British Museum Press.

Teichert, M. (2014) Game-boards and gaming-pieces in Old Norse-Icelandic fiction. In D. H. Caldwell and M. A. Hall (eds), *The Lewis Chessmen: New Perspectives*. Edinburgh: NMS Publishing, 307–20.

Tolkien, C. (ed. and trans.) (1960) *The Saga of King Heidrick the Wise*. London and Edinburgh: Thomas Nelson and Sons Ltd. http://vsnrweb-publications.org.uk/The%20Saga%20Of%20King%20Heidrek%20The%20Wise.pdf [Last viewed: 18 September 2020].

Tunstall, P. (2005) *The Saga of Hervor and King Heidrick the Wise*. http://www.germanicmythology.com/FORNALDARSAGAS/HervararSagaTunstall.html [Last viewed: 18 September 2020].

Wingfield, C. (2017) Collection as (re)assemblage: Refreshing museum archaeology. *World Archaeology* 49(5), 594–607.

Part VI

Economy and Exchange

As *Vikings in Scotland* understood, most Scotto-Scandinavians probably experienced everyday life through the prism of local and/or regional subsistence economies. For elites, environmental evidence highlights the importance of farming and fishing surpluses for redistribution and feasting strategies, which were in turn used as a social and political mechanism for influence and loyalty (see Part V).

Beyond the local, assemblages and hoards suggest some Scotto-Scandinavians also had access, at least intermittently, to 'exotic' long-distance market networks and the precious metals used as money within them. Unlike the coin-based economies of England, though, the limited commercial transactions that did occur in Scotland were more commonly facilitated with a bullion (metal-weight) currency popular in Scandinavia and parts of the Danelaw. These economies saw silver, and less frequently gold, used as cash based on weight and purity. Here, silver ornament (commonly arm-rings), ingots and coins were regularly fragmented into 'hack-silver' to make smaller denominations, being weighed in balances using specialised weights of the sort discovered on Colonsay and Gigha (Horne, this section).

As Graham-Campbell and Batey discussed, the region's natural wealth would have created surpluses that underpinned and financed this exotic, if likely rare, form of market-based activity (1998: 226). Over time, elites developed increasingly sophisticated and presumably lucrative trade, such as the exchange of timber or combs (Ashby, this section), perhaps traded directly for fish or textiles, or bought using such products as a form of cash known as 'commodity money'.

Although no permanent Scotto-Scandinavian market has been discovered outwith Whithorn (Galloway), temporary beach and *thing* markets (Sanmark, this volume) may have been held in both the north and west, perhaps explaining concentrations of burials around a natural harbour like Pierowall, Orkney. In any case, wealth was certainly entering Scotland, whatever the underlying mechanism: the Galloway Hoard, deposited around 900, contains a remarkable volume of silver ingots and Hiberno-Scandinavian arm-rings alongside artefacts derived from trade routes stretching to Central Asia, attesting to the potential liquidity of at least some settlers and their membership of wider exchange networks (Goldberg, this section).

As outlined above, precious metals used as bullion were likely gained via selling surplus natural resources, combined with shipping tolls and piracy, bringing the wealth seen in thirty-six hoards (Graham-Campbell, this section). From this, Scotto-Scandinavians adopted their own currencies, rejecting coin minting and instead developing a plain silver arm-ring (known as 'ring-money') from the mid-10th century. Popular both whole and fragmented until the mid-11th century, this ornament operated alongside imported, largely Anglo-Saxon, whole coin and was likely an example of the 'dual' economy seen in the Danelaw, where coin could be spent per its face *and* its bullion value.

Two or more decades ago, it was thought bullion use largely disappeared after the 11th century, with the most likely explanation being that its payment role was taken by other commodities such as dried fish, dairy and textiles. However, thanks to recent discoveries of bullion economies at Bornais (South Uist) and Earl's Bu (Orkney), we now know bullion persisted into the later Norse period (see Sharples, and Batey, this volume).

Chapter 20

The Viking-Age Silver and Gold of Scotland

James Graham-Campbell

When *The Viking-Age Gold and Silver of Scotland (AD 850–1100)* was published in 1995, the catalogue detailed the contents of thirty-four hoards containing coins and/or ornaments and bullion (in the form of ingots and hack-silver) which could be linked to Viking activity and Norse settlement in Scotland during the 9th to 11th centuries, together with all of the known single finds. A subsequent paper (Graham-Campbell 2008) brought to attention more recent discoveries and some further (lost) antiquarian material (summarised below). In this update, it was pointed out (ibid.: 194) that the total of thirty-four hoards was in no way definitive, given the likelihood of some duplication, with [7] being recommended for deletion, as subsequently [16] and now also [21], but with the addition of a (lost) coin hoard reportedly discovered in St Kilda in the 18th century [2a], and since then a small gold hoard from Jura, found in 1869 [25a], and the Galloway (2014) Hoard [35]. Finally, renewed consideration is given to the inclusion of two further hoards, both from south-west Scotland [6a] and [30a], originally rejected as probably 'non-Viking'. Their addition to the overall total means that the revised corpus currently consists of thirty-six hoards. For a recent survey of the use of silver in Scotland 75–1000 AD, see Blackwell, Goldberg and Hunter, *Scotland's Early Silver* (2017), and for Scandinavian Scotland, see Horne (2021).

Hoards: Addenda and corrigenda

[1] Port Glasgow (near), Renfrewshire (1699)

Hugh Pagan (2014) has recovered important information pertaining to this mixed hoard, augmenting our knowledge of both its provenance and contents, from letters written by (or addressed to) the Rev. Robert Wodrow (1679–1734), who at the time of its discovery was the newly appointed Librarian of the University of Glasgow. Pagan confirms that 'a date of deposit of c. 970' is 'appropriate' (ibid.: 419) and concludes that:

252 James Graham-Campbell

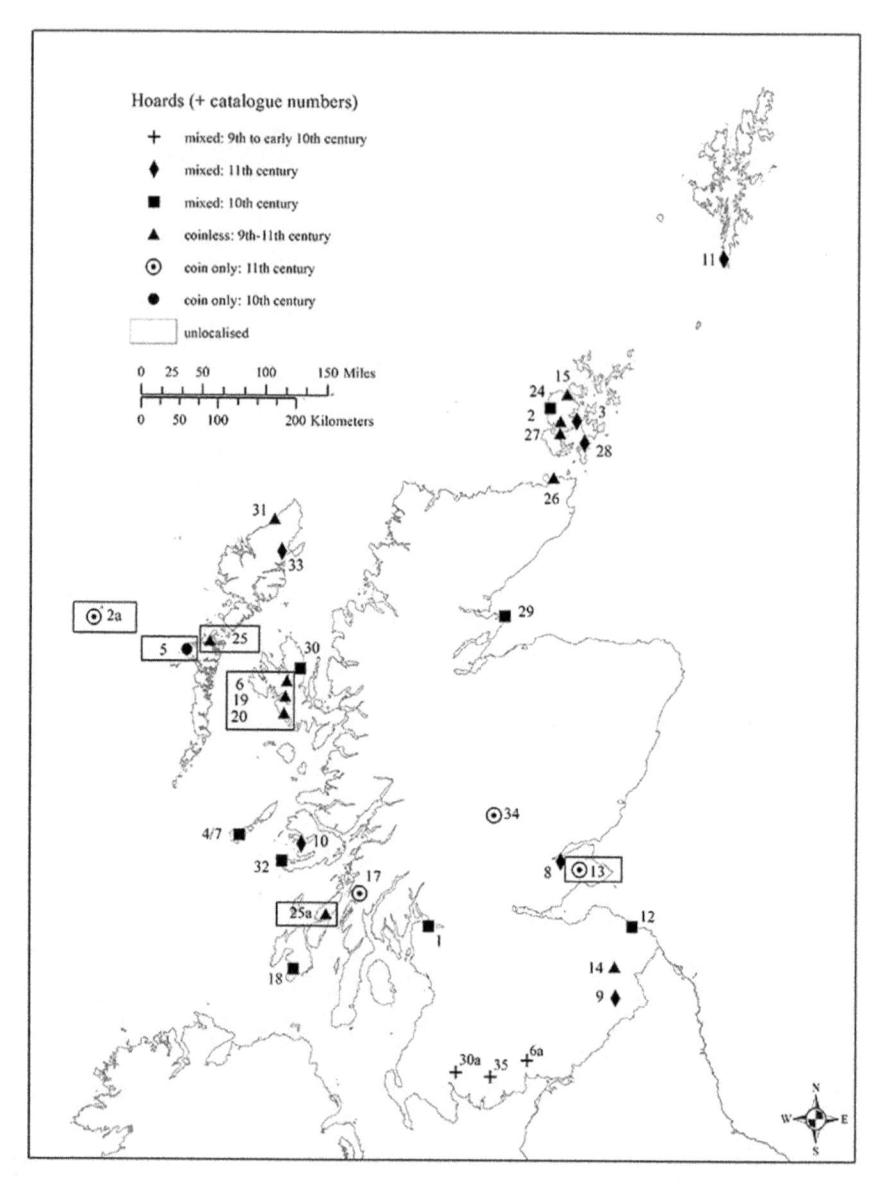

Figure 20.1 Distribution map of the Viking-Age silver and gold hoards of Scotland. J. Kershaw.

... it can now be seen that the hoard was found 'within a mile of Port Glasgow' and on a 'brae' ['by the falling doun of some earth'], i.e. not within what was at the time the urban centre of the newly created town of Port Glasgow; that its discovery presumably took place around the end of June 1699; that it contained a 'considerable' number of Anglo-Saxon coins; that it contained at least two penannular arm-rings and part of a third, adding the fragment given by Wodrow to [Sir Robert] Sibbald in 1710 [when described by Wodrow as 'part of a fibula of silver or mixed mettall'; ibid. 2014: 417] to the two whole arm-rings that James Sutherland had acquired and sold to the Faculty of Advocates in 1705 [Graham-Campbell 1995: 95, pl.1a]; and that it may also have contained some further items of Viking-age metalwork, presumably in the form of hack-silver. (Pagan 2014: 418)

[2] Ring of Brodgar, Stenness, Orkney (pre-1688)

As described by Graham-Campbell (2008: 193–4), this hoard should have been [1] in the (1995) catalogue because it was demonstrably found before the discovery of 'Port Glasgow' in 1699 (see above). The book by the Rev. James Wallace, containing his account and illustration of the find (ibid.: 95–6, pl. 2), was published posthumously by his son in 1693, following his father's death in 1688.

[2a] St Kilda

According to *The Scots Magazine* (June 1767):

> Edinburgh, May 11. We hear from Glasgow, that some fishermen lately dug up on the island of St Kilda, two antique urns, containing a quantity of Danish silver coin, which by the inscription appears to have lain there upwards of 1800 years.

The assumption is that '1800 years' is a misprint for '800' and that, although the 'description of the coins as "Danish" should not necessarily be taken literally', they 'might well have been of Cnut' (Graham-Campbell 2008: 194).

[3] Caldale, Mainland, Orkney (1774)

A letter written by William Lindsay (of Caldale House), on 27 July 1774, to an unidentified friend in Edinburgh, containing the fullest description of the discovery of the Caldale Hoard, was published in the *Caledonian Mercury* (13 August 1774). In the absence of this reference (which I owe to Brian Smith), it was only possible for me to quote part of its contents, from a copy (Graham-Campbell 1995: 96), but it commences:

> In digging lately for peats in a moss near my house at Caldale, there were found, about two feet below the surface of the ground, two cows horns, containing a number of small coins of which you have six enclosed. On the mouths of the horns, and lying near them, were several pieces of fine silver, in the form of crescents of different dimensions, nearly meeting at the ends, some of them flat made, others angled and cornered, and some round; one piece like the staple for a door for receiving the bolt of the lock, and another much like those hooks usually fastened to partitions for hanging clothes upon. In the bottom of one of the horns were several bits of the same metal, but coarser, which seem

to have been cut with an instrument; and appear to have been parts of such like crescents as have been mentioned. The horns were found in a sloping position, are much decayed, and about the size of Orkney's cattle's horns ...

[4] and [7] Tiree: nos. 1 (1780) and 2 (1782)

In his review of Graham-Campbell (1995), Mark Blackburn suggested (*Numismatic Circular* April 1996, 104(4): 87–8) that it was 'a mistake to have divided the (1780) Tiree Hoard into two finds' (Graham-Campbell 2008: 194).

[6a] Lochar Moss, Dumfriesshire (c. 1770/1782)

Ninth-century hoard found in the late 18th century, consisting of 'a leather bag, containing silver coins of the Saxon heptarchy, and a silver crucifix' (Walker 1803: 16). It has been proposed by Hugh Pagan that the coins were most likely stycas, but the 'crucifix' (presumably a pendant cross) is lost (Graham-Campbell 1995: 4–5, 85, no. 2; 2020: 455; see also below), so that the exact nature (and date) of this hoard remains uncertain.

[10] Inchkenneth, off Mull (c. 1830)

In addition to its published contents (Graham-Campbell 1995: 100), this mixed hoard is recorded as having included 'some weights of lead bound with iron', on the occasion of its exhibition in London to the Archaeological Institute (MacDonald 1849: 72); their fate, as that of the three arm-rings, is unknown (Graham-Campbell 2008: 194).

[11] Quendale (Garthbanks), Mainland, Shetland (1830)

For further discussion of this mixed hoard, see now Graham-Campbell (2010).

[16] 'Dunrossness (Skelberry), Mainland, Shetland (pre-1884)'

To be deleted: the coin of Harald Hardrada from Skelberry, in the Royal Coin Cabinet, Copenhagen, 'is best regarded as a single find' (Graham-Campbell 2010: 19).

[18] Machrie, Islay (1850)

Deposited in a horn. According to the *Glasgow Herald* (28 October 1850), this mixed hoard 'was found by labourers while excavating a drain on a farm ... deposited in a horn, which on being thrown on the ground, burst, and the coins were discovered' (Pagan 2014: 426, note 27). This becomes the fourth hoard from Scotland 'known to have been deposited in one or more cattle horns' (Graham-Campbell 1995: 59), including Caldale [3] (see above).

[21] 'Unprovenanced (pre-1851)'

This coinless silver hoard, apparently consisting exclusively of Hiberno-Scandinavian broad-band arm-rings, is generally thought to have been 'found in Scotland' but is now suggested for deletion. It is of uncertain size, seemingly having consisted of three or four rings, rather than the five previously suggested by Graham-Campbell and Sheehan (1995). There are three rings in the British Museum (Graham-Campbell 2011: 256, no. 16, pl. 78), two of which are first recorded in Edinburgh at the (1851) sale of the C. K. Sharpe collection. The rings were unprovenanced in his sale catalogue, with the only evidence for their discovery being the statement in the BM Register that they 'were found in Scotland'. However, this could well have been no more than an assumption, based on Sharpe's residence at Hoddam, whereas the sale catalogue demonstrates that his collection included a considerable number of Irish antiquities. Furthermore, there are lead copies of these rings in the National Museum of Ireland, from the collection of George Petrie, who left them to the Royal Irish Academy on his death in 1866. This mid-19th-century hoard [21] has become altogether too doubtful a proposition to be considered realistically as having been 'found in Scotland' – rather than in Ireland.

[24] Skaill, Sandwick, Orkney (1858)

For further discussion of this large mixed hoard, see now Graham-Campbell (2019), including the redating of its deposition (by Gareth Williams) to c. 960–80 (ibid.: 296). Research by David Griffiths has enabled its find-place to be more precisely determined as 'on the east side of the mound known as the Castle of Snusgar' (ibid.: 295), as in fact plotted on the second edition OS 25-inch map (Griffiths 2019: fig. 2.7), rather than on its south side, as previously suggested (Graham-Campbell 1995: fig. 49).

[25a] Isle of Jura (1869)

The gold finger-ring thought to be a single find from Skye [S13], once owned by Countess Latour (the Austrian widow of a McLeod chieftain), which she presented to her farm-manager on Skye on his retirement in

1931, was consigned by his descendants for auction in 1979. It was then, not unreasonably, catalogued by Christie's as having a Skye provenance; however, Katinka Dalglish has recently recognised it as the gold finger-ring that had belonged to (and had occasionally been worn by) the Rev. Dr Peter Hately Waddell (1816–91), of Glasgow, from its (reversed) image in his remarkable book, *Ossian and the Clyde, Fingal in Ireland, Oscar in Iceland or Ossian Historical and Authentic* (1875), where it is stated by him to be one of two discovered together in the Isle of Jura, in 1869; the second ring is lost (Dalglish with Graham-Campbell 2017).

[30a] Talnotrie, Kirkcudbrightshire (1912)

Mixed hoard (Maxwell 1913; Webster and Backhouse 1991: 273, no. 248; Graham-Campbell 1995: 4, 85, no. 4, fig. 4; 2001: 20–6, figs 10–15; 2020: 454; see further below), deposited in the mid-870s, containing Anglo-Saxon ornamental metalwork (a pair of silver pins and a silver strap-end, with a plain gold finger-ring), an Insular Viking lead weight, a couple of Abbasid dirhams and a fragment of Frankish denier, with six Northumbrian copper-alloy stycas and four silver pennies of Burgred of Mercia (852–874), one of which had been adapted for use as a brooch, as well as a cake of wax, etc. (Clarke et al. 2012: fig. 1.52).

[35] Balmaghie, Galloway (2014)

In 1995, the most recent silver hoards to have been found were (i) the accumulated result of metal-detecting at Lews Castle, Stornoway, Lewis, between 1988 and 1990 [33], and (ii) a small hoard [34] of Hiberno-Norse pennies from Dull, Perthshire (1989), so that the discovery of the Galloway Hoard in 2014, on church-land at Balmaghie, came after a long interval (see Goldberg, this section). It is by far the most important Viking hoard to have been found in Scotland for over 150 years and, although it contains only one (demonetised) Anglo-Saxon coin, its deposition can be dated to the end of the 9th or the beginning of the 10th century, making it one of the earliest Viking hoards known from Scotland (Graham-Campbell 2017; 2020; Goldberg and Davis 2021; Goldberg, this section).

The hoard of most immediate relevance to the Galloway Hoard is that from Gordon, Berwickshire [14], which can readily be overlooked because it is both small and lost. This is likewise coinless, but it can also be dated to the late 9th or early 10th century, with its five objects being suggestive of an Irish Sea origin (Graham-Campbell 1995: 27–8, 102, pl. 6; see Horne, this section). It has, consequently, been postulated that it was connected 'with the plundering of Lowland Scotland by Ivarr and his kinsmen during the year after his expulsion from Dublin in 902, or with the slightly later activities of Ragnall' (ibid.: 62).

In 1995, none of the thirty-four hoards in the catalogue was from south-west Scotland, so that the broad picture was one of hoard deposition – and non-recovery – across the Northern and Western Isles (Graham-Campbell 1995: fig. 2; compare with Figure 20.1), corresponding with the areas of most intensive Scandinavian settlement as documented from other sources (for a general survey, see 'Silver and gold' in Graham-Campbell and Batey 1998: 226–47). Chronologically, these appear to begin with the small hack-silver hoard, from the Isle of Skye (Storr Rock), deposited c. 935–40 [30], and then peaking in terms of size (>8kg) and diversity of content with the Skaill Hoard, Orkney, deposited c. 960–80 [24]. On the other hand, later hoards, such as that from the churchyard at Tarbat (Portmahomack), which was deposited c. 990–1000 [29], are generally less complex, being characterised by the plain penannular silver arm-rings known as 'ring-money' – now the subject of an unpublished PhD by Aaron Critch (2015).

However, as already noted, there were two 9th-century hoards on record from south-west Scotland by 1995, when discounted as 9th-century Anglo-Saxon (Northumbrian) treasures, both of which are in need of re-evaluation in light of the Galloway Hoard, from Balmaghie: (i) Lochar Moss, Dumfriesshire, said to have consisted of 'silver coins of the Saxon heptarchy, and a silver crucifix' [6a]; and (ii) Talnotrie, Kirkcudbrightshire, with its unusual mixed contents [30a].

The presence of the (lost) 'silver crucifix' in the Lochar Moss Hoard is clearly relevant to the fine pendant cross of late 9th-century Northumbrian workmanship in the Galloway Hoard, whereas the Talnotrie Hoard, deposited c. 875, is of wider significance in demonstrating that there already existed a degree of Anglo-Saxon/Viking interaction in south-west Scotland at this earlier date, given its combination of Anglo-Saxon ornamental metalwork with an Insular Viking weight, together with Arabic and Frankish coins, alongside the Northumbrian stycas and pennies of Burgred. In 1995 I suggested (p. 4), as again more recently (Graham-Campbell 2001: 20–6), that Talnotrie's somewhat unusual contents might be indicative of a Northumbrian metalworker's hoard rather than a Viking treasure, but I now tend to the latter interpretation (as Graham-Campbell 2020: 454; see also Horne, this section) in the light of Blackburn's comment that its coin 'assemblage is likely to have come as a group from the York region', being 'typical of that found at [the Viking winter-camp of] Torksey' (Blackburn 2005: 145), as also of recent work by Williams in establishing that Northumbrian copper-alloy stycas played an active role in the Viking economy (Williams 2020: 104–6, 129–31).

Single finds: Corrigenda

The following corrections concerning the single finds catalogued in 1995 consist of the removal of two entries [S5] and [S13], and the reinterpretation of a third [S4]:

[S4] Clibberswick, Unst, Shetland (1863)

Although this (lost) plain silver arm-ring has recently been republished by Graham-Campbell (2016: 33) as 'a simple example of John Sheehan's Hiberno-Scandinavian broad-band type' (after Graham-Campbell 1995: 154–5, pl. 71, b), its small size and marked taper to what could have been a rod-shaped end (width c. 3mm) suggest that it may well have had a twisted-rod terminal and thus originally have been annular in form (Graham-Campbell 2011: 92–4), similar to a plain annular ring of comparable form and size (ibid.: 206, no. 1:573, pl. 28) and a complete 'narrow-band annular arm-ring' with two rows of stamped decoration (ibid.: 197, no. 1:426, fig. 5.8, pl. 19), both from the Cuerdale Hoard (deposited c. 905–10).

[S5] Oxtro Broch, Birsay, Mainland, Orkney (c. 1866)

To be deleted: Anna Ritchie has convincingly argued that this (lost) silver rod fragment 'must have been deposited before the broch was demolished and the cist cemetery created. Its date is thus more likely to lie in Pictish or even Roman times' (Scott and Ritchie 2014: 196, note 4).

[S13] 'Isle of Skye (pre-1916)'

To be deleted: as demonstrated above, this gold finger-ring is now known to form part of the Isle of Jura (1869) Hoard [25a].

Single finds: Addenda

The following additions comprise five items found before 1995; for single finds reported between 1995 and 2007, see Graham-Campbell (2008).

[S1a] Pierowall, Westray, Orkney (pre-1778)

A (lost) 'gold ring', supposedly 'encircling a thigh bone', from a pagan Norse burial uncovered 'on the Links of Trenaby' (Low 1778; Graham-Campbell 2008: 194).

[S2a] Cliffdale, Shapinsay, Orkney (pre-1796)

A (lost) gold finger-ring of Viking-Age type was well described by the Rev. George Barry in the *Statistical Account of Scotland* 17 (1796), 237, as found 'a short time ago' in 'a subterraneous building' near Cliffdale on Shapinsay (RCAHMS, *Orkney and Shetland*, II, 280, no. 802; Graham-Campbell 2008: 195, 202, note 4):

> The outside of that ring was broad and large, composed, as it were, of three cords twisted or plaited together; the inside was much narrower, and pretty well fitted for the use of the finger. No inscription whatever appeared on any part of it; and at the joining, instead of being soldered, it seemed to have been beaten together with a hammer.

[S17a] Kildonan Machair, South Uist (c. 1964)

This cut fragment of silver 'ring-money' (NMS: X.GS 213) is a surface find (Graham-Campbell 2008: 196, illus. 3).

[S23a] Brough of Birsay, Mainland, Orkney (1976–81)

Cut terminal fragment of silver 'ring-money' (RF 2129, BB77FI), 'initially identified as lead' (Colleen Batey in Morris 2021: 318–19, 475, 477, illus. 15.37); 'from an unallocated episode/phase' on Site IV North – in addition to the small fragment of gold [S23], from Phase Z1 (ibid.: 315, 475, 477, illus. 15.34).

[U1a] Bannockburn, Stirling (pre-1846)

A (lost) gold finger-ring, of twisted or plaited rods, 'dug up . . . on the field of Bannockburn' in the mid-19th century (*Archaeological Journal* 3 (1846), 269), has been 'attributed an 11th/12th-century date' (Graham-Campbell 2008: 195).

References

Archaeological Journal (1846) Archaeological intelligence. *The Archaeological Journal*, vol. 3 (1846), 67–361.

Barry, Rev. Mr G. (1796) Shapinsay, Parish of Orkney. *Statistical Account of Scotland*, Vol. XVII. Edinburgh: William Creech.

Blackburn, M. (1996) *The Numismatic Circular* April 1996, 104(4), 87–8.

Blackburn, M. (2005) Coinage and contacts in the North Atlantic during the seventh to mid-tenth centuries. In A. Mortensen and S. V. Arge (eds), *Viking and Norse in the North Atlantic: Select Papers from the Proceedings of the*

Fourteenth Viking Congress, Tórshavn, 19–30 July 2001. Tórshavn: The Faroese Academy of Sciences, 141–51.

Blackwell, A., M. Goldberg and F. Hunter (2017) *Scotland's Early Silver: Transforming Roman Pay-Offs to Pictish Treasures.* Edinburgh: NMS.

Clarke, D., A. Blackwell and M. Goldberg (2012) *Early Medieval Scotland: Individuals, Communities and Ideas.* Edinburgh: NMS.

Critch, A. J. (2015) *'How are princely gifts repaid by your powerful friends?': 'Ring-money' and the appropriation of tradition in Insular Viking politics, AD 900–1065.* Unpublished PhD thesis, University of Cambridge.

Dalglish, K., with J. Graham-Campbell (2017) Ossianic gold: An enhanced object biography of a Viking Age or Late Norse finger-ring from the Isle of Jura in the collection of Glasgow Museums. *Proceedings of the Society of Antiquaries of Scotland* 147, 285–301.

Goldberg, M. and M. Davis (2021) *The Galloway Hoard: Viking-Age Treasure.* Edinburgh: NMS.

Graham-Campbell, J. (1995) *The Viking-Age Gold and Silver of Scotland (AD 850–1100).* Edinburgh: NMS.

Graham-Campbell, J. (2001) *Whithorn and the Viking World: The Eighth Whithorn Lecture.* Whithorn: Friends of the Whithorn Trust.

Graham-Campbell, J. (2004) 'Danes . . . in this Country': Discovering the Vikings in Scotland. *Proceedings of the Society of Antiquaries of Scotland* 134, 201–39.

Graham-Campbell, J. (2008) Viking Age and Late Norse gold and silver from Scotland: An update. *Proceedings of the Society of Antiquaries of Scotland* 138, 193–204.

Graham-Campbell, J. (2010) The Viking-age silver hoard(s) from Dunrossness, Shetland. *Northern Studies* 41, 13–21.

Graham-Campbell, J. (2011) *The Cuerdale Hoard and Related Viking-Age Silver and Gold from Britain and Ireland in the British Museum.* London: British Museum Research Publications 185.

Graham-Campbell, J. (2016) Pagan Norse burial in Viking Age Shetland. In V. E. Turner, O. A. Owen and D. J. Waugh (eds), *Shetland and the Viking World: Papers from the Seventeenth Viking Congress, Lerwick.* Lerwick: Shetland Heritage Publications, 31–7.

Graham-Campbell, J. (2017) The Galloway (2014) hoard: Some preliminary observations. In C. Biggam, C. Hough and D. Izdebska (eds), *The Daily Lives of Anglo-Saxons.* MRTS 519; Essays in Anglo-Saxon Studies 8. Tempe: Arizona Center for Medieval and Renaissance Studies, 99–117.

Graham-Campbell, J. (2019) The 1858 Skaill Viking-Age silver hoard. In D. Griffiths, J. Harrison and M. Athanson, *Beside the Ocean: Coastal Landscapes at the Bay of Skaill, Marwick, and Birsay Bay, Orkney: Archaeological Research 2003–2018.* Oxford: Oxbow Books, 293–9.

Graham-Campbell, J. (2020) The Galloway Hoard: Viking/Anglo-Saxon interaction in south-west Scotland. In A. Pedersen and S. Sindbæk (eds), *Viking Encounters: Proceedings of the 18th Viking Congress.* Århus: Århus University Press, 445–58.

Graham-Campbell, J. and C. E. Batey (1998) *Vikings in Scotland: An Archaeological Survey.* Edinburgh: Edinburgh University Press.

Graham-Campbell, J. and J. Sheehan (1995) A hoard of Hiberno-Viking arm-rings, probably from Scotland. *Proceedings of the Society of Antiquaries of Scotland* 125, 771–8.

Griffiths, D. (2019) Past archaeological research. In D. Griffiths, J. Harrison and M. Athanson, *Beside the Ocean: Coastal Landscapes at the Bay of Skaill, Marwick, and Birsay Bay, Orkney: Archaeological Research 2003–2018.* Oxford: Oxbow Books, 15–30.

Griffiths, D., J. Harrison and M. Athanson (2019) *Beside the Ocean: Coastal Landscapes at the Bay of Skaill, Marwick, and Birsay Bay, Orkney: Archaeological Research 2003–2018.* Oxford: Oxbow Books.

Horne, T. J. (2021) Silver threads – How Scandinavian Scotland connected with a wider economic world. In D. H. Steinforth and C. C. Rozier (eds), *Britain and its Neighbours: Cultural Contacts and Exchanges in Medieval and Early Modern Europe.* London and New York: Routledge, 69–86.

Low, G. [1778] (1915) *Tour through the North Isles and part of the Mainland of Orkney in the Year 1778.* G Goudie (ed.). London: Viking Society for Northern Research.

MacDonald, K. (1849) Antiquities and works of art exhibited, Proceedings of the meeting of the Archaeological Institute, January 5, 1849. *The Archaeological Journal* 6, 72–3.

Maxwell, H. (1913) Notes on a hoard of personal ornaments, implements, and Anglo-Saxon and Northumbrian coins from Talnotrie, Kirkcudbrightshire. *Proceedings of the Society of Antiquaries of Scotland* 47 (1912–13), 12–16.

Morris, C. D. (2021) *The Birsay Bay Project, Volume 3. The Brough of Birsay, Orkney, Investigations 1954–2014.* Oxford: Oxbow Books.

Pagan, H. (2014) The 1699 Port Glasgow Hoard. In R. Naismith, M. Allen and E. Screen (eds), *Early Medieval Monetary History: Studies in Memory of Mark Blackburn.* Farnham: Ashgate, 413–26.

RCAHMS (1946) *Twelfth Report with an Inventory of the Ancient Monuments.* Edinburgh: RCAHMS.

RCAHMS (1946) *The Royal Commission on the Ancient and Historical Monuments of Scotland: Twelfth report with an Inventory of the Ancient Monuments of Orkney and Shetland. Volume II: Inventory of Orkney.* Edinburgh: RCAHMS.

Scott, I. G. and A. Ritchie (2014) Pictish symbol stones and early cross-slabs from Orkney. *Proceedings of the Society of Antiquaries of Scotland* 144, 169–204.

Waddell, P. H. (1875) *Ossian and the Clyde, Fingal in Ireland, Oscar in Iceland or Ossian Historical and Authentic.* Glasgow: James Maclehose.

Walker, J. (1803) An essay on peat, containing an account of its origin, of its chymical principles and general properties. *Prize Essays and Transactions of the Highland Society of Scotland* 2, 1–137.

Wallace, J. (1693) *A Description of the Isles of Orkney.* Edinburgh: John Reed.

Webster, L. and J. Backhouse (eds) (1991) *The Making of England: Anglo-Saxon Art and Culture* AD *600–900.* London: British Museum Press.

Williams, G. (2020) Viking hoards from Yorkshire, c. 866–954: A survey, and Metals and exchange in Viking-Age Yorkshire: An overview. In G. Williams (ed.), *A Riverine Site Near York: A Possible Viking Camp?* British Museum Research Publication 224. London: British Museum, 103–12, 128–38.

Chapter 21

The Galloway Hoard
Martin Goldberg

The Galloway Hoard was discovered by a metal-detectorist in 2014 on what is now Church of Scotland land at Balmaghie in Kirkcudbrightshire (Nicholson 2014). It was declared Treasure Trove and allocated to National Museums Scotland in 2017. Archaeological features, interpreted as evidence for a building around where the hoard was buried, were recorded in a short phase of work immediately after discovery. The first mention of a church in the vicinity is in Bagimond's Roll in 1275 *Kirkanders Balimeth* with Kirkandrews – the church of St Andrew – perhaps reflecting links to the Northumbrian church and Hexham as an important centre for the Cult of Saint Andrew. The formation of the name uses Old Norse *kirk* but the order and how it is used to form church-names is Gaelic – what Gilbert Márkus refers to as a multi-cultural hagio-toponym (Márkus 2019) – with a range of influences we see reflected in the material of the hoard. There is currently no evidence for an earlier church and further investigation of the immediate site context for the hoard is also required. What follows can only be an interim statement as at the time of writing both conservation and research of the hoard are ongoing and have been substantially disrupted in 2020–21.

Buried around the end of the 9th century, the Galloway Hoard contains a variety of materials and objects from diverse cultural backgrounds, some originating from as far away as Asia. The hoard was buried in two layers with four separate parcels, a structure which gives a rare insight into how the collection was brought together.

The upper layer

Silver bullion made up of three intact Hiberno-Scandinavian broad-band arm-rings (Sheehan 2011) and eight hacked arm-rings and eleven ingots formed the upper layer of the Galloway Hoard as recovered on the day of discovery (Nicholson 2014). The intact ornaments have never been shaped to be worn and seem to have been buried as bullion. Silver bullion was also recovered from the surrounding area before the hoard was discovered (TT 36/14) and during topsoil stripping in the days after. Some pieces may have been displaced from the hoard, but others seem more likely to be from activity on the site. A slim rod ingot and a small hacked fragment of a similar shaped ingot came from topsoil stripping. This type of rod ingot is not found in the hoard, and there are no hacked ingots of any type. The recovery of silver droplets also suggests processing of precious metals in the vicinity (Goldberg and Davis 2021: 38–9).

There was also a silver pectoral cross with a fine spiral chain wrapped around it (Figure 21.1). To form the chain, sub-millimetre silver wire was wrapped around an organic material identified as gut (Goldberg and Davis 2021: 34). Chains this fine rarely survive, and its presence suggests the cross could have been worn shortly before burial. The cross is decorated in a distinctive Trewhiddle (late Anglo-Saxon) style (Webster 2012: 146–52) with the symbols of the Four Evangelists in each arm, and the carved designs inlaid with niello for contrast against the bright silver. Important features are picked out with gold leaf. A central circular feature has no decoration, suggesting that a raised boss or perhaps gemstone (and, given the Evangelists symbols on the arms, likely to be symbolic of Christ) has been removed. Was the central feature carefully removed as a token of the whole or was the cross also bullion, destined

Figure 21.1 Trewhiddle-style pectoral cross with a fine silver chain wrapped around it. © National Museums Scotland.

to be melted down into the types of ingots with which it was found? If proximity to a contemporary church site at Balmaghie could be proved, then this would be an important factor in the burial of the hoard, as has been shown in Ireland (Sheehan 2019). The cross is the first indication that there is something unusual about the Galloway Hoard.

The lower layer

The Galloway Hoard was much bigger and more complex than the initial discovery indicated. Beneath the top layer, hidden under a layer of natural-looking gravel, was a much richer deposit of three parts: a lidded silver-gilt vessel wrapped in textiles; a cluster of four silver ribbon arm-rings bound together and surrounding a small wooden box containing three gold items; and more than double the amount of silver bullion when compared to the upper layer (forty-six pieces, including fifteen ingots and thirty-one arm-rings or fragments of arm-rings – Figure 21.2), bound together with leather. In comparison to the upper layer, there are more complete arm-rings in the lower layer, but similarly the majority have never been formed into arm-rings to be worn.

Figure 21.2 The lower deposit of silver bullion comprised of incomplete Hiberno-Scandinavian arm-rings, hack-silver and ingots. © National Museums Scotland.

Within the silver bullion of the lower layer there are clues to four owners. There are four Hiberno-Scandinavian broad-band arm-rings inscribed with Anglo-Saxon runes forming Old English words that were frequently used as personal name-elements (Elisabeth Okasha, pers. comm.). It is unusual for these inscriptions to use Anglo-Saxon rather than Scandinavian runes. But the Anglo-Saxon runic inscriptions are also part of a small regional group of inscriptions in south-west Scotland (Parsons forthcoming), which during the 9th century was part of western Northumbria and referred to as the Saxon shore in Irish sources (Woolf 2007: 253). A complete Old English name (EGGBRECT – Egbert) was also inscribed onto a small hacked arm-ring recovered from the plough-soil of the surrounding area (Parsons forthcoming). If this is not a dispersed part of the upper layer of the hoard, then shared letter forms and a guideline feature still link the inscription on this hacked arm-ring to the inscriptions on complete arm-rings in the lower layer of the hoard.

Each of the runic-inscribed arm-rings in the lower bullion deposit are complete but unworn, and have been either left flat, or flat and then folded in a distinctive way. There are corresponding groups of arm-rings which match each of the four folding patterns (one end pinched tight, two ends pinched tight, flat, and one half bent – Goldberg and Davis 2021: 42–5). Of the twenty-four complete arm-rings in the lower bullion, twenty-two fall into these four groups. It seems likely that each group of arm-rings belonged to a different person who was identified with runes on one example of each folding pattern. This treatment of folding the arm-rings is relatively unusual in Viking-Age hoards. The Huxley Hoard from Cheshire is one of the few other examples (Sheehan 2009: 68), also composed of an ingot and Hiberno-Scandinavian broad-band arm-rings all folded roughly in half. This was interpreted as probably for ease of packing, transport and/or concealment (Sheehan 2009: 69), but the Galloway Hoard presents many different examples of folding and in combination with the runes suggests a means of identifying portions of bullion. The four groups are uneven in weight and number, suggesting the owners were unlikely to have been equals because the share of bullion was not an even split. The largest runic-inscribed arm-ring is more than twice as heavy as the other inscribed examples and it features the longest (still undeciphered) inscription (Goldberg and Davis 2021: 51).

A second group of arm-rings in the lower layer are different from the rest of the bullion because they are complete and shaped as they would have been worn. These silver ribbon arm-rings are much more elaborately decorated than the broad-band arm-rings (Type Aii in Graham-Campbell 2011: 91–3). Again there are four, bound together tightly by a smaller band arm-ring into a single cluster that cannot now be separated. The closest parallel for this treatment is the Silverdale (Lancashire)

Hoard, where three ribbon arm-rings are concentrically nested (Graham-Campbell 2020: 454). The four ribbon arm-rings in the Galloway Hoard have had different lives. One is very well worn, another is warped but with little wear. The third is barely worn with fine detail in the punched decoration. The fourth and largest is a double arm-ring, twice the size of the others, with the tongues of four pointed-eared beasts combining to form the connecting terminal knot, like the lost Hare Island example (Graham-Campbell 1995: fig. 18). Again, these four ribbon arm-rings suggest four owners, unequal in status, but the unusual cluster bound together seems almost like a contract (Goldberg and Davis 2021: 53–5). This cluster of arm-rings surrounded a small wooden box containing three gold objects – an oval-shaped, round-section ring, a small ingot and a pin with a bird-shaped head. Gold is much rarer than silver in Viking-Age hoards (Blackburn 2007; Kershaw 2019).

Silver bullion summary

Hiberno-Scandinavian broad-band arm-rings are the most common objects in the hoard found in both the lower and the upper layer. Based on coins in other hoards containing Hiberno-Scandinavian broad-band arm-rings, they were circulating 880–930 (Sheehan 2011: 94). This suggests that the Galloway Hoard is Scotland's earliest Viking-Age hoard (Graham-Campbell 2020). Many of the arm-rings in the hoard have never been shaped to be worn, even if they are decorated. Most are flat and folded, intended as bullion and valued for their weight, like the ingots they were found with. One of the differences between the upper and lower bullion is that there are more hacked arm-rings in the top layer, and more intact/unused arm-rings below. The lower deposit also contains one annular rod arm-ring (Goldberg and Davis 2021: 48), a Scandinavian type found at Torksey, Lincolnshire, the site associated with the overwintering of the Great Army in 872 (Graham-Campbell 2004), and is very like one in the Cuerdale Hoard (1:883–4 Sheehan 2011: 103 and illustrated on pl. 40). A gold rod arm-ring in the Hoen Hoard (Norway) has been dated to the mid-9th century (Graham-Campbell in Fuglesang and Wilson 2006: 79).

There are also two different types of ingots in the hoard: larger bar-shaped ingots in the top layer and finger-shaped ingots in the lower (Goldberg and Davis 2021: 27, 48). The bullion shows evidence of standardised weights: multiples of the 26.6g unit (equivalent to an ounce of silver), familiar from the many lead weights from the Viking-Age settlement of Dublin (Wallace 2015). There is also some evidence for other weight standards, including the Scandinavian unit of c. 24g (Goldberg and Davis 2021: 28). The Galloway Hoard bullion was part of a common silver economy around the Irish Sea and in northern England, connected to Scandinavia, the Baltic and beyond (Graham-Campbell and

Williams 2007), but the Anglo-Saxon runes complicate interpretations of ownership. The mixed contents of this Viking-Age hoard speak of the complexities of life at the time – nowhere more so than in the fourth parcel: the lidded vessel and its contents.

The wrapped, silver-gilt lidded vessel

This is only the third silver-gilt decorated vessel to be found as part of a Viking-Age hoard in Britain. There are some key differences that make the Galloway Hoard vessel distinct in its use, treatment and form. This vessel was carefully wrapped with evidence for at least two layers of textile (Susanna Harris, pers. comm.). Recording and preserving these rare survivals is ongoing, including exploring how they were made and whether they were coloured or embellished. They may provide important clues about the burial of the hoard. For instance, were they garments or whatever was close at hand, hastily grabbed to stash this precious vessel? Or were they specially made covers for a lidded vessel that was only ever meant to be revealed/opened to particular people at special moments? A radiocarbon date of 670–780 cal AD (SUERC-64280) from the wool wrapping the vessel pre-dates the traditional beginning of the Viking Age and is at least a century older (possibly two centuries) than when the vessel was buried with the bullion.

Three-dimensional X-ray imaging has allowed a glimpse of the decorated surface of the vessel beneath the textiles (Figure 21.3). This is not a Carolingian, or even a Christian, vessel like the otherwise close comparanda from Halton Moor (Wamers 2011) and the Vale of York hoards (Williams and Ager 2010; Ager 2020). A central icon has been identified as a Zoroastrian fire altar with a crown emerging from the flames. Beneath this is another crown motif with feathers/stylised wings atop. Leopards and tigers inhabit vegetal scrolls either side. These are all elements recognisable from Sasanian imperial iconography (Harper and Meyers 1981). Zoroastrianism was the state religion of the Sasanian Empire centred on modern-day Iran from the mid-3rd to the mid-7th centuries AD (Stewart et al. 2013). Sasanian metalwork was also hugely influential on wider Central Asian metalwork even after the Islamic conquests of the 7th century (Marshak 2017), and it seems likely that this vessel was derivative, either made beyond the imperial boundaries or made later and taking inspiration from earlier models. Barry Ager has already suggested that the form of the Carolingian cups, like the one in the Vale of York Hoard, may lie in Central Asian prototypes (2020: 8 note 33), but finding one so far west is unprecedented. Could this vessel have, in turn, inspired the production of others? The mechanisms for how this vessel arrived in western Northumbria will be a target of future research. Although the silks in the vessel (Walton Rogers 2015) and

Figure 21.3 Three-dimensional digital model of the vessel showing the surface decoration beneath the textile wrapping. © National Museums Scotland.

some of the silver bullion may ultimately have an Asian origin, the identification of the vessel and the preliminary date from textile wrappings suggests that time and distance are factors that need to be considered in the assembling of the Galloway Hoard. Other differences with the Halton Moor and Vale of York vessels then become more meaningful. The Galloway Hoard vessel is the only one used as a treasure container which has a surviving lid. This lid sealing the vessel helped to create unusual conditions within for leather and textile preservation. But the final difference is that other Viking-Age hoard vessels contained silver bullion. In the Galloway Hoard, the silver bullion was buried in separate parcels outside the vessel and the contents of the vessel are unlike any other Viking-Age hoard in Britain and Ireland.

A collection of five glass beads, a bead and coin mounted in a silver pendant, a rock crystal sphere in a damaged pendant fitting (Figure 21.4) and a spherical mineral called a rattlestone (perhaps a charmstone – Meaney 1981; Höfig 2019) were bundled and strung together at the top of the vessel (Goldberg and Davis 2021: 77–83). They were resting as a group on a silver bossed penannular brooch-hoop almost identical to a brooch-hoop in the Goldsborough (Yorkshire) Hoard of c. 925 (Graham-Campbell 2011: 234) with a beast head at either end of the hoop and openwork birds on the outside of the disc terminals. This is the only piece of Viking-Age silver in the vessel. It separated the bundle of beads, pendants and curios at the top from the Anglo-Saxon metalwork and textile-wrapped bundles below.

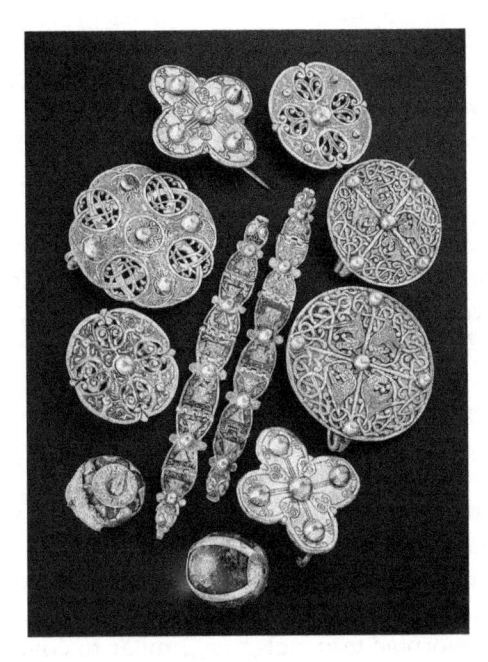

Figure 21.4 Anglo-Saxon metalwork from within the vessel: five disc brooches; two quatrefoil 'face' brooches (top and bottom); two multi-hinged straps (centre); a rock crystal pendant (bottom); and a composite bead/coin pendant (bottom left). © National Museums Scotland.

Everything at the top of the vessel was wrapped, but the evidence has only partly survived. As metals in the hoard have corroded, the copper leaching out helped create the environment for preserving organic materials. Glass does not corrode in the same way and so the beads have not preserved their textile wrappings. But everywhere there was contact with metal at the top of the vessel, there are microscopic survivals of the textile wrappings that bundled this group of beads, pendants and curios together. Where the wrapped objects touched the brooch-hoop the silver corroded, but in the process it preserved minute fragments of textile wrapping (Goldberg and Davis 2021: 84–5). The best evidence for wrapping at the top of the vessel survives on the unusual 'relic' pendant made from a polychrome bead enclosed in silver and capped with a perforated coin. The coin was minted for Coenwulf, the king of Anglo-Saxon Mercia (d. 821) (Rory Naismith, pers. comm.). It is likely the coin was minted several generations before the hoard was buried. This is the clearest clue that this unusual collection were heirlooms. Two of the ribbed/melon beads are old and well worn, and the pendant fitting and a strap were missing from the rock crystal sphere. It seems that these objects were valued for their age and/or past ownership (Goldberg and Davis 2021: 77).

The contents of the vessel include the first collection of Late Anglo-Saxon brooches from Scotland – seven in total (Goldberg and Davis 2021: 88–9; Figure 21.4). Among three close pairs of brooches, none is exactly the same. One disc-brooch is a scale version of the other, made to the same openwork silver design over a gilded copper-alloy disc. The small silver openwork pair has a finer example and one with less skilled carving. Disc-brooches are not common in Scotland. They are more normally found in the Anglo-Saxon kingdoms of southern and eastern Britain, for example the Pentney Hoard from Norfolk (Webster and Backhouse 1991: 229–31, no. 187). Two unusual cross-shaped, quatrefoil brooches are related to the more common disc-brooches in how they were made and worn, but this new design is unique to the Galloway Hoard. Using similar sensory themes to the Fuller brooch (Webster and Backhouse 1991: 281, no. 287), the iconography depicts two of the five senses – sight and hearing. On one, all the emphasis is on the eyes and on the other the ears are exaggerated – their ears are ringing because blast horns are being blown.

A pair of multi-hinged straps placed with the brooches within the vessel are also unique for Anglo-Saxon metalwork. They have five plates, with the two zoomorphic terminals very similar to contemporary strap-ends. The closest comparison is a double-hinged plate from Plumpton, Sussex (Thomas 2013), but the plates on the Galloway Hoard straps are much more elaborate, connected by four hinges that make them flexible. Detached hooks that were soldered on either end suggest these flexible straps were attached to leather or fabric, perhaps as elaborate dress accessories (Goldberg and Davis 2021: 94–7). First signalled by the cross in the top 'decoy' layer, this collection of Anglo-Saxon metalwork is exceptional not just in a Scottish context, but also compared to hoards from England (with the closest comparison perhaps the Trewhiddle Hoard, itself from a western peninsula at the southern end of the Irish Sea – Webster and Backhouse 1991: 246). Like the Anglo-Saxon runes on the silver arm-rings, this range of objects complicates the stereotype of a 'Viking' hoard. During the 9th century, Galloway occupied an ambiguous position, being at the westernmost extent of fluctuating Anglo-Saxon Northumbrian political influence, but also connected to this Irish Sea zone. As noted above, Galloway was referred to as 'the Saxon coast' in Ireland (Woolf 2007: 253). The material in the Galloway Hoard encapsulates these changing political influences. The hoard is found in Northumbria, the most intact dress accessories are Anglo-Saxon and the bullion normally interpreted as 'Viking' objects have Anglo-Saxon runes on them, but whether it is a 'Viking' or a 9th-century Northumbrian hoard is perhaps not the most crucial interpretation. The different values and histories represented by the heirloom qualities of the objects within the vessel (a family treasury?) versus the more recent wealth of bullion suggest a variety of motivations in assembling this collection.

Lower down within the carefully packed and sealed vessel, the conditions for textile preservation were exceptional. Two bundles containing leather, linen and silk (as both cord and fabric) have been preserved, wrapped around golden jewels. Between the two complex bundles was a hammered rectangular gold ingot and a twisted rod of gold. The Galloway Hoard includes the (numerically) largest collection of gold objects surviving from Viking-Age Britain and Ireland. All of the gold objects are unusual and distinct from one another, perhaps coming from distant places and different manufacturing traditions. Even the two gold ingots (one inside the vessel and one outside with the bird-pin) are different in form, chemical composition and colour (Goldberg and Davis 2021: 104).

In contrast with gold and silk, two balls of dirt seem mundane at first glance, but must have been of great significance to their owners. Analysis has shown that the dirt contains microscopic traces of gold and bone (Goldberg and Davis 2021: 114–16). The Vatican collections contain earth relics gathered during the mid-7th to 10th centuries from places in the Holy Land relating to the life of Christ (Luchterhandt 2017: 39–40). This comparison provides a thesis still to be tested through soil or chemical analysis.

Three gold filigree-decorated jewels were wrapped in a bundle with silk-woven cord (Walton Rogers 2015; Goldberg and Davis 2021: 105–7). Previously, these gold socketed mounts were single finds and thought to be bejewelled manuscript pointers, known as 'aestels' (Webster and Backhouse 1991: 282). This is the first time a group has been found together, and the relationship with the bundle of silken cord suggests these are not aestels at all – the tubular sockets of all three had cord remaining in them. The working premise is that this could have been a single composite object of woven silk with gold fittings, perhaps a girdle, priestly *cingulum* or belt-set (Leslie Webster, pers. comm.). A larger gold-filigree decorated pendant was connected to this bundle, strung on the same silken cord. A carefully shaped quadrangular black stone of schist is contained within the gold pendant and a pyramidal cap with gold clasps allowed the stone to be removed (Goldberg and Davis 2021: 108–13). Scanning Electron Microscope analysis has recorded streaks of precious metals, especially gold, on the surface of the black stone, which suggest it is a touchstone used for assaying (Ježek 2017).

A gold-mounted jar of rock crystal in a silk-lined leather pouch (Walton Rogers 2015) may be one of the oldest 'heirloom' objects (Goldberg and Davis 2021: 118–21). The technology needed to carve rock crystal was relatively rare in the ancient world. During the later 10th century, the centres of production were in the Islamic Caliphate, in modern-day Iraq and Egypt (Shalem 1998). However, although the silk wrapping the crystal jar would have travelled from Asia to reach these shores (Vedeler 2014), the Galloway Hoard was buried 50–100 years before the boom in rock crystal production attributed to the Fatimid dynasty (Contadini 1999; although earlier Abbasid carving of rock crystal is increasingly being recognised – Pilz 2020). The complex three-dimensional forms of rock crystal produced in Imperial Rome suit the high-relief carving of the surface of the Galloway Hoard jar better than Islamic jars. It resembles the acanthus lobes of a Corinthian column capital, but upside down. The square base and round top of the jar also suggest the inversion of a column capital where a round base would have connected to the column below and the expanding square top to the architecture above. Inverting the crystal column capital made it more stable to function as a container. There are rock crystal columns of a similar scale and a variety of forms in the Vatican Collection, one from the Early Christian cemetery of Domitilla in Rome (Fremersdorf 1975: 114). They all have a drilled cavity in the centre. This feature is what has allowed the Galloway Hoard rock crystal to be repurposed and function as a vial, jar or liquid container with a golden spout on the top aligning with the drilled cavity in the centre. The Galloway Hoard rock crystal was possibly more than five hundred years old when it was converted into a container using gold filigree decorated mounts on the square base and the round top, connected by a gold mesh that wraps around the well-worn acanthus scrolls of the carved crystal surface. CT scanning has shown that there is a Latin inscription on the base executed in gold filigree – it reads +HYGUALD EP~FAC~IUSS and has been translated as 'Bishop Hyguald ordered [this] to be made' (Elisabeth Okasha, pers. comm.). Hyguald is a Northumbrian name listed in the Durham Liber Vitae (British Library, MS Cotton Domitian A.VII - Rollason and Rollason 2007) although not in the section for bishops. There is a paucity of historical records for ninth century Northumbria (McGuigan 2015: 58–63) and the Bishop Hyguald named on the rock crystal jar may be an otherwise unattested Northumbrian bishop. The 12th-century historian William of Malmesbury describes an architectural fragment of crystal (*Fastigium cristallinum* in Latin) placed on the shrine of St Aldhelm in Malmesbury by King Aethelwulf of Wessex (Alfred's father, ruled 839–55), on which could be read the saint's name in golden letters (Hinton 2013: 158). Like the Alfred Jewel (another reused Roman rock crystal – Kornbluth 1989), these types of objects were commissioned by the highest levels of society and could be gifted to the most sacred places.

The many organic materials from the Galloway Hoard, including leather, wood, gut, silk, linen and wool, can also inform us about the objects they wrap and connect. Radiocarbon dating of associated organics will tell us more about how this collection came together over time. This unique mix of organic and inorganic materials provides exciting opportunities for multi-disciplinary research and analysis. The 2021 exhibition and book *Galloway Hoard: Viking-age Treasure* (Goldberg and Davis

2021) presents what we know so far, and in more detail than this brief summary, but is nowhere near the final word on this remarkable hoard.

References

Ager, B. (2020) The Carolingian cup from the Vale of York Viking Hoard: Origins of its form and decorative features. *The Antiquaries Journal* 100, 86–108.

Blackburn, M. (2007) Gold in England during the 'Age of Silver' (eighth–eleventh centuries). In J. Graham-Campbell and G. Williams (eds), *Silver Economy in the Viking Age*. Walnut Creek: Left Coast Press, 55–98.

Contadini, A. (1999) The cutting edge: Problems of history, identification and technique of Fatimid rock crystals. In M. Barrucand (ed.), *L'Egypte fatimide, son art et son histoire*. Paris: Presse de l'Université de Paris Sorbonne, 319–29.

Fremersdorf, M. (1975) *Antikes, islamisches und mittelalterliches Glas sowie kleinere Arbeiten aus Stein, Gagat und verwandten Stoffen in den Vatikanischen Sammlungen Roms, Catalogo del Museo Sacro della Biblioteca Apostolica Vaticana*, vol. 5. Vatican City: Catalogo del Museo Sacro.

Fuglesang, S. H. and D. M. Wilson (eds) (2006) *The Hoen Hoard. A Viking Gold Treasure of the Ninth Century*. [Acta ad archaeologiam et artium historiam pertinentia XIV/Norske Oldfunn XX]. Rome: Bardi.

Goldberg, M. and M. Davis (2021) *Galloway Hoard: Viking-Age Treasure*. Edinburgh: NMS.

Graham-Campbell, J. (1995) *The Viking-Age Gold and Silver of Scotland, AD 850–1100*. Edinburgh: NMS.

Graham-Campbell, J. (2004) The archaeology of the 'Great Army' (865–79). In E. Roesdahl and J. P. Schjødt (eds), *Beretning fra treogtyvende tværfaglige vikingesymposium*. Højbjerg: Aarhus Universitet, 30–46.

Graham-Campbell, J. (2011) *The Cuerdale Hoard and Related Viking-Age Silver and Gold from Britain and Ireland in the British Museum*. British Museum Research Publication 185. London: British Museum.

Graham-Campbell, J. (2020) The Galloway Hoard: Viking/Anglo-Saxon interaction in south-west Scotland. In A. Pedersen and S. Sindbaek (eds), *Viking Encounters: Proceedings of the 18th Viking Congress*. Århus: Århus University Press, 445–58.

Graham-Campbell, J. and G. Williams (eds) (2007) *Silver Economy in the Viking Age*. Walnut Creek: Left Coast Press.

Harper, P. and P. Meyers (1981) *Silver Vessels of the Sasanian Period, vol. I*. New York: The Metropolitan Museum of Art.

Hinton, D. A. (2013) An Anglo-Saxon bone acanthus-leaf mount from Malmesbury Abbey, Wiltshire. In A. Reynolds and L. Webster (eds), *Early Medieval Art and Archaeology in the Northern World: Studies in Honour of James Graham-Campbell*. The Northern World series 58. Leiden: Brill, 153–62.

Höfig, V. (2019) Births, belts, and the Brísingamen. *Viking and Medieval Scandinavia* 15, 127–50.

Ježek, M. (2017) *Archaeology of Touchstones: An Introduction Based on Finds from Birka, Sweden*. Leiden: Sidestone Press.

Kershaw, J. (2019) Gold as a means of exchange in Scandinavian England (c. AD 850–1000). In J. Kershaw and G. Williams (eds), *Silver, Butter, Cloth: Monetary and Social Economies in the Viking Age*. Oxford: Oxford University Press, 227–50.

Kornbluth, G. A. (1989) The Alfred Jewel: Reuse of Roman spolia. *Medieval Archaeology* 33, 32–7.

Luchterhandt, M. (2017) The popes and the *loca sancta* of Jerusalem: Relic practice and relic diplomacy in the Eastern Mediterranean after the Muslim conquest. In R. Bartal, N. Bodner and B. Kuhnel (eds), *Natural Materials of the Holy Land and Visual Translation of Place 500–1500*. London: Routledge, 38–63.

McGuigan, N. (2015) *Neither Scotland nor England: Middle Britain, c.850–1150*. Unpublished PhD thesis, University of St Andrews.

Márkus, G. (2019) 'Unpacking Balmaghie' blog for the Galloway Glens Place-names Project https://kcb-placenames.glasgow.ac.uk/unpacking-balmaghie/ [Last viewed: 21 September 2021].

Marshak, B. (2017) *History of Oriental Toreutics of the 3rd–13th centuries and Problems of Cultural Continuity*/Маршак Б И. История восточной торевтики III–XIII вв. и проблемы культурной преемственности / Под ред. В. П. Никонорова. СПб., 2017. [Edited by V. P. Nikonorov]. St Petersburg: Academy of Cultures Research.

Meaney, A. (1981) *Anglo-Saxon Amulets and Curing Stones*. British Archaeological Reports British Series 96. Oxford: BAR publishing.

Nicholson, A. (2014) Balmaghie excavation, preliminary report. Unpublished Treasure Trove report.

Parsons, D. N. (Forthcoming) *The Riddle of the Runes: The Early Medieval Inscriptions of Dumfries and Galloway*. Whithorn lecture series.

Pilz, M. (2020) Beyond Fatimid: The iconography of medieval Islamic rock crystal vessels and the question of dating. In A. Shalem and C. Hahn, *Seeking Transparency: Rock Crystals across the Medieval Mediterranean*. Berlin: Gebr. Mann Verlag, 169–82.

Rollason, D. and L. Rollason (eds) (2007) *The Durham Liber Vitae*. London, British Library, MS Cotton Domitian A.VII. Edition and Digital Facsimile. London: The British Library.

Shalem, A. (1998) *Islam Christianized: Islamic Portable Objects in Medieval Church Treasuries in the Latin West*. Frankfurt am Main: Peter Lang.

Sheehan, J. (2009) The Huxley Hoard and Hiberno-Scandinavian arm-rings. In J. Graham-Campbell and R. Philpott (eds), *The Huxley Viking Hoard: Scandinavian Settlement in the North West*. Liverpool: National Museums Liverpool, 58–69.

Sheehan, J. (2011) Hiberno-Scandinavian broad-band arm-rings. In J. Graham-Campbell, *The Cuerdale Hoard*. London: British Museum, 94–100.

Sheehan, J. (2019) Reflections on kingship, the church and Viking-age silver in Ireland. In J. Kershaw and G. Williams (eds), *Silver, Butter, Cloth: Monetary and Social Economies in the Viking Age*. Oxford: Oxford University Press, 104–22.

Stewart, S., F. Punthakey Mistree, U. Sims-Williams, A. Hintze and P. Godjrej (eds) (2013) *The Everlasting Flame: Zoroastrianism in History and Imagination*. London: I.B. Tauris.

Thomas, G. (2013) A casket fit for a West Saxon courtier: The Plumpton Hoard and its place in the minor arts of Late Anglo-Saxon England. In A. Reynolds and L. Webster (eds), *Early Medieval Art and Archaeology in the Northern World: Studies in Honour of James Graham-Campbell*. The Northern World series 58. Leiden: Brill, 425–58.

Vedeler, M. (2014) *Silk for the Vikings*. Oxford: Oxbow Books.

Wallace, P. (2015) *Viking Dublin: The Wood Quay Excavations*. Sallins: Irish Academic Press.

Walton Rogers, P. (2015) Unpublished report on Balmaghie textiles commissioned by Historic Environment Scotland.

Wamers, E. (2011) The Halton Moor cup and the Carolingian metalwork in the Cuerdale Hoard. In J. Graham-Campbell, *The Cuerdale Hoard*. London: British Museum, 133–9.

Webster, L. (2012) *Anglo-Saxon Art: A New History*. London: British Museum Press.

Webster, L. and J. Backhouse (eds) (1991) *The Making of England: Anglo-Saxon Art and Culture AD 600–900*. London: British Museum Press.

Williams, G. and B. Ager (2010) [2nd printing 2015] *The Vale of York Hoard*. London: British Museum Press.

Woolf, A. (2007) *From Pictland to Alba: 789–1070*. Edinburgh: Edinburgh University Press.

Chapter 22

Viking and Norse Bullion Economies in Scandinavian Scotland
Tom Horne

For Scandinavian Scotland, the study of bullion economies – where metal is weighed and tested to assess its monetary value – is dynamic, with recent finds changing our perceptions of both its origins and longevity. Regarding the former aspect, the Galloway Hoard (Goldberg, this section) suggests knowledge of bullion in the south-west by at least c. 900. At the other end of the chronological scale, recent and forthcoming publications from Late Norse contexts at Cille Pheadair (Paterson 2018) and Bornais on South Uist (Sharples 2020), and at Orkney's Earl's Bu (Batey, this volume; forthcoming) suggest bullion use was more widespread than thought and, at least in Scotland's Northern and Western Isles, was used for longer than previously considered.

Old finds and theories are being reassessed via these new discoveries. In this chapter, for example, the author evaluates suggestions linking the beginnings of bullion use in south-west Scotland with the Great Army and Hiberno-Scandinavians. New finds also refine the picture of the changing Scotto-Scandinavian relationship to metallic currencies across time and, as *Vikings in Scotland* understood, this refinement tends towards a spectrum of functioning, if not especially wealthy, bullion economies across the region.

Background

Metrological assessment of bullion could be complemented by testing via nicking, 'pecking' or even bending to confirm the metal's purity. The most common bullion was silver, with 'hack-silver' the term for deliberately fragmented pieces, apparently created to provide smaller denominations. The influx of silver into Scotland from the years around 900 was likely due to a mixture of looting, trade and migration.

Bullion is commonly associated with hoards, with hoarding having been assessed at both regional (for example, Hårdh 1996; 2008 for Scandinavia and the Baltic) and more local levels (Gruszczyński 2019 for Gotland; Williams 2020b for Yorkshire). They are generally seen as depositions reflecting conscious collection of the currency available in the region, either deposited ritually with no intention of recovery, or used as temporary safes before returning to commercial or gift-giving circulation. Common components are ingots, coins and decorative metalwork like arm-rings, often reduced to hack-silver in regions with evidence of market trade (commerce) with its requirement for multiple denominations. Bullion was measured by scales and weights, as found together at the Kiloran Bay boat burial on Colonsay in the Inner Hebrides (Anderson 1907; Graham-Campbell and Batey 1998: 118–22).

Weights could take the form of iron-cored copper-alloy 'oblate spheroids', copper-alloy 'cubo-octahedrals' and a lead type usually topped with gilded (often Insular) copper-alloy ornament, which this author calls 'Insular mounts' due to their probable genesis within Scandinavian Britain and Ireland (Horne 2014). Several Insular mounts were found at Kiloran Bay (Kilger 2008b: 285), and there are examples from Talnotrie, Gallaberry and Whithorn in Galloway (Horne 2014). These three bullion weight types, used from the c. 860/70s, can be seen in Figure 22.1.

Early forms of bullion currency developed in the 9th-century Scandinavian Baltic and market-rich Danish regions of southern Scandinavia, probably in response to Carolingian coinage and the massive dirham influx from the Abbasid Caliphate, notably Baghdad, and subsequently the Samanid emirate in Central Asia, most likely as payment for slaves (Kilger 2008a, 2008b; Jankowiak 2020). Dirhams, which underwrote Scando-Baltic bullion economies, first appear in a datable context in Britain in the c. 871/2 Croydon Hoard (which has a clear Great Army association: Brooks and Graham-Campbell 2000) and at the Torksey (Lincolnshire) winter-camp, used by the Great Army in c. 872-3. In Ireland, the apparently slightly earlier Woodstown Viking *longphort* (OIr 'ship camp', pl. *longphuirt*) has also produced a dirham fragment among its hack-silver, alongside an Insular mount (Russell and Hurley 2014). The discovery of Insular mounts at Woodstown, Kilmainham-Islandbridge (Dublin), Kiloran Bay and Talnotrie (see below) in western Scotland, Llanbedrgoch (Anglesey), 'ARSNY' (Yorkshire) and Torksey winter-camps, and in the southern Scandinavian market of Kaupang (Vestfold), indicates a shared, bi-directional, monetary region in which Scotto-Scandinavians operated, however intermittently (Horne 2014; Hadley and Richards 2016: 49; Williams 2020c: 43; Horne 2022).

The author argues that seemingly related groups (arguably largely of southern Scandinavian origin) operating out of Dublin and other *longphuirt* from 853 onwards and within the Great Army (from 865) imported a silver-based bullion market economy to Ireland and Britain, where local adaptations like Insular mounts (Hadley and Richards 2016: 49) or minting occurred. Beyond hoards and single-finds, the evidence

Figure 22.1a Insular mount weight (Darrington, PAS SWYOR-8A1BCA). West Yorkshire Archaeology Advisory Service (CC BY 2.0) and courtesy of the Portable Antiquities Scheme.

Figure 22.1b Oblate spheroid weight (PAS PUBLIC-9A7372) (CC-BY-SA 4.0) courtesy of the Portable Antiquities Scheme.

Figure 22.1c Cubo-octahedral weight (Torksey, PAS SWYOR-21CA16). West Yorkshire Archaeology Advisory Service (CC-BY-SA 4.0) and courtesy of the Portable Antiquities Scheme.

for this is seen in winter-camps and *longphuirt*, where commerce along southern Scandinavian lines flourished (Williams 2020a; Horne 2022). This interpretation suggests Viking leaders like Dublin's Ívarr (see below) involved themselves in both Ireland and the Great Army with the aim of creating a market and trade route orientated 'network-kingdom' (Blomkvist 2009) linking the 'nodal markets' (Sindbæk 2007) they established at Dublin and Jórvík to their apparent southern Scandinavian homelands (Sheehan 2020: 415, 425; Horne 2022).

Great Army connections?

The first datable deposition of dirhams in Scotland was in the c. 875 Talnotrie Hoard (Williams 2020c: 37), deposited perhaps a generation before its Galloway neighbour. Talnotrie contains two fragments of the dirhams that are key markers of Scandinavian bullion economies and an indicator of sites associated with the Great Army and seemingly related groups active earlier in Frisia, Frankia and Ireland. Critical for any argument suggesting a Great Army vector for a southern Scandinavian bullion economy entering Scotland is the presence at Talnotrie of several key elements: fragmented ornaments, dirhams, other silver coins, Northumbrian copper-alloy styca coins and an Insular mount.

If there is a standardised 'package' of Great Army bullion paraphernalia from both sides of the scales (dirhams, ingots and/or Anglo-Saxon coin on one side and specialised weights on the other), then Talnotrie displays more than a passing resemblance, suggesting influence from there (Graham-Campbell, pers. comm.). It seems Talnotrie and related finds in the region point to the Great Army and an associated group in Dublin as sources of monetary influence in southern and western Scotland (Hadley and Richards 2016: 49). Indeed, as Hadley and Richards, Williams (2020c: 37, 44, 46) and Graham-Campbell (2020: 458) all now note, it is necessary to think of both the Great Army and, particularly in light of an Irish Sea Region-type hoard like Galloway with its multiple Hiberno-Scandinavian broad-band arm-rings, also Dubliners being politically and monetarily influential on south-west Scotland, via looting or trade, in the 870s. On this, Downham (2007: 173; cf. Williams 2020c: 37) wrote: 'it is possible that Vikings were responsible [for Talnotrie]. The hoard's date corresponds with the North British [Great Army] campaigns of Hálfdan, brother of Ívarr'. It is conceivable then that Hálfdan and Ívarr's Dubliners may have left a bullion legacy amid the raiding.

The Talnotrie and Galloway hoards and Kiloran Bay assemblage make most sense if we accept a bullion economy imparted via Great Army groups and Hiberno-Scandinavians connected to Ívarr. Therefore, while on current evidence most silver was deposited in Scotland between c. 935 and 1060 (Graham-Campbell and Batey 1998: 245–7), it appears appreciation of its economic potential was planted in south-western parts in the last quarter of the 9th century. In short, then, networks of conflict, migration and trade represented best by the Great Army (and other Scandinavians linked to southern Scandinavia, like those in Dublin and Woodstown) connected Scotland to a wider economic world centred on and originating in dirham-rich southern and Baltic Scandinavia.

870s–900s: Arm-rings and early adopters

The Gordon Hoard (Berwickshire), with gold finger-ring, ingots and hack-silver, includes a fragment of Hiberno-Scandinavian broad-band arm-ring of the type well represented in Galloway. Possibly dating to the late 9th century (but just as easily the early 10th), Gordon could also fit this picture of early influence in southern Scotland from bullion-using Vikings connected to England, Ireland and southern Scandinavia. This could also be true for the Danish or Hiberno-Scandinavian broad-band fragment from Blackerne (Kirkcudbrightshire), as well as a fragment potentially from Largo in Fife (Graham-Campbell 1995: 26–7, 156; Graham-Campbell and Batey 1998: 103).

Ingot-derived 'broad-band' arm-rings originated in Danish/southern Scandinavian regions before being developed in Hiberno-Scandinavian contexts, likely Dublin, by the 880s (Sheehan 2011: 99–100; cf. Downham 2007: 63; Horne 2014: 296). The aforementioned Ívarr, arguably a Dublin king who campaigned with the Great Army, was potentially connected with these developments (Sheehan 2011: 98). If so, these arm-rings may be viewed as another example of Danish (and Danish-influenced Norwegian) economic influence on the Insular world, via Great Army types from southern Scandinavia.

For Scotland, 'hoards, like that of Gordon [demonstrating] the presence of [. . .] hack-silver and [. . .] ingots as early as the late 9th century, should shift the appreciable increase in the use of silver as a medium of exchange from the mid-10th century, as suggested by the coin-dated hoards, to a period around 900, if not earlier' (Horne 2014: 231–2). Indeed, as Williams (2007: 204) notes, single-find coins at Scotto-Scandinavian settlements, from possibly as early as the early 10th century, are also evidence regarding 'early' economic silver use, paraphrased by Blackburn (2007: 136) as suggesting that, because coins 'occurred in a large proportion of the known Scandinavian settlements, [this] indicates that within these small communities, coinage [was] used from the early 10th'. While uncertain of this, Blackburn (2007: 136) conceded: 'Perhaps we are then seeing something of a dual economy, where arm-rings, hack-silver and mixed English and continental coins remained an essential part of the economy, but individual coins could be used within settlements for daily transactions.' Note, however, that Graham-Campbell (pers. comm.) argues for this only applying in Scotland from the 930s, when the Storr Rock Hoard was deposited.

930s–960s: Storr Rock and Skaill

If knowledge of bullion existed in southern and western parts of Scotland by 900, what of 10th-century developments, and what of the north? To answer this, we turn to two hoards, both of which include dirhams as well as ornament and ingot fragments. The older, from Storr Rock, was deposited on Skye c. 935–940. It contains hack-silver and dirhams alongside Anglo-Saxon coins. While Graham-Campbell (1995) and Metcalf (1995) suggested it was of almost entirely Hiberno-Scandinavian nature, it deserves reappreciation. Given growing evidence for early bullion use in western Scotland, it should perhaps be considered more Scotto-Scandinavian than previously thought.

The Skaill Hoard, deposited on Orkney c. 960–980 (Williams, in Graham-Campbell 2019: 296; Graham-Campbell, this section), contains strong Irish Sea Region elements alongside dirhams and Scotto-Scandinavian 'ring-money' arm-rings (see below). Posited as a 'chieftain's hoard' (Graham-Campbell 1995: 48; cf. Crawford 1987: 126, 127; Horne 2014: 223, 243), it is argued here that Skaill might have been owned by a Scotto-Scandinavian version of Ohthere, whose travels were recorded at Alfred the Great's court. Ohthere was a wealthy farmer-trader from the rural north of Norway who transacted business in southern markets, likely aided by a range of currencies (Horne 2014: 114–15), something Skaill's owner would have also been able to do.

In any case, both hoards are reminders that Irish Sea Region and Great Army elements were not the sole entry mechanism for bullion use (Graham-Campbell, pers. comm.). Precious metals were likely entering Scotland via 'round-Scotland' maritime raiding, migration and trade routes between Scandinavia and Dublin. As this author remarked, following Skre (2011a, 2011b), 'the owners of Storr Rock [...] and Skaill [...] were probably following regularized routeways to the Irish Sea Region established in the early 9th century by those travelling between the Danish Corridor [my term for the Danish-dominated southern Scandinavian market zone] and the Irish Sea' (Horne 2014: 228). Moreover, the discovery of market activity with bullion use, plus an Insular mount, at Sandtorg i Tjeldsund in Troms (Krokmyrdal 2020), a site potentially known to Ohthere, strengthens the possibility of bullion influence also emanating from northern Norway.

950s–1050s: Increasing fragmentation and regularisation

A key *Vikings in Scotland* section (1998: 243–4) concerns changes in hoards after the Storr Rock and Skaill depositions and what this tells us about Late Norse bullion. Their comparison with the Burray (Orkney, c. 997–1010) and Lews Castle (Lewis, c. 990–1040) hoards centres on proportions of hack-silver to whole artefacts, levels of fragmentation and intensity of testing. The argument runs that the more hack-silver present and the more fragmented it is, the more likely a hoard represents use moving away from complete ornaments given within gift economies to commercial use as cash.

Compared to their 10th-century cousins, Graham-Campbell and Batey (1998: 243–4) noted Burray and Lews Castle display higher fragmentation but fewer test marks. While the former suggests increasing demand for smaller units of cash to facilitate a presumably growing volume of commerce, the latter is at odds with this, suggesting low circulation (1998: 243–4). However, the majority of the hack-silver is of a penannular arm-ring known as 'ring money' (Warner 1976; Graham-Campbell and Batey 1998: 243–4; Critch 2015). As this type is first seen in a datable context in Skaill (c. 960–80), and thus had been in circulation relatively briefly up to that period, this could explain a misleading picture of low circulation (Graham-Campbell and Batey 1998: 243–4).

Later hoards suggest Scotto-Scandinavian 'ring-money' dominated bullion use in the region. It was developed from an earlier (short-lived) Hiberno-Scandinavian type that, in undecorated form, became popular in Scotland between c. 960 and the 1040s. Approximated to a Scandinavian ounce (øre) of 24g ± 0.8g (Warner 1976: 141), Graham-Campbell and Batey (1998: 238) were unconvinced it was a standardised currency, but noted 'it clearly provided a convenient means of payment'. Convenient or not, the mid-11th century saw the beginning of a silver debasement that, combined with silver seemingly leaving the region or spent on the church, heralded the slow decline of Scotto-Scandinavian bullion use (Graham-Campbell and Batey 1998: 246–7; Critch 2015).

1050s–1450s: Late Norse bullion

Debasement, increasing fragmentation and a very loose ounce made precise weighing increasingly important from the mid-11th century, perhaps explaining the growing corpus of precision weights like oblate spheroids in Late Norse contexts like Cille Pheadair (South Uist). Of a type synonymous with Baltic bullion economies since its introduction there in c. 870 and associated with the dirham influx to that region, the Cille Pheadair oblate spheroid (Paterson 2018) provides evidence of continued Western Isles bullion use into the 1100s. This is also the case for Bornais, where Sharples (2020, this volume) and the author (Horne 2020a; Horne and Smith 2020a; 2020b) suggest the late continuity of bullion at this relatively nearby site via the presence of a solid copper-alloy oblate spheroid (c. 11th to 14th centuries), a fragment likely from a balance arm hinge of a type associated with bullion (c. 11th to 12th centuries) and a piece of hack-silver (c. 13th to 14th centuries).

Both weights from the Earl's Bu site at Orphir on Orkney (Batey, this volume; forthcoming) are oblate spheroids from Late Norse contexts. Like Cille Pheadair, they have a copper-alloy coated iron core. Their presence suggests the Northern as well as the Western Isles continued to belong to (or take inspiration from) a payment zone centred on Scandinavia and markets like Sigtuna in Sweden, or possibly Norway's Trondheim and Bergen (Graham-Campbell, pers. comm.). Other weights of this form exist in Scotland, ranging from the potential solid lead example from Dumbarton Rock, perhaps dating to the late 9th century (Alcock and Alcock 1990; Graham-Campbell and Batey 1998: 98–9), to the solid copper alloy version from the Bay of Cleat on Westray, Orkney (Maleszka 2003). The latter may date to the Late Norse period (Horne, forthcoming) due to its parallel in Bornais.

Although a small dataset, the presence of these weights indicates continuation of bullion economies in northern and north-western island regions. Given the manufacture of oblate spheroids in the nodal markets of central Sweden (Birka, then Sigtuna) and southern Scandinavia (Hedeby) (Horne 2014), it may also speak to direct connections between Scandinavia and Late Norse Scotland that would continue in the later medieval period.

Poor relations?

Despite this apparent longevity, Scotland's bullion economy is not viewed as being of great scale or sophistication. However, while the apparently low volume of metals in circulation may have been an impediment to growth, a small silver economy may, nevertheless, have been pervasive, complex and disproportionately influential (if not enough to encourage permanent markets); indeed, as Barrett (1995: 169) observed, 'even a modest volume of trade could be remarkably important to a relatively diffuse rural population'.

There is also little point in comparing Scotto-Scandinavian silver circulation with that of Ireland or England in order to conclude that its bullion economies were of lesser significance, as noted by Barrett (1995: 174; 2007: 319; cf. Horne 2014: 62) and Williams (2006: 167; 2007: 203, 204; cf. Horne 2014: 245). It is more appropriate to compare its 'liquidity' with its North Atlantic peers, in which case the number of Scotto-Scandinavian silver hoards compares well with Iceland and the Faeroes (Smart 1985: 66–7; Barrett 1995: 169–70; Horne 2014: 62). Furthermore, the idea that Scandinavian Scotland was poor even within an Insular context required rectification even before the Galloway and Orphir finds, with the region producing more hoards than north-west England, Man or Wales.

Additionally, as we are learning from *longphuirt*, winter-camps (Williams 2020a: 99–102) and Sandtorg i Tjeldsund (Krokmyrdal

2020), bullion economies did not need traditional urban contexts to develop. From this point of departure of accepting markets without towns, it becomes easier to accept an almost completely townless Scandinavian Scotland as a region that integrated into wider, pan-Scandinavian, economies. In this non-town perspective, Kruse (2007: 168–9) saw a trader:

> sailing to the largest farm settlement in a place [...] with few or no towns, such as Scotland, and forging or renewing contacts with the main landowner. Gift-exchange, bribes, etc., may have followed part of the exchange, but presumably more impersonal trade would have followed.

Similarly, Woolf (1999: 67) and Barrett (1995: 170, 171, 174, 186) argued for traders visiting temporary beach markets under the aegis of wealthy families at a high-status location – perhaps like Skaill or Earl's Bu – rather than anything more permanent (cf. Horne 2014: 62–5). Whithorn in Galloway aside (Hill 1997), no major market has been found in Scotland, although the Sandtorg discovery from the Arctic region seemingly home to Ohthere brings hope a similarly 'remote' Scotto-Scandinavian market may yet be found. However, lack of a long-term market is not to say Scotto-Scandinavians were unsophisticated economically or passive in receipt of monetary trends, as Ohthere and Sandtorg indicate. Indeed, as Sindbæk (2011: 58–9; cf. Ulriksen 2009: 141) has shown for northern Scandinavia and Holm for Swedish Jämtland (2017), complex systems like Scandinavian silver currencies can spread rapidly via trade routes even to rural and 'remote' regions far from major markets (cf. Horne 2014: 159–60).

As was possibly the case for Skaill, Scotto-Scandinavian trader-farmers travelling to and from Scandinavian market regions like the Danelaw and Dublin may be another important mechanism by which bullion and monetary economies spread to rural settlements. What the monetary evidence found in Scandinavian Scotland demonstrates is this ability of non-urban inhabitants to adopt and adapt economies to their socioeconomic requirements, and that this was true for both the Viking Age and the Late Norse periods.

Conclusion

It appears Scotto-Scandinavian bullion economies started earlier than previously considered, at least in the south, and the direction of this influence speaks to origins via southern Scandinavian elements, including the Great Army, operating in the Irish Sea Region and England in the second half of the 9th century. This chronological range can also be extended in the other direction, with recent finds suggesting the continuation of Scotto-Scandinavian bullion economies, at least in the Northern and Western Isles, into the 1100s. Finally, new finds and Scandinavian parallels may offer a model for how non-urban regions adopted market and monetary practices through long-distance trading connections.

References

Alcock, L. and E. Alcock (1990) Reconnaissance excavations on Early Historic fortifications and other royal sites in Scotland, 1974–84: 4, Excavations at Alt Clut, Clyde Rock, Strathclyde, 1974–5. *Proceedings of the Society of Antiquaries of Scotland* 120, 95–149.

Anderson, J. (1907) Notice of Bronze Brooches and Personal Ornaments from a Ship-burial of the Viking time in Oronsay, and other Bronze Ornaments from Colonsay [. . .] With a description, from notes by the late William Galloway of a ship-burial of the Viking time at Kiloran Bay, Colonsay. *Proceedings of the Society of Antiquaries of Scotland* 41 (1906–7), 437–50.

Barrett, J. (1995) *Fish Middens and the Economy of the Viking Age and Late Norse Earldoms of Orkney and Caithness, Northern Scotland.* Unpublished PhD thesis, University of Glasgow.

Barrett, J. (2007) The pirate fishermen: The political economy of a medieval maritime society. In B. Ballin Smith, S. Taylor and G. Williams (eds), *West over Sea: Studies in Scandinavian Sea-borne Expansion and Settlement Before 1300.* Leiden: Brill, 299–340.

Batey, C. E., with R. Barrowman, I. Mainland, J. Huntley and J. Harland (Forthcoming) *A Norse Economic Hub: Excavation of a Horizontal Mill at the Earl's Bu, Orphir, Orkney.*

Blackburn, M. (2007) Currency under the Vikings. Part 3: Ireland, Wales, Isle of Man and Scotland during the ninth and tenth centuries. *British Numismatic Journal* 77, 119–49.

Blomkvist, N. (2009) Traces of a global economic boom that came and went. In A.-M. Pettersson (ed.), *The Spillings Hoard – Gotland's Role in Viking Age World Trade.* Visby: Gotlands Museum, 155–85.

Brooks, N. and J. Graham-Campbell (2000) Reflections on the Viking-age silver hoard from Croydon, Surrey [1986: revised]. In N. Brooks (ed.), *Communities and Warfare, 700–1400.* London: Hambledon, 69–92.

Crawford, B. (1987) *Scandinavian Scotland.* Leicester: Leicester University Press.

Critch, A. (2015) *'How are princely gifts repaid by your powerful friends?': Ring-money and the Appropriation of Tradition in Insular Viking Politics, AD 900–1065.* Unpublished PhD thesis, University of Cambridge.

Downham, C. (2007) *Viking Kings of Britain and Ireland: The Dynasty of Ívarr to AD 1014.* Edinburgh: Dunedin Academic Press.

Graham-Campbell, J. (1995) *The Viking-Age Gold and Silver of Scotland.* Edinburgh: NMS.

Graham-Campbell, J. (2019) The 1858 Skaill Viking-Age silver hoard. In D. Griffiths, J. Harrison and M. Athanson, *Beside the Ocean. Coastal landscapes at the Bay of Skaill, Marwick, and Birsay Bay, Orkney: Archaeological Research 2003–2018*. Oxford: Oxbow Books, 293–9.

Graham-Campbell, J. (2020) The Galloway Hoard: Viking/Anglo-Saxon interaction in south-west Scotland. In A. Pedersen and S. M. Sindbæk (eds), *Viking Encounters: Proceedings of the Eighteenth Viking Congress, Denmark, August 6–12, 2017*. Århus: Århus University Press, 449–62.

Graham-Campbell, J. and C. E. Batey (1998) *Vikings in Scotland: An Archaeological Survey*. Edinburgh: Edinburgh University Press.

Gruszczyński, J. (2019) *Viking Silver, Hoards and Containers: The Archaeological and Historical Context of Viking-Age Silver Coin Deposits in the Baltic c. 800–1050*. London and New York: Routledge.

Hadley, D. and J. Richards (with H. Brown, E. Craig-Atkins, D. Mahoney-Swales, G. Perry, S. Stein and A. Woods) (2016) The winter camp of the Viking Great Army, AD 872–3, Torksey, Lincolnshire. *The Antiquaries Journal* 96, 23–67.

Hill, P. (1997) *Whithorn and St Ninian: The Excavation of a Monastic Town*. Stroud: Sutton.

Holm, O. (2017) The use of silver as a medium of exchange in Jämtland, c. 875–1050. In Z. Glørstad and K. Loftsgarden (eds), *Viking-Age Transformations: Trade, Craft and Resources in Western Scandinavia*. London: Routledge, 42–58.

Horne, T. (2014) *Scandinavian Market Networks in the Viking Age*. Unpublished PhD thesis, University of Glasgow.

Horne, T. (Forthcoming) A bullion economy at the Earl's Bu. In C. E. Batey (ed.) with R. C. Barrowman, I. Mainland, J. P. Huntley and J. Harland, *A Norse Economic Hub: Excavation of a Horizontal Mill at the Earl's Bu, Orphir, Orkney*.

Horne, T. (2020a) Hack-silver? In N. Sharples (ed.), *The Economy of a Norse Settlement*. Oxford: Oxbow Books, 109.

Horne, T. (2022) *A Viking Market Kingdom in Ireland and Britain: Trade Networks and the Importation of a Southern Scandinavian Silver Bullion Economy*. Abingdon and New York: Routledge.

Horne, T. and R. Smith (2020a) Weights. In N. Sharples (ed.), *The Economy of a Norse Settlement*. Oxford: Oxbow Books, 106–8.

Horne, T. and R. Smith (2020b) Balance component. In N. Sharples (ed.), *The Economy of a Norse Settlement*. Oxford: Oxbow Books, 108–9.

Hårdh, B. (1996) *Silver in the Viking-Age: A Regional-Economic Study*. Stockholm: Almquist and Wiksell International.

Hårdh, B. (2008) Hacksilver and ingots. In D. Skre (ed.), *Means of Exchange: Dealing with Silver in the Viking Age. Kaupang Excavation Project Publication Series, Volume 2. Norske Oldfunn XXIII*. Århus: Århus University Press, 95–118.

Jankowiak, M. (2020) Dirham flows into northern and eastern Europe and the rhythms of the slave trade with the Islamic world. In J. Gruszczyński, M. Jankowiak and J. Shepard (eds), *Viking-Age Trade: Silver, Slaves and Gotland*. Abingdon and New York: Routledge, 105–31.

Kilger, C. (2008a) Kaupang from afar: Aspects of the interpretation of dirham finds in northern and eastern Europe between the late 8th and early 10th centuries. In D. Skre (ed.), *Means of Exchange: Dealing with Silver in the Viking Age. Kaupang Excavation Project Publication Series, Volume 2. Norske Oldfunn XXIII*. Århus: Århus University Press, 197–252.

Kilger, C. (2008b) Wholeness and holiness: Counting, weighing and valuing silver in the Early Viking Period. In D. Skre (ed.), *Means of Exchange: Dealing with Silver in the Viking Age. Kaupang Excavation Project Publication Series, Volume 2. Norske Oldfunn XXIII*. Århus: Århus University Press, 253–325.

Krokmyrdal, T.-K. (2020) *Vareutveksling gjennom 1100 år? Arkeologisk undersøkelse av mulig vareutveksling i jernalder og middelalder på Sandtorg, Harstad kommune*. Master's thesis, The Arctic University of Norway.

Kruse, S. (2007) Trade and exchange across frontiers. In J. Graham-Campbell and G. Williams (eds), *Silver Economy in the Viking Age*. Walnut Creek: West Coast Press, 163–76.

Maleszka, M. (2003) A Viking Age weight from Cleat, Westray, Orkney. *Proceedings of the Society of Antiquaries of Scotland* 133, 283–91.

Metcalf, D. (1995) The monetary significance of Scottish Viking-Age coin hoards, with a short commentary. In J. Graham-Campbell, *The Viking-Age Gold and Silver of Scotland*. Edinburgh: NMS, 16–25.

Paterson, C. (2018) The combs, ornaments, weights and coins (with contributions by M. Parker Pearson and E. Besly). In M. Parker Pearson, M. Brennand, J. Mulville and H. Smith, *Cille Pheadair: A Norse Farmstead and Pictish Burial Cairn in South Uist*. Oxford: Oxbow Books, 293–336.

Russell, I. and M. Hurley (eds) (2014) *Woodstown: A Viking-Age Settlement in Co. Waterford*. Dublin: Four Courts Press.

Sharples, N. (ed.) (2020) *The Economy of a Norse Settlement in the Outer Hebrides: Excavations on Mounds 2 and 2A, Bornais, South Uist*. Oxford: Oxbow Books.

Sheehan, J. (2011) Hiberno-Scandinavian broad-band arm-rings. In J. Graham-Campbell (ed.), *The Cuerdale Hoard and Related Viking-Age Silver and Gold from Britain and Ireland in the British Museum*. London: British Museum Press, 94–100.

Sheehan, J. (2020) Viking-Age bullion from southern Scandinavia and the Baltic region in Ireland. In J. Gruszczyński, M. Jankowiak and J. Shepard (eds), *Viking-Age Trade: Silver, Slaves and Gotland*. London and New York: Routledge, 415–33.

Sindbæk, S. (2007) Networks and nodal points. The emergence of towns in Early Viking Age Scandinavia. *Antiquity* 81, 119–32.

Sindbæk, S. (2011) Silver economies and social ties: Long-distance interaction, long-term investments – and why the Viking Age happened. In J. Graham-Campbell, S. Sindbæk and G. Williams (eds), *Silver Economies, Monetisation and Society in Scandinavia, AD 800–1100*. Århus: Århus University Press, 41–65.

Skre, D. (2011a) The inhabitants: Origins and trading connexions. In D. Skre (ed.), *Things from the Town: Artefacts and Inhabitants in Viking-Age Kaupang*. Århus: Århus University Press, 417–41.

Skre, D. (2011b) Kaupang: Between east and west; between north and south. In D. Skre (ed.), *Things from the Town: Artefacts and Inhabitants in Viking-Age Kaupang*. Århus: Århus University Press, 443–9.

Smart, V. (1985) The penny in the pennylands: Coinage in Scotland in the Early Middle Ages. *Northern Studies* 22, 65–70.

Ulriksen, J. (2009) Viking-Age sailing routes of the western Baltic Sea – a matter of safety. In A. Englert and A. Trakadas (eds), *Wulfstan's Voyage: The Baltic Sea Region in the Early Viking Age as Seen from Shipboard*. Roskilde: The Viking Ship Museum, 135–44.

Warner, R. (1976) Scottish silver arm-rings: An analysis of weights. *Proceedings of the Society of Antiquaries of Scotland* 107, 136–43.

Williams, G. (2006) Monetary economy in Viking Age Scotland in the light of single finds. In J. Moesgaard and H. Horsnæs (eds), *Single Finds – The Nordic Perspective*. Copenhagen: University of Copenhagen, 164–72.

Williams, G. (2007) Kingship, Christianity and coinage: Monetary and political perspectives on silver economy in the Viking Age. In J. Graham-Campbell and G. Williams (eds), *Silver Economy in the Viking Age*. Walnut Creek: West Coast Press, 177–214.

Williams, G. (2020a) Viking camps and urbanisation. In G. Williams (ed.), *A Riverine Site Near York: A Possible Viking Camp?* London: The British Museum, 99–102.

Williams, G. (2020b) Viking hoards from Yorkshire, c. 866–954: A survey. In G. Williams (ed.), *A Riverine Site Near York: A Possible Viking Camp?* London: The British Museum, 103–12.

Williams, G. (2020c) The coins, weights and bullion: Discussion and interpretation. In G. Williams (ed.), *A Riverine Site Near York: A Possible Viking Camp?* London: The British Museum, 36–45.

Woolf, A. (1999) The Russes, the Byzantines, and Middle-Saxon emporia. In M. Anderton (ed.), *Anglo-Saxon Trading Centres: Beyond the Emporia*. Glasgow: Cruithne Press, 63–75.

Chapter 23

Small Finds, Big Questions: Two Decades of Research on Combs in Viking-Age Scotland
Steven P. Ashby

Is it possible, or indeed likely, that the Picts were importing antler from Norway to make their combs? ... It is inevitable that such a suggestion has not met with universal acceptance, and the results of further studies are eagerly awaited.

(Graham-Campbell and Batey 1998: 23)

At the time of *Vikings in Scotland*'s publication, the study of combs – like many artefacts – was seen by many as a peripheral pursuit: specialist, but fundamentally empiricist, and perhaps rather old-fashioned. *Vikings in Scotland* was important in running counter to this trend, putting material culture rather than landscape at the centre of discussion.

The two decades since have seen a transformation in the study of artefacts, including Viking-Age combs. Building on experimental reconstruction (e.g. Galloway and Newcomer 1981), typological study (e.g. Ambrosiani 1981) and analysis as indicators of urbanism (Ulbricht 1978; Christophersen 1980), the application of social theory and scientific method have allowed combs to play a more central role in writing the Viking Age.

New excavations, new combs

Updates could be made to *Vikings in Scotland*'s survey. Settlement excavations in both the Northern and Western Isles have expanded our corpus, though there is little evidence of manufacture to augment the Whithorn workshop (Nicholson 1997; Graham-Campbell and Batey 1998: 222). A waste assemblage has been identified in a Late Norse phase at Bornais (Sharples 2019: 421–7) but the only new Viking-Age material is one or two fragments from the Bay of Skaill (Ashby 2019: 244–5). Graham-Campbell and Batey were correct in their assertion that the combs of Viking-Age Scotland were carried in or imported from Scandinavia (1998: 222–3).

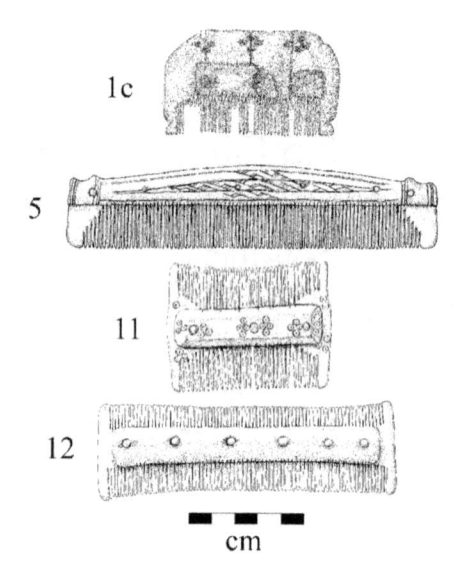

Figure 23.1 Diagnostic markers: 'native' (1c, 11, 12) and Norse (5) comb forms. Drawings by Hayley Saul (1c, 11) and Pat Walsh (5, 12). From Ashby 2009, reproduced courtesy Society for Medieval Archaeology.

The distinctiveness of 'Viking' and 'Insular' combs has allowed both to be used as diagnostic cultural indicators (Figure 23.1). In the Northern Isles, the domination of 'Norse' forms in later Viking-Age and medieval contexts has been taken to indicate cultural domination (see, for example, Barrett 2013), while the apparent intermixing of earlier material has been the subject of debate: might this indicate native–settler coexistence or co-operation (see Ritchie 1977; cf. Crawford 1981)? An obstacle to understanding the relationship between what have been variously referred to as 'native', 'Pictish' and 'pre-Norse' combs, and their 'Viking' counterparts has been a lack of stratigraphic integrity (see Hamilton 1956; Curle 1982; Buteux 1997). In order to accurately characterise the phenomena observable in the combs, we need new, stratigraphically precise, excavations.

The last two decades have seen the publication of several such projects. Pool, Sanday (Hunter 2007) was among the first, and has provided some evidence of an interface phase. More recent excavations at the Bay of Skaill (Ashby 2019; Griffiths et al. 2019) and Quoygrew, Westray (Ashby and Batey 2013; Barrett 2013) provide chronology for the later/post-Viking Age, and suggest a degree of spatial variability: the affinities of Skaill's combs lie in the Irish Sea area (see, for example, Figure 23.2), while Quoygrew apparently looks to western Scandinavia. Likewise, excavations at Cille Pheadair (Pearson et al. 2018) and Bornais (Sharples 2005, 2019) are fine-tuning our understanding

Figure 23.2 A new discovery: comb in situ at Skaill Bay, Orkney. Image from Ashby 2019 © University of Oxford.

of comb material in western Scotland. It is also now easier to place the combs of Late Iron-Age to medieval Scotland in relation to their Scandinavian and Anglo-Saxon contemporaries (Ashby 2011).

New data from old collections

Progress has also been made in the study of existing collections. In the most oft-discussed studies of Scotland's corpus, it has been proposed that reindeer antler was used in the manufacture of ostensibly pre-Viking combs in Orkney (such as Weber 1993, and further references in Ashby 2009). If correct, these results push Scandinavian contact back decades, even centuries into the pre-Viking period.

In 1993, Bjorn Myhre (1993) drew on this research to propose a long, slow start to the Viking Age. This argument met with scepticism (see, for example, Roesdahl 1994), as it demanded revision of the fundamentals of Viking-Age chronology. More pertinent here, however, are objections relating to the raw material identification in the combs. The identifications were made by an experienced zooarchaeologist, but no replicable methodology was published (see Lie in Weber 1993 for a brief overview). Smirnova (2005) independently developed a macroscopic method of identification in combs from Novgorod, Russia, and applied her techniques to the Orcadian corpus, but this was never formally published (The Sea Road, 2001).

More recently, I studied these combs and characterised raw materials using a macroscopic method developed following tutelage under Smirnova (Ashby 2009, see 2013 for critical reflection on raw material analysis). I failed to identify any reindeer antler in combs from contexts that could confidently be dated to the 8th century or before. The pattern arguably suggested some level of Norse–native coexistence in the 9th century, but not before. More recently, we applied a new, minimally destructive biomolecular approach to this material. Zooarchaeology by Mass Spectrometry (ZooMS) uses peptide mass-fingerprinting to distinguish diverse animal tissues (Hendy et al. 2018). In our sample, which included a number of 'pre-Viking' combs previously identified as reindeer, this material was only identified in diagnostically Viking-Age combs, with both ZooMS and aDNA evidencing the use of red deer antler in 'native' forms (von Holstein et al. 2014). The combs no longer support the existence of an extended period of contact between Scotland and Scandinavia prior to the traditional date of settlement in the second half of the 9th century.

Whither combs?

To summarise, the last two decades have seen significant developments in our understanding of Scotland's corpus of Viking-Age combs. These advances have emerged from more highly resolved stratigraphic data, from a rethinking of old questions in the light of more object-centred theoretical frameworks, and from the advent of new analytical techniques in the natural sciences. As a result, we now have a clearer understanding of the chronology and character of early Viking-Age Scotland. We have a better appreciation of its context with respect to wider maritime activity, and the potential to further explore the dynamics of diaspora and trade in the North Sea, Irish Sea and North Atlantic.

The future is exciting. No doubt new material will be excavated, but there is much to be accomplished from the study of existing collections, including some that have seen little recent study (e.g. Crawford 1996). The chronology of later Viking-Age and medieval comb material is still not well understood, and a priority is a systematic understanding of Late Norse comb material across Scandinavia and its North Atlantic colonies. Highly resolved comparisons with material from England, Ireland and Scandinavia might also be made, focusing on details of manufacture (tool use, for instance, could be characterised using high-powered microscopy and imaging technology). There is also potential to better understand combs as possessions, through the application of high-powered microscopy to use-wear calibrated against experimental data. Finally, systematic biomolecular analysis needs to be undertaken; given promising results in the genetic provenancing of reindeer populations in medieval Norway (Rosvold et al. 2019), this means aDNA as well as ZooMS. Once again, 'the results of further studies are eagerly awaited'.

Acknowledgements

This paper is dedicated to my friend, Anne Brundle. I would like to thank everyone for their forbearance in discussing Scottish combs over the years. Particular thanks to James Barrett, who started me on this journey, as well as Colleen Batey, David Griffiths, Niall Sharples, Jen Harland, Matthew Collins and all at BioArCh. Finally, I owe a debt of gratitude to the curatorial staff who have repeatedly facilitated access to collections in Edinburgh, Kirkwall and Lerwick.

References

Ambrosiani, K. (1981) *Viking Age Combs, Comb Making and Comb Makers in the Light of Finds from Birka and Ribe*. Stockholm: Almqvist and Wiksell.
Ashby, S. P. (2009) Combs, contact and chronology: Reconsidering hair combs in Early-Historic and Viking-Age Atlantic Scotland. *Medieval Archaeology* 53, 1–33.
Ashby, S. P. (2011) An atlas of medieval combs from northern Europe. *Internet Archaeology* 30: http://intarch.ac.uk/journal/issue30/ashby_index.html
Ashby, S. P. (2013) Some comments on the identification of Cervid species in worked antler. In S. O'Connor and A. M. Choyke (eds), *From These Bare Bones: Raw Materials and the Study of Worked Osseous Materials*. Oxford: Oxbow Books, 208–22.
Ashby, S. P. (2019) Combs. In D. Griffiths, J. Harrison and M. Athanson (eds), *Beside the Ocean: Coastal Landscapes at the Bay of Skaill, Marwick, and Birsay Bay, Orkney: Archaeological Research 2003–18*. Oxford: Oxbow Books, 243–51.
Ashby, S. P. and C. E. Batey (2013) Evidence of exchange networks: The combs and other worked skeletal material. In J. H. Barrett (ed.), *Being an Islander: Production and Identity at Quoygrew, Orkney, AD 900–1600*. Cambridge: McDonald Institute for Archaeological Research, 229–43.
Barrett, J. H. (2013) *Being an Islander. Production and Identity at Quoygrew, Orkney, AD 900–1600*. Cambridge: McDonald Institute for Archaeological Research.
Buteux, S. (1997) *Settlements at Skaill, Deerness, Orkney: Excavations by Peter Gelling of the Prehistoric, Pictish, Viking and Later Periods, 1963–1981*. British Archaeological Reports, British series 260. Oxford: Archaeopress.
Christophersen, A. (1980) Håndverket i Forandring. Studier i Horn- og Beinhåndverkets Utvikling i Lund ca. 1000–1350. *Acta Archaeologica Lundensia* 4.

Crawford, I. A. (1981) War or peace – Viking colonisation in the Northern and Western Isles of Scotland reviewed. In H. Bekker-Nielsen, P. Foote and O. Olsen (eds), *Proceedings of the Eighth Viking Congress, Århus 1977, Medieval Scandinavia Supplements Volume 2*. Odense: Odense University Press, 259–69.

Crawford, I. A. (1996) The Udal. *Current Archaeology* 147, 84–94.

Curle, C. L. (1982) *Pictish and Norse Finds from the Brough of Birsay 1934–74*. Society of Antiquaries of Scotland monograph series 1. Edinburgh: Society of Antiquaries of Scotland.

Galloway, P. and M. Newcomer (1981) The craft of comb-making: An experimental enquiry. *University of London Institute of Archaeology Bulletin* 18, 73–90.

Graham-Campbell, J. and C. E. Batey (1998) *Vikings in Scotland: An Archaeological Survey*. Edinburgh: Edinburgh University Press.

Griffiths, D., J. Harrison and M. Athanson (2019) *Beside the Ocean: Coastal Landscapes at the Bay of Skaill, Marwick, and Birsay Bay, Orkney: Archaeological Research 2003–18*. Oxford: Oxbow Books.

Hamilton, J. R. C. (1956) *Excavations at Jarlshof, Shetland*. Edinburgh: HMSO.

Hendy, J., F. Welker, B. Demarchi, C. Speller, C. Warinner and M. J. Collins (2018) A guide to ancient protein studies. *Nature Ecology and Evolution* 2, 791–9.

Hunter, J. (2007) *Excavations at Pool, Sanday: A Multi-Period Settlement from Neolithic to Late Norse Times. Investigations in Sanday Orkney: Vol 1*. (ed.) A.N.S.A.R.A.N. with Julie M. Bond. Kirkwall: The Orcadian.

Myhre, B. (1993) The beginning of the Viking Age – Some current archaeological problems. In A. Faulkes and R. Perkins (eds), *Viking Revaluations*. London: Viking Society for Northern Research, 182–204.

Nicholson, A. (1997) The antler. In P. Hill (ed.), *Whithorn and St Ninian: The Excavation of a Monastic Town, 1984–91*. Stroud: Sutton, 474–95.

Pearson, M. P., M. Brennand, J. Mulville and H. Smith (2018) *Cille Pheadair: A Norse Farmstead in South Uist: A Norse Farmstead and Pictish Burial Cairn in South Uist*. Oxford: Oxbow Books.

Ritchie, A. (1977) Excavation of Pictish and Viking-Age farmsteads at Buckquoy, Orkney. *Proceedings of the Society of Antiquaries of Scotland* 108, 174–227.

Roesdahl, E. (1994) Dendrochronology and Viking studies in Denmark, with a note on the beginning of the Viking Age. In A. B. C. Helen (ed.), *The Twelfth Viking Congress: Developments around the Baltic and the North Sea in the Viking Age*. Birka Studies 3. Stockholm: The Birka Project, 106–16.

Rosvold, J., G. Hansen and K. H. Røed (2019) From mountains to towns: DNA from ancient reindeer antlers as proxy for domestic procurement networks in medieval Norway. *Journal of Archaeological Science: Reports* 26: 101860.

Sharples, N. (2005) *A Norse Farmstead in the Outer Hebrides. Excavations at Mound 3, Bornais, South Uist*. Oxford: Oxbow Books.

Sharples, N. (2019) *A Norse Settlement in the Outer Hebrides: Excavations on Mounds 2 and 2A, Bornais, South Uist*. Oxford: Oxbow Books.

Smirnova, L. (2005) *Comb-making in Medieval Novgorod (950–1450): An Industry in Transition*. British Archaeological Reports, International series 1369. Oxford: BAR.
The Sea Road (2001) *Blood of the Vikings*. BBC2.
Ulbricht, I. (1978) *Die Geweihverarbeitung in Haithabu*. Neumünster: K. Wachholtz.
von Holstein, I. C., S. P. Ashby, N. L. van Doorn, S. M. Sachs, M. Buckley, M. Meirai, I. Barnes, A. Brundle and M. J. Collins (2014) Searching for Scandinavians in pre-Viking Scotland: Molecular fingerprinting of Early Medieval combs. *Journal of Archaeological Science* 41, 1–6.
Weber, B. (1993) Norwegian reindeer antler export to Orkney. *Universitetets Oldsaksamlings Årbok* 1991/1992, 161–74.

Part VII

Death and Burial

Perhaps one of the most enduring images in Viking studies is that of pagan burials, especially those containing swords, boats or horses. These graves allow us some understanding of Viking beliefs of the afterlife prior to Christianity and give us an intimate look at both the lives and deaths of individuals. Antiquarians discovered many Viking graves in the 18th and 19th centuries, but these tended to be poorly published (if at all) and only the 'interesting' parts of the burial, such as the weapons, were kept, and often subsequently lost. Later publications were also often riddled with errors and omissions that were perpetuated in modern academic works.

Vikings in Scotland gave a comprehensive overview of Scottish Viking burials known in the late 1990s, including questioning aspects of older interpretations of some burials such as Kiloran Bay, Colonsay. A long-term initiative called the Pagan Norse Graves of Scotland Project (Graham-Campbell et al., this section) has since sought to reassess known graves and artefacts by tracing the original written records documenting these finds to rectify any mistakes in interpretation. The result is a drastic increase in the number of known Viking graves, as well as the reinterpretation of artefacts and new insights into the origins and practices of the Norse buried here.

In addition to reassessing old finds, there have been a number of new burials found in recent years due to large-scale excavations, commercial projects and rescue digs on eroding shorelines, perhaps most notably the boat burial containing a man, woman and child at Scar, Sanday, Orkney (Owen and Dalland 1999). One highly publicised recent discovery was a boat burial found at Swordle Bay on the Ardnamurchan peninsula in Argyll in 2011 (Batey, this section). Although much was made in the popular press of this being the first Viking boat burial found on mainland Britain, its placement overlooking waters off the western coast of Scotland puts it firmly on the sailing route between the Irish Sea and North Sea areas, and it is similar to other nearby burials in the Western Isles.

A more surprising recent find is a cemetery used for centuries along the shores of Loch Lomond, a region traditionally considered outwith areas of Scandinavian settlement (Batey, also this section). Radiocarbon dates from The Carrick have revealed that use of the cemetery began in the Viking Age and continued for several hundred years. Grave goods and other finds suggest that Scandinavian men were not just passing through to raid or trade, but were living in the area with women and children. These burials alert us to unknown settlement we would otherwise know nothing about.

This section shares just a small sample of a growing area of new and exciting work in Viking studies in Scotland, such as the use of isotopes to study the origins and lifestyles of settlers (for example, Montgomery et al. 2014) and genetics to reveal movements both into and out of Scotland (Margaryan et al. 2020). Future work on both old and new Viking graves will help us further understand who these people were, their beliefs and how they lived.

References

Margaryan, A. et al. (2020) Population genomics of the Viking world. *Nature* 585 (7825), 390–6.

Montgomery, J., V. Grimes, J. Buckberry, J. A. Evans, M. P. Richards and J. H. Barrett (2014) Finding Vikings with isotope analysis: The view from wet and windy islands. *Journal of the North Atlantic* Special Volume 7, 54–70.

Owen, O. and M. Dalland (1999) *Scar: A Viking Boat Burial on Sanday, Orkney*. East Linton: Tuckwell Press.

Chapter 24

The 'Pagan Norse Graves of Scotland' Research Project

James Graham-Campbell, Caroline Paterson and Stephen Harrison

The 'Pagan Norse Graves of Scotland' Research Project (PNGS) was initiated in 1995 with the award of a research grant to James Graham-Campbell (UCL) by the Leverhulme Trust. This, together with funding from the National Museums of Scotland (NMS), enabled the creation of a temporary post at NMS to catalogue and research Viking-Age grave-finds, to which Caroline Paterson (then Richardson) was duly appointed. In 1997, NMS with Historic Scotland funded a short extension for her to accession the finds from the Norwegian excavations of the Viking cemetery at Westness, Rousay, Orkney (Kaland 1993; Sellevold 1999, 2010), then newly returned from Bergen, in part intended for display in the new Museum of Scotland.

After a fallow period, PNGS was revived in 2017 thanks again to the Leverhulme Trust, with the award to Graham-Campbell of an Emeritus Fellowship, but in the meantime there were several lesser, but no less welcome, grants in support of PNGS (to be acknowledged in the final publication). The present outline, by Graham-Campbell and Paterson, includes a review of relevant recent literature on the subject by Stephen Harrison (University of Glasgow).

The point of departure for PNGS has been the catalogue of 'Viking antiquities in Scotland', published in 1940 by the Norwegian archaeologist Sigurd Grieg, based on a study-tour undertaken during a couple of months in 1925 (1940: 9–10). It formed the basis for general studies of the material by both Brøgger (1929, 1930) and Shetelig (1945, 1954) and is an indispensable work, but 'the book teems with blunders' (Thorsteinsson 1968: 164). For anyone wishing to map the distribution of pagan Norse graves in Scotland (for example, Crawford 1987, fig. 31), it is all that there has been to go on, with the result that Grieg's inaccuracies and errors (including duplications) have inevitably been reproduced in terms of both overall numbers and individual examples of doubtful date/provenance. In the case of numbers, for example, PNGS has been able to increase Shetland's three accepted graves to maybe thirteen (Graham-Campbell 2016, with additions), and for Orkney, including the two burial places at Pierowall, Westray and Westness, Rousay (see below), the total has reached a possible ninety-seven. This makes the 'notional estimate' of an 'overall figure of about 130 pagan Norse graves from Scotland' (Graham-Campbell and Batey 1998: 47) look exceedingly conservative, with a revised total of some 223 now under consideration for inclusion in the new catalogue (Figure 24.1).

One of the main aims of PNGS has been to pursue Thorsteinsson's (1968: 164) recommendation that 'a critical and methodical study' of the sources was 'one of the most important tasks to be found in Viking archaeology in Scotland'. In so doing, we are endeavouring to overturn the pessimistic assessment that 'the random nature of the discovery of graves and the poor preservation of grave-finds means much of the material is worth little more than curiosity value' (Crawford 1987: 4). Inevitably, such remains true for some finds, but, as Thorsteinsson anticipated, the 'thorough study' of old newspaper reports, diaries and letters, museum registers and sale catalogues (for example, Graham-Campbell 2004) has revealed a wealth of evidence concerning the pagan Norse graves of Scotland which, when subjected to source criticism, can indeed be utilised 'to write cultural history over the material' (Thorsteinsson 1968: 164).

The rigorous nature of Thorsteinsson's own source criticism allowed him to accept only seventeen graves from 'The Viking burial place at Pierowall, Westray, Orkney' (1968), but further archival research, with a more sympathetic approach to the antiquarian records, has arrived at a seemingly acceptable total of thirty-three – and this almost certainly underestimates the number of pagan Norse graves to have been revealed on the Links of Pierowall during the course of two centuries of wind erosion (Graham-Campbell, forthcoming).

A good example of the potential of archival research combined with museum study has been the boat-grave at Kiloran Bay, Colonsay (Grieg 1940: 48–61, figs 26–32; Graham-Campbell and Batey 1998: 118–22, figs 7.3–4), for which there exists a long and tangled trail of both fact and fiction, such that even the accepted date of the second of the two excavations, in the 1880s, has been out by a year (for aspects of the work in progress, see Bill 2005; Paterson and Stanford 2020; Graham-Campbell 2021).

The PNGS project is, however, far from being a purely antiquarian exercise and the artefactual research, largely undertaken by Paterson, has involved looking anew at every extant assemblage and individual grave-find, most of which have been photographed by NMS, with select illustrations by Marion O'Neil. Although some of the old Scandinavian typologies, such as Petersen's seminal *De norske vikingesverd* (1919), remain unsurpassed, numerous artefact studies and excavation reports published both within Scandinavia and elsewhere since Grieg's catalogue

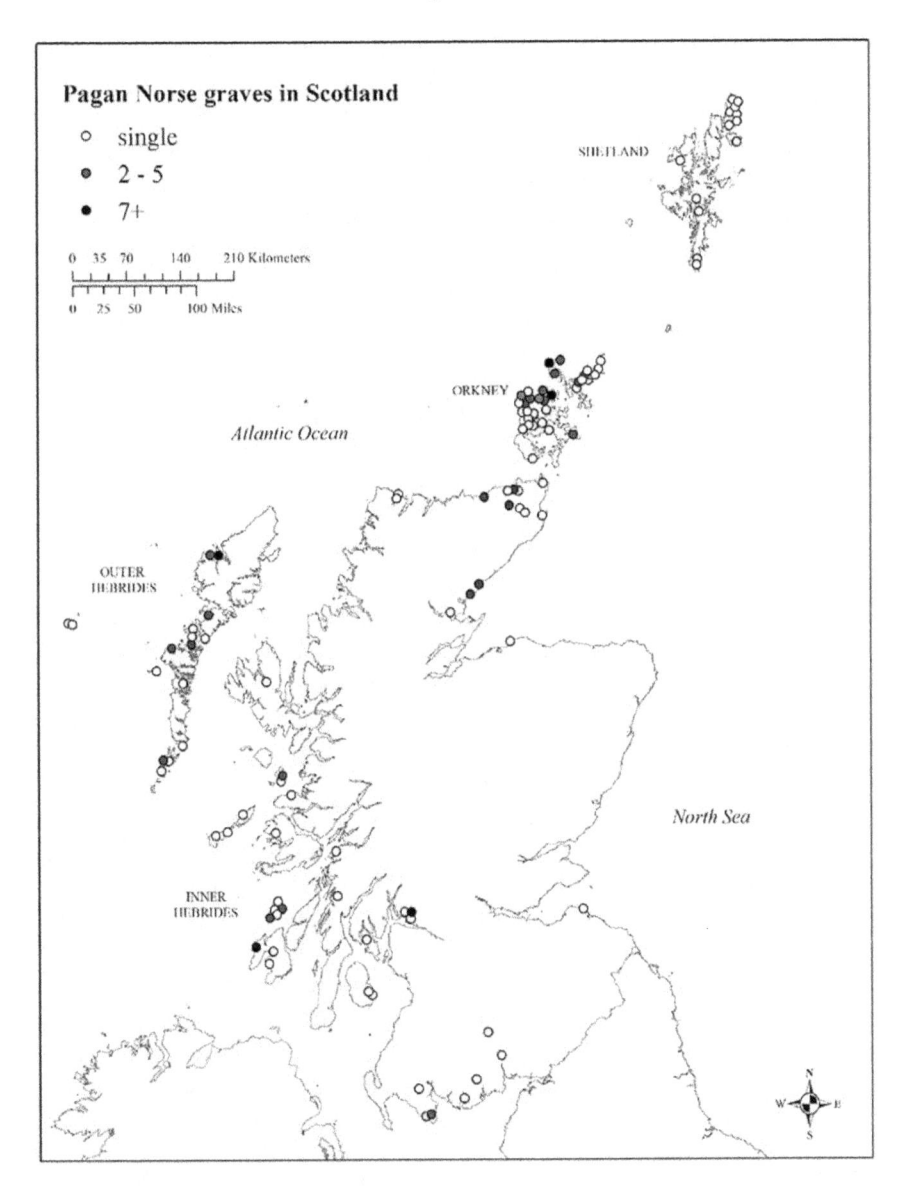

Figure 24.1 Distribution map of the pagan Norse graves of Scotland. PNGS/Jane Kershaw.

have led to many reappraisals and new identifications. The initial recording by Paterson was primarily based in the old National Museum of Antiquities, Queen Street, Edinburgh, where finds were housed prior to their redisplay in the new Museum of Scotland, which opened in 1997. In addition, study-trips were made to record assemblages housed elsewhere, namely Glasgow, Kirkwall, Lerwick, Stornoway, Cambridge,

Oxford, Salisbury and the British Museum, with other objects being brought from elsewhere to the NMS for study.

The benefits of the retention of all associated finds, including exfoliated iron corrosion, were realised with the X-raying of iron artefacts under the direction of Katherine Eremin at the NMS Granton facility. This has resulted in new identifications of antiquarian and recent finds alike and has proved to be of particular importance for the collection of swords, revealing not only decorative inlaid hilt details, but also previously unidentified pattern-welding and inlay in some of the blades. Eremin also undertook the metallurgical analysis, by non-destructive X-ray fluorescence and scanning electron microscopy, of a selection of copper-alloy artefacts, which has proved a useful scientific aid to their provenancing when used in conjunction with stylistic analysis (Paterson 2001; Eremin et al. 2002). Specialist reports have been contributed by the late Gabra-Sanders (textiles; for an interim report, see Gabra-Sanders 1998), Bill (rivets; see Bill 2005, for Kiloran Bay) and Hather (wood); most recently, in the few cases where adequate human remains have survived, isotope and aDNA analyses have been undertaken (Montgomery et al. 2014; Margaryan et al. 2020).

Since the publication of Grieg's catalogue in 1940, the quantity and quality of 'Viking' material known from Scotland has increased dramatically, largely due to the scientific excavation of a number of key settlement sites (see elsewhere in this volume). Some of these settlement excavations have also produced burial evidence, as at Gurness (Hedges 1987) and Buckquoy (Ritchie 1977; Brundle et al. 2003), both on Mainland, Orkney. Erosion has continued to produce new discoveries, with the quality of the resulting reports far exceeding those of the 19th century. These include publications on a new cemetery at Cnip (Kneep), Lewis (Welander et al. 1987; Cowie et al. 1993; Dunwell et al. 1995; Graham-Campbell 2006), a boat burial at Scar, Sanday, Orkney (Owen and Dalland 1999), and single graves at Balnakeil, Sutherland (Batey and Paterson 2013) and Cnoc nan Gall, Colonsay (Becket and Batey 2013). Other research- and development-driven excavations have revealed previously unknown cemeteries at Westness, Rousay and Carrick (Midross), West Dunbartonshire, both awaiting full publication (for summaries, see Kaland 1993; MacGregor 2009; Batey, this section), boat burials at Swordle Bay, Ardnamurchan and Wick of Aith, Fetlar (initial reports: Batey 2016; Harris et al. 2017; see also Batey, below), and a 'Viking' burial in an ecclesiastical context – rare for Scotland – at Auldhame, East Lothian (Crone and Hindmarch 2016; Graham-Campbell 2021). A badly disturbed assemblage from a site at Carronbridge, Dumfries and Galloway (Owen and Welander 1995; Graham-Campbell 2001b: 34–5; McLeod 2014) almost certainly represents another burial. All of these graves and their grave goods follow well-established patterns, but research is also producing evidence for more poorly furnished and even unfurnished burials that seem to be those of Scandinavian settlers, as at Cnip (above) and on the shores of Birsay Bay, Mainland, Orkney (Morris 1989). These burials, presumably common at the time, have been difficult to identify in the past, but new scientific techniques, particularly isotope analysis, are increasing our chances of recognising them. The current project will record all potential Viking graves discovered up to 2010 (together with a hand-list of more recent finds in process of publication).

General surveys of existing burials have been carried out at different levels: from individual cemeteries such as Pierowall (above); to regions such as Caithness (Batey 1993), Argyll (Brown 1997) and Dumfries and Galloway (Graham-Campbell 2001a); and general surveys of Scotland, most obviously by Barbara Crawford (1987) and by Graham-Campbell and Batey (1998); see also Harrison (2015). Surprisingly, there have been relatively few reinterpretations of older graves (such as Graham-Campbell 2019, 2021), particularly outside the PNGS project, with exceptions including Millhill, Arran (Harrison 2000) and 'Ardvonrig', Barra (McLeod 2015b).

General interpretations of the Scottish burial corpus have often been conservative, building on the work of others, as was the case with Eldjárn (1984), who developed a theory first published by Brøgger (1929) to argue for 'peasant' burials in the Northern Isles, representing the full spectrum of Norse society, and more 'Viking' graves in the Western Isles, representing a military elite – an interpretation now very difficult to sustain. By the 1980s, Eldjárn was unusual in arguing that any Scottish graves were 'Viking' in the narrow sense of being associated with raiding. Since Shetelig (1945), most general commentators have been happy to accept the overwhelming majority as those of settlers, even as others continue to argue that many similar graves in England and Ireland are the result of raiding.

In the last two decades, there has been some new interpretative work, on themes such as landscape (Harrison 2007; McLeod 2015a), site reuse (Batey 2002; McLeod 2015c) and the relationship between burial and conversion (Barrett 2003), but gender remains under-researched, as does ethnicity, and new interpretative Scandinavian models, notably the work of Price (for example, 2002, 2010, 2019), have yet to have a substantial impact on Scottish research. By providing a single systematic overview of the evidence, directly comparable to modern surveys of Iceland (Eldjárn 2000) and more recently Ireland (Harrison and Ó Floinn 2014), PNGS hopes to enable new research on this material at all levels.

References

Barrett, J. (2003) Christian and pagan practice during the conversion of Viking age Orkney and Shetland. In M. Carver (ed.), *The Cross goes North: Processes of Conversion in Northern Europe AD 300–1300*. York: York Medieval Press/Boydell, 207–26.

Batey, C. E. (1993) The Viking and Late Norse graves of Caithness and Sutherland. In C. E. Batey, J. Jesch and C. D. Morris (eds), *The Viking Age in Caithness, Orkney and the North Atlantic*. Edinburgh: Edinburgh University Press, 148–72.

Batey, C. E. (2002) Viking and late Norse re-use of broch mounds in Caithness. In B. Ballin Smith and I. Banks (eds), *In the Shadow of the Brochs: The Iron Age in Scotland*. Stroud: Tempus, 185–90.

Batey, C. E. (2016) Viking burials in Scotland: Two 'new' boat burial finds. In V. E. Turner, O. A. Owen and D. J. Waugh (eds), *Shetland and the Viking World: Papers from the Seventeenth Viking Congress, Lerwick*. Lerwick: Shetland Heritage Publications, 39–45.

Batey, C. E. and C. Paterson (2013) A Viking burial at Balnakiel, Sutherland. In A. Reynolds and L. Webster (eds), *Early Medieval Art and Archaeology: Studies in Honour of James Graham-Campbell*. Leiden: Brill, 631–61.

Becket, A. and C. E. Batey (2013) A stranger in the dunes? Rescue excavations of a Viking Age burial at Cnoc nan Gall, Colonsay. *Proceedings of the Society of Antiquaries of Scotland* 143, 303–18.

Bill, J. (2005) Kiloran Bay revisited – confirmation of a doubtful boat-grave. In A. Mortensen and S. V. Arge (eds), *Viking and Norse in the North Atlantic: Select Papers from the Proceedings of the Fourteenth Viking Congress, Tórshavn, 19–30 July 2001*. Tórshavn: The Faroese Academy of Sciences, 345–58.

Brown, M. M. (1997) The Norse in Argyll. In G. Ritchie (ed.), *The Archaeology of Argyll*. Edinburgh: Edinburgh University Press, 205–35.

Brundle, A., D. H. Lorimer and A. Ritchie (2003) Buckquoy revisited. In J. Downes and A. Ritchie (eds), *Sea Change: Orkney and Northern Europe in the Later Iron Age AD 300–800*. Balgavies: Pinkfoot Press, 95–104.

Brøgger, A. W. (1929) *Ancient Emigrants: A History of the Norse Settlements of Scotland*. Oxford: Oxford University Press.

Brøgger, A. W. (1930) *Den norske bosetningen på Shetland-Orknøyene: studier og resultater*. Oslo: Skrifter utgitt av Det Norske Videnskaps-Akademi i Oslo II, Hist.-Filos. Klasse 3.

Cowie, T. G., F. Bruce and N. Kerr (1993) The discovery of a child burial of probable Viking-age date on Kneep Headland, Uig, Lewis, 1991: Interim report. Appendix to C. E. Batey, The Viking and Late Norse graves of Caithness and Sutherland. In C. E. Batey, J. Jesch and C. D. Morris (eds), *The Viking Age in Caithness, Orkney and the North Atlantic*. Edinburgh: Edinburgh University Press, 165–72.

Crawford, B. E. (1987) *Scandinavian Scotland*. Leicester: Leicester University Press.

Crone, A. and E. Hindmarch, with A. Woolf (2016) *Living and Dying at Auldhame, East Lothian. The Excavation of an Anglian Monastic Settlement and Medieval Parish Church*. Edinburgh: Society of Antiquaries of Scotland.

Dunwell, A. J., T. G. Cowie, M. F. Bruce, T. Neighbour and A. R. Rees (1995) A Viking Age cemetery at Cnip, Uig, Isle of Lewis. *Proceedings of the Society of Antiquaries of Scotland* 125, 719–52.

Eldjárn, K. (1984) Graves and grave-goods: Survey and evaluation. In A. Fenton and H. Pálsson (eds), *The Northern and Western Isles in the Viking World: Settlement, Continuity and Change*. Edinburgh: J. Donald, 2–11.

Eldjárn, K. (ed. by A. Friðriksson) (2000). *Kuml og Haugfé*. 2nd edn. Reykjavík: Fornleifastofnun Íslands, Mál og menning and Þjóðminjasafn Íslands.

Eremin, K., J. Graham-Campbell and P. Wilthew (2002) Analysis of copper-alloy artefacts from pagan Norse graves in Scotland. In E. Jerem and K. T. Biró (eds), *Archaeometry 98. Proceedings of the 31st Symposium: Budapest, April 26–May 3, 1998*. BAR International Series 1043 (II). Oxford: British Archaeological Reports, 343–9.

Gabra-Sanders, T. (1998) A review of Viking-Age textiles and fibres: An interim report. In L. Bender Jørgensen and C. Rinaldo (eds), *Textiles in European Archaeology*. Göteborg: Department of Archaeology, Gothenburg University, 177–85.

Graham-Campbell, J. (2001a) *Whithorn and the Viking World: The Eighth Whithorn Lecture*. Whithorn: Friends of the Whithorn Trust.

Graham-Campbell, J. (2001b) National and regional identities: The 'glittering prizes'. In M. Redknap, N. Edwards, S. Youngs, A. Lane and J. Knight (eds), *Pattern and Purpose in Insular Art: Proceedings of the Fourth International Conference on Insular Art held at the National Museum and Gallery, Cardiff, 3–6 September 1998*. Oxford: Oxbow Books, 27–38.

Graham-Campbell, J. (2004) 'Danes . . . in this Country': Discovering the Vikings in Scotland. *Proceedings of the Society of Antiquaries of Scotland* 134, 201–39.

Graham-Campbell, J. (2006) Valtos. *Reallexikon der Germanischen Altertumskunde* 32, 64–6.

Graham-Campbell, J. (2016) Pagan Norse burial in Viking Age Shetland. In V. E. Turner, O. A. Owen and D. J. Waugh (eds), *Shetland and the Viking World: Papers from the Seventeenth Viking Congress, Lerwick*. Lerwick: Shetland Heritage Publications, 31–7.

Graham-Campbell, J. (2019) The 1888 Skaill Viking grave. In D. Griffiths, J. Harrison and M. Athanson (eds), *Beside the Ocean: Coastal Landscapes at the Bay of Skaill, Marwick, and Birsay Bay, Orkney: Archaeological Research 2003–2018*. Oxford: Oxbow Books, 300–4.

Graham-Campbell, J. (2021) Equestrian burial in Viking-Age Scotland. In M. S. Bagge and A. Pedersen (eds), *Horse and Rider in the Late Viking Age. Equestrian Burial in Perspective*. Århus: Åarhus University Press, 270–9.

Graham-Campbell, J. (Forthcoming) The pagan Norse graves of Westray. In O. A. Owen, *Tuquoy, Westray: Home to a Norse Chieftain in the Orkney Earldom*.

Graham-Campbell, J. and C. E. Batey (1998) *Vikings in Scotland: An Archaeological Survey*. Edinburgh: Edinburgh University Press.

Grieg, S. (1940) Viking antiquities in Scotland. In H. Shetelig (ed.), *Viking Antiquities in Great Britain and Ireland, Part II*. Oslo: Aschehoug and Co.

Harris, O. J. T., H. Cobb, C. E. Batey, J. Montgomery, J. Beaumont, H. Gray, P. Murtagh and P. Richardson (2017) Assembling places and persons: A tenth-century boat burial from Swordle Bay on the Ardnamurchan peninsula, western Scotland. *Antiquity* 91(355), 191–206.

Harrison, S. H. (2000) The Millhill burial in context. Artifact, culture, and chronology in the 'Viking West'. *Acta Archaeologica* 71 (= *Acta Archaeologica Supplementa* 2), 65–78.

Harrison, S. H. (2007) Separated from the foaming maelstrom: Landscapes of Insular 'Viking' burial. In S. Semple and H. Williams (eds), *Anglo-Saxon Studies in Archaeology and History 14: Early Medieval Mortuary Practices*. Oxford: Oxford University School of Archaeology, 173–82.

Harrison, S. H. (2015) 'Warrior graves'? The weapon burial rite in Viking Age Britain and Ireland. In J. H. Barrett and S. J. Gibbons (eds), *Maritime Societies of the Viking and Medieval World*. Society for Medieval Archaeology Monograph 37. Leeds: Maney, 299–319.

Harrison, S. H. and R. Ó Floinn (2014) *Viking Graves and Grave-Goods in Ireland*. Medieval Dublin Excavations 1962–81, ser. B, vol. 11. Dublin: National Museum of Ireland.

Hedges, J. W. (1987) *Bu, Gurness and the Brochs of Orkney*. BAR British Series 164, 2 vols. Oxford: British Archaeological Reports.

Kaland, S. H. H. (1993) The settlement of Westness, Rousay. In C. E. Batey, J. Jesch and C. D. Morris (eds), *The Viking Age in Caithness, Orkney and the North Atlantic*. Edinburgh: Edinburgh University Press, 308–17.

MacGregor, G. (2009) Changing people, changing landscapes: Excavations at the Carrick, Midross, Loch Lomond. *Historic Argyll*, 8–13.

McLeod, S. (2014) A traveller's end? – a reconsideration of a Viking-Age burial at Carronbridge, Dumfriesshire. *Transactions of the Dumfries and Galloway Natural History and Antiquarian Society* 88, 13–20.

McLeod, S. (2015a) *Viking Burials in Scotland: Landscape and Burials in the Viking Age*. https://vikingfuneralscapes.wordpress.com/ [Last viewed: 26 July 2021].

McLeod, S. (2015b) 'Ardvonrig', Isle of Barra: An appraisal of the location of a Scandinavian accompanied burial. *Proceedings of the Society of Antiquaries of Scotland* 145, 299–305.

McLeod, S. (2015c) Legitimation through association? Scandinavian accompanied burials and prehistoric monuments in Orkney. *Journal of the North Atlantic* 28, 1–15.

Margaryan, A. et al. (2020) Population genomics of the Viking world. *Nature* (September 17, 2020) 585(7825), 390–6 (with 'Supplementary Information').

Montgomery, J., V. Grimes, J. Buckberry, J. A. Evans, M. P. Richards and J. H. Barrett (2014) Finding Vikings with isotopic analysis: The view from wet and windy islands. *Journal of the North Atlantic* Special Volume 7, *Viking Settlers of the North Atlantic: An Isotopic Approach*, 54–70.

Morris, C. D. (1989) *The Birsay Bay Project Volume 1: Coastal Sites beside the Brough Road, Birsay, Orkney Excavations 1976–82*. Department of Archaeology Monograph 1. Durham: Department of Archaeology, University of Durham.

Owen, O. and M. Dalland (1999) *Scar: A Viking Boat Burial on Sanday, Orkney*. East Linton: Tuckwell Press.

Owen, O. and R. Welander (1995) A traveller's end? – an associated group of Early Historic artefacts from Carronbridge, Dumfries and Galloway. *Proceedings of the Society of Antiquaries of Scotland* 125, 753–70.

Paterson, C. (2001) Insular belt-fittings from the pagan Norse graves of Scotland: A reappraisal in the light of scientific and stylistic analysis. In M. Redknap, N. Edwards, S. Youngs, A. Lane and J. Knight (eds), *Pattern and Purpose in*

Insular Art: Proceedings of the Fourth International Conference on Insular Art held at the National Museum and Gallery, Cardiff, 3–6 September 1998. Oxford: Oxbow Books, 125–39.

Paterson, C. and C. Stanford (2020) Power dressing in the Irish Sea area: An interesting group of Hiberno-Scandinavian strap-fittings. In C. Thickpenny, K. Forsyth, J. Geddes and K. Mathis (eds), *Peopling Insular Art: Practice, Performance, Perception (Proceedings of the Eighth International Conference on Insular Art, Glasgow 2017)*. Oxford: Oxbow Books, 87–98.

Petersen, J. (1919) *De norske vikingesverd*. Kristiania, Videnskapsselkskapets Skrifter II, Hist.-filos. Klasse 1919, 1.

Price, N. (2002) *The Viking Way: Religion and War in Late Iron Age Scandinavia*. AUN 31. Uppsala: Department of Archaeology and Ancient History, Uppsala University.

Price, N. (2010) Passing into poetry: Viking-Age mortuary drama and the origins of Norse mythology. *Medieval Archaeology* 54, 123–56.

Price, N. (2019) *The Viking Way: Magic and Mind in Late Iron Age Scandinavia*. Oxford: Oxbow Books.

Ritchie, A. (1977) Excavation of Pictish and Viking-age farmsteads at Buckquoy, Orkney. *Proceedings of the Society of Antiquaries of Scotland* 108, 174–227.

Sellevold, B. J. (1999) *Picts and Vikings at Westness: Anthropological Investigations of the Skeletal Material from the Cemetery at Westness, Rousay, Orkney Islands*. NIKU Scientific Report 10. Oslo: Norwegian Institute for Cultural Heritage Research.

Sellevold, B. J. (2010) Life and death among the Picts and Vikings at Westness. In J. Sheehan and D. Ó Corráin (eds), *The Viking Age: Ireland and the West. Papers from the Proceedings of the Fifteenth Viking Congress, Cork, 18–27 August 2005*. Dublin: Four Courts Press, 369–79.

Shetelig, H. (1945) The Viking graves in Great Britain and Ireland. *Acta Archaeologica* 16, 1–55.

Shetelig, H. (1954) The Viking graves. In H. Shetelig (ed.), *Viking Antiquities in Great Britain and Ireland: Viking Settlers in Relation to their Old and New Countries, Part VI*. Oslo: Aschehoug and Co., 67–111.

Thorsteinsson, A. (1968) The Viking burial place at Pierowall, Westray, Orkney. In B. Niclasen (ed.), *Proceedings of the Fifth Viking Congress, Tórshavn, July 1965*. Tórshavn: Føroya Fróðskaparfelag, 150–73.

Welander, R. D. E., C. E. Batey and T. G. Cowie (1987) A Viking burial from Kneep, Uig, Isle of Lewis. *Proceedings of the Society of Antiquaries of Scotland* 117, 147–74.

Chapter 25

Swordle Bay, Ardnamurchan: A Viking Boat Burial

Colleen E. Batey

In the farthest reaches of the Western Scottish mainland, a fully-furnished Viking boat burial (Figure 25.1) was excavated in 2011 as part of the Ardnamurchan Transitions Project (Harris et al. 2012). Although the Western Isles are rich in Viking burial remains, the adjacent mainland has mere hints of contemporary activity. A study of the place-names by Anne Bankier (2006) has demonstrated a Norse presence in the immediate area and indeed the place-name of the burial location, Swordle, is ON in origin (ON *svör r* (m), gen *svar ar*, 'svard/turf' + *dalr*, 'valley'= turf valley: Simon Taylor, pers. comm.). This is, however, the first tangible archaeological evidence for the period in the area.

A low-lying cairn, with edges defined by earth-fast stones and oriented in a west-south-west–east-north-east direction, was identified on an old beach line in close proximity to a massive Neolithic burial mound (Claidh Aindreis) (Harris et al. 2012: 334). The water-worn boulders of the cairn, 5.1m x 1.6m in extent, had collapsed inwards onto a small wooden boat, surviving as an impression with 213 in situ iron rivets and containing several distinctive Viking grave goods. The detailed excavation of the small boat, roughly 5m in length, is described elsewhere (Harris et al. 2012). It is clear there was no defined inner chamber within the boat, as found at both Westness (Kaland 1993: fig. 17.7) and Scar (Owen and Dalland 1999: 27, fig. 23), and that the items had been placed within the grave not only at various stages of the burial process, but also throughout the western and central area of the vessel itself.

Due to the acidic soil, two molars were the only surviving human remains, but enough to suggest the body was laid with its head to the west end of the boat. Strontium and lead isotope analysis of the teeth suggests a childhood with a maritime diet spent a distance away from the burial location, with eastern Ireland, north-eastern mainland Scotland, Norway and Sweden all contenders (fully discussed by Janet Montgomery in Harris et al. 2017: 198–200 and accompanying material).

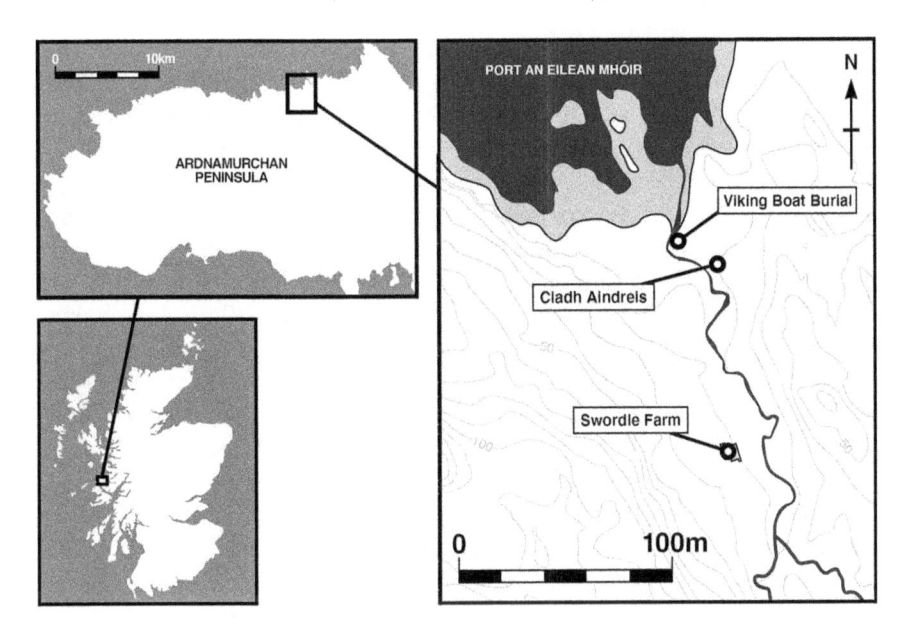

Figure 25.1 Location map of the Swordle burial, Ardnamurchan. Redrawn from the original by Ardnamurchan Transitions Project by Walter Newton.

The significance of the burial, in addition to its location, lies in the rich range of grave goods accompanying the body. Much has been written about the performative nature of burial practice, and the rite of boat burial has been subject to considerable discussion. A rite which is identified throughout most of the Viking world, and well represented in Scotland and the Isles at sites such as Kiloran Bay, Colonsay (Anderson 1907: 443–9), Scar (Owen and Dalland 1999) and Westness (Kaland 1993), it is brought more sharply into focus in the writings of Ibn Fadlān and his travels among the Volga Rus' (Montgomery 2000) and amplified in the discussions of the mortuary theatre by Price (2010), with extended activities taking place around the deposition. The later placement in the burial at Swordle of the shield and the spearhead, above the infilling cairn material defined by a kerb which lay over the body and other grave goods, is part of this ritualisation. The spearhead (Petersen Type E: Petersen 1919: 26–8) had been deliberately broken before deposition and the shield boss had damage on its upper surface and was distorted along the flange, potentially occurring when torn from the shield board (which did not survive in this burial environment). The boss is of the domical type Rygh 562 (Rygh 1885) dating to the 9th to 10th century (Petersen 1919: 47) and a type commonly found in Scottish Viking graves such as Balnakeil (Batey and Paterson 2013: 641–2).

The rest of the assemblage, positioned around the body, is exceptional in Scottish terms (these are discussed in more detail by Batey in Harris et al. 2017: 194–8). The wide range of inclusions provides a variety seldom recovered: a ladle with hammer and tongs in the scale pan, a ringed-pin, a drinking horn mount, a whetstone, flint strike-a-lights, a sickle, a sword and an axe (see Harris et al. 2017, fig. 5 for distribution of the main finds in the grave). The ladle was placed at the west end of the burial, presumably near the head, and had a pan of 270mm diameter with an impressive and complete handle of 500mm length with its terminal hook. While examples are known from Scandinavia, in a Scottish context the Kiloran Bay find is the closest geographically and is defined, on the basis of its flattened base, as a probable saucepan with a handle at least 140mm in length (Paterson, pers. comm.). The hammer and tongs were accompanied in the scale pan with organic material, potentially foodstuffs (Greaves 2011). Placed on or near the body, a knobbed ringed-pin of Irish origin may have held a garment in place. To one side of the head lay a drinking horn, represented by the copper alloy rim/mount. Both items have potentially Insular origins (Paterson et al. 2014: 149–51), although such rims have been identified in Norwegian contexts. Placed more centrally within the grave, potentially either under or on the body, is the whetstone of Norwegian schist, flint strike-a-lights and iron sickle. Sickles are known from several Scottish graves (such as Westness and Pierowall, illustrated in Graham-Campbell and Batey 1998, figs 7.10 and 7.11) and also from the western Norwegian coast (Petersen 1951: 515–16).

On the left-hand side of the body, along the edge of the boat, lay the sword. This is of particular interest because of the good preservation of the hilt, which has silver and copper wire decoration. The typology of the sword hilt is somewhat challenging, as it seems to be an amalgam of styles (Harris et al. 2017: 196), potentially any of Petersen Types K, P or O; this remains subject to debate. What is now clearer than in the paper of 2017 is the treatment of the blade and origins of its distortion. The blade appears bent into a shallow S-form with its tip removed, and was suggested by Batey as having been ritually damaged prior to burial. The reviewer pointed out, quite reasonably, that if indeed the leather scabbard remained in place among the corrosion products (which had textile materials as well), such distortion was unlikely to have been associated with the burial, rather a feature of post-depositional pressures. The displacement of the tip of the sword was clear, but only during the detailed illustrative process by Alan Braby did more interpretative detail become obvious. The tip section was not totally missing, but placed with a length of the lower blade along a higher point on the blade. It was this transposition that gave the shallow S-shaped appearance rather than a bending of the blade itself, but was indeed related to destruction of the

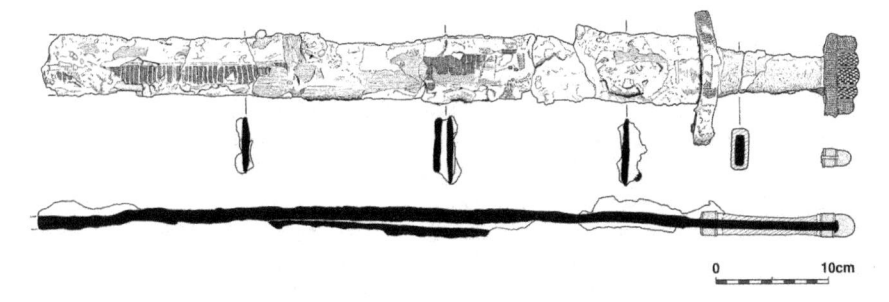

Figure 25.2 Line drawing of the sword from the burial, indicating position of repositioned tip. Courtesy of Ardnamurchan Transitions Project, drawing by Alan Braby.

weapon prior to burial (Figure 25.2). This breakage at the tip pre-deposition is noted also from Balnakeil in Sutherland (Batey and Paterson 2013: 637). Finally, located in the east of the burial, in the region of the feet, lay a broad-bladed axe that had traces of the wooden hafting preserved in the corrosion products.

Where dating permits in the assemblage, it is of necessity based on typological studies, and there is a concurrence in the late 9th to 10th century range. This does not take into account object biographies of each of the distinctive elements; it is, for example, unclear how many generations it may have been between the creation of the sword and its destruction and committal to the ground. Setting this issue aside, however, there are a number of significant points that can be headlined: the grave is both exceptionally rich in its contents and uniquely located geographically. The evidence indicates continuity of the burial landscape here, with the proximity of two prehistoric burial mounds, one of which had a secondary disturbance including a Viking-Age bead (Batey 2016: 44), and the burial itself shows evidence of the burial sequence and potential performative scene. Maritime connections both north and south are indicated, with Insular items in the assemblage and strontium/lead indications of a Scandinavian or eastern Scottish origin of the individual. Offshore movement would have been a common sight in the Viking Age and small rowing boats of this type would have been part of a flotilla of larger, more robust vessels, more suited to the sea conditions of the route between Norway and the Irish Sea. Burial in such smaller vessels is common in Scandinavian Scotland and represents a considerable investiture of resources in keeping with the rest of the artefact assemblage. This was a landscape united by maritime activity rather than a land-based focus, and this is clearly demonstrated at this, the most westerly point of mainland Scotland.

References

Anderson, J. (1907) Notice of bronze brooches ... with a description ... of a ship-burial of the Viking time at Kiloran Bay, Colonsay. *Proceedings of the Society of Antiquaries of Scotland* 41 (1906–7), 437–50.

Bankier, A. (2006) *Norse Place-names in Western Argyll*. Unpublished MLitt dissertation, University of Glasgow.

Batey, C. E. (2016) Viking burials in Scotland: Two 'new' boat burial finds. In V. E. Turner, O. A. Owen and D. J. Waugh (eds), *Shetland and the Viking World: Proceedings of the 17th Viking Congress*. Lerwick: Shetland Heritage, 39–45.

Batey, C. E. and C. Paterson (2013) A Viking burial at Balnakeil, Sutherland. In A. Reynolds and L. Webster (eds), *Early Medieval Art and Archaeology in the Northern World, Studies in Honour of James Graham-Campbell*. Leiden: Brill, 631–62.

Graham-Campbell, J. and C. E. Batey (1998) *Vikings in Scotland: An Archaeological Survey*. Edinburgh: Edinburgh University Press.

Greaves, P. (2011) Appendix six: Conservation report. In O. J. T. Harris, H. Cobb, H. Gray and P. Richardson, *Viking Boat Burial, Swordle Bay, Ardnamurchan: Season Six, 2011: Archaeological Excavations Data Structure Report (Ardnamurchan Transitions Report Number 17)*. Unpublished report prepared for the Ardnamurchan Transitions Project.

Harris, O. J. T., H. Cobb, H. Gray and P. Richardson (2012) A Viking at rest: New discoveries on Ardnamurchan. *Medieval Archaeology* 56, 333–9.

Harris, O. J. T., H. Cobb, C. E. Batey, J. Montgomery, J. Beaumont, H. Gray, P. Murtagh and P. Richardson (2017) Assembling places and persons: A tenth-century Viking boat burial from Swordle Bay, on the Ardnamurchan peninsula, western Scotland. *Antiquity* 91(355), 191–206.

Kaland, S. H. H. (1993) The settlement of Westness, Rousay. In C. E. Batey, J. Jesch and C. D. Morris (eds), *The Viking Age in Caithness, Orkney and the North Atlantic*. Edinburgh: Edinburgh University Press, 308–17.

Montgomery, J. E. (2000) Ibn Fadlān and the Rūsiyyah. *Journal of Arabic and Islamic Studies* 3, 1–25.

Owen, O. and M. Dalland (1999) *Scar: A Viking Boat Burial on Sanday, Orkney*. East Linton: Tuckwell Press.

Paterson, C., A. J. Parsons, R. M. Newman, J. Johnson and C. Howard Davis (2014) *Shadows in the Sand: Excavation of a Viking Age Cemetery at Cumwhitton, Cumbria*. Lancaster Imprint 22. Lancaster: Oxford Archaeology North.

Petersen, J. (1919) *De norske vikingesverd. En typologiskk-kronologisk studie over vikingetidens vaaben*. Kristiania: Jacob Dybwab.

Petersen, J. (1951) *Vikingetidens Redskaper*. Oslo: Det Norske Videnskaps-Akademi.

Price, N. (2010) Passing into poetry: Viking-Age mortuary drama and the origins of Norse mythology. *Medieval Archaeology* 54, 123–56.

Rygh, O. (1885) *Norske Oldsager*. Christiania: A Cammermeyer.

Chapter 26

Carrick, Mid Ross: A Viking Cemetery on Loch Lomond

Colleen E. Batey

Excavations were undertaken by GUARD (Glasgow University) between 2003 and 2005 in advance of a leisure development on the western shore of Loch Lomond in the Central Lowlands of Scotland (MacGregor et al. forthcoming) (Figure 26.1). As part of the multi-period occupation of the loch-side, a substantial penannular ring-ditch (inner diameter a maximum 45m by 4m) with primary infilling dated to the 8th to 9th centuries was identified enclosing several burials (Batey forthcoming). Among these there are potentially fourteen Viking-Age burials, six with grave goods and eight related by orientation, the presence of single nails or radiocarbon dates. These are spread across the whole interior but are defined within an inner perimeter of postholes to the north-west, and to the south roughly clustered along the south wall of a post and trench-built structure, oriented east–west, and here identified as a 10th-century chapel. Beyond the ring-ditch, an antiquarian find of Viking weapons is noted from 1851 with an additional shield boss of Viking type recovered from the upper layers of the ring-ditch fill, assumed to have been redeposited by later agricultural activity.

An early discovery: Boiden

In 1851, a mound located at Boiden on the west side of Loch Lomond was disturbed and found to include a bent sword with lower and upper guard (but lacking the pommel), a dented domical shield boss and a spearhead. No mention was made of a skeleton. The finds are now lost and are only known from three 19th-century illustrations (Ms 498 Society of Antiquaries of Scotland) drawn by Hope J. Stewart (Anderson 1874: 569). Identified as a cenotaph, due to the lack of human remains (Graham-Campbell and Batey 1998: 99, 144), it is clear from recent work that local ground conditions do not permit bone survival.

The original report by Stewart notes the finds were recovered from the 'top of a mound where a large cairn had formerly stood . . . all lying together within a space of 1½ or 2 feet square' (Stewart 1854: 144).

314 Colleen E. Batey

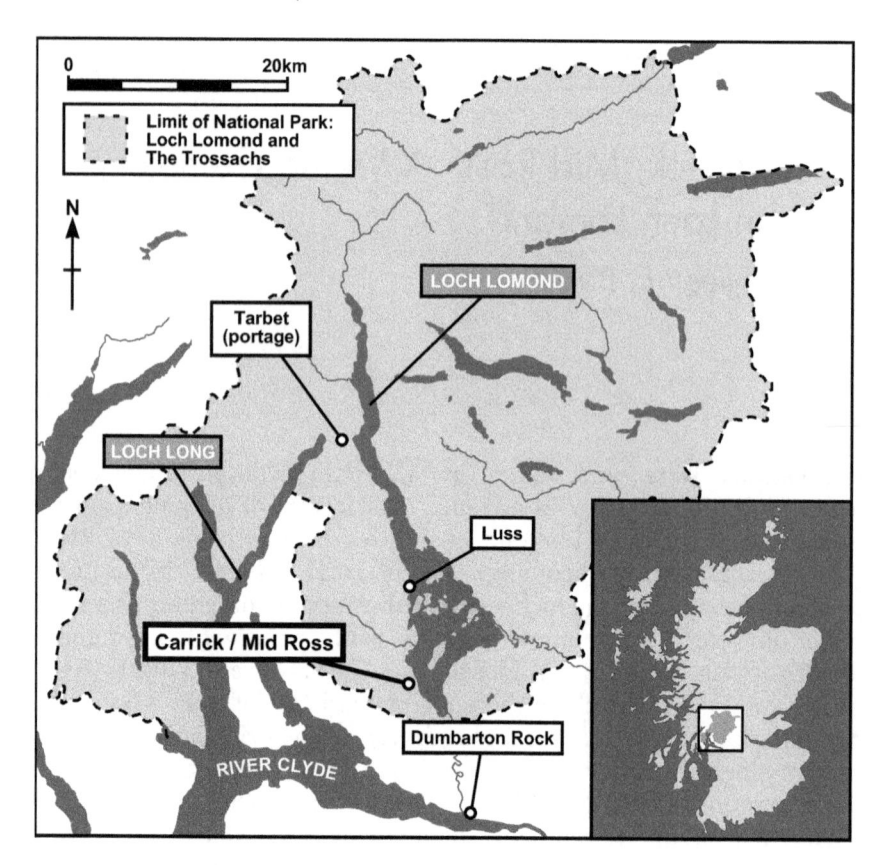

Figure 26.1 Location of Carrick, Mid Ross, Loch Lomondside. Redrawn by Walter Newton and amended by David Battley.

The sword suggests a 9th-century type, originally with a pommel of triangular form (such as Kilmainham WK42, Harrison and O'Floinn 2014: 398; Petersen type H) or 3/5 lobate form (ibid. W78, 393; Petersen type K). It is similar to the cross guard discovered in excavations at Clyde Rock, Dumbarton (Alcock and Alcock 1990: 115, illus. 14, SF 26). From the drawing it is also clear that the upper part of the scabbard survived above the area where the blade has been deliberately bent. There are several examples of bent or 'killed' swords in Scandinavia, but the rite is less commonly identified in the British Isles (for example, Swordle Bay, Ardnamurchan [Batey, previous chapter]). The spearhead is of a type which is also known from Viking-Age contexts (such as Ballinderry Crannog, illus. Peirce 2002: 64). The complete domical shield boss has slight damage to its flange and a single slash across the centre of the boss. In form it closely resembles a common Viking-Age type, such as at Balnakeil, Sutherland (Batey and Paterson 2012: 641–2).

The Mid Ross group

A damaged shield boss was recovered within the upper ring-ditch fill, suggesting a disturbed second male grave. It is of smaller diameter, slightly more pointed, with a broad flange similar in type to that recovered from Lamlash on Arran (NMS IL 726) and likely an Irish Sea variant. The only surviving in situ nail suggests a shield board of approximately 7.5mm thickness. Of significance is the survival of part of the flat, round-ended grip (L 131.5mm). These are rare finds; a more complete but useful parallel is from Ballinaby, Islay (Anderson 1880: 51–69; illustrated in Graham-Campbell and Batey 1998: 123, fig. 7.5). The recovery of this piece, in addition to the 1851 grave group, suggests the likelihood of a pair of weapon graves outside the ring-ditch.

The group of graves from the new excavations within the ring-ditch (Figure 26.2) comprises six burials with grave goods which are assigned to the Viking Age, and a potential further eight graves lacking grave goods. They are clearly delimited by the massive ring-ditch, which also encloses the cemetery of later east–west-oriented burials.

Graves with grave goods

Group 1: West

This western group comprises three graves, in addition to four others which share alignment and are grouped together here due to stratigraphical and dating considerations (these are graves 0510088, 0510280, 0510276 and 0510480).

0510270

The orientation of the grave cut is roughly east–west, which differs from those to its south but is more similar to those associated grave cuts to the north (0510088 and 0510280). The single find is a child-sized shale arm-ring of D-shaped section.

0511190/0511191

This grave cut is adjacent to grave 0510248 to its immediate east and on the same orientation, roughly north-east to south-west. The finds recovered include a whetstone of Scandinavian origin, a knife blade with textiles, and an iron rod with wood at each end and a slotted tool which included a small fragment of an Anglo-Saxon penny (Bateson, pers. comm.) within its corrosion. With comparisons for the slotted tool in Norse contexts (such as Brough of Birsay, Curle 1982: ill. 27, 44)

316 Colleen E. Batey

and a further, perforated, Anglo-Saxon coin elsewhere among the grave assemblages, this small group is likely to be of the Viking Age.

0510248

This grave cut, oriented roughly north-east to south-west, included grave goods and a few fragments of human bone. A lignite arm-ring and a shale finger-ring were recovered, as well as three non-conjoining

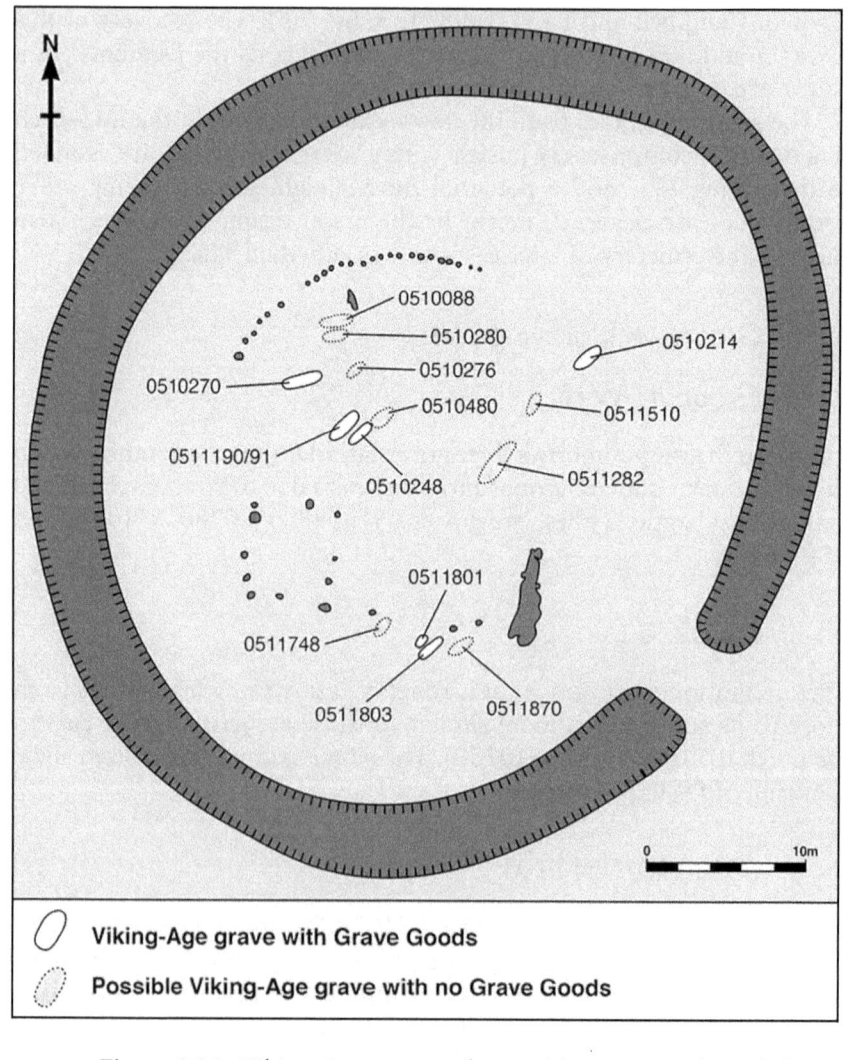

Figure 26.2 Viking-Age graves, those with grave goods and those without, within the penannular ring-ditch. Redrawn by Walter Newton from an original by GUARD.

and worn fragments of an S-twisted copper alloy wire in the bottom fill of the grave. This combination is unusual, although several single armrings of jet/lignite/shale have been noted and discussed by Hunter (2008: table 2, 113–15).

The adjacent grave cut 0510480 which lies immediately to its northeast includes in its uppermost layer a single blue glass bead of Viking type which may have been displaced from grave 0510248.

Group 2: East

This linear group of three burials share a north-east to south-west orientation, two of which have been assigned a possible Viking-Age date on the basis of C_{14} dating (0511510 and 0511282) and one which included a knife (0510214).

0510214

A single knife of Viking-Age type was recovered from the grave, having originally been placed near the waist. This is interpreted as a token grave good and is mirrored in grave 0511803 in Group 3.

Group 3: South

This group is separated from the previous two groups by approximately 10m. These graves form a discrete cluster of two graves with goods (0511801 and 0511803) and a further two without (0511748 and 0511870), oriented roughly north-east to south-west. All respect the footprint of the timber structure to their north, but none share the orientation of that structure, which is essentially east–west and identified here as a chapel.

0511801

This grave cut has no skeletal material surviving, but contains an incomplete, worn and perforated Anglo-Saxon silver penny of Aethelred I of Wessex (865/6–871), dated by Bateson to the last quarter of the 9th century. Bateson notes that this is the first recorded coin of Aethelred I of Wessex from Scotland. Stevenson has conveniently summarised other Scottish coins, pierced and non-pierced (1986: 339).

0511803

Located adjacent to 0511801 and with the common orientation of north-east to south-west, this grave included teeth fragments and indeterminate iron fragments. However, in the upper part of the burial, possibly at the right-hand side of the thigh, an intact iron knife blade was recovered.

9th/10th-century graves lacking grave goods

This secondary group of graves, identified on the basis of a relatively consistent orientation of north-east to south-west, is distinguished from the later cemetery of predominantly east–west orientation. It is comprised of grave-sized cuts without human remains, and which in some cases contain single iron nails, possibly the remains of a simple grave marker securing two planks in cross form. These could represent Christian Norse burials, as distinguished at Newark Bay in Orkney (see, for example, Barrett et al. 2000).

Group 1

Grave cuts 0510088 and 0510280 are located to the farthest north of the group. Grave 0510276 includes a single nail, as does grave 0510480 immediately to its south, which also contains a redeposited glass bead.

Group 2

Two graves fall within this group: 0511510 shares the north-east to south-west orientation with the large grave cut of 0511282, which lies to its south-west and is itself cut by several later graves. This rare inter-cutting suggests a lack of surviving grave markers at the time.

Group 3

This lies to the south of the overall complex. Both graves in this category, 0511748 and 0510870, are assigned on the basis of orientation alone.

There is a lack of surviving skeletal material, but the range of artefacts would be consistent with both male and female presence. There are individual knives which have been found in non-grave contexts here, which may suggest craft-working or small-scale industrial activity in the vicinity, but the recovery of an arm-ring fragment in a posthole, as well as a perforated shale roughout for an arm-ring from the ditch fill, suggests that such items had a wider currency. Whether there was contemporary settlement in the immediate vicinity of the graves is unknown, but likely indicated by a saga reference to the destruction of relatively dense settlement in the Loch Lomond district in the mid-13th century (*Hakon's Saga*, Anderson 1990: 625).

The potential contemporaneity of Viking-Age graves with grave goods and without can be matched at two well-known Scottish sites: Westness, Rousay, Orkney (Kaland 1993; Sellevold 1999: fig. 2 and table 1) and Cnip/Bhaltos, Isle of Lewis (Welander et al. 1987; Dunwell et al. 1995). Montgomery has identified a non-mainland Scandinavian origin for the individuals at Cnip despite Grave A having a rich and diagnostic assemblage of grave goods (Welander et al. 1987; Montgomery and Evans 2006). This is of significance as the Mid Ross graves tell little of the origin of the buried individuals.

The combination of a pierced coin and C_{14} dates provide an indication of late 9th- to 10th-century dating for these graves with goods. The Mid Ross assemblage demonstrates wider connections for this population as it contains items both potentially relatively local in origin – especially the arm-rings and finger-ring – and more distant, such as the weaponry and whetstone from Scandinavia and Anglo-Saxon coins.

The marking of graves

Viking-Age graves marked by cairns, as at Boiden, are rare in the Scottish record (Graham-Campbell and Batey 1998: 145–6). The marking of graves by posts is under-represented in the archaeological record as a whole, but at this site it is likely that other graves were marked, as only in a single case (0511282) are there indications of serious overlapping of grave cuts.

Discussion: Regional background

There has been nothing directly comparable to this number of graves in Lowland Scotland. Viking-Age activity is documented at Clyde Rock, Dumbarton, just to the south of Loch Lomond, in 871 (*Annals of Ulster*, Anderson 1990: 301), with a sword pommel and lead weight of Irish type (Alcock and Alcock 1990: illus. 14) providing archaeological support. To the north of the Mid Ross area, the lone find of a hogback stone at Luss (Lang 1974: 217–18) lies in isolation to the north of the major concentration of hogbacks on the River Clyde at Govan. Both the burials and the hogback may owe much to the same north–south routeway which passed along the west side of Loch Lomond, and linked in to the portage route between Loch Long and Loch Lomond at Tarbet, which was used later by the Norwegian fleet in 1263 (*Hakon's Saga*, Anderson 1990: 625). The significance of this newly identified focus with wider connections is considerable in the context of Lowland Scotland and indeed in Scotland as a whole.

References

Alcock, L. and E. A. Alcock (1990) Reconnaissance excavations on Early Historic fortifications and other royal sites in Scotland, 1974–84: 4, Excavations at Alt Clut, Clyde Rock, Strathclyde, 1974–5. *Proceedings of the Society of Antiquaries of Scotland* 120, 95–149.

Anderson, A. O. (1990) *Early Sources of Scottish History AD 500–1286*. Collected and translated by A. O. Anderson, edited by M. Anderson. Vol. 2. Stamford: Paul Watkins.

Anderson, J. (1874) Notes on the relics of the Viking Period of the Northmen in Scotland, illustrated by specimens in the Museum. *Proceedings of the Society of Antiquaries of Scotland* 10 (1872–4), 536–94.

Barrett, J. H., R. P. Beukens and D. R. Brothwell (2000) Radiocarbon dating and marine reservoir correction of Viking Age Christian burials from Orkney. *Antiquity* 74, 537–43.

Batey, C. E. and C. Paterson (2012) A Viking Burial at Balnakeil, Sutherland. In L. Webster and A. Reynolds (eds), *Early Medieval Art and Archaeology in the Northern World: Studies in Honour of James Graham-Campbell*. Leiden: Brill Academic Publishing, 631–59.

Batey, C. E. (Forthcoming) Mid Ross: A Viking Age cemetery. In G. MacGregor, A. Becket, D. M. Maguire, C. Rennie and D. Sneddon, *Life and Death on the Bonnie Banks: Nine Thousand Years at the Carrick, Midross, Loch Lomond*. Edinburgh: Society of Antiquaries of Scotland Monograph.

Curle, C. L. (1982) *Pictish and Norse Finds from the Brough of Birsay 1934–74*. Society of Antiquaries of Scotland Monograph Series No. 1. Edinburgh: Society of Antiquaries of Scotland.

Dunwell, A. J., T. G. Cowie, M. F. Bruce, T. Neighbour and A. R. Rees (1995) A Viking Age cemetery at Cnip, Uig, Isle of Lewis. *Proceedings of the Society of Antiquaries of Scotland* 125, 719–52.

Graham-Campbell, J. and C. E. Batey (1998) *Vikings in Scotland: An Archaeological Survey*. Edinburgh: Edinburgh University Press.

Harrison, S. H. and R. Ó Floinn (2014) *Viking Graves and Grave-Goods in Ireland*. Medieval Dublin Excavations 1962–81, Series B vol. 11. Dublin: National Museum of Ireland.

Hunter, F. (2008) Jet and related materials in Viking Scotland. *Medieval Archaeology* 52, 103–18.

Kaland, S. H. H. (1993) The settlement of Westness, Rousay. In C. E. Batey, J. Jesch and C. D. Morris (eds), *The Viking Age in Caithness, Orkney and the North Atlantic*. Edinburgh: Edinburgh University Press, 308–17.

Lang, J. (1974) Hogback monuments in Scotland. *Proceedings of the Society of Antiquaries of Scotland* 105 (1972–4), 206–35.

MacGregor, G., A. Becket, D. M. Maguire, C. Rennie and D. Sneddon (Forthcoming) *Life and Death on the Bonnie Banks: Nine Thousand Years at the Carrick, Midross, Loch Lomond*. Edinburgh: Society of Antiquaries of Scotland Monograph.

Montgomery, J. and J. A. Evans (2006) Immigrants on the Isle of Lewis – combining traditional funerary and modern isotope evidence to investigate social differentiation, migration and dietary change in the Outer Hebrides

of Scotland. In R. Gowland and C. Knüsel (eds), *Social Archaeology of Funerary Remains*. Oxford: Oxbow Books, 122–42.
Peirce, I. (2002) *Swords of the Viking Age*. Woodbridge, Suffolk: Boydell Press.
Sellevold, B. J. (1999) *Picts and Vikings at Westness. Anthropological Investigations of the Skeletal Material from the Cemetery at Westness, Rousay, Orkney Islands*. NIKU Norsk institutt for kulturminneforskning Scientific Report 10. Trondheim: NINA/NIKU.
Stevenson, R. B. K. (1986) The Anglo-Saxon silver penny and its context, 339–41. In C. D. Morris and N. Emery, The chapel and enclosure on the Brough of Deerness, Orkney: Survey and excavations, 1975–7. *Proceedings of the Society of Antiquaries of Scotland* 116, 301–74.
Stewart, J. H. (1854) Notice of the discovery of some ancient arms and armour, near Glenfruin, on the Estate of Sir James Colquhoun of Luss, Baronet. *Proceedings of the Society of Antiquaries of Scotland* I (1851–4), 142–5.
Welander, R. D. E., C. Batey and T. G. Cowie (1987) A Viking burial from Kneep, Uig, Isle of Lewis. *Proceedings of the Society of Antiquaries of Scotland* 117, 149–74.

Afterword: Major Advances and Future Directions

Colleen E. Batey and James Graham-Campbell

Already by the time our volume *Vikings in Scotland: An Archaeological Survey* came to fruition in 1998, it was becoming clear that even two authors could not fully encompass the range of developing evidence. Scientific endeavours, new methodologies and the explosion of environmental data, with burgeoning analysis, were beginning to dominate research agendas beyond our specialisms. During the succeeding decades, these aspects have developed into commonly applied approaches, complementing the study of antiquarian sources, place-names and historical documentation. Taken together, all these aspects provide a unique suite of interdisciplinary tools. The contents of this current – and most timely – volume highlight both the richness of the evidence and the results of a collegiate approach within our discipline as a whole.

Several different approaches are already enabling a much fuller – and potentially more accurate – understanding of the Scandinavians in Scotland. In combination with more commonly applied methods, new approaches and new scientific methodologies are already integrated, and all are providing a much wider platform for discussion. Commencing with a reassessment of accepted narratives, a number of issues can be addressed. Making use of new refinements in C_{14} determinations, artefactual studies (for example, Ashby on combs, this volume) and isotopic/aDNA studies, it is becoming more likely that we will be able to establish more clearly the dating of the arrival of the Vikings on our shores, as well as the nature of that arrival and interaction between native and incoming populations. The thorny issue of whether this was peaceful or violent is less commonly dictating the agenda now, being replaced with a more nuanced understanding of regional variations and continuing regimes of landscape exploitation (see, for example, Dockrill and Bond, and Macniven, this volume). The nature of this potential population replacement is informed through isotopic examination where the origin of individuals can be interrogated. The consideration of ethnic identities and their expression in newly settled areas has fascinating potential.

Major datasets ripe for reinterpretation and amplification include little-understood early settlement excavations, markedly Jarlshof in Shetland. As an oft-cited archaeological sequence of developing farmsteads, the issues with the stratigraphy and associated (or otherwise) artefact groups have cast a long shadow over the interpretation of many artefact assemblages from broadly contemporary sites. Items are uncritically considered to be securely dated in the Jarlshof sequence and are cited as datable parallels, when in fact the stratigraphical sequence is problematic. New study of this site is ongoing (for example, Dockrill et al. 2005; Graham-Campbell and Henderson 2019), following that already undertaken for Freswick Links in Caithness (Batey 1987) and more recently by Morris (this volume; 2021) for the Brough of Birsay, Orkney. This chronological refinement has the potential to revolutionise artefact dating for Viking-Age Scotland.

The second major dataset which is being reviewed (see this volume, Graham-Campbell, Paterson and Harrison) is that of the pagan graves. Combining the study of valuable antiquarian records, stray finds and museum collections (chiefly NMS) with isotopic analysis, this will provide for the first time since the 1930s (Brøgger 1930; Grieg 1940) an expanded and critically assessed record of the regional grave evidence and outline some of the issues of ethnicity in identifying apparently Norse assemblages with individuals of non-Scandinavian origins. Foremost in this area of scientific development are Janet Montgomery and colleagues whose publications are widely available (for example, Montgomery et al. 2014).

Expanding the narrative of Viking Scotland beyond the conventionally defined areas of presence and of impact is an important direction to continue to explore. More recent grave discoveries shed light on locations not previously included in these main discussions, for example Ardnamurchan in the west and the cemetery at Carrick, Loch Lomond in Lowland Scotland (see Batey, this volume). This broadening of regional evidence is to be mirrored in the pulling together of settlement/market presence, as for example in the north-east of Scotland where a probable market-site at Clarkly Hill, Aberdeenshire, has been identified by Stanford (2012), and in the south-west at Luce Sands, in Galloway, recently discussed by Griffiths (2014: 6–8). Recent study of the evidence from Iona, traditionally related only to raiding activity, now has a more wide-ranging narrative of Norse involvement (Campbell et al. 2019; Campbell and Maldonado 2020). The political landscape of Viking Scotland is becoming increasingly addressed, and the work in relation to *thing*-sites of Whyte on Mull (this volume), of Sanmark in Orkney (this volume) and of O'Grady at Dingwall in Highland (O'Grady et al. 2016) is important in this discussion.

A little-understood area of landscape research, crucial in the Norse period, lies in the identification of waterways and harbours which must have played a major role in daily life. The suggestion of the role of the Great Glen near Inverness was an early exemplar of such considerations (Crawford 1987: 22; 2013: 119), more recently amplified in Orkney by Bates et al. (2020), where place-name study combined with geophysical work has revealed a water route from Birsay, in the north-west of Orkney Mainland, to Scapa Flow, which Batey believes may have been in part related to access to a *thing*-site at Maes Howe in central Mainland. In the Western Isles, the work of Martin on the harbour at Rubh' an Dunain on Skye (Martin 2009), by Petre at Dun Ara on Mull (Petre 2020) and the study by Pollard et al. on Orkney's early harbours (Pollard, Gibson and Littlewood 2016) complement our understanding of activities on land.

Two further areas of study should be highlighted here as part of the research agenda going forward. Major environmental recovery from Norse settlement sites, particularly Late Norse, has already provided a significant insight into the rural economy and land-use practices. Some evidence for the continuation of pre-Norse farming regimes indicates a likely continuation of pre-existing estate units from the Pictish period (Bond and Dockrill 2016), as well as potential regional specialist production such as dairy production in Sanday, Orkney, as suggested from Norse levels at Pool (Serjeantson and Bond 2007: 224–5), or Freswick Links where large-scale fisheries dominated (Morris et al. 1995). Evidence from the Earl's Bu, at Orphir in Orkney, suggests that the Earls dominated both grain processing at its horizontal mill and access to choice meats for feasting. With the publication in recent years of excavation projects at Skaill, Sandwick (Griffiths et al. 2019), Quoygrew (Barrett [ed.] 2012) and Birsay in Orkney (Morris 2021), Old Scatness in Shetland (Dockrill et al. 2010), as well as at Cille Pheadair (Parker Pearson et al. 2018) and Bornais (Sharples [ed.] 2020; 2021) in the Western Isles, new evidence for both landscape and marine exploitation offers insight into farming and fishing strategies, advancing considerably what was available in 1998, when Freswick Links and Beachview, Birsay were effectively the only major players in these discussions.

The final research element which is burgeoning is that of international trade to Scandinavian Scotland: Norwegian (and Shetlandic) steatite are considered in this volume by Forster and Jones, and the mechanisms of a bullion economy with links to the Eastern Viking world are discussed by Horne, the silver hoards having been treated by Graham-Campbell in earlier years – and updated here. The results of the Galloway Hoard research project are eagerly awaited (see Goldberg, this volume). Study of the bullion economy would, however, be greatly enhanced by collective publication of the stray finds from across Scotland of the coins, hack-silver and scale-weights that have been reported to Treasure Trove. The role and nature of transnational trade mechanisms is fundamental in the Viking world, and we are starting to identify closer links, either personal or more formally trade-based, which are increasingly evidenced not only within Britain (as with York and the Danelaw), but also with Ireland and the markets of the Irish Sea.

All these elements, and others which are embryonic in development and refinement, push at the current limits of our understanding of Scandinavian Scotland. An underused research resource to add to this armoury should be further study of the collections held by some of the great estates of Scotland, where artefacts from their lands are sometimes retained (such as those of the Dukes of Argyll and the Earls of Sutherland). More urgently, the collections claimed under the Treasure Trove system, in addition to those related to the bullion economy (as noted above), need to be integrated into the overall schema and regional studies, commonly brought together by PhD students, and require fuller integration into the overall picture. The role of grey literature likewise requires further consideration.

This brief summary is incomplete, no doubt, but hopefully provides an insight into the potential of interdisciplinary studies that are a hallmark of modern archaeology and which have been instrumental in Norse Studies since before our 1998 volume. The growth in knowledge has however been exponential since that volume was published, and this is due to assiduous scholarship across the range of disciplines and the result of welcome collegiality.

September 2021

References

Barrett, J. H. (ed.) (2012) *Being an Islander: Production and Identity at Quoygrew, Orkney, AD 900–1600*. Cambridge: MacDonald Institute for Archaeological Research Monograph.

Bates, R. C., M. R. Bates, B. Crawford, A. Sanmark and J. Whittaker (2020) The Norse waterways of West Mainland Orkney, Scotland. *Journal of Wetland Archaeology* 20(1–2), 1–18.

Batey, C. E. (1987) *Freswick Links, Caithness: A Reappraisal of the Late Norse Site in its Context*. 2 vols, BAR British Series 179. Oxford: British Archaeological Reports.

Bond, J. M. and S. J. Dockrill (2016) Viking settlement and Pictish estates: New evidence from Orkney and Shetland. In V. E. Turner, O. A. Owen and D. J. Waugh (eds), *Shetland and the Viking World. Papers from the Seventeenth Viking Congress, Lerwick*. Lerwick: Shetland Heritage Publications, 7–13.

Brøgger, A. W. (1930) *Den norske bosetningen på Shetland-Orknøyene: studier og resultater*. Oslo: Skrifter utgitt av Det Norske Videnskaps-Akademi i Oslo II, Hist.-Filos. Klasse 3.

Campbell, E., C. E. Batey, G. Murray and C. Thickpenny (2019) Furnishing an Early Medieval monastery: New evidence from Iona. *Medieval Archaeology* 63(2), 298–337.

Campbell, E. and A. Maldonado (2020) A New Jerusalem 'At the Ends of the Earth': Interpreting Charles Thomas's excavations 1956–63. *The Antiquaries Journal* 100, 374–407.

Crawford, B. E. (1987) *Scandinavian Scotland*. Scotland in the Early Medieval Ages 2. Leicester: Leicester University Press.

Crawford, B. E. (2013) *The Northern Earldoms: Orkney and Caithness from AD 870 to 1470*. Edinburgh: John Donald.

Dockrill, S. J., J. M. Bond and C. E. Batey (2005) *Jarlshof, Shetland: An Economic, Environmental and Chronological Reappraisal. An Interim Report.* Compiled by L. D. Brown. Bradford Archaeological Sciences Research 14, University of Bradford.

Dockrill, S. J., J. M. Bond, V. E. Turner, L. D. Brown, D. J. Bashford, J. E. Cussans and R. A. Nicholson (2010) *Excavations at Old Scatness, Shetland Volume 1: The Pictish Village and Viking Settlement*. Lerwick: Shetland Heritage Publications.

Graham-Campbell, J. and I. Henderson, with A. Ritchie and I. G. Scott (2019) A Pictish 'serpent' incised slab from Jarlshof, Shetland. *Proceedings of the Society of Antiquaries of Scotland* 148, 189–208.

Grieg, S. (1940) Viking Antiquities in Scotland. In H. Shetelig (ed.), *Viking Antiquities in Great Britain and Ireland, Part II*. Oslo: Aschehoug & Co.

Griffiths, D. (2014) *Early Medieval Whithorn: The Irish Sea Context*. 21st Whithorn Lecture 2013, Friends of the Whithorn Trust.

Griffiths, D., J. Harrison and M. Athanson (2019) *Beside the Ocean: Coastal Landscapes at the Bay of Skaill, Marwick and Birsay Bay, Orkney. Archaeological Research 2003–2016*. Oxford and Philadelphia: Oxbow Books.

Martin, C. (2009) Rubh' an Dunain, Highland (Bracadale parish), field survey. *Discovery and Excavation in Scotland*, new vol. 10, 92–3.

Montgomery, J., V. Grimes, J. Buckberry, J. A. Evans, M. P. Richards and J. H. Barrett (2014) Finding Vikings with isotopic analysis: The view from wet and windy islands. *Journal of the North Atlantic* Special Volume 7, *Viking Settlers of the North Atlantic: An Isotopic Approach*, 54–70.

Morris, C. D. (2021) (ed. R. C. Barrowman) *The Birsay Bay Project Volume 3. The Brough of Birsay, Orkney. Investigations 1954–2014*. Oxford and Philadelphia: Oxbow Books.

Morris, C. D., C. E. Batey and D. J. Rackham (1995) *Freswick Links, Caithness. Excavation and Survey of a Norse Settlement*. Inverness and New York: Historic Scotland/Highland Libraries in association with the North Atlantic Biocultural Organisation.

O'Grady, O. J. T., D. MacDonald and S. MacDonald (2016) Re-evaluating the Scottish *Thing*: Exploring a Late Norse period and Medieval assembly mound at Dingwall. *Debating the Thing in the North: The Assembly Project II, Journal of the North Atlantic* Special Volume 8, 172–209.

Parker Pearson, M., M. Brennand, J. Mulville and H. Smith (2018) *Cille Pheadair: A Norse Farmstead and Pictish Burial Cairn in South Uist*. Sheffield Environmental and Archaeological Research Campaign in the Hebrides, vol. 7. Oxford and Philadelphia: Oxbow Books.

Petre, J. (2020) Dun Ara: A Norse-period 'harbour' in Mull? *Proceedings of the Society of Antiquaries of Scotland* 149, 145–63.

Pollard, E., J. Gibson and M. Littlewood (2016) Interpreting medieval intertidal features at Wheelie's Taing on Papa Westray, Orkney, NE Scotland. *Journal of Maritime Archaeology* 11(3), 299–322.

Serjeantson, D. and J. M. Bond (2007) Cattle and sheep husbandry at Pool: Evidence from tooth wear analysis. In J. R. Hunter with J. M. Bond and A. N. Smith, *Investigations in Sanday, Orkney. Vol. 1: Excavations at Pool, Sanday. A Multi-Period Settlement from Neolithic to Late Norse Times.* Edinburgh: Historic Scotland, 221–5.

Sharples, N. (ed.) (2020) *A Norse Settlement in the Outer Hebrides. Excavations on Mounds 2 and 2A, Bornais, South Uist.* Cardiff Studies in Archaeology. Oxford and Philadelphia: Oxbow Books.

Sharples, N. (ed.) (2021) *The Economy of a Norse Settlement in the Outer Hebrides. Excavations at Mounds 2 and 2A, Bornais, South Uist.* Cardiff Studies in Archaeology. Oxford and Philadelphia: Oxbow Books.

Stanford, C. (2012) *Clarkly Hill and the Viking Network: Artefactual Evidence for Long Distance Contact during the Viking Age at a Site near Burghead, Moray.* Unpublished undergraduate dissertation, University of Aberdeen.

Index

aDNA analysis, 12, 151, 164, 165, 171, 174–5, 292, 302, 322
Adomnán, *Life of St Columba see* St Columba
agricultural practices *see* animal bone; animal foddering; animal management; barley; beef; cereal; crop manuring; dairying; feasting; flax; grazing; hay production; infield-outfield system; milk production; oats; ploughing; rye; shieling; *see also* under various animal entries
Aikerness *see* broch, Gurness
aisle, 76–7, 80
animal bone, 77, 78, 204, 231
    cat, 38, 174–5
    cattle, 38, 45, 78, 116–17, 151, 155–7, 161–2, 174–82, 189
    dog, 116, 159–60, 161–2, 174, 175
    fish, 35, 78, 91
    horse, 116, 175
    pig, 78, 116, 159–61, 174–8
    red deer, 78, 114, 116, 157–8
    sheep/goat, 78, 161, 169, 173, 176–81
    whalebone *see* whalebone
animal foddering, 158–9, 163–4, 171
animal management, 155–9, 162–5
Annals of Inisfallen [Innisfallen], 132–3, 135
Annals of Ulster, 46, 132n, 319
annexe, 89–90, 94, 95, 232
antler, 77, 78, 175, 236
    comb *see* comb, antler; reindeer
archaeomagnetic date, 36, 88, 89, 90, 94
Ardnamurchan, Argyll, 5, 141, 297, 302, 308–12; *see also* sword, Ardnamurchan
Argisbrekka, Faroe Islands, 192

arm-ring, 227, 258, 256, 265–6, 280, 282, 315, 316, 318
ash, 35, 36, 76, 77, 82, 88, 90, 93
Ash tree, 128
assembly *see* thing (Þing)
axe, 310, 311
Aðalstræti, Iceland; Aðalstræti í Reykjavík, Iceland, 79–80, 100, 106

bake plate *see* steatite, bake plates
Ballinaby, Islay, 5, 125, 315
Balnakeil, Durness, Sutherland, 5, 302, 309, 311, 314
Balta Sound, Unst, Shetland, 86, 87
barley, 30, 34, 36, 78, 88, 90, 91, 94, 115, 116, 117, 157, 172, 235
barn, 51
Barra, 148, 303
Barvas (Barabhas), Lewis, 112–18
Battle of Torfness *see* Torfness, Battle of Torfness
Bay of Skaill, Orkney, 20, 23–4, 25, 220, 282, 324
    combs, 289, 289–91
    hoard, 5–6, 255, 257, 281, 282, 284
    see also burials, Bay of Skaill
Bayesian analysis, 24, 95, 231
beads, 17, 311
    glass, 77, 88, 116, 219, 268–9, 317, 318
    steatite, 34, 98
beef, 172, 182, 192; *see also* cattle
Benbecula, 146
Biggings, Papa Stour, Shetland, 4
bird *see also* chickens, ducks, gannet hunting, geese, shag/cormorant
    bone, 35, 78
    seabirds, 35, 78, 175
Birsay Bay, Orkney, 17–18, 171, 177, 213, 220, 303

Bishopric of Sodor, 241
boat burial, 5, 23, 277, 297, 302, 308–12; *see also* burials, Viking Age/Norse
bone
  animal *see* animal, bone
  bird *see* bird, bone
  collagen analysis, 157–63
  fish *see* animal bone, fish
  mount, 236
  needle (case), 38, 77
  pin *see* pin, bone
  toggle, 236
Bornais, South Uist, 4, 75–84
  animal husbandry, 157–9, 159–61, 162–4
  bullion, 276, 282
  combs, 77, 289, 290
  copper alloy weight, 227
  dogs, 161–2
  seabirds, 175
  strontium analysis of cattle teeth, 164
Borre style, 23
Bosta (Bostadh), Lewis, 116
Brattahlíð (Qassiarsuk), Greenland, 204
Bressay, Shetland, 66
broch, 15, 215; *see also* Picts, architecture
  Gurness (Aikerness), Orkney, 22
  Lamba Ness, Sanday, Orkney, 22
  Old Scatness, Shetland, 19–20, 29–37, 38–9, 99
  Oxtro, Birsay, 258
  The Howe, Stromness, Orkney, 17, 22
  thing-, sites on, 200, 202
  Underhoull, Unst, Shetland, 85, 91–7
  Verron, Skaill Bay, Orkney, 23
brooch, 5, 256, 269–70; *see also* silver, brooch
  penannular, 268
  quatrefoil, 269–70
  ring, 236
Brough of Birsay, Orkney, 1–2, 17–18, 21, 49, 213–22
  animal husbandry, 170, 176–7
  'Celtic' enclosure, 218–19
  dating, 219
  Late Norse longhouses, 217
  Norse earldom, 213, 220
  Pictish phase, 216, 220
  Pictish smithy, 49
  ring-money, 259
Brough of Deerness, Orkney, 3

Brough Road, Birsay, 22, 177, 180
Buckquoy (Point of), Orkney, 1, 15–17, 19, 22, 39, 63, 180, 181, 182, 214, 302
buildings and structures; *see also* barn; broch; byre; farmstead; house; kiln; longhouse; Picts, architecture; pit house; roundhouse; shieling; wheelhouse
  ancillary, 30, 82
  cellular, 15, 17, 30, 60
  pre-Viking/Iron Age, 15, 17, 19, 21, 22, 30–1, 38, 39, 60–1, 113
  passage house, 82
  Pictish, 1, 4, 15, 17, 18, 19, 30–1, 38, 39, 85, 91–2, 202, 215; *see also* Picts, architecture
  rectilinear, 15, 17, 18, 21, 104, 117
  sunken-floored, 87
  timber, 19, 36, 45, 93, 219, 317; *see also* timber
  Viking Age/Late Norse, 1, 3, 17, 20, 22, 32–5, 36, 75–83, 86–94, 114, 216, 217, 219, 230, 233
bullion, 224, 251, 262, 264–5, 266–8, 274, 276–88, 324–5; *see also* currency; silver, bullion
burials
  boat *see* boat burial
  infant, 59, 61, 63–4, 66
  isotopic research, 38, 322
  mound *see* mound
burials, Pictish/pre-Viking
  Portmahomack, Tarbart, 49
  Saevar Howe, Orkney, 18
  St Ninian's Isle, Shetland, 60–3
  Westness, Rousay, Orkney, 5, 38, 63
burials, Viking Age/Norse
  Ardnamurchan, Argyll, 308–12
  Auldhame, East Lothian, 302
  Ballinaby, Islay, 5, 125, 315
  Balnakeil, Durness, Sutherland, 5, 302, 309, 311, 314
  Bay of Skaill, Orkney, 23
  Boiden, Mid Ross, 313–14
  Broch of Gurness, Orkney, 22, 302
  Brough Road, Birsay Bay, Orkney, 22
  Buckquoy, Orkney, 17, 22, 25, 63, 302
  Carrick (Mid Ross), Loch Lomond, 313–21
  Cnip, Uig, Lewis, 5, 163, 302, 303
  Kiloran Bay, Colonsay, 5, 277

burials, Viking Age/Norse (*cont.*)
   Knowe of Moan, Harray, Orkney, 22
   Knowe of Swandro, Rousay, Orkney, 22
   Lamba Ness, Sanday, 22
   Links of Pierowall, Westray, Orkney, 5, 249, 258, 300, 303, 310
   Reay, Caithness, 5
   Saevar Howe, Orkney, 18
   St Ninian's Isle, Shetland, 59–60, 61, 62–7
   Sandwick, Orkney, 23
   Scar, Sanday, Orkney, 5, 23, 302, 308, 309
   Styes of Brough, Sanday, Orkney, 22
   The Howe, Stromness, Orkney, 22
   Westness, Rousay, Orkney, 5, 22–3, 37, 38, 63, 163, 299, 300, 302, 308, 309, 310, 319
   see also boat burial; cemetery; cist; cross slab; cross; grave; hogback; pagan graves;
   and burials listed in Chapter 24
butchery, 35, 175
Bute, 199, 200, 201
byre, 89, 91, 173, 174

cairn, 61, 62, 130, 202, 308, 309, 313
Caithness, 4, 5, 82, 190, 199, 202, 303; *see also* Freswick Links, Caithness
carbonised plant remains, 24, 36, 51, 78, 115, 116
Castle of Snusgar, Skaill Bay, Orkney, 23–4
   animal husbandry/feasting, 173–183, 225
   longhouses, 24
   Skaill hoard, 5–6, 23, 255
Castle Stuart, Moray Firth, 52
cat, 174–5
   bone *see* animal bone, cat
Catpund, Shetland, 102, 104–6, 107
cattle
   bone *see* animal bone, cattle
   farming, 78, 116–17, 153, 172–82, 189, 191–2, 225
   isotope analysis, 157–9, 163–4
   vellum production, 45
cellular buildings
   Buckquoy, Orkney, 16–17
   Jarlshof, Shetland, 30
   Old Scatness, Shetland, 30–2
   St Ninian's Isle, Shetland, 60–1
   see also buildings and structures, cellular

cemetery, 5, 18, 22, 37, 38, 44–6, 49, 52, 258, 272, 313–21
ceramic
   Viking Age/Norse, 112, 116
   platters, 78
   vessels, 76, 77–8, 81
   see also pottery
cereal
   crops, 91, 172, 189
   grain, 34, 52
cetacean, 175
chapel, 130, 137, 146, 201, 214
   Carrick, 313, 317
   St Coinneach (Kenneth), Mull, 137
   St Nicholas, Papa Stronsay, Orkney, 62
   St Ninian's Isle, Shetland, 57, 61, 64, 67
charcoal, 75, 90, 91, 93, 231, 235
chess, 240–4
chickens, 172
Christian/Christianity, 3, 24, 38, 59, 61, 62, 65–6, 136, 137, 138–40, 146, 148–9, 215, 243, 267, 272, 318
church, 59, 61, 62, 65, 66, 104, 121, 130, 137, 139, 140, 143–51, 262, 264, 282
cill- names *see* place-names, *cill-*
Cille Pheadair, South Uist, 4
   bullion, 276, 282–3
   combs, 290–1
   farmstead, 117, 155, 157–61, 162, 324
   houses, 80, 82
   pig husbandry, 159–61
   pre-Norse/Pictish burial, 63
cists, 258
   long cist, 18, 61, 62–7
   short cist, 61, 62–7
Clibberswick, Unst, Shetland, 102, 104, 106, 258
Cnip, Uig, Lewis, 5, 302, 303
   strontium analysis of burials, 163, 319
coastal grazing, 157
cod, 25, 35, 116
coins, 5–6, 125, 253, 254, 257, 268, 269, 280, 315–16
   Æthelræd I of Wessex (865/6–871), 317
   Anglo-Saxon, 34, 38, 77, 256, 269, 279, 281, 316, 317
   Bornais, South Uist, 77
   Buckquoy, Orkney, 17
   Burgred of Mercia (852–74), 18, 256, 257
   Coenwulf, 269

dirham see silver, *dirham*
Eanred, 9th century, 38
Edgar (959–75), 51
Edmund of Wessex (940–6), 17
Garthbanks hoard, Shetland, 34
Knowe of Swandro, Rousay, Orkney, 38
Louis le Begue (877–9), 51
Olaf Kyrre, 77
Old Scatness, Shetland, 34
Portmahomack, Rossshire, 51
Saevar Howe, Orkney, 18
Skaill Hoard, Orkney, 5–6, 281
styca, 38, 254, 256, 257, 279
see also listings in Chapter 20
Columba *see* St Columba
combs; comb fragments, 24, 49, 77, 116, 236, 289–95
 antler, 236, 289–95
comb-making
 workshop, 82
Conan stone, Dingwall, 52
cooking area, 80
copper alloy, 88, 302, 310, 270
 coin, 256, 279
 mount, 219, 236, 279
 pin *see* pin, copper alloy
 vessels, 236
 weights, 227, 277, 283
 wire, 317
Covesea Caves, Moray Firth, 52
crabshell
 Bornais, 78
craft-working, 45, 49, 230, 318
crop manuring, 156, 165, 189
cross (stone), 45, 57, 77, 208, 125, 147
 -marked stone, 45, 61
 -slab, 45, 46, 52, 54, 61, 62, 201
 guard, 314
 place-name, 139
 see also silver, cross; steatite (soapstone) crosses
cross-incised stone, headstone, 61, 63, 136–7
Crosskirk (church), Orkney, 104, 229–30, 232, 233
crucible, 48, 227
currency, 227, 277, 282

Da Biggings, Papa Stour, Shetland *see* Biggings, Papa Stour, Shetland
dairying, 45, 116, 159, 164, 191–3; *see also* shieling

Dál Riata, 124, 143, 147, 191
Dammins, Fetlar, Shetland, 102–3
deer *see* red deer
 antler, 292
 bone *see* animal bone, red deer
Derrynaflan hoard *see* hoard, Derrynaflan
diet, 78, 117, 157–9, 160–2, 172, 176–8, 179
 marine, 63, 308
dog, 172, 174, 207
 bone *see* animal bone, dog
 butchery, 175
 stable isotope research, 160, 161–2
doorway, 35, 87, 89, 90, 92, 93
Dornoch, 52
Drimore (Driomor), South Uist, 4, 80
drinking horn
 mount *see* mount, drinking horn
drying room, 79
Dublin, 4, 140, 148, 192, 236, 257, 266, 277, 279–80, 281, 284
ducks, 35, 172
Dunrossness, Shetland, 29, 57, 254

Earl Sigurd II, 13
Earl's Bu, Orphir, Orkney, 2, 223–8
 dogs at, 160–2
 drinking hall, 223
 feasting, 159–61, 178–83, 225, 324
 geophysical survey, 225
 hall, 223, 224, 225
 horizontal mill, 223, 225–6, 234, 324
 pig husbandry, 160–1
 round church *see* St Nicholas round church
Earl Thorfinn *see* Thorfinn
earls, 325; *see also* Orkney, Earls of
East Mound, Bay of Skaill, Orkney, 20, 24
 longhouses, 20, 24
 artefactual assemblages, 24
Edinbeg and Edinmore, Bute, 200
eggshell
 Bornais, 78
Eigg, 149
enclosure, 129
 Brough of Birsay, 214, 218, 219
 Portmahomack, 43, 45, 49, 52
 Tuquoy, 233

entrance
　Bornais, 75, 76, 77
　Broch of Gurness, 22
　comparing Hebridean and Icelandic houses, 79–83
　Hamar, 87
　Scatness, 36, 38
　Tuquoy, 230, 233
　Underhoull, 92, 93

farm, farming, 29, 32, 45, 49, 85, 91, 117
farmstead, 3, 4, 24, 51
Faroe Islands, 29, 93, 99, 104
feasting, 77, 155–6, 159–61, 165, 175, 178–83, 324
Fethaland, Shetland, 102, 104, 106
field system, 114
fieldwalking, 225
fish; fishing, 20, 32–4, 95, 116, 117
　stockfish trade, 4, 25, 35
flax, 19, 24, 34, 36, 78, 116
floor; floor surface; floor deposit, 19, 21, 24, 30, 36, 46, 51, 57, 66, 75, 76, 77, 78, 80, 81–2, 86–94
　sunken, 87–8
　timber, 80
Fluetjern, Østfold, Norway, 103
Folvelseter, Akerhus, Norway, 102–3
Fortriu, Kingdom of, 52
Freswick Links, Caithness, 4, 53, 323

gable (end), 75, 76, 79, 93, 223
Gaelic, 123, 143–51, 198, 239, 241, 245
　language, 124, 125, 126, 130, 135–6, 138, 140
　place-names see place-names, Gaelic
Galloway hoard see hoard, Galloway
Galson, Lewis, 63
Garðar (Igaliku), Greenland, 10, 107, 109, 204
gaming pieces, 239–47
gannet hunting, 175
Garthbanks hoard see hoard, Garthbanks
Gaulcross hoard see hoard, Gaulcross
geese, domestic, 172
geophysical survey, 220, 225, 233, 324
glass, 24, 30
　bead see beads, glass
　vessel fragments, 95
goat, 173
　bone see animal bone, sheep/goat
　skin, 173, 236

gold, 5, 6, 77, 227, 252, 255, 256, 258, 259, 263, 264, 266, 271–2, 280;
　see also separate entries in Chapter 20
Govan, 4, 199, 319
Granastaðir, Iceland, 79–80
grave, 5, 22, 23, 32, 53, 61, 206, 207, 299–307, 308, 309, 310, 311, 313–21, 323
　grave goods, 64, 308, 309, 313–18
　grave marker, 61
graveyard, 147, 230, 233, 325
grazing, 154, 157, 159, 171, 173, 189, 191, 192, 235
　coastal see coastal grazing
Great Army, The, 266, 276, 277, 279–80, 284
Great Glen, The, 43, 53, 324
Greenland, 99, 100, 103–4, 107, 109, 171, 173, 174, 197, 204, 206, 207, 215, 216, 244; see also Igaliku, Greenland; sagas, Tale of the Greenlanders
Gungstie, Noss, Shetland, 66

hack-silver, see silver, hack-silver
Hamar, Unst, Shetland, 21, 73, 85, 86–91, 92, 95
hammer and tongs, 310; see also tools
Harald Fairhair, 13
Harald Sigurdarson, King, 243–4
Harris, 112, 145–6, 199
hay production, 159, 172, 189, 192
head box (burials), 45, 49
hearth, 19, 35, 36, 46, 48, 76, 80, 81–2, 83, 88, 89–90, 91, 93, 94, 204, 208
Hebrides, 73, 75, 80, 83, 114, 121, 122, 123, 125, 126, 129, 131, 132, 135, 136, 137, 138, 140, 143–9
　Inner, 121, 190, 191
　Outer, 112, 117–18, 121, 137–8, 157–8, 159, 160, 163, 227
　see also individual island names; Western Isles
herring, 78
hnefatafl, 241, 243, 244–5
hoard, 5, 6, 15, 54, 57, 59, 61, 62, 66, 227, 249, 250, 251–7, 258, 276–7, 280, 281–2, 283
　Burray, Orkney, 281–2
　Derrynaflan, Tipperary, Ireland, 45
　Galloway, Kirkcudbrightshire, 6, 249–50, 251, 256–7, 262–73, 276, 279, 280, 283, 324

Garthbanks, Shetland, 34
Gaulcross, Aberdeenshire, 52
Gordon, Berwickshire, 256, 280
Lewis (gaming pieces), Lewis, 196, 239–45
Lews Castle, Lewis, 256, 281–2
Machrie, Islay, 125, 254–5
Portmahomack, Ross-shire, 43, 51, 54, 257
Skaill Bay, Orkney, 5–6, 23–4, 25, 255, 257, 281–2
Storr Rock, Skye, 257, 280, 281–2
Talnotrie, Kirkcudbrightshire, 256, 257, 277, 279
Vale of York, Yorkshire, England, 267, 268
see also Chapter 20 for listing of all Viking-age silver and gold hoards in Scotland and their contents
hogbacks, 4, 57, 61, 319
  steatite *see* steatite, hogback
hone stone *see* schist; whetstone
horizontal mill *see* mill, horizontal
horse, 11, 116, 171, 172, 174, 175, 236, 297
  bone *see* animal bone, horse
houses, 73, 75–83; *see also* buildings and structures
  Greenland-type, 215
  Hebridean, 11, 75–83
  Icelandic, 79–81, 82, 83, 88, 93, 216; *see also* buildings and structures, passage house
  Norse, 37–8, 39, 73, 75–9, 81–3, 85–95, 215, 217, 218, 234
Howe (The), Stromness, 17, 22, 179, 180, 181, 182
  buildings, 17
  burials, 22
Hoxa, Orkney, 199, 200, 202
Hrísheimar í Mývatnssveit, Iceland, 100, 107
human remains (skeletal evidence), 5, 17, 23, 59, 61, 62, 65, 67, 161, 163, 302, 308, 316
hunting, 174, 175
  sea birds, 171, 175

Iceland, 14, 29, 95, 100, 103, 104, 105, 106, 107, 108, 162, 164, 171, 173, 174, 178–9, 195, 197, 203–4, 207–8, 241, 283

settlement, 14, 29, 79, 131
see also individual sites
Igaliku (Garðar), Greenland, 100, 107, 204
infant burial *see* burials, infant
infield-outfield system, 153, 189–93
ingots *see* silver, ingot
ingot mould, 49, 227
interface, Pictish/Norse *see* Picts, Pictish–Norse transition
Iona, 46, 123, 135, 137, 140, 146, 149, 323
Ireland, 123, 125, 144, 147, 148, 162, 192, 255, 264, 268, 271, 277–9, 280, 283, 303, 308, 325
Iron Age, 29, 32, 37, 57, 60–2, 76, 114, 117, 172, 174, 175–6, 178, 179, 180, 189, 202, 235–6
  artefacts, 33, 98, 291
  occupation/phase, 15, 17, 18–19, 20, 29–32, 38, 39, 60–2, 114, 170–1, 220
  see also broch; Picts, architecture; roundhouse; wheelhouse
iron
  nails, 35, 313, 315, 318
  objects, 35, 36, 77, 254, 277, 283, 302, 308, 310, 315, 318
  pin *see* pin, iron
  plates, 35
  vessel, 78
  weights, 277, 283
iron-working, 19, 35, 36, 48, 52, 218
  slag, 36
  smelting, 48
  smithing, 18, 24, 46, 48–9, 50, 52
Islay, 5, 74, 121, 123–32, 143, 144, 146, 149, 191, 199, 254–5, 315; *see also* MacDougall's *Map of the Island of Islay;* place-names, Islay
Isle of Man, 148, 241
isotopic analysis, 23, 38, 63–4, 153, 155–65, 171, 298, 302, 303, 308, 322, 323; *see also* burials, isotopic research

Jarlshof, Shetland, 2–3, 20–1, 30, 32, 34, 36–7, 39, 66, 73, 85, 153, 157, 158, 160, 161–2, 173, 232, 323

Kaupang, Norway, 99, 105, 191, 277
Kebister, Shetland, 60
kerb, stone, 36, 45, 46, 61, 62–3, 80, 309
kiln, 51, 82

Kiloran Bay, Colonsay, 5, 277, 279–80, 297, 300, 302, 309, 310
Kilphedir, South Uist *see* Cille Pheadair, South Uist
kitchen, 79, 80
kleber see steatite (soapstone)
knife, iron, 35, 36, 64, 65, 77, 78, 237, 315, 317, 318
Knowe of Moan, Harray, Orkney, 22
Knowe of Swandro, Rousay, Orkney, 22, 29, 37–9, 171
  burials, 22
  settlement, 22, 29, 38, 171

ladle, 310
Lamba Ness, Sanday, 22
Lambay, 46
landnám, 11, 13–25, 29–39, 74, 98, 99, 109, 121–2, 123, 131–2, 135, 140–1, 195
Late Norse
  animal husbandry, fishing and farming, 4, 20, 153, 162–3, 170–83, 225, 226, 324
  artefacts, 116, 225, 227, 235, 289, 292
  bullion, 227, 276, 281–3
  burials/burial ground, 59, 64, 65, 67
  economy, 4, 20, 153, 162–3, 195–6, 225, 284, 324
  feasting, 196, 223, 225–6, 324
  hall, 2, 4, 104, 174, 196, 223, 224, 225, 229–32, 233–4, 236
  houses, 22, 73, 81–3, 87, 91, 223
  settlement, 3, 19, 37, 73, 85, 116, 216, 219
  tower/castle *see* tower, Late Norse
Lavacroon, Orkney, 196, 223, 225, 227
law, 53, 131, 136, 191, 197–208
  Grágás, 204
  Gulating, 191, 207, 208n
lead, 235
  leaded bronze, 48–9, 50
  pendant, 77
  weight, 49, 254, 256, 266, 277, 283, 319
Lewis, 5, 63, 73, 112–18, 123, 145–6, 190, 196, 199, 239–45, 256, 281–2, 302, 319
Life of Saint Columba see St Columba
Lindisfarne, 46
line sinker *see* steatite, link sinker
ling, 116

Links of Pierowall, Westray, Orkney *see* Pierowall, Westray, Orkney; burials, Links of Pierowall, Westray, Orkney
Loch Lomond, 297–8, 313–19, 323
longhouse, 3, 11, 15, 19, 20–1, 22, 24, 25, 36–7, 38, 39, 73, 75–83, 85–95, 217
loom, weights, 36, 80, 93, 94; *see also* steatite, loom weights; weaving
Lunnasting, Shetland, 198–9, 202

MacDougall's *Map of the Island of Islay*, 127
machair, 75, 76, 112, 114, 259
Machair Bharabhais, Lewis (Leòdhais), 73, 112–18
Maeshowe, Orkney, 6, 199, 324
magnetic susceptibility, 93, 233
Mail, Cunningsburgh, Shetland, 66
manuring, crop *see* crop manuring
market economy, 4, 5, 7, 49, 100, 156, 163, 164, 183, 191, 196, 204, 205–6, 249–50, 276–85, 292, 298, 323, 324–5
Marwick Bay, Orkney, 24, 220
metal-working, 18, 24, 30, 46, 48–9, 52, 54, 235–6, 257; *see also* iron-working
microwear analysis, 159, 163, 173
middens, 4, 20, 22, 32, 36, 38, 60–2, 67, 89, 91, 112, 114, 115–16, 117, 179, 218, 219, 224–7
migration, 14, 54, 98–100, 126, 131–2, 193, 276, 280, 281
milk production, 45, 116, 139, 153–4, 157, 159, 164, 171, 173, 177–8, 181–2, 183, 189, 191–3, 250, 324
mill, horizontal, 2, 196, 223, 225–7, 234, 324
Moluag, St (Moluaidh), 146
monastery, 135, 136, 148, 215
  Kinneddar, Ross-shire, 48
  Portmahomack, Ross-shire, 12, 43–54
  Rosemarkie, Ross-shire, 48
mould, 48–9, 50, 227
mound, 15, 17, 18–19, 20, 22, 23, 24, 25, 29–39, 75–83, 112–14, 195, 235, 255
  assembly, 53, 195, 198, 200–1, 202, 206–8
  burial, 17, 61, 62–3, 65, 198, 202, 206–7, 308, 311, 313
  see also settlement, mound

mount
 coin, 268
 copper alloy, 218, 219, 236
 drinking horn, 310
 gold, 271, 272
 weight, 277, 278, 279, 281
Mull, 74, 122, 135–41, 144, 146, 201, 254, 323, 324; *see also* place-names, Mull
mutton, 172

Nairnshire, 126
Nave Island, 125
Newton Cottage, Islay, 125
nine men's morris, 244; *see also* chess; tables (games)
non-ferrous metalworking, 48–9, 50, 227, 235–6
North Uist, 4, 112, 123, 147
 The Udal *see* The Udal, North Uist
Northern Isles *see* Orkney; Shetland; individual sites
Northumbria, 38, 256, 257, 262, 265, 267, 270, 272, 279
Norway, 13–15, 25, 123, 131, 189, 311
 19th-century migration to US, 132
 Crown of, 117
 Gokstad ship burial, 244
 graves, 310
 imports, 93, 98, 104, 105, 107–8, 109, 227, 237, 241, 325
 influence, 88, 192, 195, 281
 Marvik, Suldal, 32, 34
 Nidaros (Trondheim), 241, 283
 Norwegian schist, 36, 310; *see also* schist, whetstone
 Oma, house, 79
 steatite quarries *see* steatite (soapstone), Norway
Norwick, Unst, Shetland, 21, 39, 99, 104

oats, 34, 78, 91, 116, 117, 172, 236
ogham, 61, 66, 218, 219
Olav Tryggvason, King, 206, 207
Old Irish, 124, 132n, 189, 277
Old Norse
 beliefs, 147–8, 165, 207
 language, 121, 125, 135–6, 139–41, 144, 190–1, 192–3, 197, 198, 203–4, 206, 207–8

 replacement by Gaelic, 74, 121–2, 124–5, 126, 129–30, 135–6, 140, 143–4, 196, 198, 239, 245
 see also place-names, Norse
Old Red Sandstone, 29–30
Old Scatness, Shetland, 4, 11–12, 19–20, 21, 29–37, 38–9, 60, 66, 85, 99, 170, 324
 artefacts, 30, 32, 34–5, 36, 38–9, 99
 bear stone, 30
 broch, 19, 20, 30
 building reuse, 4, 19–20, 21, 29, 38–9
 dating, 11–12, 19–20, 21, 29, 30
 faunal assemblage, 35, 176, 324
 Iron Age/Pictish phase, 4, 29, 30–2
 metalworking, 19
 roundhouses, 30
 Viking presence, 4, 30, 32–7
 wheelhouses, 19, 30, 34–5
Ordnance Survey, 86, 92, 125, 126, 234
Orkney
 Earls of, 161, 170, 176–7, 179, 183, 196, 225, 324
 introduction of flax, 19, 24, 34, 153, 172
 see also individual sites
Orkneyinga Saga, 2, 3, 13, 153, 170, 178, 200, 215, 223, 229
Orphir, Orkney *see* Earl's Bu
otter, 175
óðal land, 206–7

pagan graves, 4–5, 11, 15, 17, 22–3, 32, 38, 54, 59, 61–2, 64–5, 125, 148, 258, 299–303, 323; *see also* boat burial; burials; burials, Viking Age/Norse; grave
painted pebble *see* Picts, painted pebble
palaeoenvironmental analysis, 7, 153–4, 170–1, 196, 232, 235, 236–7, 249, 324
Papa Stronsay, Orkney, 62
papar see place-names, *papar*
Papil, Shetland, 63, 66
parasites, 235, 237
paving, 36, 48, 61, 62, 94, 114
pearl, 77
peat, 45, 54, 61, 76, 91, 253
penannular brooch *see* brooch, penannular
performance, 239, 309, 311

personal names, 130, 136, 145, 146, 147, 202, 265, 272
Pictish kingdom, 52, 53
Picts, 12, 17, 22, 23, 29, 31, 235, 290
  architecture, 1, 4, 15–17, 18–21, 22, 23, 30–2, 34, 36, 37, 38, 85, 91–2, 202, 215
  artefacts, 17, 57, 258, 290
  barrow see Tarradale, Black Isle
  Burghead Fort, 52
  burial see burials, Pictish/pre-Viking; cemetery; Picts, long cist; Picts, short cist
  cairn, 61, 62, 130
  cemetery, 5, 18, 22–3, 37, 38, 44, 45–6, 49, 51, 52, 53, 258, 302
  cross-slab, 46, 52, 61, 62, 136–7, 201; see also Hilton of Cadboll; Nigg; Portmahomack; Shandwick
  'dragon', 49
  estates, 12, 17–18, 29, 32, 39, 43, 171, 178, 195, 220, 324
  Kingdom of Fortriu, 52
  language, 121, 143–4
  name symbols, 52
  painted pebble, 49, 53
  Pictish–Norse transition, 1, 3–4, 5, 11–12, 15–17, 18–21, 23, 24, 29, 32, 34, 39, 54, 59, 61, 62, 171, 174, 176, 178, 190–1, 195, 216, 220, 223, 235, 290, 324
  sculpture, 18, 22, 30, 45, 46, 48, 57, 63, 66
  symbol stone, 18, 22, 30, 223
Pierowall, Westray, Orkney, 5, 249, 258, 299–300, 303, 310
pigs, 78, 116, 159–61, 164, 165, 176–7, 179, 180; see also animal bone, pig
pin, 24, 79, 237, 256, 266, 271
  bone, 17, 19, 77, 236
  copper alloy 23, 52, 77, 236, 270
  iron, 77
  ringed-pin, 23, 52, 236, 310
  stick, 46, 53, 77
pit house, 87, 88–9, 90, 95
Pitgrudy, Dornoch, 52
place-names, 11, 73, 74, 123–32, 135–41, 143–9, 189–93, 322
  baile, 129–30
  bólstaðr (-bu), 51, 54, 196
  cill-, 51, 53, 130, 137, 145–6
  ecclesiastical, 53, 130, 136–8, 139–40, 145, 146
  Gaelic 122, 123, 125, 126, 129, 130, 135–6, 138, 140, 144–5, 154, 189–93, 198
  Islay, 74, 121, 123–32, 143, 144, 146
  kirk, 262
  Mull, 74, 135–41, 144, 146, 199, 201, 323, 324
  Norse, 13, 23, 24, 26, 51, 53, 54, 98, 123–32, 135–41, 146, 154, 189–93, 195, 198–202, 308, 324
  papar, 4, 148
  Pictish, 121
  pit-, 51, 53
  predating Scandinavian settlement, 121
  related to farmland, 23, 24, 51, 74, 121, 126–30, 136–9, 189–93
  shielings, 129, 130, 137, 173, 189–93
ploughing, 19, 116, 173
'pocket deities', 95
political turmoil, 73, 118, 127, 131, 239, 270
pollen see palaeoenvironmental analysis
pollution, 235–6
Pool, Sanday, Orkney, 3–4, 18–19, 20–1, 24, 25, 32, 37, 39, 91, 99, 104, 170, 171, 173, 175, 176, 177, 180, 181, 182, 232, 290, 324
population displacement, 14, 102, 131, 136, 143, 147, 322; see also Picts, Pictish–Norse transition
porphyry, 61, 77
Portmahomack, Tarbart, 12, 43–54, 257
  sarcophagus, 46
posthole, 76, 90, 217, 313, 318
pottery, 24, 61, 77–8, 80–1, 93, 112, 115, 159; see also ceramic
  gritty, 90
  Hebridean, 76, 80–1, 112, 116
  sagging base, 115
prehistoric landscape, 13, 19, 114, 117, 156, 157, 172, 208n, 308
prehistoric structures, 13, 19, 20, 23, 117, 201–2, 308, 311
pumice, 90, 91

quatrefoil brooch see brooch, quatrefoil
Quoygrew, Westray, Orkney, 4, 25, 99, 104, 155, 170, 173, 175, 176, 180, 181, 182, 225, 290, 324

rabbits, damage by, 5, 87, 90
radiocarbon dating, 11, 17, 18, 19, 21, 23, 24, 25n, 34, 36, 38, 39, 46, 48, 53, 59–60, 61, 62–3, 75, 88, 89, 90–1, 93–5, 114, 115, 116, 201, 220, 231–2, 235, 267, 272, 298, 313
raids, Viking, 11–12, 14, 46–8, 52, 54, 57, 59, 61, 123, 131, 148, 279, 281, 298, 303, 323
  dating, 46, 59–60, 123, 131
  evidence, 43–56, 123, 279, 303
  Iona, 46, 123, 135, 149, 323
  Portmahomack *see* Portmahomack, Tarbart
rattlestone, 268
recreation, 79
red deer, 78, 114, 116, 153, 157–8, 171, 175, 292; *see also* hunting
  bone *see* animal bone, red deer
reindeer, 291–2, 293
rent, 126, 131, 177
rickets *see* Vitamin D deficiency
ring brooch *see* brooch, ring
ring-ditch, 313, 315, 316, 318
ringed-pin *see* pin, ringed-pin
Ringerike style, 77, 125
ritual, 77, 114, 170, 171–2, 175, 178–9, 183, 207, 277, 309, 310
rivets, iron, 35, 302, 308
rock crystal, 268, 269, 271–2
Rognvald Kali Kolsson, 229
Roman past, 30, 243, 258, 272
roof, 46, 76, 81, 95, 203–4
Rosemarkie, 48
  Rosemarkie Caves, 52
rotary grindstone, 35
roundhouse, 30, 37, 38; *see also* buildings and structures
rubble, 32, 36, 61, 62–3, 65, 87, 89–90, 93, 94, 201, 233, 234
Rubha Buidhe, Islay, 125
runic inscription, 6, 15, 208n, 227
  Anglo-Saxon runes, 265, 267, 270
rye, 78

sacrifice, 156, 175, 182
Saevar Howe, Orkney, 18, 177, 180, 181, 182; *see also* coins, Saevar Howe
sagas, 2, 6, 13, 173, 178, 198, 203, 204, 207, 224, 225–6, 243, 318
  Grettir's Saga, 243
  Hakon's Saga, 318, 319
  Heimskringla, 242
  Hervarar saga ok Heiðreks, 243
  Króka-Refs Saga, 243–4
  Saga of King Olav Tryggvason, 206, 207
  Saga of the Sworn Brothers, 204
  Tale of the Greenlanders, 204
  Ynglingasaga, 242
  see also Orkneyinga Saga
St Andrew, 262
St Coinneach, 137, 140
St Colman Burn, Bute, 200
St Colman's church, Portmahomack, Ross-shire, 43
St Columba, 136, 138, 139, 140
  Adomnán, *Life of St Columba*, 136, 138
St Kilda, 251, 253
St Magnus, Egilsay, Orkney, 224
St Mary's church, Lewis, 114
St Nicholas round church, Orphir, Orkney, 223
St Nicholas chapel, Papa Stronsay, 62
St Ninian's Isle, Shetland, 12, 57–67
  burials, 59–67
  chapel, 12, 57, 59, 61, 64
  chronology, 61
  crosses, 57, 61, 62, 63; *see also* steatite crosses
  hoard of Pictish silver, 57, 59, 61, 62
  hogback, 57, 61; *see also* steatite, hogback
  infant, 59, 61, 63–4, 66
  relocation of remains, 65–6
St Olaf, 146
St Peter, 23, 146
Sandwick, Unst, Shetland, 4, 99, 104
Scallastle, Mull, 139, 140
Scalloway, Shetland, 60, 180
Scandinavia, 6, 13, 35, 76, 93, 172, 174, 175, 197–8, 206, 227, 243, 244, 249, 266, 277, 280, 281, 283, 284, 289, 290, 292, 300, 310, 314, 319
  animal movement to/from, 164, 174, 178
Scandinavian
  arrival, 11–12, 14–21, 29, 30–7, 38–9, 62, 65–7, 74, 98, 99, 109, 121–2, 148, 155, 171, 322
  identity, 32, 156, 163, 165, 170, 171–2, 174, 183, 245
  reuse of buildings, 19, 35–7, 39, 196, 225, 303
  see also Picts, Pictish–Norse transition

Scar, Sanday, Orkney, 5, 23, 297, 302, 308, 309
schist, 36, 88, 90, 91, 271, 310; *see also* whetstone
Scotland
  Crown of, 117
  legal system, 136, 198, 200
sculpture, 4, 15, 57, 66, 148
  Christian, 45, 46, 48, 66, 137
  smashed, 45, 46, 48
  typology, 46
  see also Picts, sculpture
seal, 175
seascape, 13, 131, 196
seaweed, 172, 231
serpentine, 90
settlement
  continuity, 11–12, 14–21, 22–3, 25, 32–7, 38, 53, 65–7, 80–1, 117, 121–2, 130, 135–6, 138, 143, 146, 147, 149, 311; *see also* Picts, Pictish–Norse transition; Scandinavian, arrival
  distribution, 51, 54, 73, 85–6, 114, 128, 129, 190
  duration, 22, 24
  mound, 17, 18–19, 20, 22, 23, 24, 32, 37, 53, 61, 62, 63, 65, 75–6, 81, 82, 112, 114, 200–1, 202, 235, 255
  no pre-Viking settlement, 223, 232
  reorganisation, 19, 32, 37–9, 118, 126, 178
settlers, first-generation, 29, 38
sewing, 78
shag/cormorant, 35, 175; *see also* bird
shale/jet/lignite, 315, 316, 317, 318
sheep, 78, 116, 117, 157–8, 159, 163, 171, 172, 173–4, 176–8, 180, 181, 225; *see also* wool production
  bone *see* animal bone, sheep/goat
shellfish, 38, 78, 231
Shetland, 57–67, 155, 157, 170, 198–200, 254, 258, 259, 323
  'blown' fish, 35
  longhouses, 3, 15, 19–20, 21, 22, 25, 36–7, 39, 73, 85, 86–8, 90–3, 95
  steatite, 99–100, 101, 102–3, 104, 105, 106, 107–8, 109, 227, 324
  see also under individual site names
shield boss, 309, 313, 314, 315

shieling, 129, 130, 137, 153–4, 173, 189–93
sickle, iron, 310
silk, 267–8, 271, 272; *see also* textiles
silver, 5, 6, 18, 34, 43, 191–2, 251–9, 262–73, 276–85, 310; *see also* coins
  brooch, 236, 256, 268, 270
  bullion, 227, 249, 250, 251, 262–3, 264, 265, 266–8, 270, 276–85, 324–5
  cross 254, 257, 263–4
  dirham, 256, 277, 279, 280, 281, 282
  hack-silver, 52, 227, 249, 251, 253, 257, 264, 276–85, 324
  hoard, 5, 6, 23, 25, 51, 57, 125, 249–50, 251–9, 262–73, 276, 277, 279–83, 324
  ingot, 49, 50, 227, 249, 251, 262, 263, 264, 265, 266, 271, 279, 280, 281
  nicking, 276
  ring-money, 6, 51, 227, 249, 250, 253, 255, 257, 258, 259, 262–73, 281, 282
site reuse *see* settlement, continuity
Skaill Bay, Sandwick, Orkney, *see* Bay of Skaill, Orkney
Skaill, Deerness, Orkney 3, 21, 35, 39, 170, 177, 179, 180, 181, 182, 224
  animal bone 177, 179, 180–2
Skaill, Rousay 170
skaldic poetry, 6, 206
skáli, 24
Skye, 121, 123, 132n, 146, 199, 255–6, 257, 258, 281, 324
slaves, 73, 80, 83, 131, 277
smokehouse ('skeo'), 35, 79
Snorri Sturlusson, 206, 207, 242, 243
Snusgar *see* Castle of Snusgar, Skaill Bay, Orkney
soapstone *see* steatite
Sogn, Norway, 191
South Uist, 4, 63, 73, 75–83, 104, 117, 138, 155, 161, 192, 250, 259, 276, 282
spear, 309, 313, 314
spindle whorl, 32, 34, 36, 38, 77, 93; *see also* steatite, spindle whorl
spinning, 78
standing stones, 45, 201, 202, 208n
steatite (soapstone), 17, 24, 32, 33, 34, 38–9, 74, 86, 89–90, 93, 98–109, 227
  bake plates, 90

crosses, 57, 61, 65
distribution, 11, 76, 98–109
figurine, 94–5
Greenland, 100, 107
hogback, 57, 61
line sinker, 32, 34, 88, 93, 94, 95
loom weights 36, 80, 93, 94; *see also* loom, weights
Norway, 100, 103, 105, 107, 108, 324
provenance, 98–109
quarries 38–9, 99–100, 101, 102–3, 104, 105, 106, 107–8, 109
spindle whorl, 19, 32, 34, 36, 93
typology, 35, 102
vessel, 11, 35, 36, 38–9, 76, 91, 93, 94, 100, 102, 104, 109, 227
XRF analysis, 99, 103
see also Shetland, steatite
Stenness, Orkney, 224, 253
stofa, 4
stone, fire-cracked, 36, 90
storage, 35, 78, 79, 80, 82
Strathclyde Britons, 4, 11
strontium analysis, 163–4, 308, 311
structural modification, 30, 32, 34, 225, 232
sulphur isotopes, 164
Sumburgh Head *see* Jarlshof
Sveigakot, Mývatnssveit, Iceland, 100, 107
Swandro *see* Knowe of Swandro, Rousay, Orkney
sword, 46, 297, 302, 310–11, 313, 314, 319
  Ardnamurchan, 310–11
  injuries caused by, 46
  pattern welding, 302

tables (games), 244, 245
Talnotrie, Kirkcudbrightshire *see* hoard, Talnotrie, Kirkcudbrightshire
Taransay, 148
Tarradale, Black Isle, 52
taxation, 24, 177, 183, 203, 250
tech, 124
teeth, 24, 63, 157, 158–9, 163, 164, 308, 317
textiles, 80, 249, 250, 264, 267, 268–9, 271, 302, 310, 315; *see also* silk; wool production
The Biggings, Papa Stour, Shetland *see* Biggings, Papa Stour
The Udal, North Uist, 4, 112

The Wirk, Rousay, Orkney, 233
thing (Þing), 7, 53, 195–6, 197–208, 249, 323
  booths, 203–4, 205–6, 207
  Faroe Islands, 197, 205, 206; *see also* Tinganes, Tórshavn, Faroe Islands
  Greenland, 197, 204, 206
  Iceland, 197, 203–4, 206
  location in landscape, 195–6, 197–204, 206–8, 324
  place-names, 130, 199, 200–2, 205
  Scandinavia, 197–8, 206
  Scotland, 198–203, 206, 323, 324
  see also under individual site names
Thingsva, Caithness, 80, 199, 203
Thor, 95, 202
Thorfinn, Earl, 3, 51, 53, 200, 217
Thurso, Caithness, 202
tideway, 32
timber, 199, 244, 249, 264, 302, 308, 311
  building, 4, 19, 36, 45, 76, 80, 81, 92, 93, 203, 208n, 218, 219, 317
  supplies, 53, 236–7, 249
Tinganes, Tórshavn, Faroe Islands, 205
Tingwall, Orkney, 195, 199, 202–3
Tingwall, Shetland, 195, 199, 202
Tiree, 132, 137, 143, 144, 146, 202, 254
  Eibrig, 202
  Taoinis, 199, 202
Tjaldavík, Faroe Islands, 205
Toftanes, Faroe Islands, 104, 244
tools, 53, 77, 237, 292
  in grave, 315–16
  Portmahomack, 46
Torfness, Tarbatness, 43, 53
  Battle of Torfness, 51, 53, 54
Torksey, Lincolnshire, 257, 266, 277, 278
tower, Late Norse, 196, 224, 233–4
trade, 4, 49, 100, 163, 164, 183, 249–50, 276–85, 292, 298, 324–5
Treaty of Perth, 117, 198
Trewhiddle style, 263, 270
túatha, 138
Tuquoy, Westray, Orkney, 3–4, 170, 173, 179, 196, 229–37
  artefacts, 100, 103–6, 107–8
  environmental, *see* palaeoenvironmental analysis
  woodworking, 230, 236–7
turf, 45, 46, 53–4, 81, 87, 91, 92–3, 115, 202, 203, 217, 308

Uig, Lewis, 5, 112, 241
Underhoull, Unst, Shetland, 3, 21, 73, 85–6, 89, 91–5
  Alan Small excavations, 3, 86, 91–2
  broch, 85, 91–2
  longhouse, 21, 73, 85–6, 89, 91–5
Undir Junkarinsfløtti, Sandoy, Faroe Islands, 93
Unst, Shetland, 21, 73, 85–6, 97, 258; *see also* individual sites from Unst
urban sites, 4, 160, 252, 289

vellum-working, 45
Viking raids *see* raids, Viking
violence, 14, 46, 54, 322
Vitamin D deficiency, 63–4

walls, 18, 22, 34, 36, 45, 46, 51, 61, 67n, 75–6, 79, 81, 85, 86–8, 89–91, 92–4, 112, 115, 117, 203–4, 214, 219, 223, 229, 230, 233, 313
walrus ivory, 236, 239–45
walrus skull, 244
waste *see* middens; wheelhouse, infill
wealth, 5, 30, 32, 45, 54, 196, 236, 249–50, 276–85
weaning of animals, 159, 171
weapons, 11, 241, 297, 313, 315, 319; *see also* various types of weapons
  damage to, 309, 310–11, 314, 315
weaving, 53
Western Isles *see* Hebrides, Outer
Westness, Rousay, Orkney, 5, 22–3, 37–8, 63, 163, 171, 299, 300, 302, 308, 309, 310, 319; *see also* cemetery; Picts cemetery

whalebone, 175
  counter, 53
wheelhouse, 15, 19, 20, 30, 32, 34–6; *see also* buildings and structures
  infill, 32–4, 35–6, 38
whetstone, 36, 77, 88, 90, 91, 310, 315, 319; *see also* schist
Whithorn, 4, 65, 249, 277, 284, 289
willow, 235
windblown sand, 5, 49, 57, 59, 60, 61, 62, 63, 64, 65, 66, 115, 116
winkle shell, 38
wood *see* timber
Woodstown, Ireland, 277, 280
wool production, 80, 116, 173, 177, 181, 183, 267, 272
workshop, 44, 45, 46, 48, 49, 79, 82, 230, 232, 233, 240, 241, 289
worm casts, 78

XRF analysis, 48, 99, 103

York, 34, 88, 99, 104, 237, 257, 325

zooarchaeology, 155–65, 170–83, 291–2
Zoroastrianism, 267

Æthelræd II, coin, 77

øra, 191
øre, 282

Þingvellir, Iceland, 208

www.ingramcontent.com/pod-product-compliance
Lightning Source LLC
Jackson TN
JSHW081200011225
95130JS00004B/210